AF836414

Information Technology and Law Series

Volume 34

Editor-in-Chief

Simone van der Hof, eLaw (Center for Law and Digital Technologies), Leiden University, Leiden, The Netherlands

Series Editors

Bibi van den Berg, Institute for Security and Global Affairs (ISGA), Leiden University, The Hague, The Netherlands

Gloria González Fuster, Law, Science, Technology & Society Studies (LSTS), Vrije Universiteit Brussel (VUB), Brussels, Belgium

Eleni Kosta, Tilburg Institute for Law, Technology, and Society (TILT), Tilburg University, Tilburg, The Netherlands

Eva Lievens, Faculty of Law, Law & Technology, Ghent University, Ghent, Belgium

Bendert Zevenbergen, Center for Information Technology Policy, Princeton University, Princeton, USA

More information about this series at https://link.springer.com/bookseries/8857

Felix Bieker

The Right to Data Protection

Individual and Structural Dimensions of Data Protection in EU Law

ASSER PRESS

Springer

Felix Bieker
Office of the Data Protection Commissioner
Schleswig-Holstein
Kiel, Germany

ISSN 1570-2782 ISSN 2215-1966 (electronic)
Information Technology and Law Series
ISBN 978-94-6265-502-7 ISBN 978-94-6265-503-4 (eBook)
https://doi.org/10.1007/978-94-6265-503-4

Published by T.M.C. ASSER PRESS, The Hague, The Netherlands www.asserpress.nl
Produced and distributed for T.M.C. ASSER PRESS by Springer-Verlag Berlin Heidelberg

© T.M.C. ASSER PRESS and the author 2022
No part of this work may be reproduced, stored in a retrieval system, or transmitted in any form or by any means, electronic, mechanical, photocopying, microfilming, recording or otherwise, without written permission from the Publisher, with the exception of any material supplied specifically for the purpose of being entered and executed on a computer system, for exclusive use by the purchaser of the work.
The use of general descriptive names, registered names, trademarks, service marks, etc. in this publication does not imply, even in the absence of a specific statement, that such names are exempt from the relevant protective laws and regulations and therefore free for general use.

This T.M.C. ASSER PRESS imprint is published by the registered company Springer-Verlag GmbH, DE part of Springer Nature.
The registered company address is: Heidelberger Platz 3, 14197 Berlin, Germany

Series Information

The *Information Technology & Law Series* was an initiative of IT*e*R, the national programme for information Technology and Law, which was a research programme set up by the Dutch government and The Netherlands Organisation for Scientific Research (NWO) in The Hague. Since 1995 IT*e*R has published all of its research results in its own book series. In 2002 IT*e*R launched the present internationally orientated and English language *Information Technology & Law Series*. This well-established series deals with the implications of information technology for legal systems and institutions. Manuscripts and related correspondence can be sent to the Series' Editorial Office, which will also gladly provide more information concerning editorial standards and procedures.

Editorial Office

T.M.C. Asser Press
P.O. Box 30461
2500 GL The Hague
The Netherlands
Tel.: +31-70-3420310
e-mail: press@asser.nl

Simone van der Hof, Editor-in-Chief
Leiden University, eLaw (Center for Law and Digital Technologies)
The Netherlands

Bibi van den Berg
Leiden University, Institute for Security and Global Affairs (ISGA)
The Netherlands

Gloria González Fuster
Vrije Universiteit Brussel (VUB), Law, Science,
Technology & Society Studies (LSTS)
Belgium

Eleni Kosta
Tilburg University, Tilburg Institute for Law, Technology, and Society (TILT)
The Netherlands

Eva Lievens
Ghent University, Faculty of Law, Law & Technology
Belgium

Bendert Zevenbergen
Princeton University, Center for Information Technology Policy
USA

Acknowledgements

This book started out as my doctoral thesis, submitted to the University of Kiel in December 2019, with the defence taking place in May 2021. Case law and literature were updated for publication in August 2021.

I would like to thank my supervisor, Prof. Dr. Kerstin von der Decken, who provided helpful advice. Further, I would like to thank Prof. Dr. Andreas von Arnauld for his comments and thoughts on my topic and perspective.

I was in the lucky and privileged position to embark on and finish this project only due to an expansive network of support. This fills me with gratitude for the many wonderful people in my life.

This project would not have been possible without the insights I gained working at the Office of the Data Protection Commissioner Schleswig-Holstein (ULD). I had the great fortune of learning about data protection from Marit Hansen and Martin Rost, who have both shaped my understanding and sharpened my sense of purpose. While they made this process more than just a one-directional exchange and were eager for my input, I am deeply indebted to both of them for their mentorship. I greatly appreciate the vast amount of trust, which Marit has shown consistently throughout these years.

There were many other outstanding people in this stimulating environment: I would like to specifically thank Rasmus Robrahn, Benjamin Bremert, Kirsten Bock as well as Dr. Malte Engeler for their insightful feedback or discussions at various stages of this process. However, as I could not possibly name everybody who contributed in one way or another to my understanding of data protection, thanks especially to the current and former members of the *Kaffeerunde*.

Beyond ULD, there have been many people who have engaged with my work and have helped me learn and grow in different ways. Dr. Jörg Pohle provided valuable feedback on my ideas for this project. I was very fortunate to be able to discuss parts of this work with Eleanor Sharpston, Q.C. I would also like to thank Professor Charles Raab for his feedback on aspects of this book. And I am still grateful for Professor Niamh NicShuibhne's outstanding classes at the University of Edinburgh, which laid important foundations for my understanding of EU law and let me appreciate AG Opinions.

Through my work I also had the chance to engage with many interesting and insightful people at conferences, workshops and meetings. I would like to thank Dr. Dara Hallinan, Dr. Nóra Ni Loideain and Prof. Dr. Gloria González Fuster for some great discussions.

I am also thankful for friends found during this intense phase of my life, who shared thoughts, dinners, rants and exasperation. Katharina Wommelsdorff and Isabelle Haßfurther have been particularly good companions in this endeavour. With them, Sarah Sultan, Chris Shaheen and Anna Kostekidou I was also lucky to take inspired and inspiring breaks.

I would not have been able to pursue this project without the foundations laid by my parents, Barbara and Ullrich. My brother, Fabian, raised my awareness to the issue of data protection very early on, for instance by handing down his copies of *Datenschleuder*.

My parents and Erika Theilen I owe many thanks for their ideational support and the invisible labour they performed during the intense phases of writing.

And lastly, and most importantly, thanks to Jens. Going through this process as well as breaking out of it together at times, has kept me on track over the years.

Contents

Abbreviations

AFSJ	Area of Freedom, Security and Justice
AG	Advocate General
AI	Artificial Intelligence
App. No.	Application Number
BCBP	Bureau of Customs and Borders Protection
BDSG	Bundesdatenschutzgesetz (Federal Data Protection Act)
BT-Drs.	Bundestags-Drucksache (Official Records of the German Federal Parliament)
BVerfG	Bundesverfassungsgericht (German Federal Constitutional Court)
BVerfGE	Entscheidungssammlung des Bundesverfassungsgerichts (Official Records of the German Federal Constitutional Court)
BYIL	*British Yearbook of International Law*
Cf.	Confer
CFI	Court of First Instance of the European Union
CFR	Charter of Fundamental Rights of the European Union
CFSP	Common Foreign and Security Policy
CILJ	*Cambridge International Law Journal*
CJEU	Court of Justice of the European Union
CLSLR	*Computer Law & Security Law Review*
CMLRev	*Common Market Law Review*
CoE	Council of Europe
CUP	Cambridge University Press
CYELS	*Cambridge Yearbook of European Legal Studies*
DÖV	*Die Öffentliche Verwaltung*
DPC	Data Protection Convention
DPD	Data Protection Directive
DPIA	Data Protection Impact Assessment
DPR-EC	Data Protection Regulation for the European Community
DPR-EU	Data Protection Regulation for the European Union

DRD	Data Retention Directive
DuD	*Datenschutz und Datensicherheit*
DVBl	*Deutsches Verwaltungsblatt*
DVR	*Datenverarbeitung im Recht*
e.g.	Exempli gratia
EC	European Community
ECHR	European Convention on Human Rights
ECJ	European Court of Justice
ECtHR [GC]	Grand Chamber of the European Court of Human Rights
ECtHR	European Court of Human Rights
edn.	Edition
EDPB	European Data Protection Board
EDPL	*European Data Protection Law Review*
EDPS	European Data Protection Supervisor
EDPS	European Data Protection Supervisor
EEC	European Economic Community
EJLT	*European Journal of Law and Technology*
EJRR	*European Journal of Risk Regulation*
EL	Ergänzungslieferung (Supplement)
ELRev	*European Law Review*
ENISA	European Union Agency for Cybersecurity (formerly European Union Network and Information Security Agency)
ePD	ePrivacy Directive
ePR	ePrivacy Regulation
et seq./et seqq.	Et sequentes
ETS	European Treaty Series
EU	European Union
EuConst	*European Constitutional Law Review*
Eur Law J.	*European Law Journal*
EuR	*Europarecht*
EuZW	*Europäische Zeitschrift für Wirtschaftsrecht*
GC	General Court
GDPR	General Data Protection Regulation
GLJ	*German Law Journal*
GYIL	*German Yearbook of International Law*
i.e.	Id est
Ibid.	Ibidem
ICLQ	*International and Comparative Law Quarterly*
IDPL	*International Data Privacy Law*
IEEE	Institute of Electrical and Electronics Engineers
IJLIT	*International Journal of Law and Information Technology*
IP	Internet Protocol
IPRev	*Internet Policy Review*
ISP	Internet Service Provider
IT	Information Technology

JHA	Justice and Home Affairs Council
JR	*Juristische Rundschau*
JZ	*Juristenzeitung*
LED	Law Enforcement Directive
LGBTIQ	Lesbian, Gay, Bisexual, Trans, Inter, Queer
MIT	Massachusetts Institute of Technology
MJ	*Maastricht Journal*
MLR	*The Modern Law Review*
MMR	*MultiMedia und Recht*
MN.	Marginal Note
NGO	Non-Governmental Organisation
NILR	*Netherlands International Law Review*
NJW	*Neue Juristische Wochenschrift*
NVwZ	*Neue Zeitschrift für Verwaltungsrecht*
OJ	Official Journal of the European Union
OUP	Oxford University Press
ÖVD	*Öffentliche Verwaltung und Datenverarbeitung*
p.	Page
para.	Paragraph
paras.	Paragraphs
PNR	Passenger Name Records
pp.	Pages
RDV	*Recht der Datenverarbeitung*
SA	Supervisory Authority
SCC	Standard Contractual Clauses
SIM	Subscriber Identification Module
Stan. L. Review	*Stanford Law Review*
TEU	Treaty on European Union
TFEU	Treaty on the Functioning of the European Union
U. Pa. L. Rev.	*University of Pennsylvania Law Review*
UK	United Kingdom
UNSW Law Journal	*University of New South Wales Law Journal*
URL	Uniform Resource Locator
US	United States
viz.	Videlicet
ZD	*Zeitschrift für Datenschutz*
ZEuS	*Zeitschrift für Europarechtliche Studien*

Chapter 1
Introduction

Contents

Abstract This chapter introduces the issue of data processing and the need for data protection. It lays down the foundational terminology that will be used throughout this book and provides an overview of the individual chapters. The chapters cover an introduction to and analysis of the primary EU law on data protection as well as the secondary EU data protection legislation. The book then considers the case law of the CJEU, before turning to the current approaches to data protection in the literature. In the final chapter, the dualistic approach to data protection is introduced and used to conceptualize the right to data protection as an independent fundamental right of EU law.

Keywords Data Processing · Individual Data Protection · Structural Data Protection · Systemic Data Protection · Democracy · Rule of Law · Discrimination · Bias · Artificial Intelligence · Big Data

1.1 Data Protection and the Issue of Data Processing

Everything has already been said about data protection.

While data protection has been discussed in Europe in these specific terms at least since the 1960s, it is—though perhaps to a lesser extent than the notion of privacy—an essentially contested concept.[1] Since that time, many conceptions of data protection and its rationale have been developed, and only few of them have

[1] Pohle 2018, p. 3. The notion of essentially contested concept was developed by Gallie 1955–1956.

© T.M.C. ASSER PRESS and the author 2022
F. Bieker, *The Right to Data Protection*, Information Technology and Law Series 34,
https://doi.org/10.1007/978-94-6265-503-4_1

been discarded. Instead, it appears the debate periodically runs in circles, which have several sub-circles on different national, regional and global planes.[2]

Meanwhile, the processing of personal data causes damage on a scale that affects vast amounts of individuals and specifically already marginalized groups,[3] but extends even further to the very structures of the democratic State under the rule of law: through the mostly invisible accumulation of personal data, especially from the internet and electronic means of communications, private organisations claim to offer benefits of personalization in order to profile individuals on a massive scale. While these profiles may have specific negative consequences for individuals,[4] they can also be used to manipulate entire segments of a population and thereby sway democratic processes, such as elections or referenda.[5] In this regard, data processing practices affect not only the specific individuals whose data are processed, but extend further and reverberate throughout all of society and its democratic processes of negotiating various interests.

The realisation of such risks to individuals and society as a whole is not only caused by private organisations. States subject their entire populations to the processing of their personal communications data in bulk.[6] However, such practices are not limited to matters of ordre public, but also extend to the public service more generally, where the State provides welfare and other means of social policy and engages in planning and projections.[7] In both regards, the State often extends its reach beyond what is necessary to achieve a specific aim.[8] Furthermore, it has consistently been proven that any collection of data attracts law enforcement and intelligence agencies. This applies to both private collections of data[9] as well as databases of public authorities.[10]

However, when the State, and especially the executive branch, gathers comprehensive information on its citizens or specific groups of individuals by combining and linking various information systems, it acquires informational power.[11] This can

---

[2] Pohle 2018, p. 231.

[3] Buolamwini and Gebru 2018; Richardson et al. 2019; Biber 2021; Frenkel et al. 2018, The New York Times. https://www.nytimes.com/2018/11/14/technology/facebook-data-russia-election-racism.html. Accessed 28 July 2021; Bieker and Bremert 2020.

[4] Ludwig 2015, The Guardian. https://www.theguardian.com/commentisfree/2015/oct/13/your-credit-score-is-racist-heres-why. Accessed 28 July 2021.

[5] Information Commissioner's Office 2018.

[6] Taylor 2019, The Guardian. https://www.theguardian.com/technology/2019/jul/17/government-agencies-pushing-for-longer-mandatory-metadata-retention. Accessed 17 June 2021.

[7] Syal and Campbell 2017, ibid., https://www.theguardian.com/society/2017/oct/16/nhs-data-loss-scandal-deepens-with-162000-more-files-missing. Accessed 16 June 2021.

[8] Simitis 1973, p. 144; von Berg et al. 1972, p. 3.

[9] Ball 2013, The Guardian. https://www.theguardian.com/world/2013/jun/08/nsa-prism-server-collection-facebook-google. Accessed 28 July 2021.

[10] Kannenberg 2014, heise online. https://www.heise.de/newsticker/meldung/PKW-Maut-Datenschuetzer-machen-Druck-gegen-Kennzeichenerfassung-2457265.html. Accessed 28 July 2021.

[11] Steinmüller 1981, p. 173.

be used to plan and manage, but also to control and nudge the populace and implies a deep shift of the underlying power structures.[12]

Under the rule of law, the exercise of public power must be transparent to the individual, i.e. the competences of public authorities and how they exercise them must be predictable for the individual.[13] Yet, information technology can effortlessly undermine the system of checks and balances, horizontal and vertical separation of powers, allocations of competence, i.e. social segmentations, which purposefully divide power.[14] This shift, which leads to an informational power imbalance between the individual and the State, due to the latter's superior knowledge, can therefore undermine the very structures, which the rule of law requires.[15]

The risks for individuals as well as the democratic society under the rule of law, which are inherent in the processing of personal data, and may be realised by both, the State as well as by private entities, are at the heart of data protection. As the unilateral creation of those risks by entities processing data exemplifies, there is an underlying power imbalance. Data protection thus, has to mitigate these risks and address this power imbalance.

The aim of this book is not to submit yet another theory on data protection. Rather, in light of the issues posed by the processing of personal data, my objective is to explore the right to data protection in the law of the European Union (EU or Union). I will define the specific rationale and content of this right, which has not yet been attained in the practice of the courts or the academic debate. I will also consider the importance of extending these protections in horizontal relations, i.e. between individuals, and differentiate the right to data protection from the right to privacy. I will achieve these aims by considering the extensive EU secondary legislation, which predates Article 8 of the Charter on Fundamental Rights[16] (CFR or Charter), as well as the doctrinal discourse on data protection in the EU. I will then apply my own framework, which builds on a historic discourse of German legal informatics scholars, to the EU data protection rules.

In the following section, I will provide a brief outline of the specific terminology, which I introduce in order to enable a discussion of data protection on its own terms (Sect. 1.2). Based on this, I will provide an outlook on the course of my argument in this book, taking the current EU data protection legislation as a starting point to introduce this rather specific area of law (Sect. 1.3), before turning to the fundamental right to data protection, which I will firstly consider from the point of view of the CJEU (Court of Justice of the European Union), which has interpreted this right in an evolutive manner (Sect. 1.4). Secondly, I will analyse the current doctrinal approaches to the right to data protection (Sect. 1.5). Lastly, I will develop my own theory of data protection as distinct fundamental right of EU law (Sect. 1.6), as introduced in the preceding section.

---

[12] Ibid.

[13] Podlech 1988, p. 124.

[14] Steinmüller 1981, p. 173.

[15] Podlech 1987, p. 21; Podlech 1988, p. 123.

[16] Charter of Fundamental Rights of the European Union, OJ C 303 of 14 December 2007, pp. 1–16.

1.2 Terminology

In the course of this book, I will refer to certain key terms, which enable me to build a clear argument. I will present them in further detail in the course of my reasoning. Nonetheless, I will introduce them briefly in this section, so as to provide an overview of the specific terminology I use throughout this book.

The term *EU data protection legislation* (*Datenschutzgesetze*) refers to the body of EU law labelled as data protection, which does, however, not exclusively regulate data protection, but also covers other, related fields. My focus is on the general rules of the *second generation of EU data protection legislation*, i.e. the body of legislation, which has been adopted with or after the General Data Protection Regulation (GDPR)[17] in 2016, which reformed the EU's data protection legislation framework. This includes the Law Enforcement Directive (LED)[18] as well as the Data Protection Regulation (DPR-EU).[19] For the purposes of this book, my primary focus is not on the LED and Chapter IX DPR-EU: as sector-specific regulations concerning police and judicial cooperation in criminal matters, they contain many exceptions and some additional safeguards, which I will point out where relevant, but will not address in-depth. I will also refer to the ePrivacy Directive (ePD)[20] where appropriate, which due to its legislative structure must be considered part of the first generation of EU data protection legislation. It has not yet been replaced by the ePrivacy Regulation (ePR), due to intense debates between the Member States in the Council of the EU.[21] While the ePD contains rules on data protection, this legislation specifically aims to protect privacy in electronic communications. It therefore differs from the data protection legislation and is also expressly linked to Article 7 CFR, which protects the right to privacy as well as the confidentiality of communications.[22]

---

[17] Regulation (EU) 2016/679 of the European Parliament and of the Council of 27 April 2016 on the protection of natural persons with regard to the processing of personal data and on the free movement of such data, and repealing Directive 95/46/EC (General Data Protection Regulation), OJ L 119 of 4 May 2016, pp. 1–88.

[18] Directive (EU) 2016/680 of the European Parliament and of the Council of 27 April 2016 on the protection of natural persons with regard to the processing of personal data by competent authorities for the purposes of the prevention, investigation, detection or prosecution of criminal offences or the execution of criminal penalties, and on the free movement of such data, and repealing Council Framework Decision 2008/977/JHA, OJ L 119 of 4 May 2016, pp. 89–131.

[19] Regulation (EU) 2018/1725 of the European Parliament and of the Council of 23 October 2018 on the protection of natural persons with regard to the processing of personal data by the Union institutions, bodies, offices and agencies and on the free movement of such data, and repealing Regulation (EC) No 45/2001 and Decision No 1247/2002/EC, OJ L 295 of 21 November 2018, pp. 39–98.

[20] Directive 2002/58/EC of the European Parliament and of the Council of 12 July 2002 concerning the processing of personal data and the protection of privacy in the electronic communications sector (Directive on privacy and electronic communications), OJ L 201 of 31 July 2002, pp. 37–47.

[21] For the status of the ePR cf. https://oeil.secure.europarl.europa.eu/oeil/popups/ficheprocedure.do?lang=en&reference=2017/0003(COD). Accessed 28 July 2021.

[22] Bernsdorff 2014, MN. 19 and 24.

The *first generation of EU data protection legislation*, in turn, was initiated with the adoption of the EU's first regulation concerning data protection, the Data Protection Directive[23] (DPD) in 1995. Even though the old Data Protection Regulation[24] (DPR-EC) and the ePD were adopted in 2001 and 2002, respectively—and thus a considerable time after the DPD—their rules and regulatory mechanisms still rely on the structures introduced with the DPD.

With the term *data protection* (*Datenschutz*), I refer to the issue of data processing in general. Data protection is the answer to the societal issue raised by the processing of data, which cannot be resolved, but rather must be constantly negotiated by society, as it is the flipside of data processing.[25]

I use the term *data protection law* (*Datenschutzrecht*) to refer to the legal provisions on the processing of personal data, which specifically address the issue of data processing.[26] The term thus refers to an ideal state, in which the entire body of data protection legislation exclusively regulates the issue of data protection. As this is not the case in practice, the differentiation between the wider term *EU data protection legislation* (*Datenschutzgesetze*), as introduced above, and *data protection law* (*Datenschutzrecht*) is crucial, as the EU data protection legislation regulates matters concerning rationales beyond data protection as defined in this book. Thus, I will analyse the EU data protection legislation to find the matters, which specifically address the issue of processing and therefore form the body of *EU data protection law*. With this term I will describe the narrower body of law, which I will uncover from the EU data protection legislation.

I will also differentiate between the *principles of the EU data protection legislation*, i.e. the principles included in the provisions of the second generation of EU data protection legislation,[27] and the *fundamental principles of EU data protection law*. I will use the term *fundamental principles* (*Grundprinzipien*) to describe the seven fundamental principles, which I derive from the entirety of the rules of EU data protection law and which are therefore truly reflective of the content of the secondary EU data protection law: lawfulness, separation, transparency, control, confidentiality, integrity and availability. These fundamental principles will serve as the normative basis of the EU fundamental right to data protection.

I further divide data protection law into *individual data protection law* (*Individualdatenschutz*) and *structural data protection law* (*Systemdatenschutz*). The former encompasses the legal provisions, which serve to protect the specific, enforceable rights of individuals and groups. The content and rationale of the latter will be a

---

[23] Directive 95/46/EC of the European Parliament and of the Council of 24 October 1995 on the protection of individuals with regard to the processing of personal data and on the free movement of such data, OJ L 281 of 23 November 1995, pp. 31–50.

[24] Regulation (EC) No 45/2001 of the European Parliament and of the Council of 18 December 2000 on the protection of individuals with regard to the processing of personal data by the Community institutions and bodies and on the free movement of such data, OJ L 8 of 12 January 2001, pp. 1–22.

[25] Pohle 2018, p. 237; based on Steinmüller et al. 1971, p. 44.

[26] Steinmüller et al. 1971, p. 44.

[27] Article 5 GDPR, Articles 4 and 71 DPR-EU as well as Article 4 LED.

particular focus of this book, as it has not yet been generally acknowledged: structural data protection law goes beyond the prevalent individualistic understanding and encompasses the systemic side of data protection. It includes the normative and institutional requirements for the organisation and maintenance of a democratic State and society under the rule of law.

I will introduce all of these terms more comprehensively in the course of my argument throughout the following chapters.

1.3 EU Data Protection Legislation

In Chap. 2, I will consider the extensive body of EU data protection legislation. The EU Charter includes a specific fundamental right to data protection in Article 8 CFR, which is separate from the right to private life guaranteed in Article 7 CFR. The EU had already been active in the area of data protection legislation with the first generation of EU data protection legislation, namely the DPD, the DPR-EC and the ePD, which were all based on the market harmonisation clause that is now Article 114 of the Treaty on the Functioning of the European Union (TFEU)[28]. The Treaty of Lisbon,[29] in Article 16 TFEU introduced a specific EU competence to regulate the processing of personal data, which is the basis of the second generation of data protection legislation, i.e. the GDPR, DPR-EU and LED. While this legislation introduced some new principles and instruments and redefined others, the second generation is an evolution of the first generation and adheres to its general structures and principles.

In the analysis of the secondary EU data protection legislation, I will lay a particular focus on the interpretation of the principles introduced in the EU data protection legislation. However, I will demonstrate that not all of the relevant rules of the EU data protection legislation are represented in the principles of the EU data protection legislation. Rather, there are further provisions, which are equally fundamental to the system provided by the EU data protection legislation, without being included in the principles. I will build on these considerations especially in Chap. 5, Sect. 5.3, where I will derive the fundamental principles of EU data protection law, from the EU data protection law.

[28] Treaty on the Functioning of the European Union, OJ C 45 of 30 March 2010, pp. 47–199.

[29] Treaty of Lisbon amending the Treaty on European Union and the Treaty establishing the European Community, OJ C 306 of 17 December 2007, pp. 1–271.

1.4 The Right to Data Protection: The Jurisprudence of the CJEU

In Chap. 3, I consider the jurisprudence of the EU courts, i.e. the CJEU, which, according to Article 19 TEU, consists of the European Court of Justice (ECJ or the Court) and the General Court (GC). The ECJ has been seized of disputes concerning data protection since its early days, for instance in the well-known *Stauder* case.[30]

While the Court realised the fundamental rights dimension of data protection and the corresponding EU legislation early on, it only started to engage with the right to data protection under Article 8 CFR with the coming into force of the Charter after the Treaty of Lisbon. Hence, its case law on the right to data protection is limited, even though some Advocate Generals (AG), especially AG Kokott, have long advocated to engage with data protection and fundamental rights in greater detail.

The Court's engagement has further been hampered by an ambiguous judgment in the case of *Schecke and Eifert*,[31] which in consequence has led to two different approaches to Article 8(1) and (2) CFR: one approach that reads it only in conjunction with the right to privacy and another approach, which distinguishes the rights on a superficial level. However, even the latter approach ultimately stays grounded in the right to privacy, which may be due to the fact that the first generation of EU data protection legislation included a specific reference to privacy, which has only been replaced by a reference to Article 8 CFR with the second generation of secondary EU data protection legislation, which became applicable in 2018. The Court's engagement with the secondary legislation for the interpretation of the fundamental right to data protection so far remains limited. It has only referred to it sporadically.

With regard to Article 8(1) and (3) CFR it took even longer before the Court could adjudicate on a case. After a series of judgments on the independence of supervisory authorities, which it interpreted broadly, the Court ruled on the right of individuals to submit complaints and the responsibilities of the supervisory authorities in investigating and enforcing the rules of the EU data protection legislation. In this case law it has consistently held that the supervisory authorities must be able to effectively ensure a high level of protection for individuals. In that sense, the independence of the supervisory authorities is a means to an end and the Court seeks to ensure that they take on this role.

I conclude Chap. 3 by arguing that although the Court has identified several issues of the processing of data, its approach requires more consistency and would benefit from a deeper understanding of the rationale and content of the secondary EU data protection law.

---

[30] ECJ, Case 29/69 Stauder v Stadt Ulm, Judgment of 12 November 1969, ECLI:EU:C:1969:57.

[31] ECJ, Joined Cases C-92/09 and C-93/09 Volker und Markus Schecke GbR (C-92/09) and Hartmut Eifert (C-93/09) v Land Hessen, Judgment of 9 November 2010, ECLI:EU:C:2010:662.

1.5 The Right to Data Protection: The Current Doctrinal Discourse

Picking up on my criticism of the CJEU's jurisprudence, I analyse different existing conceptualisations of data protection in Chap. 4, in order to assess whether they can remedy the shortcomings of the Court's case law.

I identify seven distinct approaches to data protection, which are based explicitly on the notions of the EU data protection legislation. The transparency-focused approach considers data protection as a means to protect privacy, but also highlights that data protection provides procedural safeguards, which enhance the transparency of processing operations. The narrow self-determination approach understands data protection as an intermediate value to further privacy, but provides an early analysis of the power structures entailed by data processing practices. In opposition to this approach, the commodification approach aims to enable data subjects to market and monetize their data subject rights, while failing to consider the very power structures at work, which imply that data subjects may not be in a position to profit from such a system.

According to the privacy approach, the right to data protection can only be applied in individual cases in conjunction with the right to privacy and otherwise merely obliges the legislator to create some form of data protection provisions. The individualistic approach considers privacy as the core of the right to data protection and finds that the EU data protection legislation aims to guarantee data subjects' control over their data, while the top-down approach argues for the separate interpretation of the EU data protection legislation on the level of the primary and secondary law and restricts the scope of the former by focusing exclusively on the verbatim of Article 8 CFR. Lastly, the checks and balances approach considers the structural implications of the data protection rules and places an emphasis on the technical and organisational measures. However, while this approach provides the most comprehensive assessment of data protection under EU law to date, it bases its interpretation of the scope of the right to data protection on the Council of Europe's (CoE) Data Protection Convention No. 108 (DPC),[32] rather than the relevant secondary EU law.

I argue that almost all of the current approaches anchor data protection, at least to some extent, in notions of privacy. They can therefore address the issue posed by data processing only in terms of intrusions against an individual. On a foundational level, their analyses therefore cannot fully grasp the dangers incurred by data processing. In these current conceptions, data protection and privacy remain linked and the former contingent on the latter.

I conclude that some of the current approaches provide insights with regard to the procedural and structural dimension of data protection, such as the transparency-focused as well as the checks and balances approach. Yet, the existing approaches to EU data protection law do not provide an explanation for the scope of the EU data protection legislation and are thus not fit to fill the gaps left by the CJEU's

[32] Council of Europe, Convention for the Protection of Individuals with regard to Automatic Processing of Personal Data of 28 January 1981, ETS No. 108.

jurisprudence. In fact, many of these approaches set out to reduce the scope of the right to data protection, even though this is a compelling part of the Court's case law. Therefore, I will argue that a new approach to determine the rationale and content, i.e. scope, interferences, justifications and its essence, of the right to data protection is required.

1.6 The Right to Data Protection: The Dualistic Approach

In the final chapter, Chap. 5, I will introduce my own framework—the dualistic approach—which I use to uncover the EU data protection law from the EU data protection legislation and which allows to determine the distinct rationale and content of the right to data protection on its own terms. This approach also serves to elucidate the need for the horizontal application of the protections offered by the right and allows to differentiate the right to data protection from the right to privacy.

In Sect. 5.2, I introduce the early German discourse on data protection, led by Steinmüller, Podlech and others in the wake of the first drafts of national data protection legislation during the 1970s and 1980s. This discourse questioned the prevalent reasoning that data protection was based on privacy and instead developed data protection on its own terms. It had already identified many of the problems, which data processing entails and can be transferred to the EU level, as I demonstrate by consistently linking it to the secondary EU data protection legislation.

In order to allow for a more nuanced debate, Steinmüller, Podlech et al. introduced the differentiations between data protection and data protection law and their individual and structural dimensions, as introduced above.[33] Due to these dualities, I refer to my framework as the dualistic approach. After briefly considering the notion and potential of group rights, I argue that a dualistic approach to data protection is required in order to remedy the issue posed by the processing of personal data.

In Sect. 5.3, I apply the dualistic approach to the secondary data protection legislation in order to elucidate the issue of data processing and parse the EU data protection law from the secondary EU data protection legislation. Firstly, I consider the dual rationale of the EU secondary data protection law: addressing the risks to the rights of individuals as well as the power imbalance inherent in the processing of data. I then turn to other rationales contained in the EU data protection legislation, which extend beyond data protection.

Once I have thus uncovered the EU data protection law, I, secondly, derive the fundamental principles of EU data protection law—which reflect the entirety of the EU secondary law addressing the issue of data protection—from the body of secondary EU data protection law, which I have uncovered in the previous sections of the chapter. Furthermore, as the secondary EU data protection legislation is primarily focussed on the individual dimension of data protection law, I emphasise the structural

[33] Cf. above Sect. 1.2.

dimension of the fundamental principles, in order to demonstrate that EU data protection law acknowledges certain aspects of the structural dimension, while pointing out where these structural aspects must be taken into consideration more fully. This analysis of the content of EU data protection law, yields seven fundamental principles of EU data protection law: lawfulness, separation, integrity, availability, confidentiality, transparency and control.

In Sect. 5.4, I apply the dualistic approach to the primary EU data protection legislation in order to define the distinct rationale and content of the EU fundamental right to data protection. I argue that the right to data protection not only includes the individual, but also the structural dimension of data protection law. I will base this on the notion of fundamental rights as a value system, which has been debated at the German and European level and also applies to the EU level: it is part of the raison d'être of fundamental rights to protect the democratic society under the rule of law.

The dual rationale of the secondary EU data protection law will serve as the point of reference for defining the rationale of the right to data protection. With regard to the aim to protect individuals from the processing of personal data by mitigating the risks of data protection, I demonstrate that the fundamental principles can be used to define generic risks to the right to data protection. In order to mitigate these risks, the second part of the rationale comes into play, which is to identify data processing as instrument of power, to thus render these power structures visible and, consequently, to impose restrictions and obligations on controllers to address these power structures with appropriate safeguards.

I argue that due to the inherent risks of data processing and its power asymmetry, the scope of the right has to be wide in order to enable the substantive review of processing operations. Considering the interferences with the right to data protection, I use the fundamental principles of the secondary EU data protection law to classify the interferences in different categories. I submit that interferences with the right to data protection can be deduced from risks to the fundamental principles, which thus serve to succinctly define the extent of the fundamental right to data protection. As a consequence of the broad scope, there are various grounds to justify interferences and to achieve a balance with other fundamental rights, which I explore subsequently.

Furthermore, I argue that the fundamental principles serve to define the essence of the right to data protection in a way that ensures that the notion of essence is reserved for appropriately grave interferences with Article 8 CFR.

Lastly, I address the need for the horizontal application of the right to data protection, which has turned into a more hypothetical problem with the second generation of the EU data protection legislation: as the rules applying between private parties are now contained in regulations, rather than directives, the secondary law itself is directly applicable. Hence, I conclude that the practical issue of a gap in the protection of individual rights, which the Court has sought to solve by the horizontal application of fundamental rights, no longer persists with regard to the right to data protection.

After having laid out the rationale and content of the fundamental right to data protection, I turn to the right to privacy to illustrate that, under the dualistic approach, this right can be differentiated clearly from the right to data protection, due to their distinct rationales, scopes and essences. I conclude that the right to data protection is the only right, which addresses the issue of data processing directly. Nevertheless, I sketch how the right to privacy, just like other fundamental rights, can provide additional protection to individuals in cases of data processing.

In the last section of the chapter, Sect. 5.5, I conclude that Article 8 CFR contains a distinct right to data protection, which has to be interpreted in concordance with the EU secondary data protection law. Through the introduction of the dualistic approach, which considers the dual rationale to mitigate the risks to the right of individuals and to address the power imbalance inherent in the processing of data as well as the individual and the structural dimension of the EU data protection law, I provide a comprehensive analysis of the right to data protection. The dualistic approach is able to define the distinct rationale and content of the right to data protection and to consider its horizontal application. I achieve this by building on the fundamental principles, which I derived from the secondary EU data protection law and which are representative of its structure and characteristic provisions. This ensures that the interpretation of the right to data protection is rooted in the secondary EU data protection law and provides the necessary coherence between the two levels of EU law.

References

Articles, Books, Chapters in Books

Bernsdorff N (2014) Artikel 7. In: Meyer J (ed) Charta der Grundrechte der Europäischen Union [Charter of Fundamental Rights of the European Union], 4th edn. Nomos, Baden-Baden.

Biber S E (2021) Machines Learning the Rule of Law: EU Proposes the World's first Artificial Intelligence Act. Verfassungsblog. https://verfassungsblog.de/ai-rol/. Accessed 28 July 2021.

Bieker F, Bremert B (2020) Die Identifizierung von Risiken für die Grundrechte von Individuen [Identifying Risks to the Rights of Individuals]. ZD 7–14.

Buolamwini J, Gebru T (2018) Gender Shades: Intersectional Accuracy Disparities in Commercial Gender Classification. In: Friedler S A, Wilson C (eds) Conference on Fairness, Accountability, and Transparency. Proceedings of Machine Learning Research 81, pp. 1–15. http://proceedings.mlr.press/v81/buolamwini18a/buolamwini18a.pdf. Accessed 28 July 2021.

Gallie W B (1955–1956) Essentially Contested Concepts. Proceedings of the Aristotelian Society 56:167–198.

Podlech A (1987) Der Datenschutz und die Akzeptabilität unserer Gesellschaftsordnung [Data Protection and the Acceptability of our Societal Order]. In: Hohmann H (ed) Freiheitssicherung durch Datenschutz [Securing Political Freedom through Data Protection]. Suhrkamp, Frankfurt am Main, pp. 19–24.

Podlech A (1988) Unter welchen Bedingungen sind neue Informationssysteme gesellschaftlich akzeptabel? [Under Which Conditions Are New Information Systems Socially Acceptable?]. In: Steinmüller W (ed) Verdatet und Vernetzt [Registered and Networked]. Fischer Taschenbuch, Frankfurt am Main, pp. 118–126.

Pohle J (2018) Datenschutz und Technikgestaltung [Data Protection and Technology Design]. Berlin. https://edoc.hu-berlin.de/bitstream/handle/18452/19886/dissertation_pohle_joerg.pdf. Accessed 28 July 2021.

Richardson R, Schultz J, Crawford K (2019) Dirty Data, Bad Predictions: How Civil Rights Violations Impact Police Data, Predictive Policing Systems, and Justice. N.Y.U. L. Rev. Online 94:192–233. https://papers.ssrn.com/sol3/papers.cfm?abstract_id=3333423. Accessed 28 July 2021.
Simitis S (1973) Datenschutz – Notwendigkeit und Voraussetzungen einer gesetzlichen Regelung [Data Protection – Exigency and Requirements of Legal Regulation]. DVR 2:138–189.
Steinmüller W (1981) Die Zweite industrielle Revolution hat eben begonnen [The Second Industrial Revolution Has Just Begun]. Kursbuch 66(4):152–188.
Steinmüller W, Lutterbeck B, Mallmann C, Harborth U, Gerhard K, Schneider J (1971) Grundfragen des Datenschutzes [Fundamental Questions of Data Protection], BT-Drs. VI/3826 Anlage 1, pp. 5–193.
von Berg M, Harborth U, Jarass H D, Lutterbeck B (1972) Schafft die Datenverarbeitung den modernen Leviathan? [Is Data Processing Creating the Modern Leviathan?]. ÖVD(1):3–7.

Table of Cases: EU

ECJ, Case 29/69 Stauder v Stadt Ulm, Judgment of 12 November 1969, ECLI:EU:C:1969:57.
ECJ, Joined Cases C-92/09 and C-93/09 Volker und Markus Schecke GbR (C-92/09) and Hartmut Eifert (C-93/09) v Land Hessen, Judgment of 9 November 2010, ECLI:EU:C:2010:662.

Other Documents: National

Information Commissioner's Office (2018) Investigation Into the Use of Data Analytics in Political Campaigns. https://ico.org.uk/media/action-weve-taken/2259371/investigation-into-data-analytics-for-political-purposes-update.pdf. Accessed 28 July 2021.

Chapter 2
EU Data Protection Legislation

Contents

Abstract This chapter introduces the EU data protection legislation. EU law regulates data protection both on the level of the primary law in Articles 8 CFR and Article 16 TFEU, and on the level of the secondary law with the second generation of EU data protection legislation, i.e. the GDPR, DPR-EU, LED and ePD. The primary law has been reverse-engineered from the provisions of the first generation of secondary EU data protection legislation. The current secondary EU data protection legislation meanwhile is an evolution of the first generation. It introduces some new principles and instruments and further substantiates others that were previously established. This is particularly true for the principles of the EU data protection legislation, which form its basis. However, the principles expressly included in the relevant provisions are not representative of all of the general rules of the legislation and will therefore have to be enhanced, which will be achieved in Chap. 5.

Keywords Lawfulness · Fairness · Transparency · Purpose Limitation · Data Minimisation · Accuracy · Storage Limitation · Integrity · Confidentiality · Availability · Accountability · Necessity · Data Protection Principles · Special Categories · Sensitive Data · Supervisory Authority · Data Protection Authority · Third Country Transfers · Data Protection Impact Assessment · Data Subject Rights

© T.M.C. ASSER PRESS and the author 2022

F. Bieker, *The Right to Data Protection*, Information Technology and Law Series 34,
https://doi.org/10.1007/978-94-6265-503-4_2

2.1 Introduction

In this chapter, I will introduce the current EU data protection legislation—i.e. the body of EU law labelled as data protection—which is anchored in the primary and further defined in the secondary law. This first analysis of the content and interplay between primary and secondary law and the structure of the EU data protection legislation framework serves to introduce this specific field of EU law as well as to identify its characteristics and particular structures.

In Sect. 2.2, I introduce the primary EU data protection legislation, namely Article 8 CFR, Article 16 TFEU and Article 39 TEU. In Sect. 2.3, I introduce the secondary EU data protection legislation, i.e. the GDPR, the DPR-EU—which, according to recital 5 DPR-EU, aims to align its protections with those of the GDPR and is to be interpreted in in harmony with it—and the LED. I will also refer to the ePD, where appropriate. However, as already stated in Chap. 1, the ePD in parts goes further than the EU data protection legislation and also protects information, which is a broader notion than personal data.[1]

2.2 Primary EU Data Protection Legislation

The European Convention Responsible for Drafting the Charter of Fundamental Rights chose to include a specific right to data protection in the Charter. The EU had already gathered experience with data protection legislation with the first generation of EU data protection legislation, which was, however, based on the market harmonisation clause that is now Article 114 TFEU, as the EU competence to regulate the processing of personal data was only introduced with the Treaty of Lisbon in Article 16 TFEU.

In the following, I will firstly introduce Article 8 CFR, which contains the right to data protection (Sect. 2.2.1), before considering Article 16 TFEU and Article 39 TEU (Sect. 2.2.2), which award the EU a legislative competence with regard to data protection.

2.2.1 Article 8 CFR: A Reverse-Engineered Fundamental Right of EU Law

The EU fundamental right to data protection is enshrined in Article 8 CFR. While it has been stated that the norm itself provides little guidance,[2] it is located in Chapter II of the Charter, entitled freedoms, which consists of 14 rights, six of which consist of

[1] Cf. for instance the definition of the central term of communication in Article 2(d) ePD. Also cf. Article 5(3) ePD.

[2] Lynskey 2014, p. 570.

no more than a few lines, while the others are comprised of two to three paragraphs. Article 8 CFR, textually, is therefore one of the rights that is laid out in greater detail.

The provision states that every person has a right to the protection of their personal data. It stipulates that data must be processed fairly and for specified purposes on the basis of a legitimate legal basis. Furthermore, every person has the right of access to data concerning them and the right to have these data rectified. Lastly, the provision requires that an independent authority controls compliance with these rules.

By virtue of being elevated to a fundamental right on the level of EU primary law, data protection has been awarded constitutional value and thus been removed from the ordinary legislative procedure of Article 289 TFEU and Article 294 TFEU. In order to change the substantive principles of data protection enshrined in Article 8 CFR and as interpreted by the Court in accordance with Article 267(a) TFEU, the legislator must adhere to the ordinary revision procedure of Article 48 TEU,[3] which, inter alia, requires ratification by all Member States.

However, rights, even when they are "new" rights, are rarely taken from a vacuum.[4] With regard to data protection, a field in which the EU had already been legislating prolifically, this is particularly obvious. The Explanations to the Charter[5] (Explanations) thus point to the EU's own secondary legislation, i.e. the DPD and DPR, as well as Article 8 ECHR and the DPC as bases of the right to data protection.[6]

This mode of basing a fundamental right on secondary legislation could also be described as reverse-engineering. Reverse-engineering in the context of software engineering has been defined as "the process of analysing a subject system to identify the system's components and their interrelationships and create representations of the system in another form or at a higher level of abstraction".[7]

The EU's first regulation of data processing, the DPD, already identified the protection of fundamental rights—then in particular the right to privacy—as its objective in Article 1(1) and recital 2 DPD. The same is true for Article 1(1) DPR-EC and Article 1(1) ePD. This existing body of secondary law, along with the principles of Article 8 ECHR and the DPC, which it had incorporated in some regards,[8]

---

[3] The ordinary revision procedure applies to primary law in its entirety, cf. Ohler 2017, MN. 22.

[4] von Arnauld and Theilen 2020, pp. 36–38, esp. fn. 36.

[5] Explanations Relating to the Charter of Fundamental Rights. OJ C 303 of 14 December 2007, pp. 17–35.

[6] As González Fuster points out, however, none of the instruments referred to as bases contain any reference to a fundamental right to data protection, cf. González Fuster 2014, pp. 206 and 260.

[7] Chikofsky and Cross 1990, p. 15.

[8] The original DPC recognised the protection of rights and fundamental freedoms in Article 1, defined notions such as personal data or controller in Article 2, contained principles on data quality according to its Article 5, as well as a general prohibition of processing of special categories of data in Article 6, required the implementation of data security measures in Article 7 and contained a more basic set of data subject rights in Article 8. Building on this, the DPD introduced, inter alia, a legal definition of processor and included the collection of data in the definition of processing in Article 2(e) and (b), respectively, laid down a general requirement for a legal basis for any processing of personal data in Article 7 and procedural rules such as notifications and prior checking in Articles 18 and 20, respectively as well as the establishment of independent supervisory authorities according to Article 28. This, in turn, inspired the Additional Protocol to the DPC of 2001: Council of Europe,

created a system of data protection legislation. It thus, according to the analysis of the legislator, served as the basis of the conception for the right to data protection.

The legislator then enshrined the requirements of this system in the EU's catalogue of fundamental rights. In that sense, the legislator reverse-engineered the fundamental right to data protection, as it was modelled after the secondary legislation and transferred back unto the more abstract constitutional plane.

Reverse-engineering, further, does not involve changing the subject system or creating a new system.[9] Although the system of data protection itself was untouched by enshrining it in the primary law, the rationale of protection was indeed, at least to a certain degree, changed. The initial secondary legislation followed the express rationale of protecting the fundamental rights of individuals. However, as there was not yet an explicit right to data protection and given the historic link of EU data protection legislation to the right of privacy, the secondary law referred in particular to the obvious normative anchor, i.e. the right to privacy, as its objective.[10]

After the changes in the primary law under the Lisbon Treaty revision, which included an explicit competence of the EU to regulate the area of data protection, the new secondary legislation, i.e. the GDPR, the DPR-EU and the LED still state as their objective the protection of the fundamental rights of individuals. Yet, the legislation now refers in particular to the individual's "right to the protection of personal data".[11]

In this regard, Article 8 ECHR and the DPC—by virtue of their respective influence on the DPD, DPR-EC and ePD as the bases of the right to data protection—influenced the historic conception of Article 8 CFR. However, for conditions of and limitations on the exercise of the right to data protection the Explanations refer only to the secondary EU law.[12] Thus, the Explanations demonstrate that the interpretation of the right to data protection is not contingent on instruments like the ECHR or the DPC.[13] Instead, the EU data protection legislation only ever had partial roots in

Additional Protocol to the Convention for the Protection of Individuals with regard to Automatic Processing of Personal Data regarding supervisory authorities and transborder data flows of 8 November 2001, ETS No. 181. In 2018, the Treaty was updated by means of another protocol, which refers to the second generation of EU data protection legislation and now includes provisions on the legitimacy and transparency of the processing in Articles 5 and 8, extended data subject rights in Article 9 and a revised chapter on supervisory authorities, cf. https://rm.coe.int/convention-108-convention-for-the-protection-of-individuals-with-regar/16808b36f1. It entered into force after ratification by five Member States of the CoE, cf. https://www.coe.int/en/web/conventions/full-list/-/conventions/treaty/223/signatures?p_auth=6aEpR5ts. Accessed 28 July 2021.

[9] Chikofsky and Cross 1990, p. 15.

[10] Cf. especially Article 1(1) DPD. Cf. also Articles 1(1) DPR-EC and ePD.

[11] Article 1(2) GDPR, Article 1(2) DPR-EU and Article 1(2)(a) LED.

[12] In this regard, it should be noted that the reference to the DPD must be read as reference to the GDPR by virtue of Article 94(2) GDPR, which applies to the Explanations as they only relate to the primary law, but do not have the status of primary law.

[13] Cf. Explanations Relating to the Charter of Fundamental Rights, Explanation on Article 8, clause 4 states that: "The above-mentioned Directive and Regulation contain conditions and limitations for the exercise of the right to the protection of personal data." The ECHR and DPC are mentioned only in clause 1, which relates to the history of the provision and are no reference points of the secondary EU data protection legislation.

privacy[14] and the right to privacy under Article 7 CFR. As Gloria González Fuster puts it, the right to data protection must now be "un-coupled" from the right to privacy.[15] This underscores that in order to elucidate the right to data protection, the secondary law is of great importance for the interpretation of its rationale, scope and content.

2.2.2 *Article 16 TFEU and Article 39 TEU*

Article 16(1) TFEU contains the same wording as Article 8(1) CFR, while para 2 gives the EU legislator an express legal basis to regulate data protection with regard to the processing of personal data by the EU as well as by the Member States. The GDPR, DPR-EU and LED are based on this provision, while the ePD, as part of the first generation of EU data protection legislation, relies on Article 286 TEC (now Article 114 TFEU). Article 16(2) clause 2 TFEU requires that compliance with the rules on data protection must be monitored by independent authorities.

With regard to the nature of Article 16 TFEU there is a debate almost exclusively in the German commentary literature, which revolves around the question whether Article 16(1) TFEU contains a fundamental right. The Explanations only refer to Article 16 TFEU as well as Article 39 TEU in passing, stating that they replace Article 286 TEC, which was the basis of the first generation of EU data protection legislation.[16]

While some authors argue, based on the wording of Article 16(1) TFEU, that it not only mirrors, but also stipulates the right to data protection,[17] others argue that Article 16 TFEU gives the EU a mandate to act in order to guarantee the fundamental right to data protection contained in the Charter.[18] From the deliberations of the Convention on the proposal for a Constitution, which contained a similar clause in Article I-50, it transpires that a motion to remove the reference to the provision did not find sufficient support, as the members felt that without it, para 2 would not be comprehensible.[19] Schröder argues that Article 16(1) TFEU affirms the importance of the right to data protection as contained in the Charter.[20]

---

[14] According to González Fuster, it "is a misconception, thus, to claim that the protection of personal data derives, generally speaking, from privacy", cf. González Fuster 2014, p. 268; also cf. De Hert and Gutwirth 2009, p. 10.

[15] González Fuster 2014, pp. 260 and 269 et seq.

[16] Cf. Explanations Relating to the Charter of Fundamental Rights, Explanation on Article 8, clause 2.

[17] Sobotta 2017, MN. 2; Frenz 2009, MN. 1357; Zerdick 2012, MN. 7; Brühann 2015, MN. 31 et seq.

[18] Hijmans 2016, pp. 4 and 127.

[19] Brühann 2015, MN. 30.

[20] Schröder 2018, MN. 5; less clear, but ultimately finding that Article 16 TFEU is a symbolic provision rather than an operative fundamental right Simitis et al. 2019, MN. 177.

It should be stressed that this debate is of no practical consequence,[21] as even those who argue for Article 16 TFEU[22] containing a fundamental right, directly or indirectly apply the justification clause of Article 52(1) CFR to Article 16 TFEU[23] or find that, while it was unclear why Article 16(1) TFEU mirrors Article 8 CFR, the latter is the only relevant provision for the application of the right to data protection.[24]

A systematic interpretation of Title II TFEU, which contains Article 16 TFEU proves inconclusive: it includes several programmatic assurances,[25] which are directed at the Union. Yet, the following Part Two of the treaty contains individual rights, such as non-discrimination according to Article 18 or EU citizenship in Article 20 TFEU. The wording of Article 15(3) TFEU awards a right of access to documents. Unlike Article 16 TFEU, however, Article 15 TFEU does not provide the EU with a competence to legislate in the area of access to documents, it can therefore only regulate access to its own documents.

Yet, the finding that Article 16(1) TFEU is an affirmation of the importance of data protection is supported, in addition to the historic interpretation, by the telos of Article 16 TFEU. When considering Article 16(2) TFEU, it transpires that the purpose of Article 16 TFEU is to provide an express legal basis for the Union to legislate in the area of data protection, rather than mirror a right already contained in the Charter. Article 16 TFEU thus contains an organisational and structural principle, directed at the EU, emphasising the importance of data protection for the entirety of Union law.[26]

Article 16(2) subpara 1 TFEU states that it does not affect Article 39 TEU, which in turn, contains a legal basis to regulate the processing of personal data by the Member States within the scope of the Common Foreign and Security Policy (CFSP) of this chapter TEU, the former second pillar of the EU. The CFSP, under the reform of the Lisbon Treaty, has remained separate from the other policies of the EU. Due to this, the material scope of the GDPR does not extend to the processing of personal data by the Member States within the scope of the CFSP according to Article 2(2)(b) GDPR. According to Article 39 clause 1 TEU, the Council shall adopt a decision to lay down rules on data protection, while clause 2 states that these rules must also be subject to oversight by independent supervisory authorities. The Council, so far, has neglected to adopt such a decision.

---

[21] With regard to the effects of Article 16 TFEU for the Area of Security and Justice (AFSJ) and Declarations 20, Protocols No. 21, No. 22 and No. 36, cf. Boehm 2012, pp. 116–120, who argued that this would open the doors for separate legislation for general data processing and processing in the field of law enforcement and has been proven right by the GDPR, LED and DPR-EU.

[22] Even though it seems odd that the same, by extension, should not apply to Article 39 TEU.

[23] Sobotta 2017, MN. 8; Frenz 2009, MN. 1363; Zerdick 2012, MN. 9; Brühann 2015, MN. 31 et seq.; cf. also Marsch 2018, pp. 66 et seq.

[24] Kingreen 2016a, MN. 3; Kingreen 2016b, MN. 5.

[25] Cf. Articles 7–14 and 17 TFEU.

[26] Schröder 2018, MN. 6.

2.3 Secondary EU Data Protection Legislation

On the level of the secondary law, the EU data protection legislation has matured and received an update with its second generation. In the following, I will introduce the current legislation by laying out its objective—which connects it directly with the primary EU data protection legislation introduced in the preceding section—and scope (Sect. 2.3.1). I will then consider the principles of the EU data protection legislation (Sect. 2.3.2), which serve as a more abstract first part of the legislation, perhaps intended to pull more general concepts to the fore, as they can then inform the interpretation of the more specific rules. As I move on to the further provisions of the EU data protection legislation (Sect. 2.3.3), I will find, however, that the principles of the EU data protection legislation are not representative of the content of all of these rules.

2.3.1 *Objective and Scope*

The second generation of secondary EU data protection legislation states as its objective the protection of fundamental rights of individuals and explicitly refers to the right to data protection.[27] Its material scope covers the processing by automated as well as by other means where the personal data are at least intended to form part of a filing system.[28] Processing is defined as any operation or set of operations performed on personal data or datasets. It includes, inter alia, the collection,[29] storage, alteration, disclosure, transfer and erasure of personal data.[30] Similarly, the notion of personal data is defined broadly: it not only extends to identified natural persons, but also includes information that renders a natural person identifiable.[31]

The territorial scope of the GDPR covers the processing of personal data by a controller or processor, who has an establishment within the EU, or when the processing relates to the offering of goods or services to data subjects in the EU or where it serves to monitor behaviour that takes place in the EU.[32] For the LED and

[27] Article 1(2) GDPR, Article 1(2) DPR-EU and Article 1(2)(a) LED.

[28] Article 2(1) GDPR, Article 2(5) DPR-EU and Article 2(2) LED. The term filing system is defined in Article 4(6) GDPR, Article 3(7) DPR-EU and Article 3(6) LED as any structured set of personal data, which are accessible according to specific criteria, which corresponds to the definition in Article 2(c) DPD. The latter, according to the ECJ, has to be interpreted widely and does not require the data to be collected in a structured form, so long as data about a specific person can be easily retrieved, ECJ, Case C-25/17 Tietosuojavaltuutettu – Jehovan todistajat, Judgment of 10 July 2018, ECLI:EU:C:2018:551, paras 55–61, esp. paras 60 et seq.

[29] For a deconstruction of this term, cf. Benjamin 2021.

[30] Article 4(2) GDPR, Article 3(3) DPR-EU and Article 3(2) LED.

[31] Article 4(1) GDPR, Article 3(1) DPR-EU and Article 3(1) LED.

[32] Article 3 GDPR.

the DPR-EU the territorial scope is defined by virtue of the fact that these provisions address specific authorities and institutions within the EU.[33]

2.3.2 *Principles of the EU Data Protection Legislation*

After setting out the objective, scope and definitions in their respective Chapter I, the second chapters of the GDPR, DPR-EU[34] and LED define the data protection principles, which are intended to form the bases of the subsequent provisions. The DPD and the DPR-EC, with Articles 4 and 6, respectively, already contained principles "relating to data quality", which set out basic conditions for the processing of personal data in general: fair and lawful processing, purpose limitation, data minimisation, accuracy and storage limitation as well as accountability. Under the second generation of EU data protection legislation, these principles—now more appropriately labelled "Principles relating to the processing of personal data"—have been amended by the principles of transparency,[35] integrity and confidentiality. The principle of accountability has been expanded and now not only requires controllers to ensure compliance with the other principles, but also to be able to demonstrate this compliance.

The principles of Chapter II are not absolute: under Article 85(2) GDPR Member States may provide for exemptions or derogations from these principles, if they are necessary to reconcile the right to data protection with the freedom of expression and information for journalistic, artistic or literary purposes. Furthermore, the aspects of Article 5 GDPR corresponding to the rights in Articles 12–22 GDPR, i.e. the data subject rights, are subject to the restrictions clause of Article 23(1) GDPR.[36] Accordingly, Member States may pass legislation in order to safeguard exhaustively listed interests, such as national and public security or the rights and freedoms of others. However, this is subject to the explicit caveat that these restrictions must respect the essence of fundamental rights and conform to the principle of proportionality. While, with regard to Article 52(1) CFR, this caveat is mostly declaratory, the requirements of Article 23(2) GDPR and Article 25(2) DPR-EU specify that the measures must, inter alia, contain safeguards to prevent misconduct, identify the risks to the rights and freedoms of individuals and, in the case of the GDPR, the right of data subjects to generally be informed about these restrictions.

As Articles 23(1) and 85(2) GDPR as well as Article 25(1) DPR-EU allow derogations from the guarantees of the secondary legislation, which aims to award a high level of protection of fundamental rights according to recital 10 GDPR, they will

---

[33] Articles 2 DPR-EU and LED.

[34] Also cf. Chapter IX of the DPR-EU on the processing of operational personal data in the AFSJ concerning judicial cooperation in criminal matters and police cooperation.

[35] Not mentioned explicitly in Article 71 DPR-EU and Article 4 LED, cf. below Sect. 2.3.2.3.

[36] Also cf. Article 25(1) DPR-EU.

have to be interpreted restrictively. According to the case law of the ECJ, this means that restrictions and derogations must be applied only in so far as strictly necessary.[37]

2.3.2.1 Lawfulness

The principle of lawfulness[38] is central for data protection law and requires that, in order to process personal data, any entity must rely on a legal basis. Under Article 6 GDPR, Articles 5 and 72 DPR-EU as well as Article 8 LED, which further define this principle, personal data may be processed only if and to the extent that this is covered by a specific legal basis under the conditions laid out in these provisions. While they provide extensive grounds for justifying the processing of personal data, the processing of personal data without a legal basis is unlawful.

However, the potential legal bases[39] are limited for public authorities, as they may only access data necessary to perform a task for a purpose defined by a legal basis.[40] Private entities may recur to a broader range of legal bases, as they are the result of the legislator's balancing of the controller's and data subject's respective fundamental rights.[41] In either case, personal data may be processed only if the controller can rely on a legal basis, which implies that it is otherwise not allowed.

[37] ECJ, Case C-73/07 Tietosuojavaltuutettu v Satakunnan Markkinapörssi Oy and Satamedia Oy, Judgment of 16 December 2008, ECLI:EU:C:2008:727, para 56; ECJ, Joined Cases C-92/09 and C-93/09 Volker und Markus Schecke GbR (C-92/09) and Hartmut Eifert (C-93/09) v Land Hessen, Judgment of 9 November 2010, ECLI:EU:C:2010:662, para 77; ECJ, Case C-473/12 Institut professionnel des agents immobiliers (IPI) v Geoffrey Englebert and Others, Judgment of 7 November 2013, ECLI:EU:C:2013:715, para 39; ECJ, Joined Cases C-293/12 and C-594/12 Digital Rights Ireland Ltd (C-293/12) v Minister for Communications, Marine and Natural Resources and Others and Kärntner Landesregierung (C-594/12) and Others, Judgment of 8 April 2014, ECLI:EU:C:2014:238, paras 52 et seq.

[38] Article 5(1)(a) GDPR, Articles 4(1)(a) and 71(1)(a) DPR-EU as well as Article 4(1)(a) LED.

[39] According to recital 45 GDPR it is not required to provide an individual, specific law for each individual processing operation, when the controller carries out the processing based on a legal obligation of Union or Member State law, in the public interest or in the exercise of vested public authority. Rather, multiple processing operations may be based on the same legal obligation. However, the permissible purposes of that processing must be determined by the legislator.

[40] Cf. in particular the restrictions on public authorities when processing data on the basis of Union or Member State law, which must pre-define the objectives of the processing operation, in Articles 5(1)(a) and (2) and 71(1) and (2) DPR-EU, Article 8(1) and (2) LED, and Article 6(1)(e) and (3) GPDR as well as the exclusion of Article 6(1)(f) GDPR for public authorities in Article 6(1) subpara 1 GDPR. On the issue of freely given consent vis-à-vis a public authority ECJ, Case C-291/12 Michael Schwarz v Stadt Bochum, Judgment of 17 October 2013, ECLI:EU:C:2013:670, paras 31 et seq.; ECJ, Joined Cases C-92/09 and C-93/09 Volker und Markus Schecke GbR (C-92/09) and Hartmut Eifert (C-93/09) v Land Hessen, Opinion of AG Sharpston of 17 June 2010, ECLI:EU:C:2010:353, paras 81–85.

[41] Article 6 GDPR.

Some argue that the EU data protection legislation does, in fact, not include a general ban on data processing.[42] The processing of data was not generally prohibited, but rather authorised under the circumstances outlined in Article 6(1) GDPR.[43] Yet, it is unclear how the need for an authorisation is different from the general ban of an activity. If an entity requires an authorisation to pursue a certain activity, this implies that it is otherwise hindered in its exercise.

While the State cannot interfere with fundamental rights of citizens without a legal basis, the general principle between private parties is that anything that is not prohibited is allowed.[44] However, this is restricted by fundamental rights, which oblige the State to protect the individual.[45] Accordingly, the State has to intervene on behalf of the party, whose rights are infringed. In the case law of the Court on the processing personal data, which I will analyse in Chap. 3, the processing of personal data without any legal basis is a violation of Article 8 CFR.[46] Consequently, the EU legislator, by introducing a general ban of processing personal data through the principle of lawfulness, conformed to this duty to protect and implemented the general ban of processing, stipulated on the level of EU primary law, in the secondary law. However, this general ban on processing is, of course, not an absolute ban. Rather Article 6(1) GDPR, Article 5 DPR-EU and Article 8 LED include numerous legal bases, which allow processing operations.

Paul De Hert and Serge Gutwirth, who also argue against a general ban, further contend that the EU data protection legislation does not prohibit data processing, but rather ensures accountability and empowers data subjects to contest illegitimate practices.[47] They substantiate this with the claim that the EU data protection legislation was based on prior regulations in the Member States, which did not include such a general prohibition, and the fact that Article 7(f) DPD (now Article 6(1)(f) GDPR) allowed processing for a wide range of purposes, if the legitimate interests of the controller are not overridden by the rights or interests of data subjects.[48]

As to the first argument it should only briefly be recalled, that Union legislation is not contingent on prior legislation in the Member States. The legal order of the EU is autonomous from those of the Member States and the interpretation of its legislation must not be based on notions of national law.[49] Thus, the EU legislator is free to introduce rules that previously did not exist in some Member States.

---

[42] Roßnagel 2019, MN. 35 states that Article 6 GDPR barely restricts the processing and largely allows it; De Hert and Gutwirth 2006, p. 78 argue that the EU data protection legislation assumes that the processing of personal data is "in principle allowed and legal".

[43] Roßnagel 2019, MN. 35.

[44] Pötters 2017, MN. 7.

[45] As rightly pointed out by Roßnagel 2019, MN. 37.

[46] Cf. Chap. 3, Sect. 3.2.

[47] De Hert and Gutwirth 2006, p. 77.

[48] Ibid., pp. 78 et seq.

[49] ECJ, Case 26/62 Van Gend en Loos v Administratie der Belastingen, Judgment of 5 February 1963, ECLI:EU:C:1963:1, p. 12.

Concerning the second argument it should be understood that even a broad exception or several permissions do not change the fact, that the processing of personal data, under the principle of lawfulness, is generally prohibited. To paraphrase Hart, a rule that ends with "only if" is still a rule.[50] The wording of this rule states explicitly, that "processing shall be lawful only if" one of the expressly and exhaustively listed legal bases of literae (a) through (f) is fulfilled. Even if some legal bases, such as consent, performance of a contract or the legitimate interests of controllers are indeed far-reaching, the principle of lawfulness is a cornerstone of the EU data protection legislation. As the case law of the ECJ demonstrates,[51] it is even enshrined on a constitutional level: the processing of personal data is an interference with Article 8 CFR. It must thus be justified through recourse to a legitimate legal basis. Furthermore, Article 7(f) DPD, just like Article 6(1)(f) GDPR, required a balancing of the interests of controllers with the rights and interests of the data subjects, which may override the former, in order to legitimize the processing. While this is left in the hands of controllers,[52] the legitimate interest and thus the outcome of the balancing, must be documented by the controller and is subject to control by data subjects as well as supervisory authorities according to Articles 13(1)(d), 14(2)(b) and 35(7)(d) GDPR.

2.3.2.2 Fairness

Under the first generation of EU data protection legislation, fairness referred to the possibility of the data subject to know of a processing operation and to be informed comprehensively when data concerning them were collected.[53] Hence, the principle was listed as an aim of the information rights under Articles 10 and 11(2) DPD. The understanding of fairness was thus geared towards the provision of adequate information to the data subjects.[54]

Under the GDPR, recital 39 links the principle of fairness explicitly to transparency by stating that the principle of transparency concerns the provision of information "to ensure fair and transparent processing".[55] While neither the recitals nor the substantive provisions of the GDPR shed much light on the meaning of fairness,

---

[50] Hart 1994, p. 139.

[51] Cf. Chap. 3, Sect. 3.4.

[52] The EU data protection legislation and specifically the GDPR shows the somewhat unsettling tendency of the legislator to 'privatize' the duty to balance fundamental rights, which is directed first and foremost towards the EU and/or the Member States (cf. Article 51(1) CFR). Instead, controllers find themselves in the position to balance their interests with the rights of individuals. This is a challenging position for controllers, as they have to act against their interest in an increased efficiency in data processing and shows one of the core conflicts in data protection law in practice, cf. also Chap. 5, Sect. 5.3.2.2.

[53] Recital 38 DPD.

[54] Cf. ECJ, Case C-201/14 Smaranda Bara and Others v Casa Naţională de Asigurări de Sănătate and Others, Judgment of 1 October 2015, ECLI:EU:C:2015:638, para 34.

[55] Cf. also Marsch 2018, pp. 172 et seq., who does not at all mention the connection to lawfulness.

it can be observed that fairness occurs always in tandem with either the principle of lawfulness[56] or the principle of transparency.[57]

Thus, while the concept of fairness under the first generation of EU data protection legislation served to ensure transparency, which was not explicitly included in the principles of Article 6 DPD, it seems doubtful whether, with the introduction of transparency as its own principle, a separate substance remains.[58] According to the Handbook on European data protection law co-published by the EU Agency for Fundamental Rights, the CoE and the European Data Protection Supervisor (EDPS), the principle of fairness extends beyond transparency and is linked to ethical considerations, which exceed legal requirements.[59] Fairness in that sense concerns expectations of a party due to trust built in previous interactions.[60]

In a similar vein, and by reference to consumer law, Maxwell argues[61] that fairness requires the controller to act in good faith,[62] which is inter alia not the case when there is a "significant imbalance in the rights and obligations of the parties" according to Article 3(1) Directive 93/13/EEC[63]. This link is established by recital 42 GDPR, which states that consent should be phrased in an accessible manner, "should not contain unfair terms" and which refers expressly to Directive 93/13/EEC. As recital 42 GDPR demonstrates, the legislator intended to build a bridge to consumer protection law. Consumer protection is a field, which partly overlaps with data protection, although it operates under different auspices. It can also effectively help to enforce data protection law,[64] though it is limited to private entities processing data. The principle of fairness thereby expands the EU data protection legislation beyond the immediate rationale of data protection to incorporate considerations of consumer protection.[65]

---

[56] Recitals 39, 45, Article 6(2) and (3) GDPR.

[57] Recitals 42, 60, 71, Articles 13(2), 14(2), 40(2)(a) GDPR.

[58] Cf. also Roßnagel 2019, MN. 45.

[59] European Union Agency for Fundamental Rights et al., Handbook on European data protection law, p. 119. Luxembourg. https://fra.europa.eu/sites/default/files/fra_uploads/fra-coe-edps-2018-handbook-data-protection_en.pdf. Accessed 16 June 2021.

[60] Roßnagel 2019, MN. 47.

[61] Maxwell 2015, pp. 208–210.

[62] The German equivalent of good faith "Treu und Glauben" is indeed used to translate "fairly" in the German version of Article 5(1)(a) GDPR; from a cursory overview it transpires that the translations of fairness vary among the different language versions: FR: "loyale"; ES/PT: "leal"; NL: "behoorlijk"; SV: "korrekt"; IT: "corretto"; DK: "rimeligt".

[63] Council Directive 93/13/EEC of 5 April 1993 on unfair terms in consumer contracts, OJ L 95 of 21 April 1993, pp. 29–34.

[64] The fact that consumer protection organisations play an important role in the enforcement of data protection law can be seen by their engagement in legal actions, cf. for instance ECJ, Case C-191/15 Verein für Konsumenteninformation v Amazon EU Sàrl, Judgment of 28 July 2016, ECLI:EU:C:2016:612; ECJ, Case C-40/17 Fashion ID GmbH & Co.KG v Verbraucherzentrale NRW eV, Judgment of 29 July 2019, ECLI:EU:C:2019:629.

[65] Cf. in more detail Chap. 5, Sect. 5.3.1.2.

2.3.2.3 Transparency

The principle of transparency is linked to the rules on communication and information of data subjects according to Articles 12–14 GDPR and Article 14 DPR-EU, communication with data subjects on the exercise of their rights under Articles 15–22 GDPR and Articles 15 et seq. DPR-EU as well as the communication of data breaches of Article 34(2) GDPR and Article 35 DPR-EU.[66] According to recital 39 GDPR, transparency implies that all information regarding the processing operation must be easily accessible and easy to understand. The Article 29 Working Party guidelines on transparency under the GDPR, which have been endorsed by the European Data Protection Board (EDPB or the Board),[67] stress the importance of the quality, accessibility and comprehensibility of the information provided,[68] i.e. the formal aspect of transparency. This is further detailed by the specific conditions of Article 12(1) GDPR and Article 14(1) DPR-EU on the information of data subjects. These provisions aim to ensure that the information provided is comprehensive, but remains comprehensible for an average data subject.

The LED and Chapter IX DPR-EU differ in this regard from this standard: while recital 26 LED requires that every processing "must be lawful, fair and transparent" for the individuals concerned, Article 71(1)(a) DPR-EU and Article 4(1)(a) LED do not contain the principle of transparency explicitly, but only list lawfulness and fairness. Yet, the data subject rights to transparent communication and information are contained in Articles 78 et seq. DPR-EU and Articles 12 et seq. LED.

In order to comply with the obligations of data protection by design and by default under Article 25 GDPR, which is also an obligation under Article 27 DPR-EU and Article 20 LED, controllers, according to recital 78 GDPR, can implement measures in a processing operation, in order to allow for a better understanding of the functions of the processing and thus enhance transparency.[69]

The Article 29 Working Party guidelines also state that transparency is intrinsically linked to the principle of fairness, as included in Article 8 CFR.[70] Transparency is a prerequisite for data subjects to hold controllers and processors accountable and to exercise control, as they are informed about the processing operation as well as their data subject rights. Thus, transparency is a foundational requirement for processing operations, as the provision of complete and accessible information is essential for data subjects to exercise their data subject rights.

Compliance with this general obligation of transparency is also closely related to the principle of accountability according to Article 5(2), which requires the controller

---

[66] Article 29 Working Party, Guidelines on transparency under Regulation 2016/679. WP 260 rev. 01, pp. 4 and 6, paras 1 and 7.

[67] European Data Protection Board, Endorsement 1/2018 of 25 May 2018.

[68] Article 29 Working Party, Guidelines on transparency under Regulation 2016/679, p. 5, para 4 and pp. 7–11.

[69] Ibid., p. 22, para 43.

[70] Ibid., pp. 4 et seq., para 2.

to demonstrate compliance with all the principles of Article 5(1) GDPR.[71] The transparency of a processing operation is supported by the maintenance of a record of processing activities according to Article 30 GDPR and, for processing operations that pose a high risk to the rights and freedoms of natural persons—or as best practice—through a Data Protection Impact Assessment (DPIA) under Article 35 GDPR.[72]

2.3.2.4 Purpose Limitation

According to the principle of purpose limitation[73] the controller may collect data only for specific, explicit and legitimate purposes and must not process them further for incompatible purposes.[74] The principle of purpose limitation is a paramount part of data protection law, as the properly defined purpose of the processing operation is a precondition to determine whether the processing complies with the law. The purpose defines the objective, which the processing operation aims to achieve; it defines the reason of and thereby provides the substantive justification for the processing.[75]

Specification of Purposes

Therefore, the purpose has to be defined explicitly, which means that the mere description of the relevant legal basis is not sufficient, but rather must define a specific task in a sufficiently narrow and precise manner.[76] A single processing operation may serve multiple purposes. However, in that case, all of the purposes must be defined and described. This is of great relevance with regard to the principle of lawfulness, as the different purposes may require different legal bases. For instance, the processing of a data subject's address may serve the purpose of shipping goods to their address, which is based on a commercial contract on the sale of goods according to Article 6(1)(b),[77] while sending advertisements to that same address would require the data subject's consent, as it is not necessary[78] for the performance of the contract.

---

[71] Ibid.

[72] Article 29 Working Party, Guidelines on Data Protection Impact Assessment (DPIA) and determining whether processing is "likely to result in a high risk" for the purposes of Regulation 2016/679. WP 248 rev.01, p. 18.

[73] Article 5(1)(b) GDPR, Articles 4(1)(b) and 71(1)(b) DPR-EU as well as Article 4(1)(b) LED.

[74] Article 29 Working Party, Opinion 03/2013 on purpose limitation of 2 April 2013. WP 203, p. 15; which has not been endorsed by the EDPB, as it concerned the DPD, rather than the GDPR. Nevertheless, Article 5(1)(b) clause 1 GDPR has the exact same wording as Article 6(1)(b) clause 1 DPD.

[75] Roßnagel 2019, MN. 69.

[76] Article 29 Working Party, Opinion 03/2013 on purpose limitation of 2 April 2013, pp. 15 et seq.; Roßnagel 2019, MN. 89 et seq.

[77] However, with regard to the principle of data minimisation, it could well be argued that it is not the online shop that actually requires the address, but rather the delivery service, whereas the online shop could operate with pseudonyms, cf. Dix 2003.

[78] Cf. below Sect. 2.3.2.5.

Concerning the communication of the purpose or purposes to data subjects, the requirements of the principle of transparency apply fully. The purpose has to be provided to data subjects at the latest at the time of the collection under the principle of transparency and Article 12 GDPR.[79] In order to enable data subjects to make an informed choice, the reason their data are processed is of great significance.[80]

Legitimacy of the Purpose

The legitimacy of the purpose of the processing goes beyond the lawfulness of the processing operation under Article 6 GDPR, Articles 5 and 72 DPR-EU as well as Article 8 LED. While under the DPD Article 7 was the only provision in Section II entitled "Criteria for Making Data Processing Legitimate", and could therefore be held to restrict the notion of legitimacy in Article 6(1)(b) DPD,[81] the Article 29 Working Party already interpreted the notion of legitimacy widely and included legal considerations in the broadest sense, including any area or form of law and extending it to customs, codes of conducts and even ethics.[82] Under the GDPR, DPR-EU and LED, the provisions on legal bases expressly refers to lawfulness, demonstrating that this did not—or at least now does not—correspond to the legitimacy of the purpose. In order to be deemed legitimate, the purpose of the processing must not run counter to the legal order and must be in conformity to the rules and principles of data protection included in the secondary legislation.[83]

Compatible Purposes

The processing of the collected data is generally limited to those tasks initially defined and communicated to data subjects[84] or at least specifically defined in a legal provision.[85] Tasks that are not covered by the purpose for which they were collected, are generally inadmissible. An exception is made when there are compatible purposes in the sense of Article 6(4) GDPR[86] or Article 6 DPR-EU under which data may be further processed.[87] Article 5(1)(b) clause 2 GDPR lists archiving purposes, scientific or historical research purposes and statistical purposes, subject to the safeguards prescribed by the GDPR and explicated in Article 89(1), as purposes that are considered to be compatible.

[79] Article 29 Working Party, Opinion 03/2013 on purpose limitation of 2 April 2013, p. 15; cf. also Recital 39 GDPR.

[80] Ibid., p. 17.

[81] Brouwer 2011, pp. 278 et seq.

[82] Article 29 Working Party, Opinion 03/2013 on purpose limitation of 2 April 2013, pp. 19 et seq.

[83] Cf. Chap. 5, Sect. 5.3.2.2 for a more in-depth consideration of the legitimacy of purposes.

[84] Cf. for instance Articles 13(1)(f), 14(1)(e) GDPR and Articles 15(1)(e) and 16(1)(e) DPR-EU.

[85] Cf. for instance Article 6(3) subsection 1 GDPR, Article 72(2) DPR-EU or Article 8(2) LED.

[86] Article 9(2) GPDR and Article 13 DPR-EU state that they apply for purposes of archiving, scientific or historical research.

[87] Zuiderveen Borgesius and Hallinan 2020, provide an in-depth analysis of compatible purposes.

2.3.2.5 Data Minimisation

The principle of data minimisation under Article 5(1)(c) GDPR and Article 4(1)(c) DPR-EU requires that personal data are adequate, relevant and limited to what is necessary in relation to the purposes of their processing. Under Article 71(1)(c) DPR-EU and Article 4(1)(c) LED the latter requirement is phrased differently: the personal data must not be excessive in relation to the purposes for which they were collected. Yet, the requirements of Article 52(1) CFR, especially concerning the necessity of the interference, apply fully to any measure taken by EU institutions in the context of the DPR-EU or national law enforcement in order to implement the LED. The relevant provisions have to be interpreted in conformity with this requirement of primary law.

Data minimisation limits the processing of personal data with regard to the purpose by ensuring that only data that are adequate, i.e. appropriate for attaining the purpose, and relevant for attaining at least parts of the purpose are processed.[88] The principle of data minimisation is thus closely connected to the principle of purpose limitation.[89]

The necessity[90] of a processing operation is the relation between a processing operation and the fulfilment of a specific task,[91] i.e. attaining the purpose of the processing. Data are necessary when the task of the controller, which defines the purpose of the processing, cannot be attained, cannot be attained in time, cannot be attained completely or can only be attained with unreasonable effort[92] without the specific data in question.[93] It must thus be assessed, whether there is an alternative way of achieving the task and thereby attaining the purpose through a less invasive processing operation.[94] Thereby, data minimisation incorporates the general principle of proportionality with regard to finding less intrusive methods to achieve a purpose, i.e. necessity.[95] This principle is further implemented in the requirements of data protection by design and by default according to Article 25 GDPR,[96] which affirm that data protection must be implemented before any data are processed and the processed data must be as minimal as possible for the specific purpose.[97]

---

[88] Roßnagel 2019, MN. 120 et seq.

[89] Konferenz der unabhängigen Datenschutzaufsichtsbehörden des Bundes und der Länder 2020, p. 10.

[90] The requirement of necessity can already be deduced from the fact that the processing of personal data is an interference with Article 8 CFR and must thus be reduced as much as possible, Roßnagel 2019, MN. 67.

[91] Podlech 1982, p. 455.

[92] This is based on recital 39 GDPR, which states that personal data should be processed only if the purpose cannot be achieved reasonably by other means.

[93] Roßnagel 2019, MN. 122.

[94] Ibid.

[95] Sobotta 2017, MN. 8.

[96] Articles 27 and 85 DPR-EU as well as Article 20 LED.

[97] Cf. below Sect. 2.3.3.3.

2.3.2.6 Accuracy

The principle of accuracy under Article 5(1)(d) GDPR[98] requires that data are accurate, kept up to date where necessary and that it must be ensured that inaccurate data are erased or rectified.[99] Controllers are thus obliged to ensure that, when they collect data, these are factually correct and must keep them updated only where this is necessary with regard to the purpose of the processing. Whenever data are processed only in order to document the situation at the time of the collection, it is not necessary to keep them up to date.[100] The controller, by virtue of the last requirement concerning the erasure or rectification of inaccurate data, is further under an obligation to proactively ensure that data are accurate and updated, if this is necessary to attain the purpose of the processing.[101]

Data subjects have rights corresponding to these obligations: according to Article 16 GDPR[102] they have a right to rectification and under Article 18(1)(a) GDPR[103] they have a right to object to the processing of personal data. When a data subject contests the accuracy of the data, the data may be stored, but otherwise processed only for certain, exhaustively enumerated purposes with the data subject's consent or to defend legal claims according to Article 18(2) GDPR.[104]

2.3.2.7 Storage Limitation

Article 5(1)(e) GDPR[105] states that personal data must not be kept in a form which allows the identification of data subjects for longer than necessary to attain the purpose of the processing. From this wording, it could be inferred that the principle of storage limitation does not per se require the deletion of data, but rather to remove those data that render an individual identifiable according to Article 4(1) GDPR, Article 3(1) DPR-EU and Article 3(1) LED.[106] However, recital 39 GDPR[107] states that the controller should set time limits for erasure of data or at least, for a periodic review of stored data, which aims to ensure that data are not kept longer than

[98] Articles 4(1)(d) and 71(1)(d) DPR-EU as well as Article 4(1)(d) LED.

[99] On the application of the principle to opinions, cf. Hallinan and Zuiderveen Borgesius 2020.

[100] Roßnagel 2019, MN. 142; Weichert 2018, MN. 52 et seq.

[101] When data are erased or rectified, the controller is further under a general obligation according to Article 19 GDPR and Article 21 DPR-EU to inform each recipient of the data of such changes. Similarly, the controller is obliged to inform the public authority from which the data originated under Article 82(5) DPR-EU and Article 16(5) LED.

[102] Articles 18 and 82(1) DPR-EU as well as Article 16(1) LED.

[103] Articles 20(1)(a) and 82(3)(a) DPR-EU as well as Article 16(3)(a) LED.

[104] If the accuracy of the data is subsequently verified by the controller, the restriction may be lifted after the data subject has been informed according to Article 18(3) GDPR, Articles 20(3) and 82(3) subparagraph 2 DPR-EU as well as Article 16(3) subparagraph 1 LED.

[105] Articles 4(1)(e) and 71(1)(e) DPR-EU as well as Article 4(1)(e) LED.

[106] Roßnagel 2019, MN. 156.

[107] Recital 20 DPR-EU and Article 72 DPR-EU as well as Article 5 LED.

necessary.[108] This demonstrates the strong link of the principle of storage limitation to the principle of data minimisation and, more specifically, its necessity requirement.

However, the EU data protection rules also allow the storing for purposes of archiving and scientific, historical or statistical purposes,[109] which are considered compatible purposes under the principle of purpose limitation, subject to appropriate technical and organisational measures, such as pseudo- or anonymisation.[110] While the EU data protection legislation does not define the latter, pseudonymisation is the processing of personal data in a way that does not allow the data to be attributed to a specific individual without separately kept additional information, i.e. an assignment function. When data are anonymous, they no longer render an individual identifiable as required by Article 4(1) GDPR, Article 3(1) DPR-EU and Article 3(1) LED and are thus outside the scope of the EU data protection legislation. Unlike pseudonymised data, anonymised data cannot be backtracked to identify the original data subjects.

2.3.2.8 Integrity and Confidentiality

The principles of integrity and confidentiality, now expressly included in Article 5(1)(f) GDPR,[111] aim to ensure an appropriate level of security for personal data by implementing technical and organisational measures. They are, therefore, very closely related to the rules on the responsibility of the controller,[112] the security of processing[113] and data protection by design and by default,[114] which link the determination of the appropriateness of the measures to the risks for the rights and freedoms of natural persons.[115]

Integrity requires that the systems and processes conform to their specifications, and the content as well as attributes of data[116] are qualitatively intact and quantitatively complete.[117] This means that the data are verifiably unaltered and untampered. Furthermore, the controller has to ensure that changes in the data can be traced.

---

[108] These time limits have to be communicated to data subjects according to Articles 13(2)(a), 14(2)(a) and 15(1)(d) GDPR, Articles 15(2)(a), 16(2)(a), 17(1)(d), 79(2)(b) and 80(d) DPR-EU as well as Articles 13(2)(b) and 14(d) LED, and contained in the record of processing activities according to Article 30(1)(f) GDPR, Article 31(1)(f) DPR-EU and Article 24 LED.

[109] Article 5(1)(b) GDPR, Articles 4(1)(b) and 71(3) DPR-EU as well as Article 4(3) LED.

[110] Cf. above Sect. 2.3.2.4.

[111] Articles 4(1)(f) and 71(1)(f) DPR-EU as well as Article 4(1)(f) LED.

[112] Article 24 GDPR, Article 26 DPR-EU and Article 19 LED.

[113] Article 32 GDPR, Articles 33 and 91 DPR-EU as well as Article 29 LED.

[114] Article 25 GDPR, Articles 27 and 85 DPR-EU as well as Article 20 LED.

[115] Cf. on the interpretation of this notion specifically, below Sect. 2.3.3.3 and, in more detail, Chap. 5, Sect. 5.3.1.1.

[116] Such as, for instance, their creator or sender, cf. Hansen 2019b, MN. 40.

[117] Weichert 2018, MN. 67.

Confidentiality means that only authorised[118] personnel and entities can access the data.[119] Non-authorised personnel of the controller and of any potential processor as well as any third-party entities must be barred from access through technical and organisational measures.[120]

The wording of the principles encompasses intentional as well as unintentional misuse. Recital 39 GDPR states that they are intended to ensure the security of the personal data generally. This security, however, is intended for the individuals concerned by the data processing, not the controller:[121] the principles of integrity and confidentiality are not a mere implementation of principles of information security, which is built around confidentiality, integrity and availability. The EU data protection law aims to protect the rights and interests of individuals with regard to risks emanating from the sphere of the controller or third parties,[122] while information security directly serves to protect the interests of the controller: if the controller does not implement information security measures, they are putting their business at risk and potentially jeopardize their own interests.[123] However, there are few incentives for the controller to protect data subjects, who, on their own, are not in a position to defend their rights vis-à-vis the controller.[124] Thus, the EU data protection legislation here adapts a subset of information security in order to ensure that the controller's systems and processes are capable of conforming to data protection rules.[125]

2.3.2.9 Accountability

Under the principle of accountability, the controller is responsible for the adherence to the other principles and has to be able to demonstrate compliance with them.[126] The principles must be implemented, not merely taken into account or considered, and cannot be outweighed by reference to other interests, as they are already the result of a balancing exercise by the legislator.[127] Requiring the controller not only to adhere to the principles, but also to provide documentation, which demonstrates that the processing adheres to the principles, expands the responsibility of the controller according to Article 24 GDPR[128] and is an addition vis-à-vis the first generation of EU data protection legislation.

---

118 Authorisation in that sense is contingent on whether access is necessary to attain the purpose of the processing, i.e. achieve the task, cf. Roßnagel 2019, MN. 170.

119 Weichert 2018, MN. 68.

120 Ibid.

121 Roßnagel 2019, MN. 170; Frenzel 2018, MN. 51.

122 Cf. below Sect. 2.3.3.3 and in-depth Chap. 5, Sect. 5.3.1.1.

123 Steinmüller 1993, p. 664.

124 Ibid.

125 Ibid.

126 Article 5(2) GDPR, Articles 4(2) and 71(4) DPR-EU as well as Article 4(4) LED.

127 Roßnagel 2019, MN. 180.

128 Articles 26 and 71(4) DPR-EU as well as Article 19 LED.

The supervisory authority can request the documents maintained by the controller for investigations according to Article 58(1)(a) GDPR.[129] If the controller cannot provide relevant documents, this is a violation of the principle of accountability, which can incur an administrative fine under Article 83(5)(a) GDPR and Article 66(3)(a) DPR-EU. In cases of conflicts with data subjects, the controller also has to demonstrate that the processing operation is in compliance with the provisions on data protection, as otherwise they might be liable for material and non-material damage resulting from an infringement of the GDPR under its Article 82[130] or the DPR-EU under its Article 65, respectively.

Outside Article 5(2) GDPR,[131] the principle of accountability is only mentioned in recital 21 DPR-EU concerning the transfer of data within the EU institutions or bodies, which states that it should be ensured that this transfer is required for a legitimate task, and recital 85 GDPR and recital 55 DPR-EU concerning data breach notifications, where the notification of a personal data breach to the supervisory authority is required unless the controller demonstrates, in accordance with the accountability principle, that there is no risk to the rights and freedoms of natural persons.

However, there are numerous instances, where the controller is required to demonstrate that something is or is not the case: it is the responsibility of the controller to implement technical and organisational measures and demonstrate compliance according to Article 24(1) and recital 74 GDPR as well as Article 26(1) DPR-EU. In order to do so, recital 78 GDPR and recital 48 DPR-EU suggest internal policies[132] and measures, which meet the requirements of data protection by design and by default, such as minimising personal data, pseudonymisation, transparency with regard to functions and processing, enabling data subjects to monitor processing and enabling controllers to create and improve security features. The principle of accountability also presupposes that the controller has tested and approved the technical and organisational measures and other safeguards.[133]

According to Article 24(3) and recital 81 GDPR adherence to codes of conduct can be used to demonstrate compliance with the controller's obligations, while certification may be used to demonstrate adherence to data protection by design and by default according to Article 25(3) GDPR. The record of processing activities, as required under Article 30 GDPR and Article 31 DPR-EU, is an instrument specifically aimed at demonstrating compliance. It applies to both, controllers and processors, according to recital 82 GDPR and recital 52 DPR-EU, respectively. For processing operations entailing a high risk to the rights and freedoms of natural persons, this can be supplemented by a DPIA under Article 35 GDPR, the outcome of which can, according to recital 84 GDPR, be used when implementing technical and organisational measures and to demonstrate compliance. Furthermore, the controller has

---

[129] Article 58(1)(a) DPR-EU and Article 47(1) LED.

[130] Breyer 2018, p. 315.

[131] Articles 4(2) and 71(4) DPR-EU as well as Article 4(4) LED.

[132] On this cf. Jung 2018.

[133] Hansen 2019a, MN. 69.

the responsibility to use only processors, which provide sufficient guarantees under Article 28(1) GDPR and Article 29(1) DPR-EU and must be bound by a contract meeting all requirements of Article 28(3) GDPR and Article 29(3) DPR-EU.[134] These manifold provisions underscore the broad scope of the principle of accountability.

2.3.3 Further Provisions of the EU Data Protection Legislation

While the principles of the EU data protection legislation lay out the general structure of the entire legislation and are aides to the interpretation of its remaining provisions, there are further provisions, which are not included in these general concepts. In the following, I will introduce the more specific provisions of the EU data protection legislation. I will consider whether they correspond to the principles and further substantiate them or whether they are of such a nature that they relate to the system of data protection legislation, but concern rules that extend beyond the formally listed principles.

2.3.3.1 Special Categories of Data

According to Article 9 GDPR[135] there are special categories of data, which are especially protected. The list of categories in the provisions is exhaustive and, when comparing Article 8 DPD to the second generation of EU legislation,[136] it can be seen that since the first generation the legislator has added genetic and biometric data as well as data on sexual orientation to the catalogue. While paras 1 of Article 9 GDPR, Articles 10 LED/DPR-EU and 76 DPR-EU prohibit the processing of such data, paras 2 specify when an exception from the prohibition is permissible. However, the requirements of Article 9(2) GDPR are additional to those of Article 6(1) GDPR.[137]

Article 10 LED allows the processing only if it is strictly necessary, subject to appropriate safeguards for the rights and freedoms of data subjects and only where it is authorised by law to protect vital interests of the data subject or another individual or where the data have manifestly been made public by the data subject.

According to recitals 10 GDPR and 29 DPR-EU these categories of data are of a sensitive nature, which is attributed to the fact that they can be used in order to discriminate against a certain group, as emphasised in recitals 71 GDPR and 43

---

[134] If the controller or processor adheres to codes of conduct or certification mechanisms the controller can use this to demonstrate compliance with the obligation under Article 24(1) and Article 28(1) GDPR, respectively.

[135] Articles 10 DPR-EU and LED.

[136] Article 9 GDPR, Articles 10 DPR-EU and LED.

[137] Petri 2019, MN. 2. This also applies to Articles 10(2) LED/DPR-EU and 76 DPR, Article 8(1) LED and Articles 5(1) and 72 DPR-EU.

DPR-EU. This is mirrored in the restriction of profiling based on special categories of personal data in Article 22(4) GDPR.[138] Under Article 11(3) LED and Article 77(3) DPR-EU, profiling which leads to the discrimination of individuals based on special categories of data is—in accordance with EU law, for instance Article 21 CFR—prohibited. Yet, despite the emphasis placed on these special categories of data, they are not represented in the principles of the EU data protection legislation.

2.3.3.2 Data Subject and Procedural Rights

The data subject rights[139] aim to provide data subjects with a range of individual, enforceable rights. As these rights are closely linked to the principles of transparency, accuracy, storage limitation and accountability, I have already touched upon them in the previous subsections.[140] This includes the requirement that data subjects receive information about the processing operation—and about the data subject rights themselves—when the data are collected.[141] Further, it includes the rights of access to these data and to information on the processing operation when the data are being processed[142] and the right to rectification[143] of inaccurate data as well as their deletion, under certain conditions, for instance when they are no longer necessary, consent has been withdrawn or the data have been processed unlawfully.[144] The GDPR and DPR-EU also introduce a right to data portability in Articles 20 and 22, respectively, which allows data subjects to request data they have submitted to the controller to be transmitted to them or another controller, subject to technical feasibility. Additionally, data subjects may object to the processing of their data due to their particular circumstances[145] and have a right not to be subjected to a decision based solely on automated processing, which produces legal or similarly significant effects on them.[146]

The data subject rights are complemented by procedural rights, i.e. the right to lodge a complaint with a supervisory authority,[147] a right to judicial remedies against controllers, processors and supervisory authorities and to be represented in these

[138] Article 24(4) and 77(2) DPR-EU as well as Article 11(2) LED.

[139] Chapter III GDPR, Chapter III and Articles 79–83 DPR-EU as well as Chapter III LED.

[140] Cf. above Sects. 2.3.2.3, 2.3.2.6 and 2.3.2.7.

[141] Articles 12–14 GDPR, Articles 14–16 and 78 et seq. DPR-EU as well as Articles 12 and 13 LED.

[142] Article 15 GDPR, Articles 17 and 80 DPR-EU as well as Article 14 LED.

[143] Article 16 GDPR, Articles 18 and 82(1) DPR-EU as well as Article 16 LED.

[144] Article 17 GDPR, Articles 19 and 82(2) DPR-EU as well as Article 16 LED.

[145] Article 21 GDPR, Article 23 DPR-EU.

[146] Article 22 GDPR, Article 24 DPR-EU; Article 77 DPR-EU prohibits and Article 11 LED and requires Member States to prohibit, respectively, fully automated decision-making, unless it is authorised by law and provides appropriate safeguards.

[147] According to Article 77 GDPR, Article 63 DPR-EU and Article 52 LED as well as Article 15(2) ePD in conjunction with Articles 94(2) and 77 GDPR.

proceedings by not-for-profit entities[148]—which introduces a first basic element of collective protection to the EU regulations[149]—as well as a right to compensation.[150]

Both of these categories of rights are further implementations of the more abstract principles of transparency, accuracy, storage limitation and accountability. The data subject and procedural rights enable individuals to understand, why and how their data are being processed and to require a controller to provide information. Yet, even these principles do not cover the full extent of the data subject rights, as they also enable data subjects to directly intervene in or even require a controller to cease a processing operation. However, even though the data subject and procedural rights have such a central role, this possibility of data subjects to intervene in a processing operation and to impose some form of control on controllers, is not reflected in the principles of the EU data protection legislation.

2.3.3.3 Obligations of Controllers and Processors

According to Article 24 GDPR,[151] the controller, i.e. the entity that determines the purposes and means of the processing operation,[152] is under an obligation to implement appropriate technical and organisational measures in order to ensure and be able to demonstrate that the processing operation complies with the EU data protection legislation, as also required by the principle of accountability. A first step in assuming responsibility is the record of processing operations according to Article 30 GDPR.[153] It contains basic information on the controller, the purposes and personal data to be processed, recipients of those data as well as a general description of the technical and organisational measures. This enhances the transparency of a processing operation not only for data subjects, but also for the controller and the supervisory authority according to recital 82 GDPR and thus also relates to the principle of accountability.

The appropriateness of the technical and organisational measures to be taken, is determined through an analysis of the processing operation itself. Its nature, scope, context and purpose, and the risks that it poses for the rights and freedoms of natural persons, must be considered. In recital 75 the GDPR[154] elaborates that these risks—which are different from the risks to an organisation processing personal data that are considered in information security[155]—may result from processing personal data and

[148] According to Articles 78–80 GDPR, Articles 63 and 67 DPR-EU, Articles 53–55 LED, Article 15(2) ePD in conjunction with Articles 94(2) and 78–80 GDPR.

[149] Also cf. Chap. 5, Sect. 5.2.3.3.

[150] According to Article 82 GDPR, Article 65 DPR-EU, Article 56 LED, Article 15(2) ePD in conjunction with Articles 94(2) and 82 GDPR.

[151] Article 26 DPR-EU and Article 19 LED.

[152] Article 4(7) GDPR, Article 3(8) DPR-EU and Article 3(8) LED.

[153] Article 31 DPR-EU and Article 24 LED.

[154] Recital 46 DPR-EU is worded identically.

[155] Such as the ENISA risk management methodology. https://www.enisa.europa.eu/topics/threat-risk-management/risk-management?tab=articles. Accessed 16 August 2021; also cf. Macenaite 2017, pp. 518–521. Also cf. above Sect. 2.3.2.8.

may entail physical, material as well as non-material damage. The recital then lists processing operations, which could lead to certain kinds of damage, such as discrimination, identity theft or fraud, financial or reputational damage, loss of confidentiality, economic or societal disadvantages, the deprivation of rights or the loss of control over personal data, the illegitimate processing of special categories of data or data of vulnerable individuals, profiling, or processing operations involving large amounts of personal data or affecting large numbers of data subjects. These factors have to be identified and evaluated and, according to clause 2 of Article 24(1) GDPR,[156] must be reviewed and updated where necessary. The provision does not prescribe a time period for such review and update, as this would be hardly possible. Risks to the rights and freedoms of natural persons may stem from a vulnerability of an information system, which can change the risk within very short periods, as they may render affected technical measures ineffective.

With regard to the selection and implementation of appropriate technical and organisational measures and other safeguards, the controller, as required by the principle of accountability, should be able to provide a documented analysis outlining their reasoning.[157] If it is likely that a processing operation entails a high risk to the rights and freedoms of natural persons, this evaluation must be carried out in a formalised and structured way as a DPIA according to Article 35 GDPR, Article 39 DPR-EU and Article 27 LED.[158]

Under Article 24 GDPR, Article 26 DPR-EU and Article 19 LED a single entity can be controller. However, if multiple entities determine the purposes and means of processing together, they are joint controllers, as further detailed in Article 26 GDPR, Articles 28 and 86 DPR-EU as well as Article 21 LED. The provisions require that the responsibilities between the parties are attributed and laid out clearly in a written arrangement. However, data subjects may exercise their rights vis-à-vis either of the controllers pursuant to Article 26(3) GDPR[159] and, under the GDPR, both are fully liable for damages suffered by data subjects under Article 82(2)–(4) GDPR. Where a controller uses a third party to carry out processing on their behalf, i.e. a processor,[160] it is the controller's responsibility to only use processors that provide sufficient guarantees to implement technical and organisational measures and ensure the protection of data subjects.

Concerning the security of the processing both, controllers and processors, are addressees of Article 32 GDPR, Articles 33 and 91 DPR-EU as well as Article 29 LED. Considering the processing operation itself and the risks it poses to the rights and freedoms of natural persons, the controller and processor have to implement technical and organisational measures to ensure a level of security, which is appropriate to the specific risks of the processing operation. These provisions thereby implement

[156] Article 26(1) DPR-EU and Article 19(1) LED.

[157] Hansen 2019a, MN. 18, 24, 33, 36, esp. 58 et seq. and 69.

[158] For a framework to carry out a DPIA, cf. Friedewald et al. 2017.

[159] Articles 28(3) and 86(3) DPR-EU as well as Article 21(2) LED.

[160] Article 4(8) GDPR, Articles and 87 DPR-EU as well as Article 3(9) LED.

the principles of integrity and confidentiality, by ensuring that the data are intact and not disclosed without authorisation.[161]

In reaction to numerous breaches of personal data due to the lack of appropriate technical and organisational measures,[162] the EU legislator also imposed an obligation to notify supervisory authorities[163] and data subjects[164] of any "breach of security leading to the accidental or unlawful destruction, loss, alteration, unauthorised disclosure of, or access to personal data"[165] on controllers. As many of these breaches were not brought to the attention of affected data subjects, individuals were exposed to the risks of a limitation of their rights, discrimination, the loss of confidentiality, identity theft or other significant disadvantages, as detailed by recital 75 GDPR.

According to the obligation of data protection by design under Article 25(1) GDPR,[166] the controller is required to implement appropriate technical and organisational measures in order to effectively implement all of the data protection principles of Article 5 GDPR[167] as well as the corresponding provisions. Further, controllers must integrate the necessary safeguards into the processing operation, before any personal data are processed, i.e. when determining the means of the processing, as well as while processing the data.[168] This obligation is subject to the same caveats as Article 24 GDPR/Article 26 DPR-EU/Article 19 LED[169] and adds the cost of implementation as a factor. The necessary safeguards—which complement the technical and organisational measures, and implement the requirements of the GDPR, DPR-EU or LED, respectively, as a whole—are also aimed at the protection of the

[161] Hansen 2019b, MN. 12.

[162] Roberts 2015, The Guardian. https://www.theguardian.com/technology/2015/jul/10/opm-hack-director-katherine-archuleta-resigns. Accessed 28 July 2021; Silver-Greenberg et al. 2014, The New York Times. https://dealbook.nytimes.com/2014/10/02/jpmorgan-discovers-further-cyber-security-issues/?mtrref=www.startpage.com&gwh=5D92274F1A2ED8DBF299FE69AD5 4FB63&gwt=pay&assetType=PAYWALL. Accessed 28 July 2021; Hern 2014, The Guardian. https://www.theguardian.com/technology/2014/jul/24/european-central-bank-customer-inform ation-hack-attack. Accessed 28 July 2021; Vodafone Germany hack hits two million customers 2013. https://www.bbc.com/news/technology-24063621. Accessed 28 July 2021; Man arrested in Athens over ID theft of most of Greek population 2012. https://www.reuters.com/article/idU SL5E8MK80020121120. Accessed 28 July 2021; Quinn and Arthur 2011, The Guardian. https:// www.theguardian.com/technology/2011/apr/26/playstation-network-hackers-data. Accessed 28 July 2021.

[163] Article 33 GDPR, Articles 34 and 92 DPR-EU as well as Article 30 LED.

[164] Article 34 GDPR, Articles 35 and 93 DPR-EU as well as Article 31 LED.

[165] Article 4(12) GDPR, Article 3(16) DPR-EU and Article 3(11) LED.

[166] Articles 27(1) and 85(1) DPR-EU as well as Article 20(1) LED.

[167] For a detailed overview of how the individual principles can be implemented through technical and organisational measures, cf. Hansen 2019a, MN. 61–69.

[168] For an overview, cf. Bieker and Hansen 2017.

[169] Such as the state of the art, the cost of implementation, the specifics of the processing operation and the risks posed to the rights and freedoms of natural persons, which serve to ensure that the rules of the GDPR/DPR-EU/LED remain technology neutral and establish an upper and lower level of measures to be taken with regard to the principle of proportionality, Hansen 2019a, MN. 36.

rights of data subjects. This reinforces my prior argument that the secondary EU data protection legislation, unlike the related field of information security, aims to protect the rights of individuals and considers their perspective.[170]

The requirement of data protection by default according to Article 25(2) GDPR[171] further specifies the principles of purpose limitation, data minimisation and storage limitation, and demands that the controller, when they preselect a configurable option, must pre-set the option which processes only the data necessary for that specific purpose. In the course of the design of a processing operation, this leads to the subsequent question, which functionalities are built in and which options are configurable.[172] This question relates to data protection by default and demonstrates that it concerns a subset of data protection by design.[173] If a controller gives data subjects the possibility to choose an option, which extends the processing of personal data and potentially the purpose, this will require a legal basis, such as the consent of the data subject pursuant to Article 7 GDPR/DPR-EU.

As I have pointed out throughout this section, the rules on the obligations of controllers and processors further specify the more general provisions of the principles of transparency, data minimisation, integrity and confidentiality as well as accountability and are therefore reflective of these principles of the EU data protection legislation.

2.3.3.4 Transfers to Third Countries and International Organisations

In order to ensure the high level of protection of fundamental rights achieved under the EU data protection legislation, Chapters V of the GDPR, DPR-EU and the LED set out limitations for the transfer of personal data to third countries. As the transfer of data to a third country constitutes the processing of personal data, i.e. a transfer in the sense of Article 4(2) GDPR,[174] the rules of the EU secondary law naturally apply to this processing operation. If a controller aims to process personal data alone or jointly with another controller or have data processed by a processor outside the EU, this transfer must—in addition to the standard requirements of the EU data protection legislation, especially the principle of lawfulness—rely on an adequacy decision of the European Commission according to Article 45 GDPR and Article 36 LED, appropriate safeguards—such as the Commission's standard contractual clauses according to Article 46 GDPR or a binding legal instrument according to Article 37 LED, respectively—, binding corporate rules according to Article 47 GDPR or an additional legal basis which conforms to the cumulative criteria of Article 39(1) LED.

[170] Ibid., MN. 31. Also cf. above Sects. 2.3.1 and 2.3.2.8.

[171] Articles 27(2) and 85(2) DPR-EU as well as Article 20(2) LED.

[172] Hansen 2019a, MN. 23.

[173] Ibid.

[174] Article 3(3) DPR-EU and 3(2) LED.

The transfer of personal data under international agreements concluded with third countries is not addressed by the provisions of the GDPR.[175] The GDPR merely states in recital 102 that it is without prejudice to such agreements concluded by the Union and that Member States may conclude such agreements when they do not affect Union law and provide an appropriate level of protection. Recital 60 DPR-EU states that where international agreements are concluded by the Union outside the scope of the GDPR, there should be an obligation to consult the EDPS, where they concern the transfer of personal data. Yet, there is no corresponding provision in the DPR-EU. Only the LED with its Article 61 features a provision on international agreements, but merely states that such agreements concluded by the Member States will stay in force when they complied with Union law as of 6 May 2016.

With these rules on transfers outside of the Union, the EU data protection legislation reinforces the principle of lawfulness, as they introduce a further requirement on such transfers on top of the standard obligations, in order to ensure that the data will be protected even when it is not within reach of EU institutions, specifically the supervisory authorities and courts.

2.3.3.5 Independent Supervisory Authorities

While the provisions of the first generation of EU data protection legislation on the supervisory authorities were sparse, the GDPR, DPR-EU and LED contain numerous provisions on the status, tasks,[176] powers of as well as cooperation and coordination between the supervisory authorities in Chapters VI and VII. The supervisory authorities, according to Article 51 GDPR, Article 57 DPR-EU and Article 41 LED,[177] are responsible for monitoring the application of the EU data protection legislation and aide the realisation of its aims under Article 1 GDPR/DPR-EU/LED.

The supervisory authorities are to be established with complete independence under Article 52 GDPR,[178] meaning that they must be free from direct or indirect external influence and be provided with an independent budget as well as full authority over their staff.[179] This includes influence by public authorities as well as private entities. While the notion of independence in EU law is not unique to the supervisory authorities of the EU data protection rules, as it also applies, for instance, to the national regulatory authorities for the telecommunications market,[180] the scope

[175] Kuner 2017.

[176] Article 57(1) GDPR features a stunning enumeration spanning from lit. a to v. The latter states that "any other tasks related to the protection of personal data" is also covered.

[177] As well as the primary law provisions of Article 8(3) CFR, Article 16(2) TFEU and Article 39 TEU.

[178] Article 55 DPR-EU and Article 42 LED.

[179] Also cf. Chap. 3, Sect. 3.3.1.

[180] For an in-depth analysis of the notion of independence for the related field of national regulatory authorities, cf. Lavrijssen and Ottow 2011.

of independence for the supervisory authorities under the EU data protection legislation is particularly far-reaching and prescribed in great detail under the GDPR.[181] Furthermore, the EU primary law, as I outlined above,[182] mandates the independence of the supervisory authorities in Article 8(3) CFR, Article 16(2) TFEU and Article 39 TEU.

However, it should also be stressed that while the supervisory authorities must be independent from the entities they control, they cannot operate outside the rule of law. Under Chapters VII of the GDPR and LED, the supervisory authorities are under an obligation to closely coordinate their action among themselves and through the EDPB, which has succeeded the Article 29 Working Party, according to Article 68 GDPR and Article 51 LED.[183] The EDPS cooperates and coordinates their work with the Board,[184] participates in its activities and provides its secretariat according to Article 57(1)(k) and (l) DPR-EU.[185]

The EDPB, which, like the supervisory authorities, enjoys independence according to Article 69 GDPR, can review acts of a supervisory authority and may, under the consistency mechanism according to Articles 63–68 GDPR, issue decisions that are binding on the national supervisory authorities under Article 65(1) GDPR.[186]

As the Board, according to Article 68(1) GDPR, is a body of the EU, it is subject to infringement proceedings under the conditions of Article 263 TFEU, where it adopts binding decision vis-à-vis third parties. It could be argued that the supervisory authorities, which are, after all, the constitutive members of the EDPB, cannot be qualified as third parties. While recital 143 explicitly states that the supervisory authorities may take judicial remedies under Article 263 TFEU against decisions of the Board, the recitals have no legal force and are only considerations by the legislator, which may guide the interpretation of the relevant act of secondary law. Especially when interpreting a rule of primary law, their argumentative value is low.

However, the ECJ has consistently interpreted the term third parties broadly, excluding only acts which cover the internal organization of a body or organ of the EU, such as rules of procedure, while including measures affecting the status of members of such an organ.[187] Furthermore, the EDPB has legal personality according to Article 68(1) GDPR, which clarifies that it is not merely a forum for the national

---

181 Szydlo 2017, pp. 373–375.

182 Cf. above Sect. 2.2.

183 For an in-depth analysis of the rules on cooperation and coordination, cf. Bieker 2016, pp. 129–134.

184 Under Articles 29(6), 42(2), 51 DPR-EU.

185 Hörnle argues that while the rules on cooperation under the one stop shop envisioned by the Commission is controller-friendly, it created an “almost byzantine coordination structure” for the supervisory authorities, cf. Hörnle 2019, p. 150.

186 On the issue of the conformity of these binding decisions with the independence of supervisory authorities, cf. Chap. 3, Sect. 3.3 and Szydlo 2017, pp. 381–385.

187 Settled case law since ECJ, Case 294/83 Parti écologiste "Les Verts" v European Parliament, Judgment of 23 April 1986, ECLI:EU:C:1986:166, para 27; ECJ, Case 78/85 Group of the European Right v European Parliament, Order of 4 June 1986, ECLI:EU:C:1986:227, paras 10 et seq.; ECJ,

supervisory authorities. Thus, when a supervisory authority is addressed by a decision of the Board, it is affected not as a member, but as an independent entity and thus a third party. Accordingly, the supervisory authorities as legal persons can bring their actions before the General Court according to Article 263(4) in conjunction with Artcle 256(1) TFEU and Article 51 Statute of the CJEU.[188]

In order to enforce the rules of EU data protection legislation, the supervisory authorities may impose fines of up to 20 million EUR or 4% of the total worldwide annual turnover of an undertaking according to Article 83(5) GPDR or, in the case of the EDPS, of up to 25,000 EUR per infringement according to Article 66(3) DPR-EU. While Article 57 LED leaves the question of penalties entirely to the Member States, Article 83(7) GDPR allows Member States to refrain from imposing administrative fines on public authorities and bodies. In either case, Member States have to impose penalties for infringements of the secondary EU data protection legislation, especially where they are not subject to fines, which are effective, proportionate and dissuasive under Article 84 GDPR and Article 57 LED.

Yet, all of these rules, which are anchored on the level of primary law, are not reflected in the principles, which with the principle of accountability focus only on the side of the controller.

2.3.3.6 Conclusions on the Further Provisions of the EU Data Protection Legislation

As I have demonstrated, a considerable body of the EU data protection legislation is not or only partly covered by the principles enshrined in the second generation of the EU data protection legislation. While many of the rules can be traced back to certain principles, this can only hardly be achieved for others. Especially with regard to the data subject and procedural rights as well as the independent supervisory authorities, which are expressly enshrined on the level of primary law, the principles incorporate them only very indirectly. It therefore transpires that the principles, as included in Articles 5 GDPR and Articles 4 DPR-EU/LED, are not fully representative of the existing body of EU data protection legislation. After considering the case law of the CJEU in the following chapter and the doctrinal discourse in Chap. 4, I will therefore revisit the principles in Chap. 5, Sect. 5.2, when deriving the fundamental principles of EU data protection law in order to ensure that all characteristic provisions of the secondary EU data protection law are incorporated.[189]

Case C-366/88 French Republic v Commission of the European Communities, Judgment of 9 October 1990, ECLI:EU:C:1990:348, para 9; also cf. Dörr 2018, MN. 41 et seq.

[188] Cf. also Albrecht and Jotzo 2017, Teil 8, MN. 18, p. 126.

[189] Cf. Chap. 5, Sect. 5.3.2.

2.4 Conclusions on the EU Data Protection Legislation

I have thus shown that with regard to the fundamental right to data protection many questions remain open. As the interpretation of Article 8 CFR is linked to the secondary legislation, the latter is of great relevance for the interpretation of Article 8 CFR.

The EU data protection legislation has evolved into a very specific regulation, stipulating its own principles, which guide the interpretation of its provisions in conjunction with Article 8 CFR. This creates a complex interplay between norms on the level of primary and secondary law. However, while the second generation of EU secondary legislation refers extensively to Article 8 CFR, it also relates to other fundamental rights and interests, for instance when it requires controllers to take into account general risks to the rights and freedoms of natural persons with regard to their processing activities.[190]

The principles of the EU data protection legislation are of particular relevance to the interpretation of Article 8 CFR. On the one hand, there is a certain overlap and the delimitation is not always quite clear, while on the other hand, some important characteristics of data protection law are not covered. As I have elaborated in this chapter, this includes the data subject and procedural rights or the independence of supervisory authorities, which are explicitly enshrined in the primary law.

From this, it also appears that the verbatim of Article 8 CFR does not encompass all relevant principles of EU data protection law, but must—with regard to its telos, which is visible in the secondary legislation—be interpreted as non-exhaustive.[191] Introducing my own approach to data protection in Chap. 5, I will reconfigure the principles in order to more comprehensively encompass the fundamental structures of EU data protection law.[192]

However, before introducing my own approach to the fundamental right to data protection in detail,[193] I will analyse the jurisprudence of the CJEU concerning data protection as fundamental right in the following chapter. I will show that the jurisprudence evolved with the changes in legislation and that the ECJ is converging towards interpreting the primary and secondary law in relation to each other. However, it does not yet seem as though the Court settled on a definitive interpretation. Furthermore, and most importantly, the Court has not yet realized the full potential of the right to data protection and its scope.

---

[190] Also cf. Hallinan and Martin 2020.

[191] Cf. also Siemen 2006, pp. 283 et seq.; Brühann 2015, MN. 51; dismissing this with reference to the wording of Article 8 CFR Marsch 2018, pp. 177 et seq.

[192] Cf. Chap. 5, Sect. 5.3.2.

[193] Cf. Chap. 5, Sect. 5.4.

References

Articles, Books and Chapters in Books

Albrecht J P, Jotzo F (2017) Das neue Datenschutzrecht der EU [The New Data Protection Law of the EU]. Nomos, Baden-Baden.

Benjamin G (2021) What we do with data: a critique of 'collection'. IPRev 10(4). https://doi.org/10.14763/2021.4.1588.

Bieker F (2016) Enforcing Data Protection Law – the Role of the Supervisory Authorities in Theory and Practice. In: Lehmann A, Whitehouse D, Fischer-Hübner S, Fritsch L, Raab C (eds) Privacy and Identity Management. Facing up to Next Steps. Springer, Cham, pp. 125–139.

Bieker F, Hansen M (2017) Normen des technischen Datenschutzes [Norms of Technical Data Protection]. DuD 41:285–289.

Boehm F (2012) Information Sharing and Data Protection in the Area of Freedom, Security and Justice. Springer, Berlin/Heidelberg.

Breyer J (2018) Verarbeitungsgrundsätze und Rechenschaftspflicht nach Art. 5 DS-GVO [Principles of Data Processing and Accountability under Art. 5 GDPR]. DuD 311–317.

Brouwer E (2011) Legality and Data Protection Law: The Forgotten Purpose of Purpose Limitation. In: Besselink L, Pennings F, Prechal S (eds) The Eclipse of the Legality Principle in the European Union. Kluwer Law, Alphen aan den Rijn, pp. 273–294.

Brühann U (2015) AEUV [TFEU] Art. 16. In: van de Groeben H, Schwarze J, Hatje A (eds) Europäisches Unionsrecht [European Union Law], 7th edn. Nomos, Baden-Baden.

Chikofsky E J, Cross J H (1990) Reverse Engineering and Design Recovery: A Taxonomy. IEEE Software 13–17.

De Hert P, Gutwirth S (2006) Privacy, Data Protection and Law Enforcement. Opacity of the Individual and Transparency of Power. In: Claes E, Duff A, Gutwirth S (eds) Privacy and the Criminal Law. Intersentia, Antwerp/Oxford, pp. 61–104.

De Hert P, Gutwirth S (2009) Data Protection in the Case Law of Strasbourg and Luxemburg: Constitutionalisation in Action. In: Gutwirth S, Poullet Y, De Hert P, de Terwangne C, Nouwt S (eds) Reinventing Data Protection? Springer, Dordrecht, pp. 3–44.

Dix A (2003) 3.5 Konzepte des Systemdatenschutzes [Approaches to Structural Data Protection]. In: Roßnagel A (ed) Handbuch Datenschutzrecht [Handbook Data Protection Law]. C.H. Beck, Munich, pp. 363–386.

Dörr O (2018) AEUV [TFEU] Art. 263. In: Grabitz E, Hilf M, Nettesheim M (eds) Das Recht der Europäischen Union [The Law of the European Union], 64th EL. C.H. Beck, Munich.

Frenz W (2009) Handbuch Europarecht [Handbook European Law], Band 4 Europäische Grundrechte. Springer, Berlin/Heidelberg.

Frenzel E M (2018) DS-GVO [GDPR] Art. 5. In: Paal B, Pauly D (eds) Kommentar Datenschutz-Grundverordnung – Bundesdatenschutzgesetz [Commentary General Data Protection Regulation – Federal Data Protection Act], 2nd edn. C.H. Beck, Munich, pp. 65–86.

Friedewald M, Bieker F, Obersteller H, Nebel M, Martin N, Rost M, Hansen M (2017) Datenschutz-Folgenabschätzung – Ein Werkzeug für einen besseren Datenschutz [Data Protection Impact Assessment – A Tool for Improved Data Protection], 3rd edn. https://www.forum-privatheit.de/wp-content/uploads/Forum-Privatheit-WP-DSFA-3-Auflage-2017-11-29.pdf. Accessed 28 July 2021.

González Fuster G (2014) The Emergence of Personal Data Protection as a Fundamental Right of the EU. Springer, Cham/Heidelberg/New York/Dordrecht/London.

Hallinan D, Martin N (2020) Fundamental Rights, the Normative Keystone of DPIA. EDPL 6:178–193.

Hallinan D, Zuiderveen Borgesius F (2020) Opinions can be incorrect (in our opinion)! On data protection law's accuracy principle. IDPL 10:1–10.

Hansen M (2019a) Artikel 25. In: Simitis S, Hornung G, Spiecker gen. Döhmann I (eds) Datenschutzrecht [Data Protection Law]. Nomos, Baden-Baden.
Hansen M (2019b) Artikel 32. In: Simitis S, Hornung G, Spiecker gen. Döhmann I (eds) Datenschutzrecht [Data Protection Law]. Nomos, Baden-Baden.
Hart H L A (1994) The Concept of Law, 2nd edn. OUP, Oxford.
Hijmans H (2016) The European Union as Guardian of Internet Privacy. Springer, Cham.
Hörnle J (2019) Juggling more than three balls at once: multilevel jurisdictional challenges in EU Data Protection Regulation. IJLIT 27:142–170.
Jung A (2018) Datenschutz-(Compliance-)Management-Systeme [Data Protection (Compliance) Management Systems]. ZD 208–213.
Kingreen T (2016a) AEUV [TFEU] Art. 16. In: Calliess C, Ruffert M (eds) EUV/AEUV Kommentar [TEU/TFEU Commentary], 5th edn. C.H. Beck, Munich.
Kingreen T (2016b) EU-GRCharta [EU CFR] Art. 8. In: Calliess C, Ruffert M (eds) EUV/AEUV Kommentar [TEU/TFEU Commentary], 5th edn. C.H. Beck, Munich.
Kuner C (2017) Data Protection, Data Transfers and International Agreements. Verfassungsblog. https://verfassungsblog.de/data-protection-data-transfers-and-international-agreements-the-cjeus-opinion-115/. Accessed 28 July 2021.
Lavrijssen S, Ottow A (2011) The Legality of Independent Regulatory Authorities. In: Besselink L, Pennings F, Prechal S (eds) The Eclipse of the Legality Principle in the European Union. Kluwer Law, Alphen aan den Rijn, pp. 72–96.
Lynskey O (2014) Deconstructing Data Protection: the 'Added-Value' of a Right to Data Protection in the EU Legal Order. ICLQ 63:569–597.
Macenaite M (2017) The "Riskification" of European Data Protection Law through a two-fold Shift. EJRR 8:506–540.
Marsch N (2018) Das europäische Datenschutzgrundrecht [The European Fundamental Right to Data Protection]. Mohr Siebeck, Tübingen.
Maxwell W J (2015) Principles-based regulation of personal data: the case of 'fair processing'. IDPL 5:205–216.
Ohler C (2017) EUV [TEU] Art. 48. In: Grabitz E, Hilf M, Nettesheim M (eds) Das Recht der Europäischen Union [The Law of the European Union], 63rd EL. C.H. Beck, Munich.
Petri T (2019) Artikel 9. In: Simitis S, Hornung G, Spiecker gen. Döhmann I (eds) Datenschutzrecht [Data Protection Law]. Nomos, Baden-Baden.
Podlech A (1982) Individualdatenschutz – Systemdatenschutz [Individual Data Protection – Structural Data Protection]. In: Brückner K, Dalichau G (eds) Festgabe für Hans Grüner. R.S. Schulz, Percha am Starnberger See, pp. 451–462.
Pötters S (2017) Art. 5. In: Gola P (ed) Datenschutz-Grundverordnung Kommentar [General Data Protection Regulation Commentary]. C.H. Beck, Munich.
Roßnagel A (2019) Artikel 5. In: Simitis S, Hornung G, Spiecker gen. Döhmann I (eds) Datenschutzrecht [Data Protection Law]. Nomos, Baden-Baden.
Schröder M (2018) AEUV [TFEU] Art. 16. In: Streinz R (ed) Kommentar EUV/AEUV [Commentary TEU/TFEU], 3rd edn. C.H. Beck, Munich.
Siemen B (2006) Datenschutz als europäisches Grundrecht [Data Protection as European Fundamental Right]. Duncker & Humblot, Berlin.
Simitis S, Hornung G, Spiecker gen. Döhmann I (2019) Einleitung [Introduction]. In: Simitis S, Hornung G, Spiecker gen. Döhmann I (eds) Datenschutzrecht [Data Protection Law]. Nomos, Baden-Baden.
Sobotta C (2017) AEUV [TFEU] Art. 16. In: Grabitz E, Hilf M, Nettesheim M (eds) Das Recht der Europäischen Union [The Law of the European Union], 63rd EL. C.H. Beck, Munich.
Steinmüller W (1993) Informationstechnologie und Gesellschaft [Information Technologies and Society]. Wissenschaftliche Buchgesellschaft, Darmstadt.
Szydlo M (2017) The Independence of Data Protection Authorities in EU Law: Between the Safeguarding of Fundamental Rights and Ensuring the Integrity of the Internal Market. ELRev 42:369–387.

von Arnauld A, Theilen J T (2020) Rhetoric of Rights: A Topical Perspective on the Functions of Claiming a "Human Right to...". In: von Arnauld A, von der Decken K, Susi M (eds) The Cambridge Handbook on New Human Rights. CUP, Cambridge, pp. 34–49.

Weichert T (2018) DSGVO [GDPR] Art. 5. In: Däubler W, Wedde P, Weichert T, Sommer I (eds) EU-Datenschutz-Grundverordnung und BDSG-neu [EU General Data Protection Regulation and the New Federal Data Protection Act]. Bund-Verlag, Frankfurt am Main.

Zerdick T (2012) Art. 16 AEUV [TFEU]. In: Lenz C O, Borchardt K D (eds) EU-Verträge Kommentar [EU Treaties Commentary] 6th edn. Bundesanzeiger Verlag, Cologne.

Zuiderveen Borgesius F, Hallinan D (2020) Article 5 GDPR, 'Principles relating to processing of personal data. In: Cole M, Boehm F (eds) Commentary on the General Data Protection Regulation. Edward Elgar, Cheltenham.

Table of Cases: EU

ECJ, Case 26/62 Van Gend en Loos v Administratie der Belastingen, Judgment of 5 February 1963, ECLI:EU:C:1963:1.

ECJ, Case 78/85 Group of the European Right v European Parliament, Order of 4 June 1986, ECLI:EU:C:1986:227.

ECJ, Case 294/83 Parti écologiste "Les Verts" v European Parliament, Judgment of 23 April 1986, ECLI:EU:C:1986:166.

ECJ, Case C-366/88 French Republic v Commission of the European Communities, Judgment of 9 October 1990, ECLI:EU:C:1990:348.

ECJ, Case C-73/07 Tietosuojavaltuutettu v Satakunnan Markkinapörssi Oy and Satamedia Oy, Judgment of 16 December 2008, ECLI:EU:C:2008:727.

ECJ, Joined Cases C-92/09 and C-93/09 Volker und Markus Schecke GbR (C-92/09) and Hartmut Eifert (C-93/09) v Land Hessen, Judgment of 9 November 2010, ECLI:EU:C:2010:662.

ECJ, Joined Cases C-92/09 and C-93/09 Volker und Markus Schecke GbR (C-92/09) and Hartmut Eifert (C-93/09) v Land Hessen, Opinion of AG Sharpston of 17 June 2010, ECLI:EU:C:2010:353.

ECJ, Case C-473/12 Institut professionnel des agents immobiliers (IPI) v Geoffrey Englebert and Others, Judgment of 7 November 2013, ECLI:EU:C:2013:715.

ECJ, Case C-291/12 Michael Schwarz v Stadt Bochum, Judgment of 17 October 2013, ECLI:EU:C:2013:670.

ECJ, Joined Cases C-293/12 and C-594/12 Digital Rights Ireland Ltd (C-293/12) v Minister for Communications, Marine and Natural Resources and Others and Kärntner Landesregierung (C-594/12) and Others, Judgment of 8 April 2014, ECLI:EU:C:2014:238.

ECJ, Case C-201/14 Smaranda Bara and Others v Casa Naţională de Asigurări de Sănătate and Others, Judgment of 1 October 2015, ECLI:EU:C:2015:638.

ECJ, Case C-191/15 Verein für Konsumenteninformation v Amazon EU Sàrl, Judgment of 28 July 2016, ECLI:EU:C:2016:612.

ECJ, Case C-40/17 Fashion ID GmbH & Co.KG v Verbraucherzentrale NRW eV, Judgment of 29 July 2019, ECLI:EU:C:2019:629.

ECJ, Case C-25/17 Tietosuojavaltuutettu – Jehovan todistajat, Judgment of 10 July 2018, ECLI:EU:C:2018:551.

Other Documents: EU

Article 29 Working Party Opinion 03/2013 on purpose limitation of 2 April 2013. WP 203.
Article 29 Working Party Guidelines on Data Protection Impact Assessment (DPIA) and determining whether processing is "likely to result in a high risk" for the purposes of Regulation 2016/679. WP 248 rev.01.
Article 29 Working Party Guidelines on transparency under Regulation 2016/679. WP 260 rev. 01.
European Data Protection Board Endorsement 1/2018 of 25 May 2018.
European Union Agency for Fundamental Rights, Council of Europe, European Data Protection Supervisor 2018 Handbook on European data protection law. Luxembourg. https://fra.europa.eu/sites/default/files/fra_uploads/fra-coe-edps-2018-handbook-data-protection_en.pdf. Accessed 16 June 2021.

Other Documents: National

Konferenz der unabhängigen Datenschutzaufsichtsbehörden des Bundes und der Länder (2020) The Standard Data Protection Model – V.2.0b. https://www.datenschutz-mv.de/datenschutz/datenschutzmodell/. Accessed 28 July 2021.

Chapter 3
The Right to Data Protection: The Jurisprudence of the CJEU

Contents

Abstract This chapter considers the evolution of the case law of the CJEU with regard to the right to data protection. While the Court already realised the fundamental rights dimension of data protection in the *Stauder* case, it did not initially engage with the Charter or the relevant secondary EU legislation. The chapter traces how the Court, partly driven by the Opinions of its AGs, developed its own line of jurisprudence. However, while the Court has consistently strengthened the supervisory authorities and the rights of individuals with regard to complaints according to Article 8(1) and (3) CFR, it has not yet arrived at a coherent line of reasoning with regard to the right to data protection under Article 8(1) and (2) CFR.

Keywords Surveillance · Bulk Data Retention · Passenger Name Records · Supervisory Authority · Data Protection Authority · Independence · Stauder · Österreichischer Rundfunk · Schecke and Eifert · Digital Rights Ireland and Seitlinger · Google Spain · Schrems · Tele2 Sverige · Ministerio Fiscal · La Quadrature du Net · Facebook Ireland · Deferential Approach · CJEU · ECJ · General Court

© T.M.C. ASSER PRESS and the author 2022

F. Bieker, *The Right to Data Protection*, Information Technology and Law Series 34,
https://doi.org/10.1007/978-94-6265-503-4_3

3.1 Introduction

Now that I have introduced the EU data protection legislation, I will consider the jurisprudence of the CJEU on the right to data protection. I will show how the case law evolved from the very early cases, which preceded the secondary legislation, and how the Court's general reluctance to consider the Charter as standard for its fundamental rights assessment impacted the interpretation of the right to data protection. I will illustrate, that, even after the adoption of the Charter with its Article 8, the Court's jurisprudence is still lacking deeper engagement with the system and specific characteristics of EU data protection law.

In order to trace developments and different lines of arguments within the Court, I will take into account the Opinions of the AGs as appropriate, especially when their reasoning diverged from that of the Court. The AGs prepare a full analysis of the case, independent of the chamber according to Article 252 TFEU in conjunction with Article 49 Statute of the CJEU and they usually elaborate the issues more comprehensively than the Court, which is known for its apodictic style.[1] As will be seen below, the AGs Opinions in some cases have a long-term effect, which is not immediately visible: their arguments may not be adopted by the Court in the case at hand, but may be discussed by other AGs in other cases and, ultimately, be adopted or repudiated by the Court, as I will highlight in the following.

In Sect. 3.2, I will consider the jurisprudence on Article 8(1) and (2) CFR, which has, since the coming into force of the Charter, been slowly evolving towards two different interpretations of the right to data protection: one considering it an independent right, the other reading it in conjunction with Article 7 CFR.

In Sect. 3.3, I will analyse the case law on the role of the supervisory authorities, which relates to Article 8(1) and (3) CFR and has been considered separately from Article 8(1) and (2) CFR in the jurisprudence of the Court. Here, the Court has consistently strengthened the position of the supervisory authorities and the case law has served as a blueprint for the reform of the rules concerning the supervisory authorities in the second generation of EU data protection legislation. The EU legislator, therefore, has already incorporated much of the Court's jurisprudence on Article 8(1) and (3) CFR in the provisions of the GDPR, DPR-EU and LED.

3.2 Case Law on Article 8(1) and (2) CFR

The reform of the EU data protection legislation, as introduced in the previous chapter, has seen the replacement of the right to privacy as a reference point to the right to data

[1] de S-O-l'E Lasser 2009, p. 229.

protection.[2] In the following, I will analyse the case law of the Court and examine in how far it has taken the right to data protection into account in its jurisprudence.

While in its early case law, the ECJ had been mostly influenced by the ECtHR, it soon—albeit hesitantly—connected its jurisprudence on the right to data protection to the EU secondary legislation. Since the coming into force of the Charter there have been two strands of case law: one that reads Articles 7 and 8 CFR together and another that tries to differentiate between the two and awards them independent scopes.

Furthermore, while the Court, in principle, acknowledged the connection between the primary and secondary law early on, this approach has gathered substance over time and moved from the mere affirmation of a close connection to a more detailed engagement with the complex interplay between the two levels. Therefore, my analysis also takes cases into consideration, which are mostly concerned with the interpretation of secondary legislation, when this is relevant for the interpretation of the right to data protection, especially in the more recent case law. However, I will argue that the Court has to take better account of the system for the processing of personal data set out in the secondary EU data protection legislation in order to achieve coherence between the different levels of EU data protection legislation.

I will analyse the case law on Article 8(1) and (2) CFR in historical order, in order to show the long lines of the Court's jurisprudence. I will group them were appropriate, i.e. when the Court followed a similar approach for several cases, and will set it in relation to the respective Opinions of the AGs, which sometimes, as I will highlight, even when their argument is not heeded in a specific case, exert a long-term influence.

3.2.1 Early Cases

Already in the Court's famous *Stauder* judgment of 1969, data protection was at play implicitly, when the referring German court was concerned that the identification of individuals by name on vouchers for a welfare programme violated fundamental rights.[3] However, as only the German version of the contested Commission decision required the identification, while others allowed for other means of authentication,[4] the Court held that in such a case "the most liberal interpretation must prevail."[5] Thus, the identification by name was not required—or according to the principles of purpose limitation and data minimisation, which were not in force at that point,

[2] The secondary legislation has thus been adapted to the Charter, which has come into force since the first generation of EU data protection legislation, a general process which González Fuster describes as "disentangling privacy and data protection", cf. González Fuster 2014a, pp. 268 et seq.

[3] ECJ, Case 29/69 Stauder v Stadt Ulm, Judgment of 12 November 1969, ECLI:EU:C:1969:57, paras 1 et seq.

[4] Ibid., para 2.

[5] Ibid., para 4.

was not necessary to attain the purpose—and the ECJ did not further engage in a full examination of fundamental rights.[6] This certainly was one of the first decisions concerning the right to data protection.[7] However, as the Court expressly stated, an actual assessment of fundamental rights was not necessary in the case at hand, and the assumption of a right to privacy or data protection is therefore only implicit.[8]

In the year 2000 in the *Fisher* case, the Court dealt with the disclosure of field crop data to a third party[9] and found that the authorities had to strike a balance between the interest of the person concerned and the third party in need of that information.[10] While AG Alber also identified these interests,[11] the Court emphasized that when dealing with personal data, the assessment of the interests of the person concerned had to ensure the protection of fundamental rights.[12]

Even though the DPD had not yet entered into force at the time of the events at issue, the Court and the AG found that the secondary legislation implemented general principles already in force in the Member States, based on recitals 10 et seq. DPD.[13] The ECJ thus referred to Article 7(f) DPD (now Article 6(1)(f) GDPR), which allows for the processing of personal data if necessary for the legitimate interests of a third party, if these are not overridden by the fundamental rights of the data subject.[14]

---

[6] Ibid.; yet, in the final paragraph, the Court made its famous reference to general principles of Community law, which would have to be examined rather than national fundamental rights, ibid., para 7.

[7] Streinz 2018, MN. 4; other early cases concerned the protection of personal data in particular circumstances, such as the protection of the anonymity of a whistleblower in ECJ, Case 145/83 Stanley George Adams v Commission of the European Communities, Judgment of 7 November 1985, ECLI:EU:C:1985:448, para 34; or the access to medical files in ECJ, Case 140/86 Gisela Strack v Commission of the European Communities, Judgment of 7 October 1987, ECLI:EU:C:1987:427, paras 9–11; as pointed out in ECJ, Case C-553/07 College van burgemeester en wethouders van Rotterdam v M. E. E. Rijkeboer, Opinion of AG Ruiz-Jarabo Colomer of 22 December 2008, ECLI:EU:C:2008:773, para 19.

[8] Siemen 2006, p. 214.

[9] The Court had already been seized of a case concerning the disclosure of medical information of an applicant for a position at the Commission, where the AG in his Opinion mentioned a right not to communicate the state of health of an individual to third persons ECJ, Case C-404/92 P X v Commission of the European Communities, Opinion of AG Gerven of 5 October 1994, ECLI:EU:C:1994:172, paras 23 and 28. However, the Court itself examined the right to keep one's own state of health a secret as an aspect of the right to private life under Article 8 ECHR and found that it had been violated ECJ, Case C-404/92 P X v Commission of the European Communities, Judgment of 5 October 1994, ECLI:EU:C:1994:361, paras 17 and 23 et seq.; Siemen 2006, p. 224.

[10] ECJ, Case C-369/98 The Queen and Minister of Agriculture, Fisheries and Food, ex parte Trevor Robert Fisher and Penny Fisher, Judgment of 14 September 2000, ECLI:EU:C:2000:443, para 31.

[11] ECJ, Case C-369/98 The Queen and Minister of Agriculture, Fisheries and Food, ex parte Trevor Robert Fisher and Penny Fisher, Opinion of AG Alber of 10 February 2000, ECLI:EU:C:2000:79, paras 43 et seq. and 48.

[12] ECJ, Case C-369/98 Fisher, Judgment of 14 September 2000, para 32.

[13] Ibid., para 34; ECJ, Case C-369/98 Fisher, Opinion of AG Alber, para 44.

[14] ECJ, Case C-369/98 Fisher, Judgment of 14 September 2000, para 35.

Birte Siemen has argued that the Court acknowledged the existence of a fundamental right to protection of personal data in this judgment.[15] However, while the Court demonstrated an awareness of the fundamental rights dimension of the data processing, it assessed the issue in the category of legitimate interest, which, though related, is different from fundamental rights. When applying the principles it had set out, the Court framed its reasoning explicitly in reference to interests rather than fundamental rights of the applicants, while leaving the ultimate outcome for the national court to determine,[16] thereby adopting a deferential approach.

Furthermore, it cannot be determined conclusively whether the case even concerned personal data in the sense of the EU data protection legislation. The eponymous Fishers wanted to obtain information on the farming history of two farms, which may well have included data, which render an individual identifiable. However, neither the AG nor the Court considered this question.[17] As the DPD was not even in force yet, they drew on it for inspiration, rather than a conclusive legal answer. Therefore, reading the proclamation of such a fundamental right, which had not been previously considered by the Court, into this case is perhaps an overstatement. Yet, it marks the beginning of the Court's consideration of the first generation of EU data protection legislation.

3.2.2 *Article 8 ECHR with a Twist*

When the Court engaged with the processing of personal data substantively, it took Article 8 ECHR and the jurisprudence of the ECtHR as a point of reference. However, the Court, whether intentionally or not, modified the right in two important regards from the outset: It narrowed the right by finding that the storage of data did not constitute an interference, while it also broadened the right by not requiring a nexus between the data processed and the private life of the individual concerned.

3.2.2.1 Österreichischer Rundfunk

The Court's first substantive judgment on the protection of personal data as a fundamental right from 2003 concerned proceedings over an Austrian law requiring the publication of every public employee's income above a certain threshold.[18] The Court found that the relevant provisions of the DPD had to be interpreted in the light of the

---

[15] Siemen 2006, p. 254.

[16] ECJ, Case C-369/98 Fisher, Judgment of 14 September 2000, paras 36 and 38.

[17] Cf. ibid., paras 11–14.

[18] ECJ, Joined Cases C-465/00, C-138/01 and C-139/01 Rechnungshof (C-465/00) v Österreichischer Rundfunk and Others and Christa Neukomm (C-138/01) and Joseph Lauermann (C-139/01) v Österreichischer Rundfunk, Judgment of 20 May 2003, ECLI:EU:C:2003:294, paras 2 et seq.

relevant fundamental rights.[19] In this context it held, at the outset, that the provisions of the DPD itself were liable to infringe "fundamental freedoms", such as the right to privacy, and thus had to be interpreted in the light of these fundamental rights.[20] The directive acknowledged this in Article 1(1) and recitals 10 and 11 DPD, which expressly stated that it aimed to protect fundamental rights of individuals, particularly the right to privacy, while the Court held that the directive's principal aim was to ensure the free movement of personal data.[21]

AG Tizzano, in his Opinion, had followed a different path: he found the case to fall under the exception clause of Article 3(2) DPD first indent (now Article 2(2)(a) GDPR), as it was outside the scope of Union law, and argued that the need for the effective protection of fundamental rights did not call for a different outcome, as he held the free flow between the Member States to be at the heart of the directive and the protection of fundamental rights as dependent on that primary goal.[22]

In order to ascertain whether the national legislation conformed to the DPD, the Court found it first had to assess whether the former violated the right to private life under Article 8 ECHR.[23] It held—in conformity to the ECtHR's case law—that the term private life had to be interpreted broadly and professional activities were not excluded from its scope.[24] The Court then asserted that it followed necessarily that the mere recording of data concerning the income of employees did not interfere with the right to private life, while the transfer of such data to a third party was an interference regardless of their subsequent use.[25] The Court went on to state that the nature of the data as well as the question of an inconvenience for the persons concerned were irrelevant.[26]

It is interesting to note that the Court explicitly stated that the storage of the data itself did not interfere with the right to private life and relied on the case law of the ECtHR. Even though, with regard to the right of private life, the Court stayed closely

---

[19] Ibid., para 68.

[20] Ibid.

[21] Ibid., para 70. Also cf. Siemen 2004, p. 312, who agrees with the AG's reasoning; Marsch 2018, pp. 309–316, who sides with the Court.

[22] ECJ, Joined Cases C-465/00, C-138/01 and C-139/01 Rechnungshof (C-465/00) v Österreichischer Rundfunk and Others and Christa Neukomm (C-138/01) and Joseph Lauermann (C-139/01) v Österreichischer Rundfunk, Opinion of AG Tizzano of 14 November 2002, ECLI:EU:C:2002:662, paras 43 and 50–53; and already in his Opinion in Lindqvist, which was delivered before the Opinion in Österreichischer Rundfunk and Others, while the judgments were delivered in reverse order, cf. ECJ, Case C-101/01 Criminal proceedings against Bodil Lindqvist, Opinion of AG Tizzano of 19 September 2002, ECLI:EU:C:2002:513, paras 39–41.

[23] ECJ, Joined Cases C-465/00, C-138/01 and C-139/01 Österreichischer Rundfunk and Others, Judgment of 20 May 2003, para 72.

[24] Ibid., para 73; citing ECtHR [GC], Amann v. Switzerland, App. No. 27798/95, Judgment of 16 February 2000, para 65; ECtHR [GC], Rotaru v. Romania, App. No. 28341/95, Judgment of 4 May 2000, para 43.

[25] ECJ, Joined Cases C-465/00, C-138/01 and C-139/01 Österreichischer Rundfunk and Others, Judgment of 20 May 2003, para 74.

[26] Ibid., para 75; citing ECtHR [GC], Amann, App. No. 27798/95, Judgment of 16 February 2000, para 70.

connected to the ECtHR's conception in its first decision explicitly recognizing the right to private life as a part of the Community's general principles,[27] in the case at hand it did not pick up on the ECtHR's reference to the CoE's DPC. In *Amann v. Switzerland*[28] as well as *Rotaru v. Romania*,[29] the ECtHR had invoked Article 2(a) DPC, which provides that personal data is any information relating to an identified or identifiable individual, to reinforce its broad concept of private life. The Court also did not consider the secondary EU data protection legislation, when interpreting this right.[30] Had it done that, the Court would have seen that under the DPD—just as under the DPC, which influenced the DPD as well as Article 8 CFR[31]—the processing of personal data includes, inter alia, the collection, recording, storage as well as use or disclosure of such data.[32] Peter Hustinx attributes this finding of the Court to the fact that it meant to differentiate privacy and data protection ECtHR, in both judgments cited, found the storing of data itself to constitute an from one another.[33] Yet, the interference.[34] In this regard, the protection offered by the Court was lower than the standard of the ECtHR.

The ECJ did, however, award greater protection than the ECtHR concerning a different, but crucial aspect. While the ECtHR required that the data themselves must also relate to the applicant's private life,[35] this condition is notably absent from the ECJ's assessment. There is, therefore, a significant conceptual difference in the assessment of the interference with Article 8 ECHR.[36] In the case at hand, where the data concerned the income of employees and because the notion of private life extends to professional activities, it is arguable that even if the ECJ had required a nexus to private life, the measure in question would have fulfilled that requirement. Yet, already in its first major decision concerning the protection of personal data, the ECJ deviated from the case law of the ECtHR, even though it relied on its jurisprudence extensively. Thus paradoxically, the ECJ's assessment was both narrower when the

---

[27] ECJ, Case 136/79 National Panasonic (UK) Limited v Commission of the European Communities, Judgment of 26 June 1980, ECLI:EU:C:1980:169, para 17; ECJ, Joined Cases C-465/00, C-138/01 and C-139/01 Österreichischer Rundfunk and Others, Opinion of AG Tizzano, paras 43 and 50–53.

[28] ECtHR [GC], Amann, App. No. 27798/95, Judgment of 16 February 2000, para 65.

[29] ECtHR [GC], Rotaru, App. No. 28341/95, Judgment of 4 May 2000, para 43.

[30] Also cf. Classen 2004, p. 1383.

[31] Explanations Relating to the Charter of Fundamental Rights. OJ C 303 of 14 December 2007, pp. 17–35, pp. 20 et seq.

[32] Article 2(b) DPC, Article 2(b) DPD (now Article 4(2) GDPR).

[33] Hustinx 2017, p. 135.

[34] ECtHR [GC], Amann, App. No. 27798/95, Judgment of 16 February 2000, para 69; ECtHR [GC], Rotaru, App. No. 28341/95, Judgment of 4 May 2000, para 43.

[35] Cf. ECtHR [GC], Amann, App. No. 27798/95, Judgment of 16 February 2000, para 70; ECtHR [GC], Rotaru, App. No. 28341/95, Judgment of 4 May 2000, para 46; and for the first time in ECtHR, Leander v. Sweden, App. No. 9248/81, Judgment of 26 March 1987, para 48.

[36] Siemen 2006, p. 266; this is also noted by Kokott and Sobotta 2014, pp. 86 et seq. However, the latter seem surprised by this relation to private life and state that the ECJ has not "yet added these potential qualifications".

Court found that the storage is not an interference and, at the same time, broader, when the ECJ dropped the requirement of a nexus to the private life of the person concerned.

3.2.2.2 Lindqvist

In the *Lindqvist* case, an employee at a Swedish parish had published personal data of co-workers on her personal website and was subsequently prosecuted and fined.[37] Unlike AG Tizzano, who in this case also argued that Mrs. Lindqvist had no economic interests in the processing and that she did not exercise a fundamental freedom of EU law, the Court did not find that the exemptions of Article 3(2) DPD (now Article 2(2)(a) and (c) GDPR), concerning activities outside the scope of EU law and household activities, applied.[38] The Court noted that recital 12 DPD lists activities that are exclusively personal or domestic, such as correspondence or private address books. It thus concluded that this provision only encompassed activities relating to private or family life, which could not be the case when data were published online, where they were accessible for an indefinite number of users.[39] It thereby also explicitly upheld its finding of *Österreichischer Rundfunk* that the application of the DPD was not contingent on a link with free movement between Member States and thus enabled a wide application of the directive.[40] This broad interpretation of the scope of the DPD is also justified by the nature of data flows, as internet traffic, even when a website is hosted in the same Member State as the person who accesses it, may be routed through several different States.[41]

As the Court had already done in *Österreichischer Rundfunk*, it noted that the aim of the DPD was to harmonise the processing of personal data to enable their free flow between the Member States, while ensuring the effective protection of these data.[42] The Court found that these "objectives may of course be inconsistent with one another."[43] Yet, it concluded again that the DPD included provisions to balance rights and interests concerning the lawfulness of data processing and the appropriate safeguards.[44]

---

[37] ECJ, Case C-101/01 Criminal proceedings against Bodil Lindqvist, Judgment of 6 November 2003, ECLI:EU:C:2003:596, paras 15–17.

[38] ECJ, Case C-101/01 Lindqvist, Opinion of AG Tizzano, para 36; ECJ, Case C-101/01 Lindqvist, Judgment of 6 November 2003, paras 40–44.

[39] ECJ, Case C-101/01 Lindqvist, Judgment of 6 November 2003, paras 46 et seq.

[40] Ibid., paras 40 et seq.; again, the Court argued against the AG, cf. ECJ, Case C-101/01 Lindqvist, Opinion of AG Tizzano, paras 39–43; ECJ, Joined Cases C-465/00, C-138/01 and C-139/01 Österreichischer Rundfunk and Others, Judgment of 20 May 2003, paras 41–44.

[41] Marsch 2018, p. 315.

[42] ECJ, Case C-101/01 Lindqvist, Judgment of 6 November 2003, para 33. Marsch 2018, pp. 326–333, criticises this finding of complete harmonization.

[43] ECJ, Case C-101/01 Lindqvist, Judgment of 6 November 2003, paras 79–81.

[44] Ibid., para 79.

While the DPD's provisions were necessarily more general, the Court found that they were sufficiently precise to provide foreseeability for the individuals concerned and were, therefore, not themselves in conflict with fundamental rights.[45] The Court then chose a deferential approach[46] and found that it was for the national authorities and courts to find a balance that paid due regard to the fundamental rights of the individuals concerned.[47] In the case at hand, the balance between the right to freedom of expression of Mrs. Lindqvist and the rights of those individuals whose data she had published had to be struck on the level of national law.[48]

However, the national court had asked explicitly whether the DPD was in conflict with the freedom of expression as guaranteed by Article 10 ECHR.[49] The Court asserted ultimately that there was no such conflict on the level of EU law.[50] It did so without engaging in an assessment of the relevant fundamental rights. Instead, the Court stated that it was not only the DPD which had to be interpreted with regard to fundamental rights and proportionality as general principles of Community law, but also the national law implementing that directive.[51]

The Court then pointed to the issue it apparently found decisive in the case: the application of the sanctions to be implemented by the Member States, prescribed by Article 24 DPD, had to be proportionate to the violation of private life.[52] This was especially true with regard to the DPD's broad scope of application and the obligations of controllers.[53] Therefore, the national court had to consider whether, with regard to the duration of the violation and its importance for the data subjects, the fine imposed was proportionate.[54] This was the only guidance the Court offered the national court, which found that Mrs. Lindqvist interests could not prevail over the rights to private life of the individuals concerned, but also held that such a minor offence did not require a penal sanction and thus acquitted Mrs. Lindqvist of the charges.[55]

With regard to its detailed examination of fundamental rights in *Österreichischer Rundfunk*, where the Court also left ample room for the national court to interpret the

---

[45] Ibid., para 82.

[46] As it had in the assessment of justification in ECJ, Joined Cases C-465/00, C-138/01 and C-139/01 Österreichischer Rundfunk and Others, Judgment of 20 May 2003, para 79. While it had ruled in *Stauder* that the most liberal interpretation of a provision must prevail, that case, unlike both *Österreichischer Rundfunk* and *Lindqvist*, concerned an EU provision, which may have led to the Court to leave the assessment to the national court.

[47] ECJ, Case C-101/01 Lindqvist, Judgment of 6 November 2003, para 84.

[48] Ibid., paras 85–87.

[49] Ibid., paras 85 et seq.

[50] Ibid., para.18.

[51] Ibid., para 90.

[52] Ibid., para 87.

[53] Ibid., para 88.

[54] Ibid.

[55] Ibid., para 89.

national law,[56] its deferential approach in *Lindqvist* is striking. However, in the former case a national law infringed the right to data protection of individuals on the vertical level and the right had to be reconciled with a public interest. The interference with that right in *Lindqvist* was caused not only by a measure in the public interest, but also by a conflict with another fundamental right, i.e. in a triangular relationship between Mrs. Lindqvist, the State enforcing the national implementation of the DPD against her and the individuals whose data were published online. These circumstances could be seen as a reason for the Court's reluctance to strike a balance: perhaps it wanted to avoid a situation where the fundamental rights were applied horizontally. Furthermore, while data protection is regulated under secondary EU law, there are no equivalent rules on the freedom of expression, which remain within the competence of the Member States.

Siemen further argues that the reasoning of the Court in *Österreichischer Rundfunk* came close to ruling on the validity of the relevant national legislation, which it is not, however, competent to adjudicate in a preliminary ruling.[57] This might have been another factor for the restraint of the Court in the case at hand. As is clear from Article 1 ECHR, the Convention does not create obligations for individuals. While the ECtHR has introduced the concept of positive obligations, under which a Contracting Party has to pass legislation in order to prevent an individual from violating another individual's rights,[58] this was not the issue in the case at hand. Sweden had enacted its national law implementing the DPD and fined Mrs. Lindqvist for the violation of the rights of third parties. Thus, the Court only had to balance the rights with regard to the proportionality of the DPD and its national implementation,[59] as the ECtHR does when it assesses cases where conflicting rights are then reconciled. Even though Article 24 DPD left it to the Member States to impose sanctions for violations of the rules of the DPD, the substantive question of whether there has been a violation of the data protection rules is determined by the DPD itself.

Even if, in the case at hand, the Court found that the main issue was the imposition of penal sanctions against Mrs. Lindqvist, this question had to be assessed from the perspective of EU fundamental rights, as the Court itself stated in the judgment.[60] Under the *ERT* line of the Court's case law on the application of EU fundamental

[56] Cf. ECJ, Joined Cases C-465/00, C-138/01 and C-139/01 Österreichischer Rundfunk and Others, Judgment of 20 May 2003, paras 81–87; while it also left some discretion to the national court, the ECJ prescribed that the court consider a less invasive way to achieve transparency, by removing the names of the employees from the published version, ibid., paras 88–90. In its subsequent judgment, the Austrian Constitutional Court (*Verfassungsgerichtshof*) followed the hints of the ECJ and held that the publication of the remuneration with the name of the employees was not proportionate with regard to the serious interference with Article 8 ECHR, cf. Verfassungsgerichtshof, KR 1/00-33 Rechnungshof v Österreichischer Rundfunk, Judgment of 28 November 2003, pp. 29–31.

[57] Siemen 2004, p. 315.

[58] Grabenwarter 2014, Article 1, MN. 6.

[59] The Opinion of AG Tizzano did not provide the Court with any guidance on this question, as he merely held that the case was outside the scope of EU law in the sense of Article 3(2) DPD and thus the DPD did not apply. Remarkably, he did not assess any other questions raised by the national court, Röben 2013, MN. 146–149.

[60] Siemen 2006, p. 271.

rights,[61] a case such as this, where a Member State chooses the kind of sanctions it imposes to conform to Article 24 DPD, clearly falls within the notion of implementation of EU law.[62] As the EU fundamental rights at the time of this judgment were construed as part of the general principles of EU law, it would have been for the Court to interpret them authoritatively. Especially, since the balancing between the freedom of expression and the right to private life is inherent in the directive, there was ample cause to engage in a more detailed assessment of the fundamental rights in question, as the Court had done in *Österreichischer Rundfunk*. In the course of its own jurisprudence, the Court stated its mission in the vein of the *ERT*[63] case law: "where national legislation falls within the field of application of Community law the Court, when requested to give a preliminary ruling, must provide the national court with all the elements of interpretation which are necessary in order to enable it to assess the compatibility of that legislation with the fundamental rights—as laid down in particular in the European Convention on Human Rights—the observance of which the Court ensures."[64] In *Lindqvist*, the Court did not adhere to this standard.

3.2.3 *Moving Beyond the ECtHR*

In the following two judgments, AG Léger and the Court of First Instance (CFI), the precursor of the GC, assessed the right to data protection and sought to re-establish coherence with the ECtHR's case law concerning the nexus of processing personal data to private life. However, the ECJ later explicitly rejected these arguments and, instead, upheld its previous case law.

3.2.3.1 Parliament v Council and Commission—Passenger Name Records

In the case on the Passenger Name Records (PNR) Decision 2004/496/EC,[65] the ECJ's reasoning was limited to an assessment of the legal bases. The Court, without further engaging with the definition of processing, ruled that the transfer of data from the airlines to the United States (US) Bureau of Customs and Borders Protection

[61] ECJ, Case C-260/89 Elliniki Radiophonia Tiléorassi AE and Panellinia Omospondia Syllogon Prossopikou v Dimotiki Etairia Pliroforissis and Sotirios Kouvelas and Nicolaos Avdellas and Others, Judgment of 18 June 1991, ECLI:EU:C:1991:254.

[62] ECJ, Case C-101/01 Lindqvist, Judgment of 6 November 2003, para 87.

[63] ECJ, Case C-260/89 ERT v DEP, Judgment of 18 June 1991, paras 43 et seq.

[64] ECJ, Case C-159/90 The Society for the Protection of Unborn Children Ireland Ltd v Stephen Grogan and Others, Judgment of 4 October 1991, ECLI:EU:C:1991:378, para 31.

[65] Council Decision of 17 May 2004 on the conclusion of an Agreement between the European Community and the United States of America on the processing and transfer of PNR data by Air Carriers to the United States Department of Homeland Security, Bureau of Customs and Border Protection (2004/496/EC), OJ L 183 of 20 May 2004—PNR Decision, p. 83.

(BCBP) fell within a framework established by public authorities relating to public security and was therefore covered by the ordre public clause of Article 3(2) first indent DPD. The decision was thus outside the scope of the DPD and could not be based on Article 95 TEC in conjunction with Article 25 DPD.[66]

While the Grand Chamber thus did not assess the right to data protection, AG Léger examined the case in its entirety. He found that the right to the protection of personal data was an aspect of the right to respect for private life under Article 8 ECHR and was therefore part of the Community legal order by virtue of its status as a general principle.[67]

The AG then examined Article 8 ECHR, as interpreted by the ECtHR, scrupulously and found that making the personal data of airline passengers available to the BCBP was a clear interference with the private lives of those persons.[68] He also expressly mentioned that the aggregation of these data to build personality profiles interfered with the individuals' rights.[69]

However, similar to the Court in *Österreichischer Rundfunk*, he did not consider that the collection of these personal data already constituted an interference and thus also did not take into consideration the definitions provided by the secondary legislation. Yet, unlike the ECJ in *Österreichischer Rundfunk*, the AG required a nexus to the private life of the persons concerned, which was, however, fulfilled.[70]

Examining whether the interference was in accordance with the law, the AG referred to the case law of the ECtHR and found that the regime for the data transfer fulfilled the requirement of being in accordance with the law, as it was accessible and sufficiently precise.[71] He further found the purpose of combating terrorism to relate to national security, public safety as well as the prevention of disorder or crime referred to in Article 8(2) ECHR and hence to constitute a legitimate aim.[72] Due to the measure's aim of combating terrorism and its relation to national security, the AG, with regard to the scope of review when assessing proportionality—and in reference to the ECtHR's jurisprudence and the case law of the ECJ—considered that the EU legislator should be awarded a wide margin of appreciation.[73] Thus, the review of proportionality was limited to manifest errors of assessment.[74] Applying this standard to the case at hand, the AG, after examining the relation between the data transferred, the purpose of combating terrorism, the period for which the data were to be retained,

---

[66] ECJ, Joined Cases C-317/04 and C-318/04 European Parliament v Council of the European Union (C-317/04) and Commission of the European Communities (C-318/04)—PNR, Judgment of 30 May 2006, ECLI:EU:C:2006:346, paras 57 et seq. and 67–70.

[67] ECJ, Joined Cases C-317/04 and C-318/04 European Parliament v Council of the European Union (C-317/04) and Commission of the European Communities (C-318/04)—PNR, Opinion of AG Léger of 22 November 2005, ECLI:EU:C:2005:710, para 207.

[68] Ibid., para 211.

[69] Ibid., para 212.

[70] Ibid., paras 211 et seq.

[71] Ibid., paras 215–219.

[72] Ibid., paras 222 et seq.

[73] Ibid., paras 223–232.

[74] Ibid., para 231.

judicial remedies for individuals and other safeguards concerning the handling of the data in the US in great detail, ultimately held that Council and Commission had acted proportionately and there was no violation of Article 8 ECHR.[75]

While the AG followed the Court's flawed assessment of the interference with regard to the collection of the passenger data, he required the nexus to private life, perhaps supposing that the ECJ had merely failed to mention it in the previous case. With regard to the case at hand, this did not affect the outcome, as the AG found this requirement to be fulfilled, given the nature of the data.

With his supposition of a reduced standard of review, the AG set a precedent, which the Court only addressed in its *Schecke and Eifert* judgment, in order to clarify that it actually applies a strict standard of review.[76] De Hert and Gutwirth have argued that such a limited standard of review in cases of such serious interferences undermines data protection principles.[77] While it is unknown whether the Court already held this position, as it did not address this question in its judgment, this different standard certainly would have affected the outcome of the case considerably and presumably led to a similar result as in *Opinion 1/15*, where the Court found a violation of the right to data protection with regard to a passenger data agreement.[78]

3.2.3.2 Bavarian Lager

In 2007, the CFI ruled on a dispute concerning access to documents of the Commission, which invoked Article 4(1)(b) Regulation 1049/2001[79] and denied a request to disclose minutes of a meeting of its officials with UK government officials.[80] Under this clause, EU institutions can refuse access to documents where this would conflict with the privacy and integrity of individuals and, particularly, the EU data protection regime.

The CFI found, in analogy to *Österreichischer Rundfunk*, that the DPR-EC also had to be interpreted in the light of Article 8 ECHR.[81] However, at this point the court departed from the ECJ's case law. Relying on AG Léger's Opinion in the PNR case, the court also referred to the ECtHR's margin of appreciation, which it held to enable the national authorities to strike a fair balance between the public and private

[75] Ibid., paras 234–261.

[76] Cf. below Sect. 3.2.6.

[77] De Hert and Gutwirth 2009, pp. 38 et seq.

[78] Cf. below Sect. 3.2.8.10.

[79] Regulation (EC) No 1049/2001 of the European Parliament and of the Council of 30 May 2001 regarding public access to European Parliament, Council and Commission documents, OJ L 145 of 31 May 2001, pp. 43–48.

[80] CFI, Case T-194/04 The Bavarian Lager Co. Ltd v Commission of the European Communities, Judgment of 8 November 2007, ECLI:EU:T:2007:334, paras 21–37.

[81] Ibid., paras 111–114.

interests.[82] From there, the CFI went on to examine the compatibility of Regulation 1049/2001 with Article 8 ECHR and stated at the outset that exceptions from that regulation had to be interpreted restrictively, and its Article 4(1)(b) could only be applied to personal data actually and specifically undermining privacy.[83]

The court argued that while the ECtHR interpreted the concept of private life broadly and the right to data protection could be a part of the right to private life, not all personal data related to private life.[84] Thus the CFI, like AG Léger, reattached the caveat from the ECtHR's case law—concerning the nexus between personal data and private life,[85] stating that the concept of private life did not necessarily encompass all personal data, as not all personal data could undermine a person's private life[86]—which the ECJ had omitted in *Österreichischer Rundfunk*.

The CFI did not discuss the consequences of the requirement's absence in the Court's reasoning, but underscored its point by referring to recital 33 DPD, which states that data capable of infringing fundamental freedoms or privacy due to their nature should be processed only with the explicit consent of the data subject. While this recital was not directly applicable to the case at hand, the DPR-EC's aim was to ensure the consistency of the EU data protection legislation in order to protect individual rights, regardless whether personal data are processed by Member States or the EU, according to recitals 13 and 17 DPR-EC. The DPR-EC thus explicitly called for interpretation in conformity with the DPD.

The CFI thus used recital 33 DPD to substantiate that not all personal data required the same protection. It then turned to Article 10 DPR-EC (now Article 10 DPR-EU)—which corresponds to Article 8 DPD (now Article 9 GDPR) and to which recital 33 DPD alludes—on the special categories of data, assuming that recital 33 DPD referred to this differentiation.[87] Applying its findings to the case at hand, the CFI found that privacy was not necessarily affected when a document contained personal data.[88] The documents in question contained only the names of the participants in the meeting, where they acted as representatives of their respective bodies, so that their private lives were not concerned.[89] The CFI used the standard it thought to have been established by recital 33 DPD to gauge whether there was an interference with the right to private life and consequently stated that the mere publication of the names

[82] Ibid., para 115; citing ECtHR, Peck v. the United Kingdom, App. No. 44647/98, Judgment of 28 January 2003, paras 76 and 77; and ECJ, Joined Cases C-317/04 and C-318/04 Parliament v Council and Commission—PNR, Opinion of AG Léger, paras 226–228.

[83] CFI, Case T-194/04 Bavarian Lager v Commission, Judgment of 8 November 2007, paras 116 et seq.

[84] Ibid., para 118; citing ECJ, Joined Cases C-317/04 and C-318/04 Parliament v Council and Commission—PNR, Opinion of AG Léger, para 209.

[85] Cf. above Sect. 3.2.2.1

[86] CFI, Case T-194/04 Bavarian Lager v Commission, Judgment of 8 November 2007, paras 118 et seq.

[87] Ibid., para 119.

[88] Ibid., para 123.

[89] Ibid., para 125.

was not capable of affecting the protection of privacy for these persons.[90] While this outcome is in line with the ECJ's assessment in *Österreichischer Rundfunk*, the CFI adopted a different approach from the Court. Of course, under both, the DPR-EC and the DPD, any processing of personal data has to be justified in order to be lawful. However, this had not yet become the standard for the assessment of an interference with the right to data protection in the Court's case law.

As the Commission, in its arguments before the court, had relied on the prior jurisprudence of the ECJ, the CFI insisted that the circumstances of the case differed from those in *Österreichischer Rundfunk*, since the case at hand concerned the interpretation of Article 4(1)(b) Regulation 1049/2001.[91] The CFI found a difference between the publication of a list of attendees and the publication of the names of employees and their income.[92]

Comparing the case at hand with the Court's judgment in *Lindqvist*, the CFI further distinguished between the general ban of the processing of personal data, unless the criteria of Article 7 DPD (now Article 6 GDPR) are fulfilled, and the interpretation of the requirements of Article 4(1)(b) Regulation 1049/2001 as cumulative and thus requiring the processing of personal data and the undermining of the privacy of an individual.[93]

Lastly, the CFI, with regard to the ECtHR's jurisprudence, stated that while professional activities were not excluded per se from the notion of private life, not every such activity was fully covered by the protection of the right to private life.[94] Thus, the CFI concluded that the publication of a document including a list of attendees did not qualify as an interference with the protection of private life and Article 4(1)(b) Regulation 1049/2001 did not apply.[95] While the CFI's approach was in conformity with the jurisprudence of the ECtHR on Article 8 ECHR, it was narrower than that of the ECJ. Yet, the CFI's interpretation of the right to data protection as contingent on the right to privacy was not in direct contradiction of the Court's case law on Article 8 ECHR, which was still the standard and the Court did not yet examine the Charter, which was not legally binding then.[96]

Nevertheless, the Commission filed an appeal with the ECJ and argued that the CFI—which in the wake of the Lisbon Treaty reform had become the GC—had misinterpreted Article 4(1)(b) Regulation 1049/2001 and the EU data protection regime.[97] AG Sharpston based her argument on a rather different approach from the

---

[90] Ibid., para 126.

[91] Ibid., paras 127 et seq.

[92] Ibid., para 128.

[93] Ibid., para 129.

[94] Ibid., paras 130 et seq.

[95] Ibid., paras 132–139.

[96] Perhaps the Court had aimed to differentiate data protection from privacy since its judgment in *Österreichischer Rundfunk*, however, there is no information available on the motivation of the Court. Also cf. De Hert and Gutwirth 2009, pp. 41 et seq.

[97] ECJ, Case C-28/08 P European Commission v The Bavarian Lager Co. Ltd., Judgment of 29 June 2010, ECLI:EU:C:2010:378, para 40.

GC. She found that it had misinterpreted Article 4(1)(b) Regulation 1049/2001 and that the disclosure of the documents did in fact interfere with the right to privacy protected by Article 8(1) ECHR.[98] The AG nonetheless agreed with its outcome, arguing that the interference was justified by the professional context in which the document was drawn up and the legitimate interest of transparency.[99]

The Court, however, found that Article 4(1)(b) Regulation 1049/2001 could only be assessed with regard to the general data protection regime and specifically the DPR-EC in this case.[100] As Article 1(1) DPR-EC stated, its purpose was to implement the right to privacy with regard to the processing of personal data.[101] Thus, the secondary law on data protection always had to be interpreted in conjunction with Article 8 ECHR.[102] In contrast to the GC, the ECJ then found that Articles 8(b) and 18 DPR-EC (now Article 9(1)(b) and 23 DPR-EU) on the transfer of data to recipients that are not Community institutions or bodies and the right to object, respectively, were applicable.[103] By making the documents available in a form that excluded the names of the participants, the Commission therefore fulfilled its obligation of transparency. As the undertaking had not provided any reasons to justify the release of the names, the Commission could not weigh the opposing interests and thus had to reject the request in accordance with Article 8(b) DPR-EC.[104] While the Court did not carry out an in-depth assessment of Article 8 ECHR, it nonetheless rejected the GC's approach of reading the provisions of data protection narrowly, while demonstrating the strong link between the secondary legislation and the right to data protection.

The Court's approach has been criticised as awarding data protection precedence over the access to documents and failing to strike a balance when finding that the DPD applied to the case at hand.[105] However, Regulation 1049/2001 was not created in a vacuum, as AG Sharpston pointed out, but rather explicitly referred to the DPR-EC.[106] Thus, the legislator already achieved a first balance by making reference to the data protection regime and thus ensuring that the latter provision, as lex posterior, did not, by default, overrule the earlier legislation. However, as the Court explicitly stated, a balance would still need to be struck between the rights, i.e. the right to data protection of the data subjects whose names were included in the memorandum, and the right of access to documents of the undertaking requesting the memorandum. This was achieved on the level of the secondary law by virtue of Article 4(1)(b)

[98] ECJ, Case C-28/08 P European Commission v The Bavarian Lager Co. Ltd., Opinion of AG Sharpston of 15 October 2009, ECLI:EU:C:2009:624, paras 95–101, 151–155, 171–174 and 186–191.

[99] Ibid., paras 185 and 192.

[100] ECJ, Case C-28/08 P Commission v Bavarian Lager, Judgment of 29 June 2010, paras 57–63.

[101] Ibid., para 61.

[102] Ibid.

[103] Ibid., paras 64–71.

[104] Ibid., paras 72–78.

[105] Lynskey 2015b, p. 140.

[106] ECJ, Case C-28/08 P Commission v Bavarian Lager, Opinion of AG Sharpston, paras 93 et seq.

Regulation 1049/2001, which ensured that data protection would not per se take precedence over the access to documents.

3.2.4 Article 8 ECHR with Reference to the Charter: Promusicae

Eight years after the CFR had been solemnly declared, the Court, in 2008, referred to the rights contained in the Charter for the first time in the *Promusicae* case.[107] The national court had asked whether the Member States could lay down an obligation to reveal the identity of an internet service user in order to ensure the effective protection of copyrights by enabling the rights holder to instigate civil proceedings.[108]

Firstly, the Grand Chamber assessed whether either the ePD prohibited such a measure or the three Copyright Directives[109] laid this down as an obligation. It concluded that neither was the case.[110]

Secondly, the Court considered whether other rules of Community law, including the Charter, might require a different interpretation of the Copyright Directives.[111] Here, the Grand Chamber examined whether the protection of intellectual property rights under Article 17 CFR and the right to an effective remedy guaranteed in Article 47 CFR and as recognized as general principles, called for a different interpretation.[112] However, at the same time, the "right to the protection of personal data and hence of private life"[113] had to be taken into consideration, as according to recital 2 ePD it was the directive's aim to protect the rights of Articles 7 and 8 CFR.[114]

---

[107] ECJ, Case C-275/06 Productores de Música de España (Promusicae) v Telefónica de España SAU Judgment of 29 January 2008, ECLI:EU:C:2008:54. Even though the ECJ's judgment in *Bavarian Lager* was rendered in 2010, it curiously fell into its old habit of only referring to the ECHR as standard for fundamental rights in that case.

[108] Ibid., paras 2 and 30 et seq.

[109] Directive 2000/31/EC of the European Parliament and of the Council of 8 June 2000 on certain legal aspects of information society services, in particular electronic commerce, in the Internal Market ('Directive on electronic commerce'), OJ L 178 of 17 July 2000, pp. 1–16; Directive 2001/29/EC of the European Parliament and of the Council of 22 May 2001 on the harmonisation of certain aspects of copyright and related rights in the information society, OJ L 167 of 22 June 2001, pp. 10–19; Directive 2004/48/EC of the European Parliament and of the Council of 29 April 2004 on the enforcement of intellectual property rights, OJ L 157 of 30 April 2004, pp. 45–86.

[110] ECJ, Case C-275/06 Promusicae, Judgment of 29 January 2008, paras 49–59. With regard to the ePD the Court found that Article 15(1) ePD referred to the exception clause of Article 13(1) DPD, which in turn, referred to the rights and freedoms of others, Member States were not barred from laying down an exception, but were also not compelled to provide such an option, cf. ibid., paras 53–55.

[111] Ibid., para 46.

[112] Ibid., paras 61 et seq.

[113] Ibid., para 63.

[114] Ibid., para 64.

The Court found that Article 7 CFR substantially reproduced the right to private life provided by Article 8 ECHR and that Article 8 CFR proclaimed the right to data protection.[115] However, when the Court came to the balancing of these rights, it merely referred to the right to respect for private life vis-à-vis the rights to protection of property and to an effective remedy.[116] It found that the relevant secondary law as well as the national implementation legislation contained the necessary tools for striking this balance.[117]

Picking up on its *Lindqvist* judgment, the Court stated that the generality of the EU provisions awarded the Member States discretion for the transposition.[118] Nevertheless, the national authorities and courts had to achieve a fair balance between the fundamental rights and ensure that they did not interpret their implementation measures in a way that conflicted either with these rights or the relevant secondary law.[119] The Court, therefore, passed the "hot potato"[120] of reconciling the rights to the Member States and, aside from referring to the rights of the Charter, upheld the deferential approach it had taken in the *Lindqvist* judgment.

In her Opinion, AG Kokott had laid out a very different course for the Court. The AG had also referred to the Charter, although only at the outset. Regarding the link of data protection to fundamental rights, she found that data protection was based on the right to private life as guaranteed in Article 8 ECHR.[121] This provision was mirrored in Article 7 CFR, while Article 8 CFR emphasised the right to the protection of personal data and the fundamental principles of data protection.[122]

The AG then turned to Article 8 ECHR to analyse the substantive issues and took the Court's judgment in *Österreichischer Rundfunk* as a starting point. Yet, she made an important adjustment, when she went on to state that "any interference with private life—the processing of personal data—must be proportionate to the aims pursued."[123]With this interjection, the AG introduced a new standard for the interference: the processing of personal data was sufficient to constitute an interference. As in the preceding paragraph she had cited both the Charter and the DPD to interpret the notion of in accordance with the law,[124] it can be assumed that she thus relied on Article 2(b) DPD (now Article 4(2) GDPR), which defines the processing of personal data as encompassing, inter alia, the collection, recording, storage and making available.

---

[115] Ibid.

[116] Ibid., para 65.

[117] Ibid., para 66.

[118] Ibid.

[119] Ibid., para 67.

[120] Coudert and Werkers 2008, p. 51.

[121] ECJ, Case C-275/06 Productores de Música de España (Promusicae) v Telefónica de España SAU Opinion of AG Kokott of 18 July 2007, ECLI:EU:C:2007:454, para 51.

[122] Ibid.

[123] Ibid., para 54.

[124] Ibid., para 53.

Even though the AG referred to the previous judgment of *Österreichischer Rundfunk*, she refined the notion of interference with the right to private life. While the Court did not adopt this interpretation in its judgment, its reference to a right to the protection of personal data as part of the right to private life, is a shift from the notion of privacy, which it had previously invoked, towards a right to data protection, albeit still in the context of the right to private life under the ECHR.[125]

With regard to the justification of the interference, the AG found more inspiration in the Charter and the DPD when she turned to the criterion of foreseeability in her assessment of Article 8 ECHR. She argued that the data protection principle of purpose limitation laid down in Article 8(2) CFR and defined in Article 6(1)(b) DPD (now Article 5(1)(b) GDPR) as allowing the collection of data only for specific, explicit and legitimate purposes, was a specific expression of foreseeability.[126]

While the Court in the judgment reaffirmed its deferential approach laid out in *Lindqvist* and did not elucidate on the balance to be struck under Community law,[127] AG Kokott argued that the balance between the conflicting fundamental rights had to be struck firstly on the Community level.[128] She then relied on *Lindqvist* as authority to emphasise the Member States' obligation to interpret their national laws in conformity with the DPD, which in turn had to be interpreted in a way that ensured the protection of fundamental rights.[129] This reading of *Lindqvist* differs considerably from the interpretation of the Court. However, the AG found that the DPD was a specific expression of the fundamental right to data protection on the level of secondary law, and most notably extended data protection obligations to individuals.[130] She thus laid out a revised line of argument, which took more careful account of the secondary legislation for the interpretation of the right to data protection and thus introduced the concept that every processing of personal data constitutes an interference with the right to data protection. Nevertheless, this argument was not yet adopted by the Court, neither in this judgment nor in a similar case, shortly thereafter, where it expressly upheld its own ruling.[131]

3.2.5 Reference to Article 1 DPD

After this affirmation of its course, the Court, perhaps influenced by AG Kokott's substantive arguments in *Promusicae*, refined the framing of the right to data protection as part of the right to privacy by reference to the secondary legislation.

---

125 ECJ, Case C-275/06 Promusicae, Judgment of 29 January 2008, para 63.

126 ECJ, Case C-275/06 Promusicae, Opinion of AG Kokott, para 53.

127 Varju 2014, pp. 78 et seq.

128 ECJ, Case C-275/06 Promusicae, Opinion of AG Kokott, paras 55 et seq.

129 Ibid., para 56.

130 Ibid., para 57.

131 ECJ, Case C-557/07 LSG-Gesellschaft zur Wahrnehmung von Leistungsschutzrechten GmbH v Tele2 Telecommunication GmbH, Order of 19 February 2009, ECLI:EU:C:2009:107.

3.2.5.1 Satamedia

In *Satamedia* the referring national court was concerned with the scope of the exemption clause of Article 9 DPD (corresponding to Article 85 GDPR), which excludes data processing for journalistic purposes from the scope of the DPD.[132] The Grand Chamber held that any interpretation of the DPD had to be in accordance with its general aim, stated in Article 1 DPD, to protect the "right to privacy, with respect to the processing of personal data."[133] This right, however, had to be reconciled with the right to freedom of expression, which was the purpose of Article 9 DPD, as reaffirmed by recital 37 DPD and was an obligation of the Member States in implementing the directive.[134] In this regard, the right to freedom of expression demanded a broad interpretation of notions such as journalism, while the right to privacy required that derogations and limitations from the DPD were permissible only when strictly necessary.[135] The Grand Chamber thus found that Article 9 DPD could not only be applied to media undertakings, but extended to every person engaged in journalism and was not dependent on a certain kind of medium used for the circulation of information.[136] Furthermore, profit orientation did not preclude journalistic purposes.[137] Yet, aside from these rather general remarks, the Grand Chamber, again, left the finding of a balance between the rights at hand for the national court[138] and reinforced its deferential approach.

In this case, just as in *Promusicae*, AG Kokott delivered the Opinion. Unlike the Court, she laid out an extensive argument concerning Article 9 DPD and its interpretation in the light of the relevant fundamental rights: in her opinion, the provision was aimed at balancing different rights and thus had to be interpreted in accordance with these rights.[139] Referring to the case law of the ECtHR and the ECJ, the AG returned to her previous argument that the DPD implemented fundamental rights on the level of secondary law and put the directive in the context of the positive obligations under the right to respect for private life.[140] She argued that the DPD, in accordance with these obligations, extended the rules on the protection of personal data to individuals.[141]

With regard to the balance between the rights of Article 8 and Article 10 ECHR—a conflict that was also inherent in the DPD, as the strict application of its rules

[132] ECJ, Case C-73/07 Tietosuojavaltuutettu v Satakunnan Markkinapörssi Oy and Satamedia Oy, Judgment of 16 December 2008, ECLI:EU:C:2008:727.

[133] Ibid., para 52.

[134] Ibid., paras 53–55.

[135] Ibid., para 56.

[136] Ibid., paras 57 et seq. and 60.

[137] Ibid., para 59.

[138] Ibid., para 62.

[139] ECJ, Case C-73/07 Tietosuojavaltuutettu v Satakunnan Markkinapörssi Oy and Satamedia Oy, Opinion of AG Kokott of 8 May 2008, ECLI:EU:C:2008:266, paras 37 et seq.

[140] Ibid., paras 39 et seq.

[141] Ibid., paras 40 et seq.

was liable to limit the freedom of expression, e.g. with regard to investigative journalism—the AG stated that the DPD awarded the Member States discretion to adopt implementation measures in order to reconcile these conflicting positions.[142] However, a balance had to be achieved in conformity with the fundamental rights of Community law.[143]

Before turning to the interpretation of Article 9 DPD, the AG interjected a brief reflection on the ECJ's approach to the assessment of fundamental rights. While in *Promusicae* it had only pointed out the relevant rights, it had provided the national court more guidance on the balance to be achieved in *Österreichischer Rundfunk*.[144] However, in its *Viking* judgment, the Court had also found that its own purpose was to provide useful answers to the national courts, especially regarding the assessment of proportionality.[145] Yet, the AG concluded, it would be best for the Court to follow its deferential approach in this case and leave the reconciliation of fundamental rights to the national courts due to the wide scope of the DPD.[146] While the DPD was based on the harmonisation clause of Article 95 TEC (now Article 114 TFEU), it also applied to purely national cases.[147] As it thus reached far into the domain of the Member States, the Court should leave them a broad discretion in the assessment of fundamental rights.[148]

This last paragraph illustrates how the AG adapted her approach regarding the assessment of fundamental rights after the Court's judgment in *Promusicae*: she did not pick up her reference to Article 2(b) DPD as standard for the interference with Article 8 ECHR, but merely referred to the Court's judgment in *Österreichischer Rundfunk*.[149] Further, while in the earlier case she urged the Court to find a balance between the Community fundamental rights, she here advised the opposite with reference to the broad scope of the DPD.[150]

Though the Court stated that any exemptions from the DPD had to be interpreted strictly to ensure the protection of the fundamental right to privacy, it stuck to the course laid out in *Lindqvist* and merely mentioned the relevant rights.[151] Of course, it must be noted that this line of reasoning, especially in such a pronounced manner as in the case at hand, runs counter to the aim of harmonising the rules on the processing of personal data, which the legislator pursued when basing the directive on the market

[142] Ibid., paras 43 et seq.

[143] Ibid., para 45.

[144] Ibid., para 46.

[145] Ibid., para 49; citing ECJ, Case C-438/05 International Transport Workers' Federation and Finnish Seamen's Union v Viking Line ABP and OÜ Viking Line Eesti, Judgment of 11 December 2007, ECLI:EU:C:2007:772, para 85.

[146] ECJ, Case C-73/07 Satakunnan Markkinapörssi and Satamedia, Opinion of AG Kokott, paras 50 and 53.

[147] Ibid., para 52.

[148] Ibid., para 53.

[149] Ibid., para 40.

[150] Ibid., paras 50 and 53.

[151] ECJ, Case C-73/07 Satakunnan Markkinapörssi and Satamedia, Judgment of 16 December 2008, para 56.

harmonization clause. Thus, while the Court now framed the right to data protection in line with Article 1 DPD as a right to privacy with regard to the processing of personal data, it did not develop this right further, but rather left this to the national courts.[152]

3.2.5.2 Rijkeboer

The *Rijkeboer* case concerned the restriction of the data subject's right to access information on the disclosure of their personal data to third parties under Article 12(a) DPD (corresponding to Article 15(1)(c) GDPR) by means of a one-year time limit.[153] As in the previous cases, the Court turned to Article 1 DPD and highlighted the directive's objective to protect the right to privacy with respect to the processing of personal data.[154] This right to privacy, the chamber held, ensured that the data subject's personal data were processed correctly and lawfully, i.e. were accurate and disclosed only to authorised third parties.[155] In order to enable the data subject to ascertain whether that was the case, they had to have a right to access according to recital 41 DPD,[156] which was implemented in Article 12(a) DPD.[157]

AG Ruiz-Jarabo Colomer had chosen a slightly different approach in the derivation of the fundamental right and found that the right to privacy, as a general principle resulting from the common constitutional traditions of the Member States, was further developed by the DPD.[158] The inclusion of the right to data protection in the Charter, which guaranteed the right of access and the right to have data processed fairly, reflected these traditions.[159] Though the Charter was not a legally binding instrument, the AG found that it was a collection of the common constitutional traditions.[160]

As the AG stated in his characteristically poetical style, the case demonstrated the conflict between the obligation of the controller to delete personal data when they are no longer necessary and the data subject's right of access to the information.[161] The chamber ultimately concluded that the Member States enjoyed discretion regarding the imposition of a time limit for the exercise of this right.[162] However, they had to

---

[152] The Court also followed this approach in ECJ, Case C-524/06 Heinz Huber v Bundesrepublik Deutschland, Judgment of 16 December 2008, ECLI:EU:C:2008:724, paras 47 and 67; as suggested by AG Poiares Maduro, ECJ, Case C-524/06 Heinz Huber v Bundesrepublik Deutschland, Opinion of AG Poiares Maduro of 3 April 2008, ECLI:EU:C:2008:194, paras 22 and 24.

[153] ECJ, Case C-553/07 College van burgemeester en wethouders van Rotterdam v M. E. E. Rijkeboer, Judgment of 7 May 2009, ECLI:EU:C:2010:662, paras 2, 23 and 31.

[154] Ibid., para 46.

[155] Ibid., para 49.

[156] Ibid.

[157] Ibid., para 50.

[158] ECJ, Case C-553/07 Rijkeboer, Opinion of AG Ruiz-Jarabo Colomer, paras 18–21.

[159] Ibid., para 22.

[160] Ibid.

[161] Ibid., para 25.

[162] ECJ, Case C-553/07 Rijkeboer, Judgment of 7 May 2009, para 64.

strike a fair balance between the interests of the data subject to protect their privacy and the obligation of the controller to store the relevant information.[163] The AG, drawing on the verbatim of Article 8 CFR, which mentions the right of access in its first paragraph and deletion only in the second, concluded that the right to access took precedence over the obligation to delete, as it enabled the data subject to exercise control over the controller.[164] He concluded that, in order to give full effect to the data subject's fundamental rights, the one-year time limit was unlawful, if the data subject was not notified about the disclosure of their data, was not informed about the time limit in advance or was not given sufficient information about the recipients.[165]

The chamber, in substance, followed the AG's argument and concluded that the time limit did not constitute a fair balance, unless a longer period was demonstrated to pose an excessive burden on the controller. Yet, it left the resolution of this question to the national court.[166] While the judgment is thus generally in line with the Court's deferential approach from the previous case law, it here provided the national court with more guidance.

The AG, on the other hand, as AG Kokott before him, made reference to the Charter and pointed to the expressly included right to data protection. He also picked up on AG Kokott's argument that the DPD was a specific expression of the right to data protection and thus aimed to extend the coherence between the secondary and primary law.

3.2.6 *The Charter as Standard: Schecke and Eifert and Deutsche Telekom AG*

After the Charter became legally binding, the Grand Chamber, in its seminal judgment of 2010 in the case *Schecke and Eifert*, concerning the publication of information on recipients of agricultural aid, found that it had to assess the case in the light of the Charter.[167] While AG Sharpston had relied on the ECHR and the DPC as well as the Charter for her Opinion,[168] the Court thus finally shifted its standard. Furthermore, the Court awarded the right to data protection an independent scope, i.e. assessed the interference separately from the right to private life.

[163] Ibid.

[164] ECJ, Case C-553/07 Rijkeboer, Opinion of AG Ruiz-Jarabo Colomer, paras 33–35.

[165] Ibid., paras 69 et seq.

[166] ECJ, Case C-553/07 Rijkeboer, Judgment of 7 May 2009, para 66.

[167] ECJ, Joined Cases C-92/09 and C-93/09 Volker und Markus Schecke GbR (C-92/09) and Hartmut Eifert (C-93/09) v Land Hessen, Judgment of 9 November 2010, ECLI:EU:C:2010:662, paras 44–46.

[168] ECJ, Joined Cases C-92/09 and C-93/09 Volker und Markus Schecke GbR (C-92/09) and Hartmut Eifert (C-93/09) v Land Hessen, Opinion of AG Sharpston of 17 June 2010, ECLI:EU:C:2010:353, paras 65, 71 and 93–123.

However, in its preliminary observations, it found that Article 8(1) CFR was closely connected to the right to respect of private life guaranteed by Article 7 CFR.[169] Article 8(2) CFR then, the Grand Chamber held, laid down requirements under which the processing was lawful, i.e. for limited purposes and based on consent or a legal basis, and Article 52(1) CFR allowed interferences with both Article 7 and 8 CFR.[170] As a last point of these preliminary observations, it referred to Article 52(3) CFR, which provides that rights of the Charter corresponding to rights of the ECHR are to be interpreted in accordance with the Convention.[171] Furthermore, as stated in Article 53 CFR, the Charter was not intended to restrict the rights of the ECHR. From this, the Grand Chamber—referring to the ECtHR cases of *Amann v. Switzerland* and *Rotaru v. Romania*, as it had already done in *Österreichischer Rundfunk*—concluded that the "right to respect for private life with regard to the processing of personal data, recognised by Articles 7 and 8 of the Charter, concerns any information relating to an identified or identifiable individual."[172] The limitations on the right to data protection corresponded to those of Article 8 ECHR.[173]

Concerning the personal scope of this right, the Grand Chamber found that legal persons could only rely on Articles 7 and 8 CFR when their official title identified at least one natural person.[174] Aside from the names, Regulation 1290/2005[175] and Regulation 259/2008[176] also required the publication of the amounts of agricultural aid received as well as information on the place of residency and postal code of recipients.[177] As the aid was part of the income of the recipients and the information was made available to third parties, the Court, referring to its judgment in *Österreichischer Rundfunk*, found the publication to interfere with the recipients' right to private life according to Article 7 CFR.[178] Further, the publication was a processing of personal data in the sense of Article 8(2) CFR and was not based on the consent of the recipients.[179]

---

[169] ECJ, Joined Cases C-92/09 and C-93/09 Volker und Markus Schecke and Eifert, Judgment of 9 November 2010, para 47.

[170] Ibid., paras 49 et seq.

[171] Ibid., para 51.

[172] Ibid., para 52.

[173] Ibid.

[174] Ibid., para 53.

[175] Council Regulation (EC) No 1290/2005 of 21 June 2005 on the financing of the common agricultural policy, OJ L 209 of 11 August 2005, pp. 1–25.

[176] Commission Regulation (EC) No 259/2008 of 18 March 2008 laying down detailed rules for the application of Council Regulation (EC) No 1290/2005 as regards the publication of information on the beneficiaries of funds deriving from the European Agricultural Guarantee Fund (EAGF) and the European Agricultural Fund for Rural Development (EAFRD), OJ L 76 of 19 March 2008, pp. 28–30.

[177] ECJ, Joined Cases C-92/09 and C-93/09 Volker und Markus Schecke and Eifert, Judgment of 9 November 2010, paras 56 et seq.

[178] Ibid., paras 58 et seq.

[179] Ibid., paras 60–63.

The Court went on to assess the justification under Article 52(1) CFR, finding that the publication was based on Articles 1(1) and 2 Regulation 259/2008, was thus provided for by law and served the transparency of public spending as a legitimate aim of general interest.[180] Regarding the proportionality of the measure, it held that the publication of names was liable to increase transparency and public control and that this interest had to be balanced with the rights of Articles 7 and 8 CFR.[181] Referring to its judgment in *Satamedia*, the Grand Chamber reaffirmed that all derogations from the DPD had to be examined under a standard of strict necessity, due to the fundamental rights dimension of the secondary law.[182] Before this background, it criticised the legislator for failing to consider other, less invasive modes of publication and, like AG Sharpston,[183] found that the publication in the form prescribed by the regulation with regard to individuals was not necessary and thus a disproportionate interference with the rights of Articles 7 and 8 CFR.[184]

While the Court, in its preliminary observations, seemed to interpret Articles 7 and 8 CFR jointly, it consistently referred to the rights of Articles 7 and 8 CFR in the plural form and also awarded them independent scopes when examining the interferences.[185] Concerning the standard for interferences with Article 8 CFR—even if it did not refer to Article 2(b) DPD explicitly[186]—the Grand Chamber, in substance, adopted the standard advanced by AG Kokott in *Satamedia* and found that the processing of personal data constituted an interference with Article 8 CFR. Yet, the Court simultaneously stayed in line with its judgment in *Österreichischer Rundfunk* and did not consider the collection of the data, which—although it may have been found to be justified—also constituted a form of processing and thus also interfered with the right to data protection.

With the judgment in *Schecke and Eifert*, the Court—upon first engaging with the Charter—already considered Article 8 CFR to have an independent scope from the right to private life. However, it did not fully engage with the system provided by the DPD, such as the definition of processing personal data, even though the argument had already been laid out by AG Kokott.

While the coming into force of the Charter thus shifted the formal point of reference and allowed the Court to pursue its jurisprudence on data protection more independently of the ECtHR, the Court's first judgment remained tentative and cannot be said to have marked a pronounced shift in its argument. Rather, it was an adjustment

---

[180] Ibid., paras 66–71.

[181] Ibid., paras 74–76.

[182] Ibid., para 77; ECJ, Case C-73/07 Satakunnan Markkinapörssi and Satamedia, Judgment of 16 December 2008, para 56.

[183] ECJ, Joined Cases C-92/09 and C-93/09 Volker und Markus Schecke and Eifert, Opinion of AG Sharpston, paras 93–123.

[184] ECJ, Joined Cases C-92/09 and C-93/09 Volker und Markus Schecke and Eifert, Judgment of 9 November 2010, paras 79–86.

[185] Cf. also Wagner 2015, pp. 45 et seq. and 116.

[186] Ibid., pp. 68 et seq.

that still did not realise the full potential of interplay between the data protection rules from the primary and secondary law.

After *Schecke and Eifert* the chamber judgment in *Deutsche Telekom AG*, where Judge Lenaerts also served as rapporteur, was rendered. It touched upon Article 8 CFR only briefly. The Court held that with the consent of the data subject under Article 8(2) CFR, the processing of personal data could be "authorise[d]".[187] While this does not clarify whether the Court meant that the processing would be outside the scope of Article 8 CFR or consent could justify an interference, it found that once a data subject had given consent to have their address published in a public directory according to Article 12(2) ePD, this also extended to other directory services.[188] It must be noted here, that Article 12(2) ePD is a lex specialis explicitly concerning only directories and, unlike the Court, does not use the word consent, but rather the term determination.[189] This is due to Article 2(f) ePD, which states that consent is to interpreted in accordance with Article 2(h) DPD (corresponding to Articles 2(11) and 7 GDPR) and is limited to a specific processing operation and purpose with regard to a specific controller.[190]

With regard to Article 8 CFR, the Court found that the further processing of the data subject's data could not "substantively impair" their right to data protection.[191] Here, again, the wording of the Court is not very clear: the statement could be read as implying that there is a sort of de minimis threshold, which an interference has to reach in order to be considered an interference or it could mean that the Court considered that the interference caused by this transfer is proportionate. However, reading a chamber judgment in a way that establishes a de minimis approach, when the Court's previous case law has eschewed any additional requirements, is unwarranted. Especially, as the Court, again with Judge Lenaerts as rapporteur, expressly reaffirmed the argument from *Schecke and Eifert* in another chamber judgment in the *ASNEF* case.[192]

---

[187] ECJ, Case C-534/09 Deutsche Telekom AG v Bundesrepublik Deutschland, Judgment of 5 May 2011, ECLI:EU:C:2011:279, para 52.

[188] Ibid., para 65.

[189] Lynskey 2015b, pp. 191 et seq. seems to assume that the Court interpreted the general rules on consent.

[190] Cf. above Chap. 2, Sect. 2.3.2.4 and also Article 29 Working Party, Opinion 15/2011 on the definition of consent of 13 July 2011. WP 187, p. 17.

[191] ECJ, Case C-534/09 Deutsche Telekom, Judgment of 5 May 2011, para 66.

[192] ECJ, Joined Cases C-468/10 and C-469/10 Asociación Nacional de Establecimientos Financieros de Crédito (ASNEF) (C-468/10) and Federación de Comercio Electrónico y Marketing Directo (FECEMD) (C-469/10) v Administración del Estado, Judgment of 24 November 2011, ECLI:EU:C:2011:777, paras 40–42, using almost the exact wording of *Schecke and Eifert*.

3.2.7 Assessing Article 8 CFR Exclusively: The Internet-Monitoring Cases

On the same day as *ASNEF*, the Court passed a judgment, which initiated a series of cases between late 2011 and early 2012, similar in facts to *Promusicae*, as they related to the obligations of internet service providers (ISP). In these cases, which required a balancing of intellectual property rights and the right to data protection, the Court did not mention Article 7 CFR at all.

The first judgment was *Scarlet Extended*, where an organization of copyright holders, SABAM, sued the eponymous ISP, Scarlet Extended. The latter refused to install a monitoring system on its internet traffic in order to prevent peer-to-peer software from being used for copyright infringements.[193] With these demands, the copyright holders desired an even more invasive system for the protection of their rights, which would have come at the expense of the rights of internet users.[194]

The chamber, assessing the same three copyright directives invoked in *Promusicae*, found that while intellectual property rights were protected by Article 17(2) CFR, they had to be balanced with other rights, such as the right to conduct business under Article 16 CFR.[195] The filtering system envisioned by SABAM would have to preventively monitor any electronic communications on the ISP's network, would be complicated and costly for the latter and would thus, the chamber held, not strike a balance between the rights of the two parties concerned.[196] Further, it found that the systematic analysis of content and the collection of internet users' internet protocol (IP) addresses would constitute the processing of personal data and thus infringe the right to data protection under Article 8 CFR as well as the freedom of information under Article 11 CFR, due to the possibility of blocking lawful communications.[197] Thus, a request for such a filtering system could not be based on the copyright directives invoked by SABAM, as it would not strike a fair balance between the different rights at stake.[198]

While the chamber thus merely referred to Article 8 CFR and, curiously, made no mention of Article 7 CFR, AG Cruz Villalón had prepared a full examination of fundamental rights for the Court. As the national court had asked for an assessment of Articles 8 and 10 ECHR, the AG found that for the purposes of Article 52(3) CFR, these rights corresponded to those of Articles 7 and 8 CFR and Article 11 CFR, respectively.[199] Although he did not refer to any case law of the ECtHR, this implies

---

[193] ECJ, Case C-70/10 Scarlet Extended SA v Société belge des auteurs, compositeurs et éditeurs SCRL (SABAM), Judgment of 24 November 2011, ECLI:EU:C:2011:771, paras 2, 15–18.

[194] Coudert and Werkers 2008, p. 71.

[195] ECJ, Case C-70/10 Scarlet Extended, Judgment of 24 November 2011, paras 42–45.

[196] Ibid., paras 47–49.

[197] Ibid., paras 50–52.

[198] Ibid., para 54.

[199] ECJ, Case C-70/10 Scarlet Extended SA v Société belge des auteurs, compositeurs et éditeurs SCRL (SABAM), Opinion of AG Cruz Villalón of 14 April 2011, ECLI:EU:C:2011:255, paras 30 et seq.

that the AG assumed that the right to data protection, as guaranteed by Article 8 CFR, also exists under the Convention. However, this is implicit and the AG did not discuss whether a nexus to private life with regard to Article 8 ECHR was required or whether such a link would conform to Article 8 CFR. As the requested filtering system would affect these rights, the relevant copyright directives, he found, had to be interpreted in the light of these provisions.[200]

The AG started his assessment concerning the interference with Article 8 CFR and found it difficult to ascertain whether this filtering system, which would monitor the entirety of the ISP's internet traffic, would entail the collection of personal data.[201] At least concerning the static IP addresses, he concluded that the Court should regard them as personal data and thus the right to data protection was affected.[202] With regard to Article 7 CFR, as the right to confidentiality of electronic communications, the AG referred to the case law of the ECtHR on the tapping of telephone, email and internet communications, which he found comparable to the issue at hand, and concluded that the filtering system also interfered with the right to respect for correspondence and the confidentiality of communications.[203]

Assessing the justification of the measure, AG Cruz Villalón turned to Article 52(1) CFR and found the protection of the rights of the copyright holders to constitute an objective of general interest.[204] However, at the stage of examining the legal basis in domestic law, he found that the relevant provision, which allowed the national courts to issue injunctions against intermediaries whose services are used by third parties to infringe copyrights, did not conform to the requirements on the quality of the law, as such an obligation, both from the point of view of the ISP as well as its users, could not be foreseen, especially as it did not include any guarantees on the protection of personal data, the confidentiality of communications or the possibility to appeal to the blocking of certain contents.[205] Thus, there was no adequate legal basis for the adoption of the filtering system requested by SABAM.[206]

This first set-back did not prevent SABAM from bringing another case before the Court, where it sought to have an online social networking website implement the desired filtering system. The Court here merely reiterated its finding that such a system would not strike a fair balance between the fundamental rights concerned, while, again, referring only to Article 8 CFR and not Article 7 CFR.[207]

In the case of *Bonnier Audio*, as in *Promusicae*, copyright holders obtained an injunction against an ISP to disclose names and addresses of its users identified

[200] Ibid., paras 69 et seq.

[201] Ibid., para 74.

[202] Ibid., paras 74–80.

[203] Ibid., paras 81 et seq.

[204] Ibid., paras 89–92.

[205] Ibid., paras 101–106.

[206] Ibid., para 108.

[207] ECJ, Case C-360/10 Belgische Vereniging van Auteurs, Componisten en Uitgevers CVBA (SABAM) v Netlog NV, Judgment of 16 February 2012, ECLI:EU:C:2012:85, paras 2, 16–22 and 47–51.

by their IP addresses.[208] After dismissing a far-fetched claim relying on the Data Retention Directive (DRD),[209] the chamber reiterated its finding from *Promusicae* that Directive 2004/48 and the ePD neither precluded Member States from imposing such a disclosure of personal data in civil proceedings nor obliged them to do so.[210] However, it emphasised that the national law transposing the directive had to strike a fair balance and the Member States had to ensure that the national law was not interpreted in a way that was in conflict with EU fundamental rights.[211] While AG Jääskinen only mentioned the rights to data protection and privacy in passing,[212] the chamber did not even refer to any specific fundamental rights and rather applied its deferential approach, leaving this assessment to the referring court.[213]

All of these cases concern a rather specific issue, and the Court approached them in a rather peculiar fashion. As the Court continued this line of case law in 2016, it first dropped the reference to Article 8 CFR and, later, to Article 11 CFR as well.[214] However, with regard to Article 8 CFR, the judgments demonstrate that the Court, after *Schecke and Eifert*, clearly found the right to data protection to have an autonomous scope and content. It further subscribed to the standard for interferences suggested by AG Kokott. However, it did so, just like in *Schecke and Eifert*, without expressly referring to the DPD.

Yet, the Court only found the collection of IP addresses to be an interference with Article 8 CFR, even though the monitoring system also concerned the contents of communications. Perhaps, the Court felt that the collection of IP addresses was the more evident issue, whereas the contents could hypothetically contain any kind of personal data. From the perspective of data protection, the nature of the data is not crucial, as all personal data are protected. However, it would, of course, matter on the justification stage when assessing the gravity of the interference. Furthermore, as the Court would later hold, access to the contents of communications is a violation of the essence of Article 7 CFR, which it did not assess here at all.[215] As the Court

[208] ECJ, Case C-461/10 Bonnier Audio AB and Others v Perfect Communication Sweden AB, Judgment of 19 April 2012, ECLI:EU:C:2012:219, paras 2, 25–28.

[209] Directive 2006/24/EC of the European Parliament and of the Council of 15 March 2006 on the retention of data generated or processed in connection with the provision of publicly available electronic communications services or of public communications networks and amending Directive 2002/58/EC, OJ L 105 of 13 April 2006, pp. 54–63.

[210] ECJ, Case C-461/10 Bonnier Audio, Judgment of 19 April 2012, paras 38–45 and 55.

[211] Ibid., paras 49 and 56.

[212] ECJ, Case C-461/10 Bonnier Audio AB and Others v Perfect Communication Sweden AB, Opinion of AG Jääskinen of 17 November 2011, ECLI:EU:C:2011:753, para 62.

[213] ECJ, Case C-461/10 Bonnier Audio, Judgment of 19 April 2012, para 59.

[214] ECJ, Case C-484/14 Tobias Mc Fadden v Sony Music Entertainment Germany GmbH, Judgment of 15 September 2016, ECLI:EU:C:2016:689, para 82; ECJ, Case C-18/18 Eva Glawischnig-Piesczek v Facebook Ireland Limited, Judgment of 3 October 2019, ECLI:EU:C:2019:821. Also cf. ECJ, Case C-401/19 Poland v Parliament and Council, pending; ECJ, Case C-401/19 Poland v Parliament and Council, Opinion of AG Saugmandsgaard Øe of 15 July 2021, ECLI:EU:C:2021:613.

[215] Cf. below Sect. 3.2.8.2.

concluded that even with regard to IP addresses the monitoring would still not be proportionate, this ultimately did not affect the outcome of the case.

3.2.8 *Frictions and Factions: The Recent Case Law*

In the more recent case law of the Court, two strands can be identified, both of which rely on the judgment in *Schecke and Eifert*: a chamber judgment in the *Schwarz* case read Articles 7 and 8 CFR together, still referring to these rights in the plural form. This approach is essentially based on the preliminary observations in *Schecke and Eifert*.[216]

The opposing approach is based on the independent assessment of Articles 7 and 8 CFR, which the Grand Chamber had adopted in *Schecke and Eifert* for the operative part of the assessment of the interferences and which the Grand Chamber also adopted in *Digital Rights Ireland*. Since then, the Court has oscillated between these approaches to various degrees in its reasoning. As Judge Thomas von Danwitz, who also drafted the judgment in *Digital Rights Ireland*, has been rapporteur in the most recent cases, the latter approach has been prevalent.

3.2.8.1 Schwarz

In the 2013 judgment in the *Schwarz* case, the Court was concerned with a challenge of the validity of the Passport Regulation.[217] The chamber examined whether the taking of fingerprints and their subsequent storage on the passports amounted to an interference with the rights to respect for private life and data protection.[218] Reading Articles 7 and 8(1) CFR together, it concluded that any processing of personal data by a third party constituted such an interference.[219] The chamber's argument was closely linked to the Opinion of AG Mengozzi. However, in line with the submissions made to the Court and its jurisprudence in the internet-monitoring cases, he had examined only Article 8 CFR.[220]

As fingerprints contained unique information and allowed for the precise identification of an individual, the chamber, citing the ECtHR's *S. and Marper* judgment, just like the AG, concluded that these constituted personal data, which were processed,

[216] Also cf. Lynskey 2014, p. 1807.

[217] Council Regulation (EC) No 2252/2004 of 13 December 2004 on standards for security features and biometrics in passports and travel documents issued by Member States, OJ L 385 of 29 December 2004, pp. 1–6.

[218] ECJ, Case C-291/12 Michael Schwarz v Stadt Bochum, Judgment of 17 October 2013, ECLI:EU:C:2013:670, para 23.

[219] Ibid., paras 24 et seq. Also cf. González Fuster 2014b, pp. 269 et seq.

[220] ECJ, Case C-291/12 Michael Schwarz v Stadt Bochum, Opinion of AG Mengozzi of 13 June 2013, ECLI:EU:C:2013:401, para 35.

as defined by Article 2(b) DPD, and thus interfered with the rights to private life and to the protection of personal data.[221]

In order to be justified, the processing under Article 8(2) CFR had to be based either on consent—which the chamber swiftly and rightly dismissed as there was no other option for citizens to obtain a passport, which is essential for travelling, and consent could therefore not be given freely—or on a legitimate legal basis, which is required similarly under the general justification clause of Article 52(1) CFR.[222] The taking and storing of the fingerprints was authorised by Article 1(2) Passport Regulation as legal basis.[223] The second requirement of Article 52(1) CFR, concerning an objective of general interest, was met with the regulation's aims to prevent the falsification of passports and their fraudulent use as well as illegal entry into the EU.[224]

The Court did not find that there was a violation of the essence of the rights recognised by Articles 7 and 8 CFR, which it had, however, not even bothered defining.[225] In the assessment of proportionality, the Court held that, with regard to the aim of preventing falsification, the use of fingerprints was likely to reduce this risk and facilitate the work of the authorities.[226] Even though fingerprint technology was not wholly reliable, it nonetheless reduced the likelihood of misuse and was thus appropriate.[227] With regard to necessity, AG Mengozzi and the chamber noted that by taking prints of only two fingers, which was not of an intimate nature and caused no further discomfort than the taking of a picture, there were no less invasive measures, which the legislator would have had to take into consideration.[228]

While the AG, taking up the argument from AG Léger in the PNR case,[229] argued that the standard for the assessment of the legislator's choice was that of manifest error, as the case concerned an area of complex and evolving technology, where the legislator enjoyed a broad discretion,[230] the chamber made no mention of any reduction in the depth of its review. Yet, it did not address this issue at all and thus missed the opportunity to reject this long-standing line of argument advanced by several AGs.

---

[221] ECJ, Case C-291/12 Schwarz, Judgment of 17 October 2013, paras 27–30; citing the preliminary observations of ECJ, Joined Cases C-92/09 and C-93/09 Volker und Markus Schecke and Eifert, Judgment of 9 November 2010, at para 52; ECJ, Case C-291/12 Schwarz, Opinion of AG Mengozzi, paras 39 et seq. and 42.

[222] ECJ, Case C-291/12 Schwarz, Judgment of 17 October 2013, paras 31–34.

[223] Ibid., para 35; ECJ, Case C-291/12 Schwarz, Opinion of AG Mengozzi, para 43.

[224] ECJ, Case C-291/12 Schwarz, Judgment of 17 October 2013, paras 36–38; ECJ, Case C-291/12 Schwarz, Opinion of AG Mengozzi, para 48.

[225] ECJ, Case C-291/12 Schwarz, Judgment of 17 October 2013, para 39.

[226] Ibid., paras 40 et seq.

[227] Ibid., paras 42–45; ECJ, Case C-291/12 Schwarz, Opinion of AG Mengozzi, paras 48 et seq.

[228] ECJ, Case C-291/12 Schwarz, Judgment of 17 October 2013, paras 46–52; ECJ, Case C-291/12 Schwarz, Opinion of AG Mengozzi, paras 52 and 54 et seq.

[229] Cf. above Sect. 3.2.3.1.

[230] ECJ, Case C-291/12 Schwarz, Opinion of AG Mengozzi, para 53.

Further, the chamber, unlike the AG, specifically mentioned technical and organisational measures, when it held that the measure did not go beyond what was necessary to attain the goal, as the regulation included specific guarantees against abuse: the fingerprints could only be used for authentication, were secured by strong encryption and were not to be stored in a central database.[231] Therefore, both the AG and the Court concluded that the processing was necessary, justified and the regulation valid.[232]

While the chamber's assessment of the interference deviated from that of the Grand Chamber in *Schecke and Eifert*, it must be pointed out that the joint assessment, as actually carried out by the chamber, does conform to the previous standard for Article 8 CFR. However, the chamber did not examine the right to private life. Rather, its assessment of the interference considered only issues of processing personal data.

Yet, the chamber apparently considered issues of privacy in the assessment of the proportionality.[233] There, the chamber found that the taking of fingerprints did not constitute an intimate procedure, which may have been prompted by the ECtHR's assessment whether the collection of different types of biometric and genetic information interfered with Article 8 ECHR in the *S. and Marper* judgment,[234] which the chamber cited when examining the interference. This demonstrates a drawback of the joint assessment, which can lead to misconceptions concerning the respective content of the two rights. Further, the ECtHR explicitly held, with regard to an interference with Article 8 ECHR, that it did not matter whether "the applicant had been inconvenienced in any way."[235]

3.2.8.2 Digital Rights Ireland

In the case of *Digital Rights Ireland*, concerning the validity of the DRD with regard to fundamental rights, the Court delivered another seminal judgment in the evolution of the right to data protection.[236] After the judgments in *Österreichischer Rundfunk* and *Schecke and Eifert*, the 2014 judgment marked a further turning point in the interpretation of the right to data protection, as the Grand Chamber further explored its distinct scope.

---

[231] ECJ, Case C-291/12 Schwarz, Judgment of 17 October 2013, paras 54–62; only the latter point was mentioned in ECJ, Case C-291/12 Schwarz, Opinion of AG Mengozzi, paras 56 et seq.

[232] ECJ, Case C-291/12 Schwarz, Judgment of 17 October 2013, paras 64 and 66; ECJ, Case C-291/12 Schwarz, Opinion of AG Mengozzi, para 59.

[233] As pointed out by Lynskey 2015b, pp. 196 et seq. in a different context.

[234] ECtHR [GC], S. and Marper v. the United Kingdom, App. Nos. 30562/04 and 30566/04, Judgment of 4 December 2008, paras 66–86.

[235] ECtHR [GC], Amann, App. No. 27798/95, Judgment of 16 February 2000, para 70; which the Court had referred to in ECJ, Joined Cases C-465/00, C-138/01 and C-139/01 Österreichischer Rundfunk and Others, Judgment of 20 May 2003, para 75.

[236] ECJ, Joined Cases C-293/12 and C-594/12 Digital Rights Ireland Ltd (C-293/12) v Minister for Communications, Marine and Natural Resources and Others and Kärntner Landesregierung (C-594/12) and Others, Judgment of 8 April 2014, ECLI:EU:C:2014:238.

This came after the Court had faced strong criticism when Ireland challenged the legal basis of the DRD and the Court decided not to consider the pleas put forward by the Slovak Republic, which joined the proceedings, on the compatibility of the DRD with fundamental rights.[237] While the Court might have been guided by procedural considerations,[238] which were not unprecedented,[239] neither the Grand Chamber nor AG Cruz Villalón, who only mentioned the right to privacy protected by Article 8 ECHR in passing, assessed the fundamental rights implications of the case.[240]

In his Opinion on *Digital Rights Ireland*, AG Cruz Villalón analysed the rights to privacy and data protection in great detail and started his assessment by stating that the latter, as guaranteed in Article 8 CFR, was distinct from the right to privacy, as data protection was covered by an autonomous regime,[241] i.e. the secondary EU data protection legislation. The retention of metadata affected the right to the protection of personal data significantly, the AG found, as it was for the individual to consent to the disclosure of their data under the right to informational self-determination.[242]

Yet, the AG held that it was not the processing of the retained data, but rather the actual collection and retention of the data, which was at issue and posed a threat to the right to privacy.[243] Unfortunately, he thereby disregarded Article 2(b) DPD defining processing as an umbrella term for any operation performed with data,[244] such as collection and storage, which had been picked up by the Court in the previous *Schwarz* judgment.[245]

AG Cruz Villalón continued that even if the DRD was in compliance with Articles 8(2) and (3) CFR this did not prejudice the finding of a violation under the right to privacy according to Article 7 CFR.[246] In support of this, he referred to the private sphere, which was the core of the personal sphere, and linked these spheres to Article

---

[237] Cf. ECJ, Case C-301/06 Ireland v European Parliament and Council of the European Union, Judgment of 10 February 2009, ECI:EU:C:2009:68, para 34 and above in Sect. 3.2.3.1; Petri 2009; Simitis 2009; Terhechte 2009.

[238] Giegerich 2014, pp. 9 et seq. Bieker 2015, p. 80.

[239] ECJ, Case C-155/91 Commission of the European Communities v Council of the European Communities—Framework Directive on Waste, Judgment of 17 March 1993, ECLI:EU:C:1993:98; Pechstein 2011, MN. 212.

[240] ECJ, Case C-301/06 Ireland v European Parliament and Council of the European Union, Opinion of AG Bot of 14 October 2008, ECLI:EU:C:2008:558, para 95.

[241] ECJ, Joined Cases C-293/12 and C-594/12 Digital Rights Ireland Ltd (C-293/12) v Minister for Communications, Marine and Natural Resources and Others and Kärntner Landesregierung (C-594/12) and Others, Opinion of AG Cruz Villalón of 12 December 2013, ECLI:EU:C:2013:845, para 55.

[242] Ibid., paras 56 et seq.

[243] Ibid., para 59.

[244] Also observed by Lynskey 2014, p. 1809.

[245] Cf. above Sect. 3.2.8.1. and ECJ, Case C-291/12 Schwarz, Judgment of 17 October 2013, paras 27–30; ECJ, Case C-291/12 Schwarz, Opinion of AG Mengozzi, paras 39 et seq. and 42.

[246] ECJ, Joined Cases C-293/12 and C-594/12 Digital Rights Ireland and Seitlinger and Others, Opinion of AG Cruz Villalón, paras 60 et seq.

7 and Article 8, respectively.[247] Yet, he never followed up on this differentiation in any way in the course of his assessment.

The AG cited the Court's previous line of case law, stating that the rights of Article 7 and 8 CFR were closely connected and could be regarded as a right to respect for private life with regard to the processing of personal data and to this end relied on AG Kokott's Opinion in *Promusicae*, the Court's preliminary observations in *Schecke and Eifert* and the Explanations on Article 8 CFR.[248] Yet, AG Cruz Villalón went beyond these authorities and held that the link between the rights was contingent on the nature of the data.[249] Even though the data in question were always personal, a distinction had to be made between personal data as such, which identify an individual, but were neutral[250] to some extent and data that was more than personal data.[251] While the former category was sufficiently protected under Article 8 CFR with its guarantees regarding the processing, the latter was essentially related to private life, including the intimate sphere.[252] Thus, the real issue, according to the AG, was whether a person's private life had been recorded—rather than that the relevant data were subsequently processed—which was protected under Article 7 CFR.[253]

Although the AG repeatedly referred to the jurisprudence of the Bundesverfassungsgericht (BVerfG),[254] when elaborating the difference between the right to private life and the right to data protection, which he refers to as the right to informational self-determination at times, he unfortunately did not take the German court's iconic line from its 1983 census judgment stating that "under the conditions of automated data processing there is no irrelevant date"[255] into consideration. This quote provides the major argument against the differentiation proposed by AG Cruz Villalón: there are no neutral personal data. Even seemingly innocuous data like a name or a location may reveal sensitive information about a person,[256] such as their ethnic origin in the case of names or medical information, when a person visits a specialized clinic for the treatment of a health condition. Thus, the differentiation between seemingly neutral data and personal data that "relate essentially to private

---

[247] Ibid., para 61.

[248] Ibid., para 62.

[249] Ibid., para 63.

[250] Which seems to have been inspired by the jurisprudence of the ECtHR, cf. ECtHR [GC], S. and Marper, App. Nos. 30562/04 and 30566/04, Judgment of 4 December 2008, para 84.

[251] ECJ, Joined Cases C-293/12 and C-594/12 Digital Rights Ireland and Seitlinger and Others, Opinion of AG Cruz Villalón, paras 63–65.

[252] Ibid., para 65.

[253] Ibid., paras 65 et seq.

[254] Ibid., paras 72 and 79.

[255] Bundesverfassungsgericht, BVerfGE 65, pp. 1–71—Volkszählung, Judgment of 15 December 1983, p. 45.

[256] Cf. also Lynskey 2014, p. 1808.

life",[257] in practice, is impossible to achieve.[258] Further, while the AG explicitly argues for a separation between the right to private life and data protection, the right to data protection he conceptualises remains opaque and is overshadowed by the all-encompassing right to private life.[259]

The AG concluded from his preliminary remarks that the retention of data at issue related mostly to Article 7 CFR and held that this interference could not be justified due to its disproportionality.[260]

Even though the Grand Chamber ultimately reached the same verdict regarding the proportionality of the DRD as the AG, it reached this conclusion by a vastly different path, which laid down a rather structured and clear argument.

The Court's assessment started under the premise that the data retained provided detailed insights into the daily life of the persons concerned.[261] The retention therefore affected the private lives of these persons and it had to be determined under Article 7 CFR whether the data could be retained.[262] Here, the Court suddenly introduced the nexus to private life it had not mentioned when assessing Article 8 ECHR since the judgment in *Österreichischer Rundfunk*. Perhaps it felt that this was necessary here, to differentiate between the two independent rights. However, this did not affect the standard of interference, but rather only the scope of the right.

As the retention of the data was also a form of processing personal data, the measure fell under Article 8 CFR and had to conform to the requirements of data protection.[263]

Concerning the interference, the Grand Chamber referred to its judgment in *Österreichischer Rundfunk* to establish that, contrary to the proposition of AG Cruz Villalón, the right to privacy did not require that the information concerned were sensitive or the persons concerned inconvenienced in any way.[264] Nevertheless, in the next step, the Grand Chamber departed from its previous case law, holding that the obligation to collect the data itself interfered with Article 7 CFR.[265] Further, it found the access rights of the national authorities to constitute another, separate interference with Article 7 CFR.[266]

---

[257] ECJ, Joined Cases C-293/12 and C-594/12 Digital Rights Ireland and Seitlinger and Others, Opinion of AG Cruz Villalón, para 65.

[258] Cf. Kunnert 2014a, p. 104. With regard to the special categories of personal data, cf. Chap. 5, Sect. 5.3.1.2.

[259] Cf. Wagner 2013.

[260] ECJ, Joined Cases C-293/12 and C-594/12 Digital Rights Ireland and Seitlinger and Others, Opinion of AG Cruz Villalón, paras 131 and 152.

[261] ECJ, Joined Cases C-293/12 and C-594/12 Digital Rights Ireland and Seitlinger and Others, Judgment of 8 April 2014, para 27.

[262] Ibid., paras 29 et seq.

[263] Ibid., paras 29 et seq.; citing ECJ, Joined Cases C-92/09 and C-93/09 Volker und Markus Schecke and Eifert, Judgment of 9 November 2010, para 47.

[264] ECJ, Joined Cases C-293/12 and C-594/12 Digital Rights Ireland and Seitlinger and Others, Judgment of 8 April 2014, para 33.

[265] Ibid., para 34.

[266] Ibid., para 35 relying on the case law of the ECtHR.

Due to the processing of personal data entailed in the operations, the DRD also interfered with Article 8 CFR.[267] Relying on the Opinion of AG Cruz Villalón in this regard, the Grand Chamber asserted that the interferences were particularly serious due to their mass-scale and the fact that they could be used without notification of the person concerned, which was likely to create a feeling of constant surveillance.[268]

At the justification stage, the Grand Chamber mostly assessed the rights of Articles 7 and 8 CFR jointly. This can be attributed to the fact that Article 52(1) CFR, as horizontal justification clause, lays down the same requirements for all rights of the Charter. Firstly, however, it concluded that the retention of the data did not violate the essence of the rights guaranteed by Article 7 CFR, as Article 1(2) DRD expressly excluded the content of any communication.[269] Further, due to the minimal provisions on data protection and data security included in Article 7 DRD, the directive did not encroach on the essence of Article 8 CFR either.[270] Orla Lynskey and Maja Brkan have criticised this definition of the essence of the right to data protection due to the fact that technical and organisational measures were not included in the wording of Article 8 CFR.[271] However, from a teleological interpretation of Article 8 CFR, it can be gathered that when processing personal data, all the guarantees of the right to data protection, such as lawfulness or the rights of data subjects, have to be implemented by measures on a technical and/or organisational level. The definition of the essence of Article 8 CFR is therefore minimalistic, but in principle sound.[272]

However, Lynskey and Brkan raise another point, concerning the superficial level that the Court awards the essence in this case.[273] It does indeed appear that with regard to the DRD, the Court was satisfied with any provision, which so much as hinted at safeguards. While it is certainly within the nature of a directive that Member States implement it, only by applying this low standard could the Court find that Article 7 DRD did not constitute a violation of the essence of Article 8 CFR.

Furthermore, the Court's differentiation between metadata and contents of communications with regard to the essence of Article 7 CFR is questionable. As there are no innocuous data, the mere knowledge of who communicates with whom and when, can already provide detailed insights into an individual's life.[274] Especially in the context of a digital society, these data are available on mass-scale and quite literally trace every step a person takes.[275]

---

[267] Ibid., para 36; ECJ, Joined Cases C-293/12 and C-594/12 Digital Rights Ireland and Seitlinger and Others, Opinion of AG Cruz Villalón, paras 67–75; disagreeing with the finding of an interference, Dimitropoulos 2015, p. 77.

[268] ECJ, Joined Cases C-293/12 and C-594/12 Digital Rights Ireland and Seitlinger and Others, Judgment of 8 April 2014, para 37.

[269] Ibid., para 39.

[270] Ibid., para 40.

[271] Lynskey 2015b, p. 172; Brkan 2019b, p. 878.

[272] Cf. also Bock and Engeler 2016, p. 596. In more depth cf. Chap. 5, Sects. 5.4.5.3 and 5.4.3.4.

[273] Brkan 2019b, pp. 878 et seq.; Lynskey 2015b, p. 172.

[274] Brkan 2019b, pp. 872–874; Ojanen 2016, pp. 327 et seq.

[275] Bock and Engeler 2016, p. 595; Nettesheim 2015, p. 60; Ojanen 2014, p. 537.

The Grand Chamber then held that the material objectives[276] of the directive were the legitimate aims of investigation, detection and prosecution of serious crime.[277] Concerning the scope of review and departing once more from the AG's suggestion,[278] it then reiterated its finding of *Schecke and Eifert* concerning the strict standard of review[279]—which, interestingly, the Court found to have established in *Satamedia*, where in fact it had called for a strict review of any derogation from the secondary law on data protection, while leaving the actual assessment of proportionality explicitly to the national court[280]—and held that even in the case at hand concerning the combatting of terrorism and serious crime, this still applied. It thereby, unlike the chamber in *Schwarz*, expressly rebuked the suggestions of numerous AGs, who found that the review of proportionality could only be limited,[281] and to this end could rely on a reference to the margin of appreciation in *Österreichischer Rundfunk*.[282]

Instead, the Grand Chamber relied on the ECtHR's *S. and Marper* judgment[283] to establish that fundamental rights limit the discretion of the legislator depending, inter alia, on the area concerned, the nature of the rights in question, the nature and gravity of the interference and the object pursued with that interference.[284] However, while the ECtHR usually awards Contracting Parties a wider margin of appreciation in cases of national or public security,[285] as was at issue here, the Court applied a

[276] The Court was trying to distinguish its answer from that given in its previous ruling concerning the objective of the DRD in ECJ, Case C-301/06 Ireland v Parliament and Council, Judgment of 10 February 2009, para 34; also cf. Classen 2014, pp. 443 et seq.

[277] ECJ, Joined Cases C-293/12 and C-594/12 Digital Rights Ireland and Seitlinger and Others, Judgment of 8 April 2014, paras 41–45.

[278] ECJ, Joined Cases C-293/12 and C-594/12 Digital Rights Ireland and Seitlinger and Others, Opinion of AG Cruz Villalón, para 136.

[279] ECJ, Joined Cases C-92/09 and C-93/09 Volker und Markus Schecke and Eifert, Judgment of 9 November 2010, para 77.

[280] Cf. above Sect. 3.2.5.1 and ECJ, Case C-73/07 Satakunnan Markkinapörssi and Satamedia, Judgment of 16 December 2008, paras 56 and 62.

[281] ECJ, Joined Cases C-293/12 and C-594/12 Digital Rights Ireland and Seitlinger and Others, Opinion of AG Cruz Villalón, para 136; ECJ, Case C-291/12 Schwarz, Opinion of AG Mengozzi, para 53; ECJ, Joined Cases C-317/04 and C-318/04 Parliament v Council and Commission—PNR, Opinion of AG Léger, paras 223–232.

[282] ECJ, Joined Cases C-465/00, C-138/01 and C-139/01 Österreichischer Rundfunk and Others, Judgment of 20 May 2003, paras 80–90.

[283] ECtHR [GC], S. and Marper, App. Nos. 30562/04 and 30566/04, Judgment of 4 December 2008, para 102.

[284] ECJ, Joined Cases C-293/12 and C-594/12 Digital Rights Ireland and Seitlinger and Others, Judgment of 8 April 2014, para 47.

[285] ECtHR, Leander, App. No. 9248/81, Judgment of 26 March 1987, para 59; ECtHR, Weber and Saravia v. Germany, App. No. 54934/00, Decision of 29 June 2006, para 106; although, after the ECJ's ruling in Digital Rights, more reluctantly in ECtHR, Big Brother Watch and Others v. the United Kingdom, App. Nos. 58170/13, 62322/14 and 24960/15, Judgment of 13 September 2018, paras 314 et seq. However, this has been overruled by the Grand Chamber's extremely lenient approach in ECtHR [GC], Big Brother Watch and Others v. the United Kingdom, App.

strict standard of review, which it found necessary due to the high value of the rights concerned and the magnitude of the interference.[286]

In line with AG Cruz Villalón's arguments, the Grand Chamber found that even though not all means of electronic communication were encompassed by the DRD and there were technical means to circumvent the surveillance, this did not change the usefulness of the data retained for criminal investigations.[287] The Court, like the AG, thus brushed aside the empirical evidence on the inefficiency of mass-surveillance data for criminal investigations.[288]

However, concerning the necessity, the Grand Chamber made clear that even though the fight against serious crime was crucial for public security, this aim was in itself not capable of justifying the scale of the retention.[289] Rather, the Grand Chamber found, in line with its case law since *Satamedia*,[290] that any restriction in relation to the protection of personal data had to be applied only in so far as strictly necessary and that the protection of personal data explicitly laid down in Article 8(1) CFR was of prime importance for the right to respect for private life guaranteed by Article 7 CFR.[291] With regard to the standard of review, the Court had already referred to the important role of "the protection of personal data in the light of the fundamental right to respect for private life".[292] While the latter instance could be attributed to the fact that it refers to the standard of the ECtHR in the preceding paragraph and thus be seen as an emphasis of the role of data protection, the former reference could be understood to indicate that the Court finds that the requirements of Article 8(1) CFR also inform the interpretation of the right to private life.[293]

Nos. 58170/13, 62322/14 and 24960/15, Judgment of 25 May 2021. On that latest judgment cf. Zalnieriute 2021; Milanovic 2021.

[286] ECJ, Joined Cases C-293/12 and C-594/12 Digital Rights Ireland and Seitlinger and Others, Judgment of 8 April 2014, paras 47 et seq.

[287] Ibid., paras 49 et seq.; ECJ, Joined Cases C-293/12 and C-594/12 Digital Rights Ireland and Seitlinger and Others, Opinion of AG Cruz Villalón, para 137.

[288] Kunnert 2014a, p. 106.

[289] ECJ, Joined Cases C-293/12 and C-594/12 Digital Rights Ireland and Seitlinger and Others, Judgment of 8 April 2014, para 51.

[290] ECJ, Case C-73/07 Satakunnan Markkinapörssi and Satamedia, Judgment of 16 December 2008, para 56.

[291] ECJ, Joined Cases C-293/12 and C-594/12 Digital Rights Ireland and Seitlinger and Others, Judgment of 8 April 2014, paras 52 et seq.; unlike the AG, the Grand Chamber did not assess whether the subsequent retention of data known as quick freeze was a less invasive measure with regard to the period of retention, cf. ECJ, Joined Cases C-293/12 and C-594/12 Digital Rights Ireland and Seitlinger and Others, Opinion of AG Cruz Villalón, paras 142–144. González Fuster 2014b, p. 275 et seq., criticizes this as meddling the two rights.

[292] ECJ, Joined Cases C-293/12 and C-594/12 Digital Rights Ireland and Seitlinger and Others, Judgment of 8 April 2014, para 48.

[293] Ojanen argues that the separation of Articles 7 and 8 CFR rested on this as a premise. However, this argument must be rejected, as the Court only mentions it after the individual assessment of the interferences with the respective rights in the justification under the uniform justification clause of the Charter, cf. Ojanen 2014, p. 540.

The Grand Chamber, much like the AG, then held that any EU legislation had to include clear and precise rules on the scope and application of the measure at issue as well as minimum safeguards in order to protect the persons concerned against abuse and unlawful access or use of the data.[294] As the DRD encompassed the metadata of all means of electronic communication and all persons using them, it interfered with the fundamental rights of the entire European population without any distinction with regard to unsuspicious individuals[295] or individuals protected by rules of professional secrecy.[296]

In particular, the DRD contained no limits on the collection of data, neither temporally nor geographically or on the access and use by the national authorities or on the period of retention, which, the Grand Chamber found in line with the AG's assessment, was instead set arbitrarily between six months and two years.[297] While the Court did not expressly refer to the secondary legislation in the proportionality assessment, these requirements relate to the principles of purpose and storage limitation, integrity and confidentiality as well as transparency, which I introduced in Chap. 2.[298]

Just like the AG, the Grand Chamber found that the lack of specific rules governing the extent of the interference with the rights to privacy and data protection meant that the interference was exceptionally serious and wide-ranging.[299] Additionally, the failure to provide sufficient safeguards concerning abuse and unlawful access and use of the data did not meet the standard of Article 8 CFR and allowed the service providers to take economic considerations into account when determining the level of data security.[300] Thus, the Grand Chamber concluded that the DRD was disproportionate and declared it invalid.[301]

---

[294] ECJ, Joined Cases C-293/12 and C-594/12 Digital Rights Ireland and Seitlinger and Others, Judgment of 8 April 2014, para 54; ECJ, Joined Cases C-293/12 and C-594/12 Digital Rights Ireland and Seitlinger and Others, Opinion of AG Cruz Villalón, paras 120–131.

[295] As Aqilah Sandhu rightly points out, the differentiation between certain groups of individuals should be met with scepticism, as it is likely to lead to discrimination based on ethnicity, nationality or similar factors protected under Article 21 CFR, cf. Sandhu 2017, p. 463.

[296] ECJ, Joined Cases C-293/12 and C-594/12 Digital Rights Ireland and Seitlinger and Others, Judgment of 8 April 2014, paras 56–58.

[297] Ibid., paras 59–64; ECJ, Joined Cases C-293/12 and C-594/12 Digital Rights Ireland and Seitlinger and Others, Opinion of AG Cruz Villalón, paras 145–149.

[298] Cf. Chap. 2, Sect. 2.3.2.

[299] ECJ, Joined Cases C-293/12 and C-594/12 Digital Rights Ireland and Seitlinger and Others, Judgment of 8 April 2014, para 65; ECJ, Joined Cases C-293/12 and C-594/12 Digital Rights Ireland and Seitlinger and Others, Opinion of AG Cruz Villalón, paras 121–131.

[300] ECJ, Joined Cases C-293/12 and C-594/12 Digital Rights Ireland and Seitlinger and Others, Judgment of 8 April 2014, paras 66 et seq.

[301] Ibid., paras 69 et seq. However, unlike the AG had suggested, cf. ECJ, Joined Cases C-293/12 and C-594/12 Digital Rights Ireland and Seitlinger and Others, Opinion of AG Cruz Villalón, paras 154–158; the Court did not limit the temporal effects of the judgment, thereby invalidating the directive with ex tunc effect, ECJ, Joined Cases C-293/12 and C-594/12 Digital Rights Ireland and Seitlinger and Others, Judgment of 8 April 2014, para 73.

While the Court engaged with the right to data protection extensively and provided a clear affirmation of its separate nature from privacy, it did so mostly with regard to the scope of these rights. In the proportionality assessment, the Court conflated the rights to a certain degree, albeit to a lesser extent than in *Schwarz*. In the assessment of proportionality, the Court expanded its reasoning compared to *Schwarz*, where it had already hinted at technical and organisational measures, and found several measures, which also relate to the principles of the data protection legislation.

With regard to the material scope of the judgment itself and the consequences of the conditions imposed on the legislator for the mass-retention of communications data, the Court had not, as became apparent shortly after the judgment, provided a reasoning that made it sufficiently clear to the Member States that such a blunt instrument necessarily collided with EU fundamental rights.[302] Shortly after the *Digital Rights Ireland* judgment, the United Kingdom (UK) and Sweden introduced their own mass-retention legislation, which prompted a follow-up judgment in the case of *Tele2 Sverige*, which I will analyse below.[303]

3.2.8.3 Google Spain

Shortly after the judgment in *Digital Rights Ireland*, the ECJ delivered another landmark judgment in 2014, concerning a dispute between an individual and an internet search engine operator. The issue was whether an individual could demand that the operator deletes search results under "a right to be forgotten".[304]

AG Jääskinen, in his Opinion, which was delivered before the judgment in *Digital Rights Ireland*, examined whether the rights to erasure, blocking and objection as granted by Articles 12(b) and 14(a) DPD (now Articles 17 and 21 GDPR) contained such a right to be forgotten and—after he found that this was not the case[305]—whether this was compatible with the rights of Articles 8 and 7 CFR as well as Articles 11 and 16 CFR.[306]

Then, the AG, in three steps all but disposed of the right to data protection: he started by stating that Article 8 CFR confirmed the acquis on the EU and CoE level, but did not introduce new elements relevant for the interpretation of the DPD.[307] Secondly, Article 7 CFR, just like its corresponding provision of Article 8 ECHR,

[302] Cf. also Bieker 2015, p. 86; Roßnagel 2014, pp. 375–377 also found that the Court outruled bulk data retention; for the implications of the judgment on other EU surveillance measures, which largely have not been reviewed by the Court, cf. Boehm and Cole 2014, pp. 58–89.

[303] Cf. below Sect. 3.2.8.9.

[304] ECJ, Case C-131/12 Google Spain SL and Google Inc. v Agencia Española de Protección de Datos (AEPD) and Mario Costeja González, Judgment of 13 April 2014, ECLI:EU:C:2014:317, paras 14–20.

[305] ECJ, Case C-131/12 Google Spain SL and Google Inc. v Agencia Española de Protección de Datos (AEPD) and Mario Costeja González, Opinion of AG Jääskinen of 13 April 2014, ECLI:EU:C:2013:424, para 111.

[306] Ibid., paras 102 et seq.

[307] Ibid., para 113.

had to be taken into account in the interpretation of the directive, while the latter also covered aspects of the protection of personal data.[308] Lastly, the AG then referred to the joint reading of Articles 7 and 8 CFR in the preliminary observations to *Schecke and Eifert* and found that the right to the protection of private life with regard to the processing of personal data, due to the wide scope of the notion of processing, covered any electronic communication concerning an individual.[309] Thereby, the AG had dissolved the right to data protection in the right to private life. Consequently, at the stage of the interference, the AG held that a search engine operator engaged in the processing of personal data and found this to interfere with Article 7 CFR.[310]

While this interference, which he then found to pertain to both Article 7 and 8 CFR, had to be justified, the AG noted that, in the case at hand, the interference was not caused by a public authority, but rather between private parties and there would thus need to exist a positive obligation of the Member States to enforce a right to be forgotten.[311] However, this required balancing with the competing fundamental rights to freedom of expression and information under Article 11 CFR and its counterpart in Article 10 ECHR for the users of the search engine, and the right to conduct a business under Article 16 CFR of the search engine operator.[312] Answering the question whether Article 7 CFR read in conjunction with Articles 12(b) and 14(a) DPD demanded such a right to be forgotten, the AG found that in balancing this with the other fundamental rights in question, such a right would not strike a fair balance and cautioned the Court against leaving this balance to be struck by the search engine operator on a case-by-case basis.[313]

The Court did not heed the advice of the AG.[314] As a starting point, the Grand Chamber[315] stated that the DPD had to be interpreted in accordance with fundamental rights, especially the right to privacy.[316] While the right to private life was protected under Article 7 CFR, Article 8 CFR guaranteed the right to the protection of personal data and the data subject's rights contained in the DPD were enshrined in Article 8(2) and (3) CFR.[317]

The Court found that Article 7(f) DPD (now Article 6(1)(f) GDPR) was the relevant legal basis for the processing of personal data by a search engine operator.[318] As the provision allowed for processing only where the legitimate interests of the

---

308 Ibid., paras 114 et seq.

309 Ibid., paras 117 et seq.

310 Ibid., paras 118 et seq.

311 Ibid., para 119.

312 Ibid., paras 119–124.

313 Ibid., paras 127–134.

314 Also cf. Kuner 2015, pp. 32 et seq.

315 While *Google Spain* and *Digital Rights Ireland* were both decided by the Court's Grand Chamber around the same time, only four of the thirteen and 15 judges, respectively, were involved in both cases. Notably, both cases, with Judge Ilešič and Judge von Danwitz, had different rapporteurs.

316 ECJ, Case C-131/12 Google Spain and Google, Judgment of 13 April 2014, para 68.

317 Ibid., para 69.

318 Ibid., paras 70–73.

controller were not outweighed by the interests or fundamental rights of the data subject, it required a balancing of the two positions.[319]

The processing operations carried out by a search engine, i.e. the indexing of websites, allowed the aggregation of information on various aspects of an individual's private life, which otherwise would not be available in such a structured and systematic way.[320] According to the Court, the important role of the internet in contemporary society amplified the interference with the rights to privacy and data protection.[321] Therefore, the Grand Chamber ruled that it could not be justified by the purely economic interests of the search engine operator.[322]

Yet, a fair balance had to be struck with the rights of other internet users to access the data in question.[323] As a general rule, the rights of the data subject protected by Articles 7 and 8 CFR prevailed over those rights.[324] However, in certain cases, a different result might be reached due to the nature of the data at issue, its sensitivity for the private life of the individual and the public's interest, which also depended on whether the data subject was a public figure.[325] Thus, the Court concluded that the data subject could request the relevant supervisory authorities to order the removal of certain results for a name-based search, which was not contingent on an order to remove the original source of the indexed link.[326]

The indexing carried out by search engines was an additional interference with the individual's fundamental rights, separate from that of publishing information on a website.[327] While the original source could be exempt under the exception clause of Article 9 DPD (corresponding to Article 85 GDPR) concerning journalistic activities, search engine operators did not benefit from that provision, as their legitimate interests under Article 7(f) DPD were different from those of publishers and the indexing had a different impact on the data subject.[328]

With regard to the exercise of the individual's right to be forgotten, the Court found that the processing of data, which may have been collected and initially used in conformity to Article 6 DPD (now Article 6 GDPR), could become incompatible with that provision when the data were no longer necessary for their purpose, especially when they appeared to be inadequate, irrelevant or no longer relevant, or their processing became excessive in relation to the purposes for which they were

[319] Ibid., para 74.

[320] Ibid., para 80.

[321] Ibid.

[322] Ibid., para 81. Also cf. Spindler 2014, p. 987, who argues that search engine operators should also profit from a quasi-right to freedom of expression, in analogy to media.

[323] ECJ, Case C-131/12 Google Spain and Google, Judgment of 13 April 2014, para 81. On potential conflicts with other rights, cf. Boehme-Neßler 2014, p. 829; Jozwiak 2016.

[324] ECJ, Case C-131/12 Google Spain and Google, Judgment of 13 April 2014, para 81.

[325] Ibid.

[326] Ibid., para 82.

[327] Ibid., para 83.

[328] Ibid., paras 85–87.

collected and the period since then.[329] If these conditions were met, a data subject could request the deletion of data under Article 12(b) DPD (now Article 17 GDPR) from search results even when these were published lawfully by third parties and contained accurate information.[330]

While there has been broad criticism of the practical implications of this judgment,[331] the Grand Chamber's reasoning is interesting from a fundamental rights perspective.[332] The Court here engaged in-depth with the secondary legislation and based the right to be forgotten on the general data subject rights of the DPD by interpreting them in the light of fundamental rights.[333]

While the Grand Chamber, in the spirit of *Digital Rights Ireland*, awarded the right to data protection an independent scope, the reasoning concerning the balancing of the right to be forgotten with other rights puts an emphasis on the notion of private life. This can be seen especially when the Court considers the indexing function of search engines, which connects "a vast number of aspects of his personal life"[334] and considers "the sensitivity for the data subject's private life"[335] in the balancing exercise.[336] However, this emphasis on private life can also be seen in the structure of the right to be forgotten: the Court allows that while the original publication as well as the indexing by the search engine may well be covered by the legal basis allowing the processing in the legitimate interest of the respective controller, it argues that over time, this interest may have to be re-evaluated.[337] Yet, this is not done with regard to the purpose of the processing, but rather by balancing the data subject's right to private life with the right to information of the general public.[338]

It thus becomes apparent that the right to be forgotten relates to the right to private life,[339] rather than the right to data protection. It can be connected to the jurisprudence on the media reporting details concerning the private lives of individuals, which the ECtHR has established.[340] Hence, the judgment in *Google Spain* is relevant for the right to data protection only insofar as it reaffirms the independent scope of Article 8 CFR.

---

329 Ibid., paras 92 et seq.

330 Ibid., para 94.

331 Spindler 2014; Masing 2014; Jozwiak 2016.

332 On the scope of the right to be forgotten, which is not relevant to the analysis here, cf. ECJ, Case C-507/17 Google LLC v Commission nationale de l'informatique et des libertés (CNIL), Judgment of 24 September 2019, ECLI:EU:C:2019:772; also cf. Van Alsenoy and Koekkoek 2015.

333 Also cf. Kuner 2015, pp. 37 et seq.

334 ECJ, Case C-131/12 Google Spain and Google, Judgment of 13 April 2014, para 80.

335 Ibid., para 81.

336 With regard to the special categories of data, often referred to as "sensitive" data, cf. Chap. 5, Sect. 5.3.1.2.

337 ECJ, Case C-131/12 Google Spain and Google, Judgment of 13 April 2014, paras 92 et seq.

338 Ibid., para 93 and especially paras 97 et seq.

339 Similarly, cf. Kühling 2014, p. 531. Also cf. Lynskey 2015a, pp. 528–531, who argues, however, that the right to be forgotten is part of the right to data protection.

340 ECtHR [GC], Von Hannover v. Germany (No. 2), App. Nos. 40660/08 and 60641/08, Judgment of 7 February 2012.

Yet, it is a missed chance that only in a judgment that considers a facet of the right to private life, the Court engages substantively with the secondary EU data protection legislation. Perhaps this as well as the AG's Opinion, which dissolved data protection in privacy, illustrates the lack of a clear concept within the Court of what exactly the right to data protection entails.

3.2.8.4 YS and Others

In the case of *YS and Others*, applicants for a residence permit requested access to the minutes of the administrative proceedings under their right of access to personal data according to Article 12(a) DPD (now Article 15 GDPR) and Article 8(2) CFR.[341] The national court's first question was whether the content of the minutes, which consisted of personal information of the applicant and a legal analysis regarding the residence permit, were personal data in the sense of Article 2(a) DPD.[342]

While the chamber found it to be evident that the personal information, such as name or date of birth, was personal data, it concluded that this was not the case for the legal analysis.[343] Although the latter contained personal data, it was not such data itself: the analysis reflected the application of the law by the competent authority, which was also achieved by consideration of the applicant's personal data.[344]

The notion of personal data, the chamber held in accordance with AG Sharpston's assessment, could not only be defined with regard to the wording of Article 2(a) DPD (now Article 4(1) GDPR), but the objective and general scheme of the directive itself also had to be considered.[345] The rights of the data subjects served to protect their right to respect for private life;[346] with the right of access, the directive aimed to enable the data subject to ensure that the data processed were correct and processed in a lawful manner and, if that was not the case, have the data rectified, erased or blocked.[347] However, the right of access to personal data did not aim to allow for a check of the accuracy of the legal analysis, as it did not grant a right of access to administrative documents for ensuring the transparency of public administration and thus the notion of personal data did not extend to the legal analysis as part of the minutes.[348]

---

[341] ECJ, Joined Cases C-141/12 and C-372/12 YS (C-141/12) v Minister voor Immigratie, Integratie en Asiel and Minister voor Immigratie, Integratie en Asiel (C-372/12) v M and S, Judgment of 17 July 2014, ECLI:EU:C:2014:2081, paras 1 et seq.

[342] Ibid., para 33.

[343] Ibid., paras 38 and 48.

[344] Ibid., paras 39 et seq.

[345] Ibid., para 42; ECJ, Joined Cases C-141/12 and C-372/12 YS (C-141/12) v Minister voor Immigratie, Integratie en Asiel and Minister voor Immigratie, Integratie en Asiel (C-372/12) v M and S, Opinion of AG Sharpston of 12 December 2013, ECLI:EU:C:2013:838, paras 44–61.

[346] This limitation of scope has rightly been criticized by Brouwer and Zuiderveen Borgesius 2015, p. 266.

[347] ECJ, Joined Cases C-141/12 and C-372/12 YS and Others, Judgment of 17 July 2014, para 44.

[348] Ibid., paras 45–48.

Concerning the scope of the right to access, the chamber held that Article 12(a) DPD implemented the right to access guaranteed by Article 8(2) CFR and made no further assessment of fundamental rights, as it relied on the provisions of the secondary law to find that the right to access covered only those parts of the minutes that contained personal data, but not the full file.[349] Thus, as there was no right to obtain a full copy of the document, it was sufficient to provide a full summary of all personal data in an intelligible form.[350]

While the Opinion of AG Sharpston reached a similar conclusion, she explored the fundamental right in question in more detail and, citing the Explanations, found that Article 8 CFR, which was drafted against the background of the DPD, set out an independent right to the protection of personal data.[351]

However, similar to AG Jääskinen in his Opinion for *Google Spain*,[352] she held that the right of access under Article 8(2) CFR did not go beyond what was prescribed by Article 12(a) DPD.[353] Curiously, she argued that the principle of proportionality should be applied to reduce the scope of the right to access under Article 8(2) CFR to "what is necessary in order to achieve its objectives [...]".[354] While, of course, this would be a reverse application of the principle against the individual, rather than its intended function as limitation of the State's power to interfere with the individual's rights, this argument stresses that the purpose of data protection, i.e. the DPD, limits the right of access in Article 12 DPD, as well as Article 8(2) CFR, to considerations of enabling the data subject to exercise the "follow-up" rights of rectification, erasure or blocking. In the case at hand, it could thus not be transformed into a right of access for reasons of transparency or freedom of information in order to challenge the administration's findings.[355]

While the Court here laid down limitations of the scope of the secondary law, this, as is clear from the judgment, also relates directly to the right to data protection under Article 8(2) CFR, which is to be interpreted in the light of the secondary law. However, this limitation is not surprising, as there are specific legal provisions on the right of access to documents according to Article 42 CFR and respective national

---

349 Ibid., paras 55, 58–60. Also cf. Tracol 2015, pp. 115 and 119.

350 ECJ, Joined Cases C-141/12 and C-372/12 YS and Others, Judgment of 17 July 2014, paras 58 et seq.

351 ECJ, Joined Cases C-141/12 and C-372/12 YS and Others, Opinion of AG Sharpston, paras 49–61 and 70. Critical of this assessment and perhaps foreshadowing the decision in *Nowak*: Brouwer and Zuiderveen Borgesius 2015, p. 268.

352 ECJ, Case C-131/12 Google Spain and Google, Opinion of AG Jääskinen, para 113.

353 ECJ, Joined Cases C-141/12 and C-372/12 YS and Others, Opinion of AG Sharpston, para 70; NB: the Grand Chamber's judgment in Google Spain had not been delivered yet at the time of AG Sharpston's Opinion.

354 Ibid., para 70.

355 Apparently, the right of access to a file and the duty to state reasons under Article 47 CFR had not been raised in the national proceedings, even though they would have been highly relevant for the cause of the individuals concerned. Following the suggestion of AG Sharpston, the chamber did not expand the scope of the proceedings to include this right and thus did not mention this issue in the judgment, cf. ibid., paras 34 and 92.

legislation as well as Article 47 CFR. However, it must be borne in mind that this has to be seen in the context of the right of access to personal data, which is specifically geared at implementing the principle of transparency and the fulfilment of the rights to rectification or erasure. This must not be taken to imply that the Court in any way restricts the right to data protection to these specific rights.

3.2.8.5 Ryneš

In the *Ryneš* case an individual, relying on the household exemption of Article 3(2) second indent DPD (now Article 2(2)(c) GDPR), installed a video surveillance system at his house, which also extended into public space.[356] Interpreting this exemption, the chamber held that the directive aimed for a high level of fundamental rights protection and that the right to private life under Article 7 CFR demanded that derogations and limitations with regard to the protection of personal data had to be applied only in so far as strictly necessary.[357]

Although it also cited the judgment in *Digital Rights Ireland*, the chamber did not mention Article 8 CFR.[358] Nevertheless, just like the Grand Chamber, it found that the provisions of the DPD were likely to infringe the right to privacy, as they governed the processing of personal data, and thus the household exemption had to be interpreted narrowly.[359] As the provision expressly stated that only purely personal or household activities were excluded from the scope of the DPD, the chamber followed AG Jääskinen's suggestions and concluded that video surveillance of a public space did not fall within its ambit.[360] However, it pointed out that Articles 7(f), 11(2) and 13(1)(d) and (g) DPD (now Articles 6(1)(f), 13(1)(d) and 14(2)(b) GDPR) allowed to take the legitimate interests, such as the protection of the health and life of the individual concerned in the case as well as his family and their property, into account.[361]

AG Jääskinen had found both rights of Articles 7 and 8 CFR to be relevant to the case at hand, as there was a conflict between the rights of the controller to carry out video surveillance of a public space to protect his private life and the right of all

[356] ECJ, Case C-212/13 František Ryneš v Úřad pro ochranu osobních údajů, Judgment of 11 December 2014, ECLI:EU:C:2014:2428, paras 13 et seq.

[357] Ibid., paras 27 et seq.

[358] Ibid., para 28; although the chamber cited ECJ, Joined Cases C-293/12 and C-594/12 Digital Rights Ireland and Seitlinger and Others, Judgment of 8 April 2014, para 52, there the Grand Chamber referred to the right to data protection and the right to privacy in the following paragraph; most likely, the chamber in the case at hand merely relied on ECJ, Case C-473/12 Institut professionnel des agents immobiliers (IPI) v Geoffrey Englebert and Others, Judgment of 7 November 2013, ECLI:EU:C:2013:715, para 39, where the chamber had only relied on the right to privacy.

[359] ECJ, Case C-212/13 Ryneš, Judgment of 11 December 2014, para 29.

[360] Ibid., paras 30–33; ECJ, Case C-212/13 František Ryneš v Úřad pro ochranu osobních údajů, Opinion of AG Jääskinen of 10 July 2014, ECLI:EU:C:2014:2072, paras 48–58.

[361] ECJ, Case C-212/13 Ryneš, Judgment of 11 December 2014, para 34; ECJ, Case C-212/13 Ryneš, Opinion of AG Jääskinen, paras 59–67.

persons in that public space to respect for their personal data.[362] Such a balance, he found, could be achieved under Article 7(f) DPD (now Article 6(1)(f) GDPR), but pointed out that this exercise was to be carried out by the referring court, which he pointed towards a relevant opinion of the Article 29 Working Party on the notion of legitimate interest.[363] Despite this generally deferential approach, the AG provided some further guidance and reiterated the Grand Chamber's ruling in *Google Spain* concerning the respective scopes of the rights, according to which Article 7 CFR protected the right to respect for private life, while Article 8 proclaimed the right to the protection of personal data and was implemented in the provisions and principles of the DPD.[364]

AG Jääskinen also adopted the categorization of the interference from *Digital Rights Ireland*, stating that the storage of data fell within the scope of both rights.[365] He went on to reiterate that the right to data protection according to Article 8 CFR was of particular significance for the right to the protection of private life under Article 7 CFR and later stated that the publication, recording or storing of data as well as the disclosure to public authorities were all independent interferences with the rights guaranteed by Article 7 CFR, however, without referring to the definition of Article 2(b) DPD or Article 8 CFR.[366]

While this case does not have a focus on the fundamental right to data protection, it illustrates how, within the Court, even after *Digital Rights Ireland* and *Google Spain*, where the Grand Chamber engaged with the right to data protection to a greater extend, the fundamental rights dimension of the secondary data protection legislation was still not fully realized. However, the AG here also engaged with the case more fully and provided the national court with more guidance, while not engaging with the conflict between the fundamental rights to the same degree as the Grand Chamber in *Google Spain*.

3.2.8.6 Willems and Others

The 2015 judgment in *Willems and Others*, just as *Schwarz*, concerned the use of biometric data in passports.[367] The national court asked whether Article 4(3) Passport Regulation read in the light of Articles 7 and 8 CFR and the principle of purpose

[362] ECJ, Case C-212/13 Ryneš, Opinion of AG Jääskinen, para 22.

[363] Ibid., para 23; Article 29 Working Party, Opinion 06/2014 on the notion of legitimate interests of the data controller under Article 7 of Directive 95/46/EC of 9 April 2014. WP 217.

[364] ECJ, Case C-212/13 Ryneš, Opinion of AG Jääskinen, para 28.

[365] Ibid., paras 29 and 34.

[366] Ibid., paras 39 and 59 et seq.; citing ECJ, Joined Cases C-293/12 and C-594/12 Digital Rights Ireland and Seitlinger and Others, Judgment of 8 April 2014, paras 53 and 34, respectively.

[367] ECJ, Joined Cases C-446 to C-449/12 W. P. Willems and Others v Burgemeester van Nuth and Others, Judgment of 16 April 2015, ECLI:EU:C:2015:238, paras 2 and 16 et seq.

limitation[368] had to be interpreted in a way that ensured that the data were not used for other purposes.[369]

With regard to the compatibility with the Charter, the chamber merely referred to the judgment in *Schwarz*.[370] Concerning the use of the data for other purposes under national law, it held that this was expressly not covered by the regulation and thus remained in the exclusive competence of the Member States.[371] Accordingly, the Passport Regulation was not applicable to other uses of the data and their further use thus not within the scope of EU law, which meant that under the *Åkerberg Fransson* test,[372] the Charter did not apply either.[373] Therefore, the national court had to examine the case under the national law as well as the rights of the ECHR.[374] Further, the chamber stated that the national court had requested only an interpretation of the Passport Regulation and held that there was no need to examine whether the DPD applied to the use of the data by the Member States.[375]

The Court had decided to proceed with a judgment without an AG's Opinion,[376] presumably due to the similarities with the *Schwarz* judgment. However, the chamber's contention that it did not have to apply the DPD to the case at hand is astonishing. While the national court only submitted questions about the Passport Regulation, it is for the Court to give an answer about the applicable EU law. In other instances, the Court is in no way shy to reformulate a national court's questions in the preliminary reference procedure,[377] as it has found itself to be under a duty to interpret all provisions of EU law necessary to enable the national court to decide the case at hand, even if the national court does not expressly indicate them.[378]

While the Passport Regulation includes no provisions on the further processing of data, this assertion of the chamber seems dubious, especially with regard to the Grand Chamber's requirement in *Digital Rights Ireland* concerning the inclusion of

---

[368] The national court also included Article 7(f) DPD (now Article 6(1)(f) GDPR) in its question, however, this provision on the processing in the legitimate interest of a controller does not apply to the processing of personal data by public authorities.

[369] ECJ, Joined Cases C-446 to C-449/12 Willems and Others, Judgment of 16 April 2015, para 29.

[370] Ibid., para 46.

[371] Ibid., para 47.

[372] ECJ, Case C-617/10 Åklagaren v Hans Åkerberg Fransson, Judgment of 26 February 2013, ECLI:EU:C:2013:105.

[373] ECJ, Joined Cases C-446 to C-449/12 Willems and Others, Judgment of 16 April 2015, paras 49 et seq.

[374] Ibid., para 51.

[375] Ibid., para 53.

[376] The Court may decide that an Opinion is not necessary according to Article 20 Statute of the CJEU when a case raises no new point of law.

[377] Cf. inter alia ECJ, Case C-334/95 Krüger GmbH & Co. KG v Hauptzollamt Hamburg-Jonas, Judgment of 17 July 1997, ECLI:EU:C:1997:378, para 23; ECJ, Case C-15/15 New Valmar BVBA v Global Pharmacies Partner Health Srl, Judgment of 21 June 2016, ECLI:EU:C:2016:464, para 28.

[378] Cf. inter alia ECJ, Case C-280/91 Finanzamt Kassel-Goethestrasse v Viessmann KG, Judgment of 18 March 1993, ECLI:EU:C:1993:103, para 17; ECJ, Case C-15/15 New Valmar, Judgment of 21 June 2016, para 28.

technical and organisational measures in EU legislation prescribing the storage of such data.

Furthermore, the subsequent use of the data would fall under the DPD, unless it was covered by one of the exception clauses. However, from the facts of the case, it does not seem that this would have been the case.[379] Therefore, the subsequent processing of national public authorities would have to be in accordance with the DPD and the chamber, following the Court's case law, would have had to interpret those provisions in the light of Articles 7 and 8 CFR, as they were fully applicable.

3.2.8.7 Coty

In another 2015 chamber judgment concerning proceedings where a holder of intellectual property rights requested that a bank reveal the identity of an account holder, who had infringed these rights, the Court held that the rights to intellectual property, an effective remedy and data protection had to be reconciled.[380] The Court, when linking the provision of the Copyright Directive 2004/48 to the right to data protection, held that this fundamental right was "guaranteed by Article 8 of the Charter and by Directive 95/46"[381] and thus directly linked the primary and secondary EU data protection legislation.[382] It found that, if the bank could refuse to reveal the identity of the account holder without any qualification, this violated the obligation of Member States to ensure that such information could be obtained through court-ordered enquiry measures.[383] Like the AG,[384] the Court adopted a deferential approach and left this question to be resolved by the national court, but found that the national provision read in isolation seemed to allow for such unlimited and unqualified refusal and thus did not strike a fair balance between the competing rights.[385]

The judgment in *Coty* fits into the line of case law started in *Promusicae* and continued in the internet-monitoring cases.[386] The Court here also does not mention Article 7 CFR and thus, at least superficially, underlines the independent scope of Article 8 CFR. It addresses the balancing of fundamental rights in more detail, even though it also leaves the national court to carry out the final assessment with regard to the national provision at issue. Perhaps, this indicates a learning curve of the Court,

---

[379] The Court may not have dwelled on this in detail, due to the fact that the centralisation of thc relevant databases was to be carried out in the future.

[380] ECJ, Case C-580/13 Coty Germany v Stadtsparkasse Magdeburg, Judgment of 16 July 2015, ECLI:EU:C:2015:485, paras 9–12 and 33 et seq.

[381] Ibid., para 30.

[382] Cf. also van der Sloot 2017, p. 12.

[383] ECJ, Case C-580/13 Coty Germany, Judgment of 16 July 2015, para 36.

[384] ECJ, Case C-580/13 Coty Germany v Stadtsparkasse Magdeburg, Opinion of AG Cruz Villalón of 16 April 2015, ECLI:EU:C:2015:485, paras 30–32, 39 and 44.

[385] ECJ, Case C-580/13 Coty Germany, Judgment of 16 July 2015, paras 38–43.

[386] Cf. above Sects. 3.2.4 and 3.2.7.

as the measure in question, i.e. the disclosure of the name of an account holder, was a much less serious interference than the internet-monitoring filters desired by copyright holders in the previous cases. Therefore, it is also not surprising that the Court here leaned in favour of the rights to an effective remedy and intellectual property, as it would be easy to foresee a provision, which balances the interests at stake more diligently.

3.2.8.8 Schrems

In its first substantive judgment on Articles 7 and 8 CFR since *Digital Rights Ireland*, the Grand Chamber in *Schrems* was concerned with a challenge to the validity of the Commission's Safe Harbour Decision[387] in the context of the transfer of Facebook users' personal data to the US in the wake of Edward Snowden's revelations on mass-surveillance.[388] As in *Digital Rights Ireland*, Judge von Danwitz was rapporteur in this case. However, the structure of the judgment is noticeably less clear than that of its predecessor. This discrepancy could simply be attributed to the fact that the assessment of fundamental rights in this judgment was carried out incidentally within the assessment of the Safe Harbour Decision's validity. However, especially considering the assessment of the interference, it could be seen as a sign that there were individual reservations after *Digital Rights Ireland* within the Grand Chamber.

In the assessment of the interference, the difference to *Digital Rights Ireland* is striking: the Grand Chamber here only stated that the unspecified scope of the derogation clause in the Safe Harbour Decision, which awarded primacy to US interests of national and public security as well as law enforcement requirements, led to an interference "with the fundamental rights of [data subjects]."[389] Subsequently, the Court only referred to an interference with Article 7 CFR, even though it named both Article 7 and Article 8 CFR when laying out the requirements for the proportionality of such measures in reference to *Digital Rights Ireland*.[390]

Meanwhile, AG Bot, in a scrupulous and separate examination of Articles 7 and 8 CFR as interpreted in *Digital Rights Ireland*, had found that the mere access, i.e. processing, of US intelligence services to the data constituted its own interference with Article 8 CFR.[391]

Turning to the justification stage, the Grand Chamber reiterated its finding that Articles 7 and 8 CFR required clear and precise provisions on the scope of application

[387] Commission Decision 2000/520/EC of 26 July 2000 pursuant to Directive 95/46/EC of the European Parliament and of the Council on the adequacy of the protection provided by the safe harbour privacy principles and related frequently asked questions issued by the US Department of Commerce, OJ L 215 of 25 August 2000, pp. 7–47.

[388] ECJ, Case C-362/14 Maximillian Schrems v Data Protection Commissioner, Judgment of 6 October 2015, ECLI:EU:C:2015:650, paras 1 and 27 et seq.

[389] Ibid., paras 86 et seq.

[390] Ibid., paras 87 and 91.

[391] ECJ, Case C-362/14 Maximillian Schrems v Data Protection Commissioner, Opinion of AG Bot of 23 September 2015, ECLI:EU:C:2015:627, para 170.

of the measures as well as minimum safeguards against abuse and unlawful access to personal data.[392] It further stressed that it exercised a strict review of proportionality whenever provisions allowed for the indiscriminate processing of personal data.[393]

Just as AG Bot had suggested in his Opinion, it concluded with regard to the provisions of the Safe Harbour Decision that these allowed public authorities access to personal data contained in electronic communications on a generalised basis, including their contents, and therefore infringed the essence of Article 7 CFR.[394]

The Grand Chamber did not mention the essence of Article 8 CFR, while AG Bot voiced doubts as to the compatibility with the essences of both Article 7 and 8 CFR,[395] although he did not engage substantively with the concept of essence.[396] With regard to the essence of Article 8 CFR, the AG found the exception allowing to suspend the adherence to the Safe Harbour Principles for requirements of national security, the public interest or law enforcement, to compromise the essence of the right to data protection.[397] Perhaps, the Court was reluctant to engage in an assessment of US law to this extent.[398]

Overall, the Court's judgment demonstrates a certain restraint, which barred it from fully engaging with the facts of the case. Rather, the Court focused on the role of the Commission and expressly stated that the assertions in the Safe Harbour Decision as to the level of protection of fundamental rights were insufficient.[399]

While many reactions to the judgment placed an emphasis on the practical consequences of the invalidation of the Safe Harbour Decision with regard to data transfers to the USA,[400] it must be pointed out that these are even more far-reaching, as the general terms of the judgment also apply to other third countries as well as the other instruments for the transfer of data to third countries, i.e. the binding corporate rules or standard contractual clauses.[401] On these the Court later ruled in the Schrems II judgment and reaffirmed the lines set out in this judgment.[402]

However, this must not distract from the fact that the fundamental rights assessment in this judgment is lacking, especially when compared to *Digital Rights Ireland*.

---

[392] ECJ, Case C-362/14 Schrems, Judgment of 6 October 2015, para 91.

[393] Ibid., paras 92 et seq.

[394] Ibid., para 94; ECJ, Case C-362/14 Schrems, Opinion of AG Bot, para 177; also cf. Brkan 2019b, pp. 874–877, who severely criticises this reasoning and argues that the Court should have merely found this to constitute a grave interference.

[395] ECJ, Case C-362/14 Schrems, Opinion of AG Bot, para 177.

[396] Tridimas and Gentile 2019, p. 810.

[397] ECJ, Case C-362/14 Schrems, Opinion of AG Bot, para 177.

[398] Cf. also Bock and Engeler 2016, p. 596.

[399] ECJ, Case C-362/14 Schrems, Judgment of 6 October 2015, paras 79–91; Azoulai and van der Sluis 2016, p. 1359 note that the apparent mistrust of the Court towards the Commission might be well placed, as the latter treated the negotiations for the Safe Harbour Decision as trade talks.

[400] Tracol 2016; Eichenhofer 2016, pp. 86–88; Kühling and Heberlein 2016; for a particularly crass example, which completely ignores the fundamental rights dimension of the mass-surveillance at issue, cf. Cohen 2015.

[401] For an in-depth analysis cf. Kuner 2017b, pp. 904–910.

[402] Cf. below Sect. 3.2.8.15.

The Court did not apply the same standard set out in the previous case. This reluctance might be due to the fact that the revelations concerning the activities of US intelligence agencies were—obviously—never officially confirmed.[403] While it is advisable for the Court not to engage in speculation, a lingering feeling that the final outcome of the case overshadowed the assessment of the fundamental rights remains.

3.2.8.9 Tele2 Sverige

The 2016 judgment in the *Tele2 Sverige* case is essentially a follow-up to *Digital Rights Ireland*.[404] Sweden and the UK kept their national implementation measures for the DRD in place, arguing that they no longer fell within the scope of EU law.[405] However, it was contentious whether Article 15(1) ePD—which stipulates that Member States may impose retention measures for a limited amount of time for reasons of ordre public, if they are proportionate and respect EU fundamental rights—applied to such measures.

The Court, as well as AG Saugmandsgaard Øe, held that general data retention obligations were indeed within the scope of Article 15(1) ePD.[406] Much like the AG,[407] the Grand Chamber found that the inclusion of Article 15(1) ePD with its requirement for data retention measures, implied that such measures would not be excluded from the ePD's scope under Article 1(3) ePD, as the former provision would otherwise have no scope of application.[408] Article 15(1) read together with Article 3 ePD thus extended to the provisions requiring service providers to retain communications data as well as the provisions on the access of national authorities to these retained data.[409] While it can be debated whether this connection is convincing, there is certainly no substantive reason, why the protection of the EU right to data protection would not be required in instances of criminal investigations. With regard to the invasive nature of surveillance measures, perhaps there is an even greater need for such protection. As is apparent from the second generation of EU data protection legislation, the legislator agreed and thus adopted the LED, which now brings such measures within the scope of EU law.

---

[403] Cf. also Azoulai and van der Sluis 2016, p. 1366.

[404] Cf. already above Sect. 3.2.8.2.

[405] ECJ, Joined Cases C-203/15 and C-698/15 Tele2 Sverige v Post- och telestyrelsen (C-203/15) and Secretary of State for the Home Department v Tom Watson, Peter Brice and Geoffrey Lewis (C-698/15), Judgment of 21 December 2016, ECLI:EU:C:2016:970, paras 62–65.

[406] Ibid., para 80; ECJ, Joined Cases C-203/15 and C-698/15 Tele2 Sverige v Post- och telestyrelsen (C-203/15) and Secretary of State for the Home Department v Tom Watson, Peter Brice and Geoffrey Lewis (C-698/15), Opinion of AG Saugmandsgaard Øe of 19 July 2016, ECLI:EU:C:2016:572, paras 88–97.

[407] ECJ, Joined Cases C-203/15 and C-698/15 Tele2 Sverige, Opinion of AG Saugmandsgaard Øe, paras 121–125.

[408] ECJ, Joined Cases C-203/15 and C-698/15 Tele 2 Sverige, Judgment of 21 December 2016, paras 69–73.

[409] Ibid., paras 68 and 82–87.

The Court further found that, according to Article 1(1) ePD, the directive served to protect fundamental rights, particularly the right to privacy and confidentiality[410] and its provisions were geared at this protection.[411] While Article 15(1) ePD provided for exceptions from that protection, this provision had to be interpreted narrowly and could not allow that exception to become the rule,[412] as the Court had first held in *Satamedia*. Hence, the provision had to be interpreted in light of the rights of Articles 7 and 8 as well as 11 CFR.[413] Yet, even though Article 15(1) ePD itself provided that the measures had to be strictly proportionate, the national provisions were of a general and indiscriminate nature, relating to all means of electronic communications, without exceptions.[414] For a change, the AG, with regard to the scope of the measure, had also called for a strict standard of review.[415]

The Grand Chamber, just like AG Saugmandsgaard Øe, swiftly established that there were serious interferences with the rights of Articles 7 and 8 CFR, respectively, as had been established in the *Digital Rights Ireland* judgment.[416] While it thus did not provide any additional insights, in an obiter dictum, relating to a question of the national court on the relationship between Articles 7 and 8 CFR and Article 8 ECHR, the Court found that EU law had to be interpreted solely in the light of the Charter and expressly stated that Article 8 CFR, which was independent from Article 7 CFR, had no equivalent provision in the ECHR.[417]

On the justification stage, the Grand Chamber, in line with the AG's Opinion,[418] did not change its earlier standard concerning the essence.[419] However, in a previous paragraph, the Grand Chamber, explicitly picking up a point made by AG Saugmandsgaard Øe, had found that the profiles derived from this data were "no less

[410] Which demonstrates that the ePD is still part of the first generation of EU data protection legislation, as in 2002, when the directive was adopted, the Charter had not yet become legally binding and thus, the right to data protection was not yet included.

[411] ECJ, Joined Cases C-203/15 and C-698/15 Tele 2 Sverige, Judgment of 21 December 2016, paras 74–80.

[412] Ibid., para 89; also already Boehm and Cole 2014, pp. 92 et seq.

[413] ECJ, Joined Cases C-203/15 and C-698/15 Tele 2 Sverige, Judgment of 21 December 2016, paras 91 et seq.

[414] Ibid., paras 95–97.

[415] ECJ, Joined Cases C-203/15 and C-698/15 Tele2 Sverige, Opinion of AG Saugmandsgaard Øe, para 209.

[416] ECJ, Joined Cases C-203/15 and C-698/15 Tele 2 Sverige, Judgment of 21 December 2016, para 100; ECJ, Joined Cases C-203/15 and C-698/15 Tele2 Sverige, Opinion of AG Saugmandsgaard Øe, para 128.

[417] ECJ, Joined Cases C-203/15 and C-698/15 Tele 2 Sverige, Judgment of 21 December 2016, paras 126–129. Meanwhile, AG Saugmandsgaard Øe had referred extensively to the ECtHR's case law, cf. ECJ, Joined Cases C-203/15 and C-698/15 Tele2 Sverige, Opinion of AG Saugmandsgaard Øe, paras 136–143.

[418] ECJ, Joined Cases C-203/15 and C-698/15 Tele2 Sverige, Opinion of AG Saugmandsgaard Øe, paras 156 et seq.

[419] ECJ, Joined Cases C-203/15 and C-698/15 Tele 2 Sverige, Judgment of 21 December 2016, para 101.

sensitive, having regard to the right to privacy, than the actual content of communications."[420] Yet, it appears the Court was too reluctant to draw the consequences of that statement with regard to the essence of Article 7 CFR.[421]

With regard to the essence of Article 8 CFR, the AG had stated that the Court, in its previous judgment on data retention, had held that the DRD did not violate the essence of the right to the protection of personal data, as "the principles of data protection and data security [...] had to be observed".[422] Though only a slight deviation, the Court in *Digital Rights Ireland* was satisfied that the DRD included "certain" principles of data protection and data security, namely technical and organisational measures.[423] The AG thus perhaps aimed to clarify that the essence of Article 8 CFR included all principles of data protection law.[424] However, this was not picked up by the Court.

Further, the Grand Chamber, like the AG,[425] found that only the objective of fighting serious crime could be a legitimate aim to pursue through such a bulk data retention measure.[426] The AG had rebuked the UK government's argument, which relied on *Promusicae* to claim that any of the broad objectives included in Article 15(1) ePD were capable of justifying a blanket retention of communications data.[427] He pointed out that, due to the serious interference of such a measure with fundamental rights, this could not be the case.[428] In this regard, it must be emphasised that the blanket data retention, which is carried out without any concrete reason, stands in stark opposition to the principle of purpose limitation.[429] According to the AG, the fight against serious crime could provide the only justification for general data retention in that provision with regard to the principle of proportionality.[430] This argument would become relevant in the continuation of this case law in *La Quadrature du Net* and *Privacy International*, which I will discuss below.[431]

---

[420] Ibid., para 99.

[421] Cf. Brkan 2019b, pp. 873 et seq.; Tridimas and Gentile 2019, p. 810.

[422] ECJ, Joined Cases C-203/15 and C-698/15 Tele2 Sverige, Opinion of AG Saugmandsgaard Øe, para 158.

[423] ECJ, Joined Cases C-293/12 and C-594/12 Digital Rights Ireland and Seitlinger and Others, Judgment of 8 April 2014, para 40.

[424] Cf. Chap. 2, Sect. 2.3.2 and Chap. 5, Sect. 5.3.3.

[425] ECJ, Joined Cases C-203/15 and C-698/15 Tele2 Sverige, Opinion of AG Saugmandsgaard Øe, paras 172 et seq.

[426] ECJ, Joined Cases C-203/15 and C-698/15 Tele 2 Sverige, Judgment of 21 December 2016, para 102.

[427] ECJ, Joined Cases C-203/15 and C-698/15 Tele2 Sverige, Opinion of AG Saugmandsgaard Øe, paras 162–169.

[428] Ibid., paras 170 et seq.

[429] Kunnert 2014a, p. 107. Arguing for the need of general retention by evoking general fears of terrorist threats: Cameron 2017, esp. pp. 1481–1483.

[430] ECJ, Joined Cases C-203/15 and C-698/15 Tele2 Sverige, Opinion of AG Saugmandsgaard Øe, paras 172 et seq.

[431] Cf. below Sect. 3.2.8.16.

The Grand Chamber then reiterated its finding of *Digital Rights Ireland* as to the nature of the data retention and the lack of safeguards and held that the national provisions were not proportionate.[432] However, in what can now be read as a shift towards the implementation of such bulk data retention measures, rather than an attempt to block it, the Court stated that in order to adopt data retention as a preventive measure, national law would have to lay down transparent rules on the scope and application of such a measure, impose minimum safeguards against misuse, establish—with objective criteria—the connection between the retained data and the pursued objective and identify a part of the public whose data were likely to be at least indirectly linked to serious criminal offences, for instance, by setting a geographical limitation of the retention.[433]

The AG had not prescribed to the submission of some Member States that a lower standard for one safeguard could be compensated by strengthening another,[434] arguing that a lack in one of the requirements would entail serious consequences for the weight of the interference with fundamental rights and pointing out that the safeguards were rather to be seen as minimum requirements.[435] He found this to be underscored by the ECtHR's judgment in *Szabó and Vissy*, which had adopted the standard in express reference to the ECJ's judgment.[436] The Grand Chamber also reaffirmed the cumulative criteria it had laid out in *Digital Rights Ireland*, and found that any further access to the data would have to be subject to prior review and required the notification of data subjects as soon as possible.[437]

While the AG had apparently convinced the Grand Chamber with many of his arguments, he ultimately left the assessment of the criteria he provided for the national courts to determine.[438] The Grand Chamber, here, took a less deferential approach and instead found that Article 15(1) ePD, read in the light of the Charter, precluded blanket data retention.[439] It cannot yet be said whether this marks a departure from the Court's deferential approach, which it took in certain cases since *Lindqvist*.

---

[432] ECJ, Joined Cases C-203/15 and C-698/15 Tele 2 Sverige, Judgment of 21 December 2016, paras 103–107.

[433] Ibid., paras 108–111; this suspicion seems confirmed by von Danwitz 2015, p. 583.

[434] Unlike the ECtHR under its "global assessment", cf. ECtHR [GC], Big Brother Watch and Others, App. Nos. 58170/13, 62322/14 and 24960/15, Judgment of 25 May 2021, paras 360 and 370.

[435] ECJ, Joined Cases C-203/15 and C-698/15 Tele2 Sverige, Opinion of AG Saugmandsgaard Øe, paras 216–227.

[436] Ibid., para 226; ECtHR, Szabó and Vissy v. Hungary, App. No. 37138/14, Judgment of 12 January 2016, para 68.

[437] ECJ, Joined Cases C-203/15 and C-698/15 Tele 2 Sverige, Judgment of 21 December 2016, paras 115–123; also cf. ECJ, Joined Cases C-203/15 and C-698/15 Tele2 Sverige, Opinion of AG Saugmandsgaard Øe, paras 232–243. Also cf. Møller Pedersen et al. 2018, pp. 167–170.

[438] ECJ, Joined Cases C-203/15 and C-698/15 Tele2 Sverige, Opinion of AG Saugmandsgaard Øe, paras 154, 207–215, 245 and 262 et seq.

[439] ECJ, Joined Cases C-203/15 and C-698/15 Tele 2 Sverige, Judgment of 21 December 2016, paras 112 and 125.

However, this is the first time the Court invalidated national law in all but name in a case concerning the right to data protection.

While the judgment, in substance, did not add much to the interpretation of Article 8 CFR, it confirmed the notion of an independent right to data protection and further elaborated on the Court's approach concerning procedural and substantive safeguards for the processing of data. However, it is unfortunate that the Court did not link these safeguards to the principles of the secondary EU data protection law.

3.2.8.10 Opinion 1/15

The Grand Chamber with Judge von Danwitz as rapporteur set out its Opinion on the PNR agreement with Canada, delivered in 2017, by stating that while both Article 16(1) TFEU and Article 8 CFR set out the right to the protection of personal data, only Article 8(2) CFR contained conditions for the processing of data.[440] The transfer of PNR data and the framework to facilitate this were interferences with Article 7 as well as Article 8 CFR under the established standards.[441]

AG Mengozzi, in his Opinion, established an interference with Article 7 CFR and "the 'closely connected' but nonetheless distinct right to protection of personal data".[442] However, he did not elaborate on the distinct nature beyond the previously settled case law concerning the interference. Even though the agreement recognised these interferences and included provisions aimed at reconciling public security and fundamental rights, he argued that the scope of this bulk data retention measure still systematically affected several tens of millions of persons a year, all of whom were turned into potential suspects.[443]

The Grand Chamber concurred that the transfer and the framework concerned all air passengers' travel details, including their financial situation or state of health, which would be used for systematic automated checks and could lead to additional security checks or other binding decisions concerning these individuals without due regard to whether the person concerned posed an actual risk to public security.[444] These aspects, which it did not contextualize explicitly, concerned the gravity of the interference and were revisited in the assessment of the necessity of the interference.[445]

On the justification stage, the Court stressed that the right to data protection required a high level of protection, which had to be upheld on an essentially equivalent

[440] ECJ, Avis 1/15, Opinion of 26 July 2017, ECLI:EU:C:2017:592, para 120.

[441] Ibid., paras 122–126. However, Kuner holds that the Court based its analysis on Article 8 CFR, while also considering Article 7 CFR, without differentiating between them, cf. Kuner 2018, p. 873.

[442] ECJ, Avis 1/15, Opinion of AG Mengozzi of 8 September 2016, ECLI:EU:C:2016:656, paras 170 et seq.

[443] Ibid., paras 174–176.

[444] ECJ, Avis 1/15, Opinion of 26 July 2017, paras 127–132.

[445] Ibid., paras 154–217.

level when data were transferred outside the EU.[446] Thus, a strict standard of necessity applied and the relevant legal basis had to define the scope and application of the measure in clear and precise terms, including minimum safeguards to protect against risks of misuse.[447] However, in its actual assessment, the Grand Chamber seems to have applied a more lenient approach to some of the issues posed by the PNR framework.[448]

The Court held that the fight against terrorism and serious transnational crime was a legitimate aim and that the measure did not violate the essences of either Article 7 or 8 CFR, as it was limited to flight passengers between the EU and Canada and included rules on purpose limitation as well as security, confidentiality and integrity.[449] According to the Court, the requirements for safeguards, however, were even greater when sensitive data, such as racial or ethnic origin, political opinions or data concerning health or sex life, as foreseen by Article 2(e) of the agreement, were at stake and the processing was automated, which entailed a significant margin of error and thus required review by an individual before any measures were taken.[450] With regard to the former, AG Mengozzi explicitly stated that it was likely to stigmatise a large number of individuals and was thus not proportionate.[451]

Yet, the Grand Chamber held, the provisions of the agreement, inter alia, did not define, which data exactly were to be transferred, included a free text field where any supplementary information could be entered and allowed the transfer of data for purposes of oversight and accountability of Canadian authorities as well as in order to comply with court-ordered measures and were, in these regards, not sufficiently clear and precise.[452] Concerning the provisions on the legal definitions of terrorism, serious transnational crime and the Canadian authorities, which receive the transferred data, the Court generally followed the AG's line of reasoning and found that they adhered to the standard of strict necessity.[453] Furthermore, it even considered the fact that the agreement covered all air passengers to meet the standard of strict necessity,[454] as the exclusion of specific categories of persons or specific areas of origin could prevent the identification of any person, who could present a risk to public security, and,

[446] Ibid., para 134.

[447] Ibid., paras 139–141.

[448] Vogiatzoglou 2019, at 3.1; Kuner 2017a.

[449] ECJ, Avis 1/15, Opinion of 26 July 2017, paras 148–150, 179 and 181.

[450] Ibid., paras 141 and 164–174.

[451] ECJ, Avis 1/15, Opinion of AG Mengozzi, paras 221–223 and 252–261.

[452] ECJ, Avis 1/15, Opinion of 26 July 2017, paras 156–163; also cf. ECJ, Avis 1/15, Opinion of AG Mengozzi, paras 211–220 and 237.

[453] ECJ, Avis 1/15, Opinion of 26 July 2017, paras 175–180 and 182–185; also cf. ECJ, Avis 1/15, Opinion of AG Mengozzi, paras 226–236 and 274 et seq., who argued that Canada should provide an exhaustive list of offences it considered as serious transnational crime and clearly specify, which government officials would have access to the data.

[454] Also observed by Vogiatzoglou 2019, at 2.3.

because the PNR data verification process was part of the national border controls, regulated in Article 13 Chicago Convention.[455]

With regard to the use of the data by Canadian authorities, the Grand Chamber held that the agreement was proportionate with regard to the carrying out of checks on individuals, who wanted to enter.[456] Once they had been allowed to do so, the use of their data—generally subject to prior review—had to be based on specifically laid down substantive and procedural conditions regulating their use, for instance to protect the data against risks of abuse, and justifying the processing by linking it to the purpose of effectively contributing to the combat of terrorism and serious transnational crime.[457]

Once individuals had left the country, their data could generally no longer be processed, unless objective evidence in specific cases and also subject to prior review justified the further storage of the data by identifying a certain passenger as a risk.[458] Even though the Grand Chamber found the fact that the PNR data were stored for a maximum of five years, was a particularly long period earlier in the judgment,[459] it, unlike the AG,[460] ultimately found this period not to exceed the standard of strict necessity.[461]

Concerning the disclosure of PNR data to other government authorities within or outside Canada, the Grand Chamber found this proportionate, as long as it was safeguarded that the receiver of the data ensured a level of protection essentially equivalent to that of the EU, which had to be ensured by an agreement between the EU and the receiving country or a Commission decision under Article 25(6) DPD (now Article 45 GDPR), while it held that the provisions on the disclosure to individuals were too vague and not linked to the purposes of the agreement.[462]

In addition to the considerations on proportionality, the lack of a right to individual notification when the Canadian authorities used an individual's data for more than security and border control checks, once the investigations were no longer liable to be jeopardised,[463] ultimately led the Court to find that the PNR agreement was incompatible with Articles 7, 8, 21 and 52(1) CFR. The AG had adopted a different framing and concluded that the PNR agreement generally complied with Article 16 TFEU as well as Articles 7, 8 and 52(1) CFR, if several conditions concerning more

---

[455] Convention on International Civil Aviation (Chicago Convention), 15 UNTS pp. 295–375. ECJ, Avis 1/15, Opinion of 26 July 2017, paras 186–189. In this regard it also followed the AG, cf. ECJ, Avis 1/15, Opinion of AG Mengozzi, paras 238–245.

[456] ECJ, Avis 1/15, Opinion of 26 July 2017, paras 190–199.

[457] Ibid., paras 199–203; also cf. ECJ, Avis 1/15, Opinion of AG Mengozzi, para 224.

[458] ECJ, Avis 1/15, Opinion of 26 July 2017, paras 204–210. Also cf. Bossong 2017.

[459] ECJ, Avis 1/15, Opinion of 26 July 2017, para 132.

[460] ECJ, Avis 1/15, Opinion of AG Mengozzi, paras 278–290.

[461] ECJ, Avis 1/15, Opinion of 26 July 2017, para 209.

[462] Ibid., paras 212–217. AG Mengozzi, on the other hand, did not find the provisions on disclosure to authorities sufficiently clear and precise, but also found the disclosure to individuals disproportionate, cf. ECJ, Avis 1/15, Opinion of AG Mengozzi, paras 246–251 and 291–305.

[463] ECJ, Avis 1/15, Opinion of 26 July 2017, paras 218–227.

precise definitions and procedural safeguards were fulfilled, while also finding several especially far-reaching provisions to be incompatible with the Charter provisions.[464]

Despite the different frames for the results that the Grand Chamber and the AG reached, the former seems reluctant to draw consequences from the aspects of mass-surveillance it points out throughout the judgment, especially concerning the fact that all air passengers are affected and the sensitive nature of the data processed.[465] The Court admonishes these practices in the same register as it had in its previous decisions in *Digital Rights Ireland* and *Tele2 Sverige*, but seems appeased that they are limited to affect only passengers flying between the EU and the Canada[466] and gives the legislator in-depth feedback on how to legislate in this matter.[467]

However, this constructive role of the Court comes at a price: it does not pick up the AG's explicit argument of stigmatization of large parts of society, especially when additional checks are performed based exclusively on a person's religious beliefs. Instead, it merely finds that the safeguards must then be increased, which does, however, not question this problematic practice itself and may serve to legitimise it. Instead, the Court should have asked whether such a processing operation in itself can be legitimate.[468]

3.2.8.11 Puškár

In 2017, the Court delivered a chamber judgment in *Puškár*, a case concerning the publication of the names, national identity and tax identification numbers of individuals on a list of persons suspected of acting as fronts for companies.[469] The Court and AG Kokott very briefly considered issues of the right to the protection of private life and the right to data protection. While the Court stated that the requirements of the rights of Articles 7 and 8 CFR were deemed to be fulfilled when the processing of personal data was in conformity with the DPD,[470] AG Kokott elaborated this by showcasing that the assessment under the DPD was essentially the same as under Articles 7 and 8 CFR.[471] In this assessment, the AG did not explicitly examine the rights in detail, but made clear that both applied to the case at hand.[472] Hence, the

[464] ECJ, Avis 1/15, Opinion of AG Mengozzi, para 328.

[465] Kuner 2017a.

[466] Brkan 2019b, pp. 877 et seq., who agrees with the Court that the interference should not infringe the essence of Article 7 CFR. However, Kuner argues that the Court lessened its review from *Tele2 Sverige*, cf. Kuner 2018, pp. 871 et seq.; while Vedaschi 2018, p. 134 argues the opposite.

[467] Hijmans 2017.

[468] Also hinted at by Woods 2017; with regard to the AG's Opinion, cf. Zanfir-Fortuna 2016.

[469] ECJ, Case C-73/16 Peter Puškár v Finančné riadite'stvo Slovenskej republiky and Kriminálny úrad finančnej správy, Judgment of 27 September 2017, ECLI:EU:C:2017:725, para 2.

[470] Ibid., para 102.

[471] Ibid., paras 102–110 and 114–116.

[472] Ibid., paras 114 et seq.

case demonstrates that the Court considers the rights to be closely connected and now interprets them with more regard for the rules of the secondary law.

3.2.8.12 Nowak

In another chamber judgment from the same year, concerning the question whether an exam candidate's answers to written exams constituted personal data, the Court stated that the DPD was "very wide" in scope, which extended to the definition of personal data under Article 2(a) DPD (now Article 4(1) GDPR), as it referred explicitly to "any information".[473] This was due to the legislator's intent to provide comprehensive protection, not limited to sensitive or private information, but all objective and subjective information.[474]

Unlike in the case of *YS and Others*,[475] it must be noted that the judgment here concerns an exam, i.e. a document written by data subjects themselves, rather than a legal analysis based on the data of the data subject, but carried out by a public authority.

When assessing the data subject rights, the Court, citing AG Kokott's assessment in verbatim,[476] found that a candidate might have a legitimate interest in being able to object to the processing of the answers to an exam based on the protection of his private life.[477] However, by basing this interest on Article 7 CFR rather than Article 8 CFR, the chamber demonstrated a limited engagement with the right to data protection. Unfortunately, AG Kokott also referred to Article 8 CFR only in the context of the data subject's right to be heard by a national supervisory authority.[478] After the previous judgment in *Puškár*, which was more considerate of the secondary EU data protection legislation, this judgment, again, demonstrates a lack of engagement with regard to the interplay between the primary and secondary law, which may, however, at least partly, have been caused by the reference of Article 1(1) DPD to the right to privacy.

3.2.8.13 Ministerio Fiscal

In 2018, the Grand Chamber delivered a judgment in the *Ministerio Fiscal* case, which, like *Tele2 Sverige*, concerned the interpretation of Article 15(1) ePD with

[473] ECJ, Case C-434/16 Peter Nowak v Data Protection Commissioner, Judgment of 20 December 2017, ECLI:EU:C:2017:994, paras 33 et seq.

[474] Ibid., para 34.

[475] Cf. above Sect. 3.2.8.4.

[476] ECJ, Case C-434/16 Peter Nowak v Data Protection Commissioner, Opinion of AG Kokott of 20 July 2017, ECLI:EU:C:2017:582, para 26.

[477] ECJ, Case C-434/16 Nowak, Judgment of 20 December 2017, para 50.

[478] ECJ, Case C-434/16 Nowak, Opinion of AG Kokott, para 33.

regard to Articles 7 and 8 CFR.[479] In this case, the police requested that the competent authority order providers to hand over the phone numbers activated on a stolen mobile phone and the identity of the respective users, which the authority refused.[480]

The national court argued that such measures had to be limited to serious offences and that the relevant national law was disproportionate to the interference with fundamental rights and requested guidance on the interpretation of the notion of serious offences.[481] As in *Tele2 Sverige*, several Member States argued that the processing of data by the police was outside the scope of the ePD and DPD, but AG Saugmansgaard Øe and the Court affirmed the previous ruling and stated that the relevant national law permitted the police to require communications providers to grant them access to personal data, which was a form of processing.[482]

The Court, relying on the AGs Opinion,[483] swiftly established that there was an interference with the right to respect for private life—albeit not a serious one—as well as the right to data protection, as the access of the police constituted the processing of personal data.[484]

With regard to the legitimate objectives, which could justify such interferences, the Grand Chamber found that the list provided in Article 15(1) clause 1 ePD provided an exhaustive enumeration, which did, however, only refer generally to criminal offences rather than serious crime.[485] While the Court had held in *Tele2 Sverige* that the access to an amount of personal data, which allowed such precise conclusions about the lives of persons as the bulk data retention in that case, could only be justified by the combat of serious crime, the requirements under the principle of proportionality were lower in cases of a less serious interference.[486] Hence, the Grand Chamber held that for such less serious interferences, the objective of fighting criminal offences in general might suffice.[487]

It then examined the measure in question, similarly to the assessment of the AG,[488] in detail and found that since it did not concern the contents of communications and was limited to subscriber identification module (SIM) cards activated with one specific mobile phone for a limited period of time, the measure did not allow to build

---

[479] ECJ, Case C-207/16 Ministerio Fiscal, Judgment of 2 October 2018, ECLI:EU:C:2018:788, para 1.

[480] Ibid., paras 20 et seq.

[481] Ibid., paras 23–26; ECJ, Case C-207/16 Ministerio Fiscal, Opinion of AG Saugmandsgaard Øe of 3 May 2018, ECLI:EU:C:2018:300, paras 38–40.

[482] ECJ, Case C-207/16 Ministerio Fiscal, Judgment of 2 October 2018, paras 29–42.

[483] ECJ, Case C-207/16 Ministerio Fiscal, Opinion of AG Saugmandsgaard Øe, paras 74–86.

[484] ECJ, Case C-207/16 Ministerio Fiscal, Judgment of 2 October 2018, para 51.

[485] Ibid., paras 52 et seq.

[486] Ibid., paras 54–56; ECJ, Case C-207/16 Ministerio Fiscal, Opinion of AG Saugmandsgaard Øe, paras 87–91.

[487] ECJ, Case C-207/16 Ministerio Fiscal, Judgment of 2 October 2018, para 57.

[488] ECJ, Case C-207/16 Ministerio Fiscal, Opinion of AG Saugmandsgaard Øe, paras 32–37.

profiles on the scale of bulk data retention and could thus be justified for the fight of criminal offences in general.[489]

In reaction to this judgment, Celeste has suggested that the ECJ walked back its previously set case law of *Digital Rights Ireland* and *Tele2 Sverige* regarding the requirements on bulk data retention.[490] However, this conclusion does not acknowledge the specific circumstances of the case, as set out comprehensively both by the AG and the Grand Chamber with regard to the limited gravity of the interference. Even though the measure in question was of a much more limited scope, the Court made sure that the requirements derived from Article 7 and 8 CFR in the previous judgments were met. As this was the case, the measure was by no means as grave as the blanket data retention. The Court then applied the principle of proportionality and accordingly set out lower requirements for the measure, due to its much more limited scope. Consequently, it can be assumed that the requirements for proportionality set out in the previous case law are very much still in force, while the standards for the legitimate aim may vary, depending on the gravity of the interference, as the Grand Chamber subsequently demonstrated with the explicit differentiation between the various aims of the bulk data retention measures at issue in *La Quadrature du Net*.[491]

3.2.8.14 Buivids

In a chamber judgment rendered in early 2019, the Court again mentioned the right to data protection, as a right separate from the right to privacy.[492] However, when balancing the relevant fundamental rights concerning the journalism derogation of Article 9 DPD (corresponding to Article 85(1) GDPR), the Court only considered the right to privacy.[493] Yet, this can be attributed to the fact that Article 9 DPD itself only refers to the striking of a balance between the right to privacy and the freedom of expression. Notably, there was not yet a distinct binding right to data protection, when the DPD came into force. Under Article 85(1) GDPR, the verbatim has now been updated to refer to the right to data protection. Perhaps in light of this, AG Sharpston, in her Opinion referred to the right to privacy and the right to data protection in tandem.[494] Yet, she also only assessed an interference with Article 7 CFR.[495]

---

[489] ECJ, Case C-207/16 Ministerio Fiscal, Judgment of 2 October 2018, paras 59–62.

[490] Celeste 2019.

[491] Cf. below Sect. 3.2.8.16.

[492] ECJ, Case C-354/17 Sergejs Buivids, Judgment of 14 February 2019, ECLI:EU:C:2019:122, para 41.

[493] Ibid., paras 63–67.

[494] ECJ, Case C-354/17 Sergejs Buivids, Opinion of AG Sharpston of 27 September 2018, ECLI:EU:C:2018:780, paras 60 et seq. and 66.

[495] Ibid., para 65.

3.2.8.15 Schrems II

In *Schrems II* the Court revisited the transfer of personal data to the US and the local regime for data retention, including the PRISM and UPSTREAM surveillance programmes.[496] In his Opinion, AG Saugmansgaard Øe focussed on the validity of the Standard Contractual Clauses (SCC) Decision 2010/87,[497] which he found not to be in violation of Articles 7, 8 and 47 CFR.[498] In his assessment he focussed on the data subject rights and effective remedies required by Article 46(1) GDPR. However, he did not further engage with Articles 7 and 8 CFR and their respective requirements from the case law, thereby leaving the implications of the mass-surveillance regime for those rights under-examined.[499]

With regard to the Privacy Shield Decision[500] he argued on procedural grounds that the Court should not assess this.[501] Nevertheless, the AG provided "with certain reservations, some non-exhaustive observations".[502] Consequently, he embarked on an analysis along the lines of the case law of the Court, however, often not providing definitive answers and remaining rather vague in many instances.[503] The AG found that the transfer, access and retention were three different interferences with the rights of Articles 7 and 8 CFR and examined the relevant US provisions as legal bases, concluding that they did not meet the requirements of accessibility and foreseeability.[504] On the basis of the Court's jurisprudence, he further concluded that the essence of Article 7 CFR was violated due to the generalised access to the content of communications.[505] Regarding the essence of Article 8 CFR the AG, even though he expressed doubts as to the description of the purposes of the processing, concluded that this would not be sufficient to find a violation.[506] As he leaned towards finding the aims of national security to be legitimate, the AG—applying a strict standard of

[496] ECJ, C-311/18 Data Protection Commissioner v Facebook Ireland Ltd. and Maximillian Schrems—Schrems II, Judgment of 16 July 2020, ECLI:EU:C:2020:559, para 165.

[497] Commission Decision 2010/87/EU of 5 February 2010 on standard contractual clauses for the transfer of personal data to processors established in third countries under Directive 95/46/EC of the European Parliament and of the Council (notified under document C(2010) 593), OJ L 39 of 12 February 2010, pp. 5–18.

[498] ECJ, C-311/18 Data Protection Commissioner v Facebook Ireland Ltd. and Maximillian Schrems—Schrems II, Opinion of AG Saugmansgaard Øe of 19 December 2019, ECLI:EU:C:2019:1145, paras 121–160.

[499] Cf. also Woods 2019.

[500] Commission Implementing Decision (EU) 2016/1250 of 12 July 2016 pursuant to Directive 95/46/EC of the European Parliament and of the Council on the adequacy of the protection provided by the EU-U.S. Privacy Shield (notified under document C(2016) 4176), OJ L 207 of 1 August 2016, pp. 1–112.

[501] ECJ, C-311/18 Facebook Ireland and Schrems—Schrems II, Opinion of AG Saugmansgaard Øe, paras 161 and esp. 178–186.

[502] Ibid., para 187.

[503] Cf. ibid., paras 280, 282, 289, 297, 301, 308.

[504] Ibid., paras 255–262 and 263–271.

[505] Ibid., paras 272–278.

[506] Ibid., para 280.

review—was uncertain, whether the safeguards provided by US law could be seen as essentially equivalent to the level of the GDPR, read in the light of Articles 7 and 8 CFR.[507] He thus concluded that there were certain doubts concerning the conformity of the Privacy Shield Decision with Articles 7 and 8 CFR.[508]

In its judgment, delivered in July 2020, the Grand Chamber also found that the SCC Decision did not violate Articles 7, 8 and 47 CFR.[509] Much like the AG, it emphasised the data subject rights to compensation and to lodge a complaint and merely pointed to the fact that, where the general level of protection in a third country was not adequate, the controller or processor established in the EU had to take additional measures or suspend the transfer.[510] In this first part of the judgment, the Court makes sure to repeatedly point out that the relevant provisions are interpreted in the light of Articles 7, 8 and 47 CFR,[511] though it never quite states how these rights inform the interpretation of the secondary law.

However, when assessing the Privacy Shield Decision, the successor of the Safe Harbour Decision previously annulled by the Court,[512] this time, and different from the path suggested by the AG, the Grand Chamber examined the US provisions in more detail with regard to the interferences with Articles 7 and 8 CFR.[513] It found that there was not an adequate level of protection in the sense of Article 45 GDPR, as the Commission had found, provided by US law.[514]

Examining Articles 7 and 8 CFR, the Court reiterated its case law on both rights being affected by the processing of information and data, respectively, and established that the communication of data to a third party, the retention as well as the subsequent access to this data by public authorities were three different interferences with Articles 7 and 8 CFR.[515]

However, both rights were subject to limitations under Article 8(2) CFR and/or Article 52(1) CFR.[516] Under these provisions, the legal basis had to include specific rules on the scope and application of the measures as well as the minimum safeguards laid down by the Court to protect individuals from risks of abuse.[517] Referring back to Opinion 1/15, the Court emphasised the increased need for safeguards when data was processed by automated means.[518]

---

[507] Ibid., paras 290–301.

[508] Ibid., para 342.

[509] ECJ, C-311/18 Facebook Ireland and Schrems—Schrems II, Judgment of 16 July 2020, para 149.

[510] Ibid., paras 122–149.

[511] Ibid., paras 122, 132, 137, 140, 149.

[512] Cf. above Sect. 3.2.8.8.

[513] ECJ, C-311/18 Facebook Ireland and Schrems—Schrems II, Judgment of 16 July 2020, paras 165 and 168 et seq.

[514] Ibid., para 168.

[515] Ibid., paras 170 et seq.

[516] Ibid., paras 173 et seq.

[517] Ibid., paras 175 et seq.

[518] Ibid., para 176.

It thus went on to assess the US surveillance regime in detail and found that the US provisions did not meet the required standards, as they allowed for bulk data retention without sufficiently clear and precise rules or minimum safeguards.[519] It also found that there were no actionable rights for individuals from the EU, which led to a violation of the essence of Article 47 CFR, in line with its established case law.[520]

With regard to the interpretation of Article 8 CFR, much is not to be gained from this case. Essentially, it is the application of the standards set previously with the addition of the new secondary EU data protection legislation, which regulates third country transfers in more detail. Applying these established standards to the sweeping mass-surveillance regime in the US, was generally expected to yield this outcome.[521] Following the Grand Chamber's declaration of invalidity, the General Court dismissed proceedings brought by the non-governmental organisation (NGO) La Quadrature du Net, which had also challenged the validity of the Privacy Shield Decision.[522]

3.2.8.16 La Quadrature du Net, Privacy International and Prokuratuur

In January 2020, AG Campos Sánchez-Bordona delivered three Opinions in the cases of *Ordre des Barreaux*, *La Quadrature du Net* and *Privacy International*, all concerning various national bulk data retention schemes.[523] While the AG laid out his argument comprehensively in the first Opinion and referred back to it in the others, the Court ruled on *Ordre des Barreaux* as joined case with *La Quadrature du Net*.

In his Opinions AG Campos Sánchez-Bordona did not assess the fundamental rights in question in detail, but rather just pointed to them in a few instances. Instead, he summarized the standards established by the Court.

The AG started out in *Ordre des Barreaux* with a comprehensive recapitulation of the Court's case law on *Tele2 Sverige* and *Ministerio Fiscal*.[524] He then went on to consider the Member States' objections to this case law, which were, firstly, that strict rules on access to the data retained by the communication services would serve as

---

[519] Ibid., paras 180–185.

[520] Ibid., paras 181 and 186–197. Also cf. above Sect. 3.2.8.8.

[521] Churches and Zalnieriute 2020; Irion 2020; Kuner 2020.

[522] GC, Case T-738/16 La Quadrature du Net and Others v European Commission, Order of 14 December 2020, ECLI:EU:T:2020:638.

[523] ECJ, Case C-520/18 Ordre des barreaux francophones and germanophone and Others, Opinion of AG Campos Sànchez-Bordona of 15 January 2020, ECLI:EU:C:2020:7; ECJ, Joined Cases C-511/18, C-512/18 and C-520/18 La Quadature du Net and Others v Premier ministre and Others, Opinion of AG Campos Sànchez-Bordona of 15 January 2020, ECLI:EU:C:2020:6; ECJ, C-623/17 Privacy International v Secretary of State for Foreign and Commonwealth Affairs and Others, Opinion of AG Campos Sànchez-Bordona of 15 January 2020, ECLI:EU:C:2020:5.

[524] ECJ, Case C-520/18 Ordre des barreaux francophones and germanophone and Others, Opinion of AG Campos Sànchez-Bordona, paras 32–67.

sufficient safeguards.[525] Secondly, the Member States argued that under the right to security guaranteed by Article 6 CFR, they needed to adopt effective measures which they could select with discretion.[526] This argument had initially been introduced by the Court itself in *Digital Rights Ireland*.[527] In *La Quadrature du Net*, the AG briefly dismissed the reliance on Article 6 CFR, by rightly pointing out that as a fundamental right, it could be violated by the State, but was not necessarily capable of justifying an interference, especially as the notion of security was not synonymous with public security.[528] Rather, in correspondence to Article 5 ECHR, it covered the freedom from arbitrary arrest or detention.[529]

In *Ordre des Barreaux*, the AG continued by arguing that the Court should principally uphold its previous case law, which could, however, be refined with regard to the possibility of limited retention of communications data.[530] If there were specific rules on retention that ensured that there was no general and indiscriminate retention, this would be a feasible route.[531]

Generally, the AG argued that it was difficult to refute the usefulness of data retention to prevent or combat terrorism and that the selection was indeed in the discretion of Member States.[532] However, he thereby disregarded the fact, that the Member States must exercise their discretion within the limits of the principle of proportionality and that within the examination of the necessity of a given measure, this measure would have to be able to further the legitimate aim pursued. In this step, the question of the effectiveness of those measures must be examined. However, the Court has not considered such arguments, even when the effectiveness of the retention was challenged explicitly in *Digital Rights Ireland*.[533]

From the premise of their general effectiveness, the AG went on to lay out rules for limited bulk data retention, which he found permissible under the case law and Charter. This entailed the temporary retention of certain categories of traffic and location data, which would be limited to ensure that it would not lead to the creation of a detailed profile of the persons concerned by this measure.[534] The categories of data retained should therefore encompass only the minimum amount deemed absolutely

[525] Ibid., para 70.

[526] Ibid., para 71.

[527] ECJ, Joined Cases C-293/12 and C-594/12 Digital Rights Ireland and Seitlinger and Others, Judgment of 8 April 2014, para 42. Also pointed out by Sajfert 2020.

[528] ECJ, Joined Cases C-511/18, C-512/18 and C-520/18 La Quadrature du Net, Opinion of AG Campos Sànchez-Bordona, paras 95–97.

[529] Ibid., para 98.

[530] ECJ, Case C-520/18 Ordre des barreaux francophones and germanophone and Others, Opinion of AG Campos Sànchez-Bordona, paras 72 et seq.

[531] Ibid., paras 77–79.

[532] Ibid., para 81.

[533] ECJ, Joined Cases C-293/12 and C-594/12 Digital Rights Ireland and Seitlinger and Others, Judgment of 8 April 2014, paras 49–51.

[534] ECJ, Case C-520/18 Ordre des barreaux francophones and germanophone and Others, Opinion of AG Campos Sànchez-Bordona, para 93.

necessary for the measure to remain effective.[535] He also suggested that the period of retention could be adjusted according to the degree of detail that the category of data revealed about an individual by storing more invasive data for a shorter period of time, which would thus limit the interference with Article 8 CFR.[536]

Further, the AG pointed out that the distinction between metadata and content was difficult to maintain, especially with regard to the uniform resource locators (URLs) accessed, as they could simultaneously reveal the content of the communication.[537] Ultimately, it would be for the legislator to strike a balance, while heeding the premise that a State bound by fundamental rights under the rule of law would not be able to pursue the most effective route of retention at all cost.[538]

As last point of his general remarks on the case law, the AG considered that there could be extreme circumstances under which, by declaring an official state of emergency, a Member State could impose "an obligation to retain data that is as extensive and general as is deemed necessary" for a limited time.[539]

With regard to the specific Belgian legislation at hand in *Ordre des Barreaux*, the AG merely pointed out that it imposed a general and indiscriminate bulk data retention obligation, which was incompatible with the Court's case law and, hence, the Charter. After having laid out his reasoning in detail, he thus seemingly adopted a deferential approach when concluding that the modalities for access to the data were for the national court to assess.[540]

Concerning the French legislation at issue in *La Quadrature du Net*, the AG found that the retention of the data was not solely based on the prevention and combat of terrorism and the categories of data affected were largely the same as in *Digital Rights Ireland* and *Tele2 Sverige*, i.e. were also general and indiscriminate and thus entailed a very far-reaching and particularly serious interference with the rights of Articles 7 and 8 CFR.[541] As the Court in those previous cases had also considered legislation that served the fight against terrorism to violate these rights, the AG argued that the same principles should apply here.[542] Instead, he argued, the Member State could pursue selective retention, focused on the essential categories of data, which were for the legislator to determine.[543]

Concerning the access to the data, AG Campos Sánchez-Bordona found that the legislation had to lay out the substantive and procedural requirements and had to be

---

535 Ibid., para 94.

536 Ibid., para 96.

537 Ibid., para 99.

538 Ibid., para 102. Also cf. ECJ, Joined Cases C-511/18, C-512/18 and C-520/18 La Quadrature du Net, Opinion of AG Campos Sànchez-Bordona, paras 130–136.

539 ECJ, Case C-520/18 Ordre des barreaux francophones and germanophone and Others, Opinion of AG Campos Sànchez-Bordona, para 105.

540 Ibid., paras 119–143.

541 ECJ, Joined Cases C-511/18, C-512/18 and C-520/18 La Quadrature du Net, Opinion of AG Campos Sànchez-Bordona, paras 109–112.

542 Ibid., paras 114–123 and 127.

543 Ibid., paras 133–136.

subject to prior review following a reasoned request by the competent authorities.[544] Addressing the real-time collection of data foreseen in the French legislation, he argued that this was no different from the usual retention regime and thus had to follow the same rules, i.e. the criteria for the processing had to be specific, reliable and non-discriminatory.[545]

In the assessment of the bulk data retention regime at issue in *Privacy International*, the AG referred to his previous Opinion to the extent that the analysis from *La Quadrature du Net* was quoted extensively and—as there were few differences in the eyes of the AG—applied to that case. As the regime at hand amounted to general and indiscriminate collection, he found it to be precluded by EU law.[546]

The Grand Chamber of the Court delivered the judgments in *La Quadrature du Net*, now joined with *Ordre des Barreaux*, and *Privacy International* all on the same date in October 2020.[547] In the former judgment the Court started out by somewhat laboriously differentiating the application of Article 1(3) ePD from its previous PNR judgment that the transfer of personal data did not fall under the scope of the DPD, which I have briefly analysed above.[548]

Interpreting Article 15(1) ePD in the light of Articles 7 and 8 CFR, the Court found that metadata could reveal significant information on the private lives of individuals and could help to build a profile, which, under the right to privacy, was no less sensitive than the content of the communications concerned.[549] The Court here reaffirmed its adoption of AG Saugmandsgaard Øe's point in *Tele2 Sverige*.[550]

In the beginning of the actual assessment, the Court reiterated the points concerning the non-absolute nature of the rights in question and the balancing required.[551] It also picked up the AG's assessment of Article 6 CFR and found that this provision did not impose an obligation on Member States to enact specific measures or punish specific criminal offences.[552] With regard to the proportionality of the bulk data retention measures, it stated that the right to privacy required a strict standard of review and that the seriousness of the interference had to be balanced against the importance of the public interest objective.[553] Furthermore, as established in the previous case law, the legislation had to contain clear and precise rule on the application of the measure, include minimum safeguards to protect individuals

[544] Ibid., paras 137–139.

[545] Ibid., paras 142–146.

[546] ECJ, C-623/17 Privacy International, Opinion of AG Campos Sànchez-Bordona, paras 37–39.

[547] In all three cases, just as in *Digital Rights Ireland*, the *Schrems* cases, *Ministerio Fiscal* and *Tele2 Sverige* Judge von Danwitz acted as rapporteur.

[548] ECJ, Joined Cases C-511/18, C-512/18 and C-520/18 La Quadature du Net and Others v Premier ministre and Others, Judgment of 6 October 2020, ECLI:EU:C:2020:791, paras 100–104. Also cf. above Sect. 3.2.3.1.

[549] Ibid., paras 130–136.

[550] Cf. above Sect. 3.2.8.9.

[551] ECJ, Joined Cases C-511/18, C-512/18 and C-520/18 La Quadrature du Net, Judgment of 6 October 2020, paras 120–122.

[552] Ibid., paras 123–125.

[553] Ibid., paras 130 et seq.

against abuse, be legally binding and foreseeable.[554] Especially when special categories of data that are considered sensitive were at stake and there were additional risks due to the use of automated processing as well as a significant risk of unlawful access to the data, the need for safeguards was increased.[555]

After setting out these initial requirements—curiously only with regard to Article 7 CFR, not Article 8 CFR—the Grand Chamber went on to assess the various objectives pursued by the legislation in question. Considering the objective of national security, the Court held that due to Article 4(2) TEU, which provides that national security lies within the exclusive competence of the Member States, it had a different status from the other objectives listed in Article 15(1) ePD and could justify more serious interferences than the other objectives,[556] which mirrors its earlier reasoning in *Ministerio Fiscal*.[557] Accordingly, under Articles 7 and 8 CFR, a serious threat to national security could legitimise the general and indiscriminate retention of all user data for a limited period of time, which could be extended, if the situation persisted.[558] However, strict safeguards against abuse had to be included and a legally binding previous authorisation by a court or independent administrative body, which could review the measures in place, was required. Further, the retention could not be systematic in nature.[559]

Concerning the objectives of combating crime and safeguarding public security, the Court held that only serious crime and serious threats to public security could justify the likewise serious interferences with Articles 7 and 8 CFR entailed by the retention of traffic and location data.[560] On the one hand this meant that non-serious interferences, i.e. the retention of other metadata, could indeed be ordered for a more general set of criminal offences.[561] On the other hand, the Court held that the general and indiscriminate retention of traffic and location data for serious crime was not justified due to their sensitive nature under Article 7 CFR.[562] In the judgment, the Court does not make it clear, how these notions of national security, combatting crime and safeguarding public security are to be differentiated. Especially on the oft invoked reason of fighting terrorism, the Court is silent and does not offer any categorisation.[563]

---

[554] Ibid., para 132.

[555] Ibid.

[556] Ibid., paras 134–137.

[557] Cf. above Sect. 3.2.8.13.

[558] ECJ, Joined Cases C-511/18, C-512/18 and C-520/18 La Quadrature du Net, Judgment of 6 October 2020, paras 137 et seq.

[559] Ibid., paras 138 et seq.

[560] Ibid., para 140.

[561] Ibid.

[562] Ibid., paras 141 et seq. Here, the Court also found Article 7 CFR to be relevant with regard to the ensuing deterrent effect of such a measure, whereas it later found that this only concerned Article 11 CFR, cf. ibid., paras 170 and 186.

[563] Cf. with regard to the AG's Opinion Vogiatzoglou 2020; on the distinction in the context of the LED cf. Vogiatzoglou and Fantin 2019.

The Court went on to reiterate its previous case law since *Digital Rights Ireland* on general and indiscriminate bulk data retention, but also cited *Tele2 Sverige*, where it had held that targeted retention would be permissible for the objectives at hand, subject to limitations in personal, temporal, geographical and material scope.[564] It emphasised that the selection of a geographical area had to be based on objective and non-discriminatory criteria and while the duration may not exceed what is strictly necessary, an authorisation could be extended.[565]

With regard to the retention of IP addresses and data on the identity of internet service users, the Grand Chamber found that these data were "less sensitive than other traffic data."[566] However, as these data revealed a user's entire browsing history, i.e. the URLs visited, it enabled the compilation of a detailed profile and therefore was a serious interference with both Articles 7 and 8 CFR.[567] Nevertheless, the Court argued that the IP addresses were the only means of investigation for offences committed online and would be lost if only stored for as long as necessary for purposes of billing by ISPs. In order to combat serious crime or prevent serious threats to public security, inter alia particularly serious child pornography offences, the extended retention would be a proportionate measure, even though it entailed a blanket retention of all internet users' data, if strict compliance to substantive and procedural conditions was ensured.[568] Concerning the data on the identity of internet service users, the Court held that this data did not have the same effect as metadata in revealing information about the user and therefore was not a serious interference. Hence, it could be stored even in absence of a connection between all users affected and the objectives pursued for combating crime in general, even without imposing a specific time limit.[569]

The Court then turned to the expedited retention of traffic and location data retained by communications providers under the ePD even after their purposes have been attained in order to investigate serious criminal offences or threats to national security, which are at least reasonably expected.[570] Noting that similar obligations existed under the CoE Cybercrime Convention,[571] the Court found this to be permissible, where such an authorisation was subject to effective judicial review.[572] However, as the purpose of the processing was changed after collection contrary to Article 8(2) CFR, this was a serious interference with Articles 7 and 8 CFR and therefore only allowed for serious crime or, a fortiori, safeguarding national security, if the

[564] ECJ, Joined Cases C-511/18, C-512/18 and C-520/18 La Quadrature du Net, Judgment of 6 October 2020, paras 143–147 and 150.

[565] Ibid., paras 150 et seq.

[566] Ibid., para 152.

[567] Ibid., para 153.

[568] Ibid., paras 154 et seq.

[569] Ibid., paras 157–159.

[570] Ibid., paras 169 et seq.

[571] Council of Europe, Convention on Cybercrime of 23 November 2001, ETS No. 185.

[572] ECJ, Joined Cases C-511/18, C-512/18 and C-520/18 La Quadrature du Net, Judgment of 6 October 2020, paras 162 et seq.

conditions of the application of the measure were transparent and the storage duration limited.[573] The Court even found that this measure could be extended to persons who were not suspected of any serious criminal acts or acts adversely affecting national security, if their data, on the basis of objective and non-discriminatory criteria, might further an investigation.[574]

Furthermore, the Court considered the automated analysis of all traffic and location data by service providers at the request of national authorities justifiable, albeit only for serious threats to national security.[575] In line with its previous case law, it found that this general and indiscriminate bulk data retention constituted a particularly serious interference with Articles 7 and 8 CFR due to the automated analysis and the potential to reveal a person's browsing history and would have to be subject to strict safeguards.[576]

With regard to the automated analysis, the Court referred back to its Opinion 1/15 to state that in automated processing, the pre-established models and criteria on which the processing is based had to be specific and reliable to only identify persons under reasonable suspicion and "should be non-discriminatory".[577] Processing by automated means in this context could, due to the infringement of Articles 7 and 8 CFR read in conjunction with Article 21 CFR, not be based on special categories of data alone.[578] Additionally, with regard to the margin of error of such automated systems, the Court found that before an individual measure was taken, it would have to be subject to human review and it had to be ensured that the models and criteria were and remained non-discriminatory as well as stayed reliable and updated through regular review.[579]

When considering the continuous real-time collection of traffic and location data foreseen in national law, the Grand Chamber found that this allowed for very precise insights into the private lives of the persons concerned and was a particularly serious interference with Articles 7 and 8 CFR as it allowed for a "virtually total" monitoring.[580] While the Grand Chamber found that the aim of preventing terrorist acts could justify this interference, it could only do so with regard to persons who were suspected of engaging in terrorist activities and the authorisation was based on objective and non-discriminatory criteria and subject to prior review.[581] Lastly, the Court considered that the notification of persons concerned was a necessary requirement in order to enable them to exercise their data subject rights, which the Court considered to be guaranteed by both Articles 7 and 8 CFR.[582]

---

573 Ibid., paras 164 and 166.
574 Ibid., para 165.
575 Ibid., paras 172 and 177.
576 Ibid., paras 173–179.
577 Ibid., para 180.
578 Ibid., para 181.
579 Ibid., para 182.
580 Ibid., paras 183–187.
581 Ibid., paras 188 et seq.
582 Ibid., paras 190 et seq.

The judgment in *Privacy International* concerned the retention of all metadata for reasons of national security. It relied heavily on the judgment in *La Quadrature du Net* and reiterated that in adopting the ePD, the EU legislator had given concrete expression to the rights of Articles 7 and 8 CFR and that therefore derogations under Article 15(1) ePD could not become the rule.[583] It argued that any such measure affected both Article 7 and 8 CFR and that therefore, under Article 52(1) CFR, the legal basis had to lay out the required safeguards to ensure its proportionality.[584]

However, as it carried on its assessment, the Grand Chamber found that the transmission of the data to the security and intelligence agencies was only a particularly serious interference with to the right to privacy under Article 7 CFR, due to the possibility of compiling a profile from the metadata, which was just as sensitive as the content of the communications and was likely to make them feel that their lives were under constant surveillance.[585] While it did mention the fact that, given the sheer amount of data, the mere retention entailed a risk of abuse and unlawful access—which the Court usually sees as the object of Article 8 CFR—it did not make any reference to the right to data protection here.[586] However, as was to be expected from its established case law, the Grand Chamber concluded that the general and indiscriminate nature of the data transmitted to the security and intelligence agencies did not include the necessary safeguards to ensure the proportionality of the measure, even though the objective of national security was generally capable of justifying more serious interferences.[587]

In March 2021 the Court again delivered a judgment on a case concerning bulk data retention. This time, the issue was the access of the prosecutor's office to metadata retained by service providers in a criminal case concerning theft.[588]

The Estonian provisions at issue allowed for the general and indiscriminate retention of traffic and location data for one year in order to combat crime in general and the Court swiftly and by extensive reference to its earlier jurisprudence concluded that due to the seriousness of the interference entailed by this measure it was not proportionate.[589] It did not share the national court's view that due to the one year period of retention the quantity of the data retained would be lower, as the interference with the rights of Articles 7 and 8 CFR was serious regardless of the time period, because the data in question allowed precise insights into the private lives of the persons concerned.[590] Furthermore, the quantity of the data could only be assessed after the data had been accessed and thus, the interference had already

[583] ECJ, C-623/17 Privacy International v Secretary of State for Foreign and Commonwealth Affairs and Others, Judgment of 6 October 2020, ECLI:EU:C:2020:790, paras 50–59 and 69.

[584] Ibid., paras 60–70.

[585] Ibid., paras 71 et seq.

[586] Ibid., para 73.

[587] Ibid., paras 74–82.

[588] ECJ, Case C-746/18 Criminal proceedings against H. K.—Prokuratuur, Judgment of 2 March 2021, ECLI:EU:C:2021:152, paras 16 et seq.

[589] Ibid., paras 28–36.

[590] Ibid., paras 37–39.

taken place so that consequently, this could not affect the question of whether the data at hand actually revealed sensitive information.[591] The Grand Chamber here differed from AG Pitruzzella's Opinion, which had been delivered shortly after AG Campos Sánchez-Bordona's Opinions, discussed above, in January 2020. The AG extensively laid out the previous case law and suggested that the retention period should indeed be considered, but ultimately adopted a more deferential approach when he concluded that it was for the referring court to ascertain the proportionality of the interference.[592]

The three cases demonstrate that the Court has now established its case law with regard to mass-surveillance measures and is merely refining it with regard to the specific data retained and objectives pursued. However, they also show that, as could already be seen in *Digital Rights Ireland*, the Court's line is not strictly against any form of data retention measures.[593] It now rather focuses on the question which circumstances render it is permissible. Unfortunately, the Court has not even ruled out the general and indiscriminate bulk data retention it holds to be the most serious interference, but rather has been swayed by the apparently paramount needs of national security. With IP addresses and subscribers' identity information it has now also found categories of data that it deems less relevant. This will encourage the Member States and the Commission to further pursue their legislative efforts with regard to bulk data retention regimes. Especially with regard to the Court's requirement that the retention must be limited in duration, while explicitly opening up the possibility to extend an authorisation creates leeway for legislators.[594] Any retention regime is sure to use this and it seems likely that the Court will again be seized of such a measure in the future. It will then have to further elucidate what it means by strict necessity with regard to the duration of the retention.

Concerning the interpretation of the fundamental right to data protection, these latest judgments give a somewhat murky impression. While the Grand Chamber generally refers to the rights of Articles 7 and 8 CFR, indicating that they are indeed two different rights, it mostly considers them in tandem, without differentiating further. Even when it does consider individual aspects of the rights, such as the sensitive nature of the data under Article 7 CFR[595] or the principle of purpose limitation in Article 8(2),[596] it moves on to establish an interference with both rights. In the operative part of the rights assessment in *Privacy International*, the Grand Chamber does not even mention Article 8 CFR, when it considers the risks of abuse, which it has established as a—rather limited—substantive guarantee of the right to data protection.

---

[591] Ibid., para 40.

[592] ECJ, Case C-746/18 Criminal proceedings against H. K.—Prokuratuur, Opinion of AG Pitruzzella of 21 January 2020, ECLI:EU:C:2020:18, paras 52–97.

[593] Ojanen 2014, pp. 539 et seq.; Kunnert 2014b, p. 777.

[594] Also cf. Sajfert 2020.

[595] ECJ, Joined Cases C-511/18, C-512/18 and C-520/18 La Quadrature du Net, Judgment of 6 October 2020, para 142.

[596] Ibid., para 164.

With regard to the use of automated processing systems—including what is commonly referred to as artificial intelligence (AI) systems—it is welcome that the Court further develops and generalises the approach of Opinion 1/15.[597] In its reasoning it has shown that it is aware of the discriminatory potential of such systems and imposed basic obligations in order to protect individuals from such outfalls. It has effectively ruled out that special categories of data are the only means of assessing a situation. It has also required that there must be human review before a decision is made, but also throughout the lifecycle of the automated processing system in order to ensure that these systems do not become black boxes for controllers. However, merely ensuring that a person checks the result of an AI system may not prove to be efficient, as can be seen by Article 22 GDPR. This provision also only applies when there is no human involved in the decision process. However, a person confronted with a decision of an AI system might be hesitant to revise it, as such systems are often, and unjustifiably, held to be unbiased.[598] If, only because a person pushes a button, rather than a machine deciding autonomously, there is a different standard of safeguards, this might leave individuals without protection.[599] It seems likely that the Court will revisit these points in the future, when it is called to adjudicate on such a system.

3.2.9 Conclusions on the Case Law on Article 8(1) and (2) CFR

In the preceding analysis, I have illustrated how the right to data protection has evolved in the jurisprudence of the Court. This analysis has shown that this right has not yet been properly defined with regard to its function in the system of EU fundamental rights, i.e. its underlying rationale and content.[600]

In its first substantive judgment on data protection, the ECJ severed the nexus to private life and set the right to data protection on a course that led it to become independent from the limitations of the right to privacy under the jurisprudence of the ECtHR. As I have pointed out, the early case law of the Court relied on general notions of proportionality, which are now incorporated in the secondary EU data protection legislation,[601] as introduced in Chap. 2. For instance, the notion of legitimate aim relates to the legitimate purpose. Further, a legitimate legal basis is required in both, the general law and the data protection legislation. The Court has also considered

[597] Cf. above and ibid., paras 180–182.

[598] Buranyi 2017, The Guardian. https://www.theguardian.com/inequality/2017/aug/08/rise-of-the-racist-robots-how-ai-is-learning-all-our-worst-impulses. Accessed 28 July 2021. For an example cf. Mysegades 2019.

[599] Cf. similarly on Article 22 GDPR Brkan 2019a, pp. 98 et seq.

[600] Also cf. González Fuster and Gellert 2012, p. 76.

[601] Cf. in this regard the assessment in ECJ, Case C-496/17 Deutsche Post AG v Hauptzollamt Köln, Judgment of 16 January 2019, ECLI:EU:C:2019:26, paras 54–68.

the notion of necessity in its case law, which, in the data protection legislation, is embodied in the requirements of purpose limitation and data minimisation.[602]

The ECJ recognised the fundamental rights dimension of the EU secondary legislation early on, even though it was reluctant to apply the Charter.[603] The Court found that its scope had to be interpreted broadly and any exceptions narrowly in order to offer appropriate protection to individuals. After several AGs, from the first PNR case to *Digital Rights Ireland*, suggested to limit the scope of review,[604] the Court has expressly rebuffed this idea.[605] Instead, the Court has always allowed a broad variety of reasons to render the processing of data lawful, where that is necessary to achieve a legitimate purpose or aim. Its judgment in *YS and Others* also demonstrates that the Court does not see data protection law as boundless and is mindful of its interplay with other legal regimes—in that instance the framework for access to documents.

However, initially, the Court did not balance the right to data protection with conflicting rights, but rather followed a deferential approach and left the national courts to determine the specific outcome of a case. It has only deviated from this as recently as *Google Spain*, *Tele2 Sverige* and has continued this in the Grand Chamber judgments in the cases *La Quadrature du Net* and *Privacy International*. Yet, there have also been cases, such as *Ryneš*, where the Court did not carry out the balancing, although this was only a chamber judgment. As the fundamental rights of EU law apply in these cases, the Court, as the ultimate judicial authority for their interpretation, should engage with them more substantively, as argued especially by AG Kokott in her Opinions in *Promusicae* and *Satamedia*.

AG Kokott also was the first member of the Court to rely on the secondary EU data protection legislation in a meaningful way for the interpretation of the right to data protection and has consistently argued for a deeper analysis of the fundamental rights at issue.[606] Over time, the Court started to interpret the right to data protection with reference to the secondary law, which could achieve coherence between the respective norms on the different levels of EU law. However, the Court has done so only reluctantly since *Schecke and Eifert* and has considered the right to data protection on its own in a very limited number of judgments. In this regard, it is apparent,

---

[602] Further, the requirement of foreseeability relates to the principle of transparency. However, since the coming into force of the Charter, the ECJ no longer considers this requirement, which is derived from the requirement that any interference must be "in accordance with the law", as included in Article 8(2) ECHR.

[603] More critically González Fuster 2014b, p. 267.

[604] ECJ, Joined Cases C-317/04 and C-318/04 Parliament v Council and Commission—PNR, Opinion of AG Léger, paras 223–232. ECJ, Case C-291/12 Schwarz, Opinion of AG Mengozzi, para 53. ECJ, Joined Cases C-293/12 and C-594/12 Digital Rights Ireland and Seitlinger and Others, Opinion of AG Cruz Villalón, para 136. AG Saugmandsgaard Øe might have broken the spell by expressly calling for a strict standard of review in ECJ, Joined Cases C-203/15 and C-698/15 Tele2 Sverige, Opinion of AG Saugmandsgaard Øe, paras 209 and 213 et seq.

[605] ECJ, Joined Cases C-92/09 and C-93/09 Volker und Markus Schecke and Eifert, Judgment of 9 November 2010, para 77. ECJ, Joined Cases C-293/12 and C-594/12 Digital Rights Ireland and Seitlinger and Others, Judgment of 8 April 2014, para 48.

[606] Cf. above Sect. 3.2.4.

as González Fuster and Gellert have argued, that the Court was still considering data protection from a perspective of privacy.[607]

The judgment in the case *Schecke and Eifert* also laid the groundwork for two different approaches with regard to Articles 7 and 8 CFR, which both rely on this judgment, as the Court, arguably, had read Articles 7 and 8 CFR jointly in its preliminary observations,[608] but assessed their scope separately.[609] *Digital Rights Ireland*, which adopted the latter approach, today still provides the most comprehensive assessment of an independent right to data protection, which the Court has delivered. Not only did the Court fully embrace the processing of personal data as standard for interference, but it, at least partly, drew the necessary consequences concerning the coherence of the different levels of norms in the proportionality assessment.

The Court perhaps realized in *Digital Rights Ireland* that data protection is not about a prohibition of processing operations for its own sake, but rather that the general ban on processing[610] serves to bring all processing operations within the scope of data protection law in order to ensure that they fulfil the relevant requirements. This may have led the Court to finally fully adopt the standard of interference in conformity to the secondary EU data protection legislation, as it understood that the broad scope of the right enables it to apply the requirements of the principles to all processing operations. Article 8(2) CFR allows for the processing of personal data only when there is a legitimate legal basis and thus enshrines the principle of lawfulness on a constitutional level. This creates a fundamental right with a very wide scope, as any processing of personal data interferes with the right to the protection of personal data.[611] The judgment in *Digital Rights Ireland* thereby, again, demonstrates how closely the principles of data protection are connected to the more general requirements of proportionality, as I have pointed out above and which the Court had already relied on in its early case law.[612]

In *Digital Rights Ireland* the Court further held that the principles of data protection and data security and their implementation through technical and organisational measures formed the essence of Article 8 CFR.[613] The Court thereby rightly assessed

607 González Fuster and Gellert 2012, pp. 79 et seq.

608 Which the chamber expressly relied on in *Schwarz* and AG Cruz Villalón and AG Jääskinen followed on in their Opinions in *Digital Rights Ireland* and *Google Spain*, respectively.

609 Which the Grand Chamber followed explicitly in *Digital Rights Ireland* and AG Bot adopted in his Opinion in *Schrems*.

610 Cf. Chap. 2, Sect. 2.3.2.1.

611 However, as I will demonstrate in Chap. 5, such a comprehensive provision is necessary to counter the risks inherent in any form of processing, cf. Chap. 5, Sects. 5.3.1.1. and 5.4.2.1.

612 Cf. already Chap. 2, Sect. 2.3.2.5.; I will also explore this point in more detail in Chap. 5, Sect. 5.2.4.

613 ECJ, Joined Cases C-293/12 and C-594/12 Digital Rights Ireland and Seitlinger and Others, Judgment of 8 April 2014, para 40; also cf. ECJ, Joined Cases C-203/15 and C-698/15 Tele2 Sverige, Opinion of AG Saugmandsgaard Øe, paras 155–158, who did not consider this question to be an issue in this case; consequently, the Grand Chamber did not consider the essence of Article 8 CFR and only briefly dealt with the essence of Article 7 CFR, ECJ, Joined Cases C-203/15 and C-698/15 Tele 2 Sverige, Judgment of 21 December 2016, para 101.

that in order for data protection law to function properly, data security is a necessary prerequisite. Yet, as pointed out by Lynskey and Brkan, it must be noted that the Court, ever since this judgment, only applies a rather superficial understanding of when legislation contains appropriate safeguards,[614] as demonstrated by the very rudimentary rules of Article 7 of the invalidated DRD.

Furthermore, it is important to note that data security as part of information security has a different focus from data protection, as it aims to ensure the interests of the entity processing data, and is beneficial to data subjects only by extension.[615] So far, the Court has demonstrated a tendency in subsequent cases[616] to not engage with this issue, but rather use data security and data protection interchangeably.

More importantly, in its *Digital Rights Ireland* judgment, the Court found that the essence of Article 8 CFR includes the principles of security, confidentiality and integrity, relating to the implementation of appropriate technical and organisational measures.[617] In Opinion 1/15, the Court expanded this by explicitly referring to the principle of purpose limitation.[618] This finding is as seminal as it is logical for the interpretation of the right to data protection. It suggests that the Court could be on track to find that the principles of data protection also form the essence of the fundamental right to data protection. However, the latest cases on bulk data retention did not further explore the right to data protection, instead merely referring back to the established case law, and overall demonstrated a murkier assessment of the right.

While the *Schrems* judgment, in its discussion of data protection, did not live up to its precursor, the Grand Chamber reiterated the requirements imposed on processing operations with regard to the principles of the EU secondary data protection legislation. In the subsequent *Tele2 Sverige* judgment on bulk data retention, the Grand Chamber further extended this jurisprudence on procedural and substantive requirements for surveillance measures and, in an *obiter dictum*, held that the right to data protection was independent of the right to privacy under the Charter and that the former did not have a corresponding provision under the ECHR.[619]

Unfortunately, the Court, even in its more recent case law and aside from the essence of Article 8 CFR, shows no sign of systematising its jurisprudence in line with the principles of the secondary EU data protection legislation.[620] While these were already enshrined in the first generation of data protection legislation, it may

---

614 Brkan 2019b, pp. 878 et seq.; Lynskey 2015b, p. 172.

615 Cf. Chap. 2, Sects. 2.3.2.8 and Sect. 2.3.3.3.

616 For instance ECJ, Avis 1/15, Opinion of 26 July 2017, para 150.

617 ECJ, Joined Cases C-293/12 and C-594/12 Digital Rights Ireland and Seitlinger and Others, Judgment of 8 April 2014, para 40.

618 ECJ, Avis 1/15, Opinion of 26 July 2017, para 150.

619 ECJ, Joined Cases C-203/15 and C-698/15 Tele 2 Sverige, Judgment of 21 December 2016, para 129. In turn, the jurisprudence of the Court, especially in *Digital Rights Ireland* and *Schrems* has visibly impacted the adjudication of the ECtHR, notably in ECtHR, Szabó and Vissy, App. No. 37138/14, Judgment of 12 January 2016; ECtHR [GC], Roman Zakharov v. Russia, App. No. 47143/06, Judgment of 4 December 2015. Also observed by Cole and Vandendriessche 2016.

620 Vogiatzoglou 2019, at 3.3.

still be hoped that in the future the Court will refer to Article 5 GDPR and thus realise the link between the secondary and primary law.

Yet, the judgments in *Schrems* and *Google Spain* illustrate that the understanding of data protection in the case law of the Court overall is limited and lacking a clear vision.[621] The subsequent case law shows that especially in the chamber judgments and perhaps under the influence of Article 1 DPD, the Court considers data protection mostly through the lens of the right to privacy and hence the differentiation between the right to privacy and the right to data protection remains on a superficial level. In many of the recent chamber judgments, the Court pays only lip-service to the right to data protection, if it even mentions it at all.[622]

With Judge von Danwitz acting as rapporteur in the three most recent Grand Chamber judgments on data retention, it would seem that the approach of two separate rights of Articles 7 and 8 CFR has been consolidated. However, while they are still highlighted as such, the rights to privacy and data protection are not assessed independently anymore. Rather, a violation of either also seems to lead to a violation of the other.[623] In this regard there would have still been plenty of opportunity to further explore the differences of both rights, rather than consolidating the case law and merely referring back to the standards established.

3.3 Case Law on Article 8(1) and (3) CFR

Concerning Article 8(3) CFR, which stipulates the requirement of control by the data protection supervisory authorities, the Court has strengthened their role since it first engaged with the rules under the first generation of EU data protection legislation. In fact, the legislator, when drafting the second generation of the EU data protection legislation, implemented much of the Court's jurisprudence in Chapters VI GDPR, DPR-EU and LED.[624]

I will, firstly, consider the case law on the independence of the supervisory authorities (Sect. 3.3.1), which the Court has developed over the course of several cases and found that it must entail complete independence from the entities they supervise. Secondly, I will turn to the individual dimension of the right contained in Article 8(1) and (3) CFR, which the Court has emphasised in its more recent case law (Sect. 3.3.2).

---

[621] Cf. also González Fuster 2014b, pp. 267 et seq. Similarly, albeit from the perspective of privacy, Nettesheim 2014, MN. 59–75, esp. MN. 74 et seq.

[622] Cf. ECJ, Joined Cases C-141/12 and C-372/12 YS and Others, Judgment of 17 July 2014; ECJ, Case C-212/13 Ryneš, Judgment of 11 December 2014; ECJ, Case C-73/16 Puškár, Judgment of 27 September 2017; ECJ, Case C-434/16 Nowak, Judgment of 20 December 2017; with the notable exception of ECJ, Case C-580/13 Coty Germany, Judgment of 16 July 2015.

[623] Particularly stark in ECJ, Joined Cases C-511/18, C-512/18 and C-520/18 La Quadrature du Net, Judgment of 6 October 2020, paras 164 and 166, as I have pointed out above Sect. 3.2.8.16.

[624] For an in-depth analysis of the case law on supervisory authorities in general and its implementation in the GDPR, cf. Bieker 2016.

3.3.1 Independence of the Supervisory Authorities

The supervisory authorities were established in EU law with the DPD in 1995. Twelve years later, the Commission brought the first cases concerning their status before the ECJ in a series of actions for failure to fulfil obligations according to Article 258 TFEU. This first line of cases concerned the independence of supervisory authorities from those it supervised, i.e. any oversight from or cooperation with public or private entities, which I will consider in the following (Sect. 3.3.1.1). Furthermore, I will address the question of horizontal independence of the supervisory authorities, i.e. the independence from each other when enforcing the rules of the secondary EU data protection legislation (Sect. 3.3.1.2), as addressed by the Court with regard to Article 8(3) CFR.

3.3.1.1 Vertical Independence

In its first judgment concerning the status of the supervisory authorities in 2010, the Court found that the high level of protection of the right to data protection was ensured in practice by these authorities, which it termed 'the guardians [...] of those fundamental rights'.[625] It thereby rejected the approach advanced by AG Mazák, who had advocated for a more restrictive interpretation of the notion of complete independence with regard to the fact that the supervisory authorities were part of the executive and oversight over them concerned the monitoring whether they carried out their functions rationally, lawfully and proportionately.[626] The AG had based his argument on a negative definition of independence to be achieved on a case-by-case basis and the supposed failure of the Commission to prove that the system of oversight in Germany did not work or that the competent oversight authorities abused their powers.[627]

The Court found that due to the supervisory authorities' purpose to protect the fundamental rights of individuals, their decision-making had to be completely independent from influence not only of those it supervised, i.e. both the public and the private sector, but also more generally from influence or pressure, whether direct

[625] ECJ, Case C-518/07 European Commission v Federal Republic of Germany, Judgment of 9 March 2010, ECLI:EU:C:2010:125, para 23.

[626] ECJ, Case C-518/07 European Commission v Federal Republic of Germany, Opinion of AG Mazàk of 22 October 2009, ECLI:EU:C:2009:694, paras 13–18 and 30.

[627] Ibid., paras 22–24 and 34. The AG upheld his view in the following Opinion, but did ultimately find the system of oversight to not fulfil his more restrictive notion of independence, cf. ECJ, Case C-614/10 European Commission v Republic of Austria, Opinion of AG Mazàk of 3 July 2012, ECLI:EU:C:2012:406, paras 25–28 and 45; unlike the Court he, again, did not assess Article 8(3) CFR, but restricted his review to the implementation of the DPD.

or indirect,[628] as now included expressly in the secondary legislation, which I have introduced in the previous chapter.[629]

While the Court assessed its first judgment concerning the supervisory authorities from the perspective of fundamental rights, it did not expressly mention the Charter, even though it had already become legally binding.[630] However, it linked the requirement of *complete* independence in the secondary legislation to Article 8(3) CFR in the subsequent cases[631] and thus interpreted the scope of the primary law broadly.

In its 2017 Opinion 1/15 the Court even applied the standards of Article 8(3) CFR to the Canadian authority tasked with supervision of the handling of the data under the PNR agreement. Like the AG, the Grand Chamber found that it was not sufficiently ensured that there would be independent oversight, as it was possible that an authority subordinate to another supervisory authority, which could instruct the former, would be in charge of supervision.[632] This illustrates the importance the ECJ attaches to the independence of supervisory authorities in order to fulfil their role as guardians of the rights under Articles 7 and 8 CFR and to enforce the EU data protection legislation.

3.3.1.2 Horizontal Independence

As the system of cooperation between the supervisory authorities changed substantively with the introduction of the second generation of the secondary EU data protection legislation,[633] a new facet concerning the independence of supervisory authorities has now come into focus. This relates to the question of whether Article 8(3) CFR requires that the authorities can operate independently from one another. As the Court has, so far, interpreted the notion of independence broadly, the introduction of a lead supervisory authority under Articles 56 and 60 GDPR and the binding dispute

---

[628] ECJ, Case C-518/07 Commission v Germany, Judgment of 9 March 2010, paras 19, 30 and 36 et seq.; ECJ, Case C-614/10 European Commission v Republic of Austria, Judgment of 16 October 2012, ECLI:EU:C:2012:631, paras 41, 43, 55 and 61–63; ECJ, Case C-288/12 European Commission v Hungary, Judgment of 8 April 2014, ECLI:EU:C:2014:237, paras 51–55 and 59 et seq. The latter had also been outlined by AG Wathelet in ECJ, Case C-288/12 European Commission v Hungary, Opinion of AG Wathelet of 10 December 2013, ECLI:EU:C:2013:816, paras 64–74 and 79–83.

[629] Cf. Chap. 2, Sect. 2.3.3.5.

[630] ECJ, Case C-518/07 Commission v Germany, Judgment of 9 March 2010. It took the Court exactly another eight months to apply the Charter in *Schecke and Eifert*, discussed above in Sect. 3.2.6.

[631] ECJ, Case C-614/10 Commission v Austria, Judgment of 16 October 2012, para 36; ECJ, Case C-288/12 Commission v Hungary, Judgment of 8 April 2014, para 47. The Court, here, as well as in *Schrems*, also mentioned Article 16(2) TFEU, cf. ECJ, Case C-362/14 Schrems, Judgment of 6 October 2015, para 40.

[632] ECJ, Avis 1/15, Opinion of 26 July 2017, paras 228–231; ECJ, Avis 1/15, Opinion of AG Mengozzi, paras 306–316.

[633] Cf. the overview in Chap. 2, Sect. 2.3.3.5; for an analysis of the new cooperation and consistency mechanism, cf. Bieker 2016, pp. 129–134.

settlement by the EDPB according to Articles 65 et seq. GDPR may collide with this facet of horizontal independence.

In the case *Wirtschaftsakademie*, the referring national court questioned whether a supervisory authority could exercise its powers under Article 28(3) DPD (corresponding to Article 58 GDPR), where the controller had an establishment in a different Member State, without being bound by a previous assessment by the supervisory authority of the other Member State.[634] The Court, in its 2018 judgment, followed an argument similar to that advanced by AG Bot[635] and found that Article 28(6) DPD only contained a general obligation concerning cooperation, but awarded neither priority with regard to an intervention by a supervisory authority nor an obligation of one supervisory authority to comply with the position of another supervisory authority.[636]

The Court then, as it had already done in its 2015 *Schrems* judgment,[637] held that under Article 8(3) CFR each supervisory authority was competent to check whether the processing of personal data within the territory of its own Member State complied with the requirements of the data protection legislation.[638] Thus, each supervisory authority had to investigate any claims brought by data subjects with complete independence.[639]

While AG Bot had not mentioned Article 8(3) CFR at all,[640] the Court, in this last paragraph referred only to the secondary legislation and not Article 8(3) CFR.[641] Though this might have been an unintentional oversight, this omission could also be read as implying that this independence from other supervisory authorities is, in the opinion of the Court, not a requirement of the primary, but only the secondary law and could thus be revised by a change in the secondary data protection legislation.

While the GDPR lays down substantial obligations of cooperation between the supervisory authorities, as I laid out in Chap. 2,[642] it still links the competences and tasks of the national supervisory authorities to the territory of their Member State under Articles 55(1) and 57(1)(a) GDPR. According to Article 56(1) GDPR, a national supervisory authority may decide to act as lead authority and, under Article

---

[634] ECJ, Case C-210/16 Unabhängiges Landeszentrum für Datenschutz Schleswig-Holstein v Wirtschaftsakademie Schleswig-Holstein GmbH, Judgment of 5 June 2018, ECLI:EU:C:2018:388, para 65.

[635] ECJ, Case C-210/16 Unabhängiges Landeszentrum für Datenschutz Schleswig-Holstein v Wirtschaftsakademie Schleswig-Holstein GmbH, Opinion of AG Bot of 24 October 2017, ECLI:EU:C:2017:796, paras 133–136.

[636] ECJ, Case C-210/16 Wirtschaftsakademie Schleswig-Holstein, Judgment of 5 June 2018, para 69.

[637] ECJ, Case C-362/14 Schrems, Judgment of 6 October 2015, para 47.

[638] ECJ, Case C-210/16 Wirtschaftsakademie Schleswig-Holstein, Judgment of 5 June 2018, para 71.

[639] Ibid., para 72.

[640] ECJ, Case C-210/16 Wirtschaftsakademie Schleswig-Holstein, Opinion of AG Bot.

[641] ECJ, Case C-210/16 Wirtschaftsakademie Schleswig-Holstein, Judgment of 5 June 2018, para 72.

[642] Cf. Chap. 2, Sect. 2.3.3.5.

60(1) and (3) GDPR, has to endeavour to reach a consensus with the other supervisory authorities and take their position duly into account. When consensus is reached, the other supervisory authorities are bound by the decision of the lead supervisory authority according to Article 60(6) GDPR.[643] When there is no agreement, the consistency mechanism of Articles 63 et seqq. GDPR is triggered and the Board has to adopt a binding decision according to Article 65(1)(a) GDPR.

Lynskey has argued that such a binding decision would limit the supervisory authorities' independence, as they would be bound to implement this decision.[644] Arguing that the supervisory authority could only ignore the decision, if it did not want to comply, she overlooks the fact that the supervisory authority concerned, as addressee of such a decision, could challenge it with an annulment action according to Article 263 TFEU before the ECJ,[645] as pointed out in recital 142 GDPR. This possibility would be a mitigating factor regarding the encroachment on independence.[646] Lynskey also concludes that this notion of independence, while implemented in the DPD, is not a violation of Article 8(3) CFR as it improves the harmonisation and effectiveness of the EU data protection legislation,[647] which the Court found to be the objective of independence.

In *Wirtschaftsakademie*, the Court further held that Article 8(3) CFR required that each supervisory authority had to be able to carry out investigations on its own territory.[648] This has not changed with the GDPR. The other observations of the Court concerning cooperation were based on the secondary law, which at that time only foresaw a very general obligation to cooperate, which, of course, has been reformed considerably with new secondary legislation.

In the recent *Facebook Ireland* judgment, the Court stressed that beside the monitoring and enforcing of the application of the GDPR, supervisory authorities also had the task of cooperation under Article 57(1)(g) GDPR.[649] It considered the actions, which the concerned supervisory authority, i.e. the authority that is not the lead, could still take and, in substance, followed the detailed analysis of AG Bobek.[650] The Court highlighted the exceptions to the rule that the lead supervisory authority is competent, which are found in Article 56(2) GDPR for cases where the subject matter relates only to an establishment in the Member State of the supervisory authority concerned, and in Article 66 GDPR, which contains the urgency procedure.[651] However, even

---

643 This consensus is considered to be reached when there are no objections within a four-week period.

644 Lynskey 2017, p. 276.

645 Cf. also already Chap. 2, Sect. 2.3.3.5.

646 Bieker 2016, p. 133.

647 Lynskey 2017, pp. 276 et seq.; also cf. Ducuing et al. 2018, p. 552.

648 ECJ, Case C-210/16 Wirtschaftsakademie Schleswig-Holstein, Judgment of 5 June 2018, paras 50–52.

649 ECJ, Case C-645/19 Facebook Ireland Limited and Others v Gegevensbeschermingsautoriteit, Judgment of 15 June 2021, ECLI:EU:C:2021:483, para 48.

650 ECJ, Case C-645/19 Facebook Ireland Limited and Others v Gegevensbeschermingsautoriteit, Opinion of AG Bobek of 13 January 2021, ECLI:EU:C:2021:5, paras 39–140.

651 ECJ, Case C-645/19 Facebook Ireland, Judgment of 15 June 2021, paras 57–59.

under the default case of the competence of the lead supervisory authority, there was still the obligation of close cooperation.[652]

The fact that a concerned supervisory authority could still bring legal proceedings against violations under Article 58(5) GDPR the Court found not to be in violation of Article 8 CFR.[653] Here, it only considered Article 8(1) CFR and made no reference to its third paragraph. It held that the allocation of competences to adopt decisions still placed an obligation to contribute to and provide a high level of protection for individuals on each supervisory authority.[654] The Court emphasised that the obligation of sincere and effective cooperation was the necessary flipside of the shared competences of the supervisory authorities to ensure the consistent application of the GDPR.[655] Therefore, from this ruling, it does not transpire that the provisions on cooperation impede the complete independence of the supervisory authorities, as enshrined in Article 8(3) CFR.

3.3.2 *Substantive Right of Individuals*

After the initial set of infringement proceedings initiated by the Commission, it took a while before the Court ruled on the individual rights dimension of Article 8(1) and (3) CFR. In the 2014 judgment *Digital Rights Ireland*, the Grand Chamber held that the failure to include an obligation to store the relevant data within the EU, as observed by AG Cruz Villalón, did not conform to Article 8(3) CFR, which required that a supervisory authority can enforce compliance with the rules of data protection and data security and which was of paramount importance for the protection of individuals.[656] With this finding the Court, for the first time, clarified that Article 8(3) CFR contains a fundamental right, which individuals can invoke, rather than just an organisational principle.

In the subsequent *Schrems* case, the Court held that the obligation of Article 28(1) DPD (corresponding to Articles 51 et seq. and 55–59 GDPR), which requires the establishment of independent supervisory authorities, was also laid down in EU primary law, namely Article 8(1) and (3) CFR and was aimed at strengthening the protection of individuals.[657] Just like AG Bot,[658] the Court stressed that the supervisory authorities were a crucial part in the system for the protection of individuals with

---

[652] Ibid., para 63.

[653] Ibid., para 66.

[654] Ibid., paras 67 et seq.

[655] Ibid., paras 71 et seq.

[656] ECJ, Joined Cases C-293/12 and C-594/12 Digital Rights Ireland and Seitlinger and Others, Judgment of 8 April 2014, para 68; ECJ, Joined Cases C-293/12 and C-594/12 Digital Rights Ireland and Seitlinger and Others, Opinion of AG Cruz Villalón, paras 76–79.

[657] ECJ, Case C-362/14 Schrems, Judgment of 6 October 2015, paras 40 et seq.

[658] ECJ, Case C-362/14 Schrems, Opinion of AG Bot, paras 207–210.

regard to the processing of personal data.[659] However, unlike the AG, who argued that independent supervision was essential in order to guarantee the right to data protection,[660] the Court held that the independence aimed to ensure the observance of the fundamental right to privacy[661] and thereby, just like in the case law on Article 8(1) and (2) CFR, demonstrated a limited understanding of data protection. This argument may, however, be attributable to the fact that privacy is the foundational right referred to in Article 1 DPD, which has been remedied in the second generation of EU data protection legislation. The Court nevertheless found that the possibility for data subjects to lodge a claim with the supervisory authority was guaranteed by Articles 8(1) and (3) CFR.[662]

In *Schrems II* the Court held that while the primary responsibility of the supervisory authorities was to monitor the application of the GDPR and enforce its rules, it also had to handle complaints lodged under Articles 57(1)(f) and 77(1) GDPR "with all due diligence".[663] When a supervisory authority found that a processing operation was not in accordance with the respective rules, it had to suspend or prohibit the transfer under Article 58(2)(f) and (j) GDPR.[664] However, the supervisory authorities were fully bound by the Commission adequacy decisions under Article 45(1) GDPR.[665] As it had already established in *Schrems*, the Court held that the supervisory authorities could not invalidate an act of EU law themselves,[666] and where they did not concur with the claim of the data subject, the data subject had to have the possibility to challenge that decision in a court under Article 28(3) DPD (now Article 78 GDPR), which could then submit a preliminary reference to the Court.[667] Conversely, if the supervisory authority considered the claim well founded and an EU measure invalid, Article 8(3) CFR required that the authority could challenge the measure before national courts.[668]

659 ECJ, Case C-362/14 Schrems, Judgment of 6 October 2015, para 41.

660 ECJ, Case C-362/14 Schrems, Opinion of AG Bot, esp. para 207.

661 ECJ, Case C-362/14 Schrems, Judgment of 6 October 2015, para 42.

662 Ibid., paras 57 et seq.

663 ECJ, C-311/18 Facebook Ireland and Schrems—Schrems II, Judgment of 16 July 2020, paras 108 et seq. and 112.

664 Ibid., para 113.

665 Ibid., paras 115–117 and 156.

666 Ibid., paras 118 and 157. Conversely, Kuner argues that it was not even for the supervisory authorities to balance the relevant fundamental rights, as that was better left to the courts, cf. Kuner 2015, pp. 39 et seq.

667 ECJ, C-311/18 Facebook Ireland and Schrems—Schrems II, Judgment of 16 July 2020, paras 119 et seq.; ECJ, Case C-362/14 Schrems, Judgment of 6 October 2015, paras 62–64.

668 ECJ, Case C-362/14 Schrems, Judgment of 6 October 2015, para 65.

3.3.3 Conclusions on the Case Law on Article 8(1) and (3) CFR

The Court, from the outset and in opposition to the advice of the AG, interpreted the notion of independence broadly. However, this independence, as the Court has made clear, is not an end in itself. Rather, it aims to ensure that the supervisory authorities are able to enforce the high level of protection required by the secondary EU data protection legislation. Therefore, it seems likely that the Court will not take issue with the new duties of coordination and cooperation introduced in the second generation of EU data protection legislation from the perspective of the Charter.

The broad notion of independence, in the conception of the Court, does not only apply to the supervisory authorities in the EU, but, in the context of transnational data transfers, even extends to supervisory bodies of third countries. This further elucidates the Court's underlying rationale: as the data moves outside the EU, there must be bodies, which ensure that the right of the individual concerned under Article 8(1) and (3) CFR is enforced. Therefore, this right also has a strong individual dimension and is not a mere organisational principle.

The Court has also explicitly held, that the individual has a right to lodge a complaint with a supervisory authority under Article 8(1) and (3) CFR. Thus, the organisational aspect of the right to data protection under Article 8(3) CFR, much like Article 47 CFR, can be enforced by an individual, as their complaints must be effectively investigated by the competent supervisory authority.

3.4 Conclusions on the Case Law of the CJEU

The case law of the CJEU on Article 8(1) and (2) CFR, on a more general level, perhaps illustrates that a substantial effort is required in order to emancipate those rights that have been awarded a greater or independent scope, from the ECHR. The Court only slowly shifted its jurisprudence with regard to Article 8(1) and (2) CFR in *Schecke and Eifert*, after the Charter entered into force and still does not fully engage with the principles and characteristics of the secondary law. It seems that the Court has been straining to maintain coherence between its own case law and that of the ECtHR. However, this has also tethered it to the Convention and could be a factor in the Court's reluctance to explore the EU data protection legislation in depth. This becomes even more apparent, when considering the case law on Article 8(1) and (3) CFR: even though it did not expressly refer to the then applicable Charter in its first judgment, the Court has always interpreted Article 8(3) CFR in accordance with the relevant secondary legislation. However, as the supervisory authorities were established under EU law and neither the ECHR nor the ECtHR have addressed them, the Court was free to establish its own path.

Although the Court has identified many issues relating to the processing of personal data, it has addressed structural issues only fleetingly in very limited instances, i.e. with regard to the requirements on the storage of communications data in *Digital Rights Ireland* and *Tele2 Sverige*.[669] While it is positive that the ECJ considers the technical and organisational measures, especially in the proportionality assessment, it has not yet consistently linked these—or the right to data protection in general—to the principles of the secondary EU data protection legislation.

However, the Court has interpreted Article 8(3) CFR—which, through its institutional provision, has a focus on the structural dimension of data protection—broadly and consistently strengthened the position of the supervisory authorities. From this case law, it transpires that the Court regards the supervisory authorities as a central element in the institutional system of the EU with regard to data protection. The independence that is awarded to them is therefore not an end in itself, but rather a necessary structural guarantee to enable them to pursue their intended objective to uphold fundamental rights with regard to the processing of data. Furthermore, the Court has made clear that Article 8(3) CFR is not only an institutional requirement, but, in combination with Article 8(1) CFR, also a substantive fundamental right, which can be enforced by the individual.

Yet, I will argue in Chap. 5 that the structural dimension of data protection law extends well beyond these isolated issues. While, of course, the Court is not tasked with an elaboration of the rationale behind each fundamental right, but rather has to solve the specific cases brought before it, I have shown through the preceding analysis that the underlying conceptualization of data protection directly affects the outcome of a case. In the following chapter, I will turn to the doctrinal debate on the right to data protection and consider whether the dogmatic criticism of the Court's interpretation of the right to data protection can remedy the shortcomings of the jurisprudence.

References

Articles, Books and Chapters in Books

Azoulai L, van der Sluis M (2016) Institutionalizing personal data protection in times of global institutional distrust: Schrems. CMLRev 53:1343–1372.

Bieker F (2015) The Court of Justice of the European Union, Data Retention and the Rights to Data Protection and Privacy—Where Are We Now? In: Camenisch J, Fischer-Hübner S, Hansen M (eds) Privacy and Identity Management for the Future Internet in the Age of Globalisation. Springer, Cham/Heidelberg/New York/Dordrecht/London, pp. 73–86.

Bieker F (2016) Enforcing Data Protection Law – the Role of the Supervisory Authorities in Theory and Practice. In: Lehmann A, Whitehouse D, Fischer-Hübner S, Fritsch L, Raab C (eds) Privacy and Identity Management. Facing up to Next Steps. Springer, Cham, pp. 125–139.

[669] It had already considered access controls and the decentralization of databases in ECJ, Case C-291/12 Schwarz, Judgment of 17 October 2013, paras 54–62; only the latter point was mentioned in ECJ, Case C-291/12 Schwarz, Opinion of AG Mengozzi, paras 56 et seq.; ECJ, Case C-524/06 Huber, Judgment of 16 December 2008, paras 61 et seq. and 66.

Bock K, Engeler M (2016) Die verfassungsrechtliche Wesensgehaltsgarantie als absolute Schranke im Datenschutzrecht [The Essence of Fundamental Rights as Absolute Limit in Data Protection Law]. DVBl 593–599.
Boehm F, Cole M (2014) Data Retention after the Judgement of the Court of Justice of the European Union. Münster/Luxemburg. http://www.zar.kit.edu/DATA/veroeffentlichungen/237_237_Boehm_Cole-Data_Retention_Study-June_2014_1a1c2f6_9906a8c.pdf. Accessed 28 July 2021.
Boehme-Neßler V (2014) Das Recht auf Vergessenwerden – Ein neues Internet-Grundrecht im Europäischen Recht [The Right to be Forgotten – A New Internet Right of European Law]. NVwZ 825–830.
Bossong R (2017) Passenger Name Records – from Canada back to the EU. Verfassungsblog. https://verfassungsblog.de/passenger-name-records-from-canada-back-to-the-eu/. Accessed 28 July 2021.
Brkan M (2019a) Do algorithms rule the world? Algorithmic decision-making and data protection in the framework of the GDPR and beyond. IJLIT 27:91–121.
Brkan M (2019b) The Essence of the Fundamental Rights to Privacy and Data Protection: Finding the Way Through the Maze of the CJEU's Constitutional Reasoning. GLJ 20:864–883.
Brouwer E, Zuiderveen Borgesius F (2015) Access to Personal Data and the Right to Good Governance during Asylum Procedures after the CJEU's YS. and M. and S. Judgment (C-141/12 and C-372/12). European Journal of Migration and Law 17:259–272.
Cameron I (2017) Balancing data protection and law enforcement needs: Tele2 Sverige and Watson. CMLRev 54:1467–1496.
Celeste E (2019) The Court of Justice and the Ban on Bulk Data Retention. EuConst 15:134–157.
Churches G, Zalnieriute M (2020) A Groundhog Day in Brussels. Verfassungsblog. https://verfassungsblog.de/a-groundhog-day-in-bruessels/. Accessed 28 July 2021.
Classen C D (2004) Joined Cases C-465/00, C-138/01 and C-139/01, Österreichischer Rundfunk, Judgment of 20 May 2003, Full Court, [2003] ECR I-4989 [Case Comment]. CMLRev 41:1377–1385.
Classen C D (2014) Datenschutz ja – aber wie? [Data Protection, yes – but how?]. EuR 441–448.
Cohen N (2015) The Privacy Follies: A Look Back at the CJEU's Invalidation of the EU/US Safe Harbor Framework. EDPL 3:240–244.
Cole M, Vandendriessche A (2016) From Digital Rights Ireland and Schrems in Luxembourg to Zakharov and Szabó/Vissy in Strasbourg. EDPL 1:121–129.
Coudert F, Werkers E (2008) In The Aftermath of the Promusicae Case: How to Strike the Balance? IJLIT 18:50–71.
De Hert P, Gutwirth S (2009) Data Protection in the Case Law of Strasbourg and Luxemburg: Constitutionalisation in Action. In: Gutwirth S, Poullet Y, De Hert P, de Terwangne C, Nouwt S (eds) Reinventing Data Protection? Springer, Dordrecht, pp. 3–44.
de S-O-l'E Lasser M (2009) Judicial Deliberations: A Comparative Analysis of Transparency and Legitimacy. OUP, Oxford.
Dimitropoulos G (2015) The CJEU's Decision on the Data Retention Directive: Transnational Aspects and the Push for Harmonisation. In: Hess B, Mariottini C (eds) Protecting Privacy in Private International and Procedural Law and by Data Protection. Nomos, Baden-Baden, pp. 71–79.
Ducuing C, Schroers J, Kindt E (2018) The Wirtschaftsakademie Fan Page Decision: A Landmark on Joint Controllership – A Challenge for Supervisory Authorities Competences. EDPL 4:547–553.
Eichenhofer J (2016) „e-Privacy" im europäischen Grundrechtsschutz: Das „Schrems"-Urteil des EuGH "[ePrivacy in European Fundamental Rights Protection: The Schrems Judgment of the ECJ]. EuR 76–89.
Giegerich T (2014) Spät kommt Ihr, doch Ihr kommt: Warum wird die Grundrechtskonformität der Vorratsdatenspeicherung erst nach acht Jahren geklärt? [You are late, but here you are: Why has the compatibility of bulk data retention with fundamental rights only been addressed after eight years?]. ZEuS 3–17.

González Fuster G (2014a) The Emergence of Personal Data Protection as a Fundamental Right of the EU. Springer, Cham/Heidelberg/New York/Dordrecht/London.
González Fuster G (2014b) Fighting for Your Right to What Exactly – The Convoluted Case Law of the EU Court of Justice on Privacy and/or Personal Data Protection. Birkbeck Law Review 2:263–278.
González Fuster G, Gellert R (2012) The Fundamental Right of Data Protection in the European Union: in Search of an Uncharted Right. International Review of Law, Computers & Technology 26:73–82.
Grabenwarter C (2014) European Convention on Human Rights Commentary. C.H. Beck, Munich.
Hijmans H (2017) PNR Agreement EU-Canada Scrutinised. EDPL 3:406–412.
Hustinx P (2017) EU Data Protection Law: The Review of Directive 95/46/EC and the General Data Protection Regulation. In: Cremona M (ed) New Technologies and EU Law. OUP, Oxford, pp. 123–173.
Irion K (2020) Schrems II and Surveillance: Third Countries' National Security Powers in the Purview of EU Law. European Law Blog. https://europeanlawblog.eu/2020/07/24/schrems-ii-and-surveillance-third-countries-national-security-powers-in-the-purview-of-eu-law/. Accessed 28 July 2021
Jozwiak M (2016) Balancing the Rights to Data Protection and Freedom of Expression and Information by the Court of Justice of the European Union. MJ 404–420.
Kokott J, Sobotta C (2014) The Distinction between Privacy and Data Protection in the Jurisprudence of the CJEU and the ECtHR. In: Hijmans H, Kranenborg H (eds) Data Protection 2014: How to Restore Trust? Contributions in Honour of Peter Hustinx. Intersentia, Cambridge, pp. 83–95.
Kühling J (2014) Rückkehr des Rechts: Verpflichtung von "Google & Co." zu Datenschutz [Return of the Law: Data Protection Obligations of Google & Co.]. EuZW 527–532.
Kühling J, Heberlein J (2016) EuGH „reloaded": „unsafe harbor" USA vs. „Datenfestung" EU [ECJ reloaded: unsafe harbor USA vs data fortress EU]. NVwZ 7–12.
Kuner C (2015) The Court of Justice of the EU Judgment on Data Protection and Internet Search Engines. In: Hess B, Mariottini C (eds) Protecting Privacy in Private International and Procedural Law and by Data Protection. Nomos, Baden-Baden, pp. 19–44.
Kuner C (2017a) Data Protection, Data Transfers and International Agreements. Verfassungsblog. https://verfassungsblog.de/data-protection-data-transfers-and-international-agreements-the-cjeus-opinion-115/. Accessed 28 July 2021.
Kuner C (2017b) Reality and Illusion in EU Data Transfer Regulation Post Schrems. GLJ 18:881–918.
Kuner C (2018) International agreements, data protection, and EU fundamental rights on the international stage. CMLRev 55:857–882.
Kuner C (2020) The Schrems II judgment of the Court of Justice and the future of data transfer regulation. European Law Blog. https://europeanlawblog.eu/2020/07/17/the-schrems-ii-judgment-of-the-court-of-justice-and-the-future-of-data-transfer-regulation/. Accessed 28 July 2021.
Kunnert G (2014a) Das Ende der Vorratsdatenspeicherung? [The End of Bulk Data Retention?]. DuD 103–108.
Kunnert G (2014b) EuGH zur Vorratsdatenspeicherung [ECJ on Bulk Data Retention]. DuD 774–784.
Lynskey O (2014) The Data Retention Directive is incompatible with the rights to privacy and data protection and is invalid in its entirety: Digital Rights Ireland. CMLRev 51:1789–1812.
Lynskey O (2015a) Control over Personal Data in a Digital Age. MLR 78:522–548
Lynskey O (2015b) The Foundations of EU Data Protection Law. OUP, Oxford.
Lynskey O (2017) The 'Europeanisation' of Data Protection Law. CYELS 19:252–286.
Marsch N (2018) Das europäische Datenschutzgrundrecht [The European Fundamental Right to Data Protection]. Mohr Siebeck, Tübingen.
Masing J (2014) RiBVerfG Masing: Vorläufige Einschätzung der "Google-Entscheidung" des EuGH [Judge Masing of the Bundesverfassungsgericht: Preliminary Assessment of the Google Judgment

of the ECJ]. Verfassungsblog. https://verfassungsblog.de/ribverfg-masing-vorlaeufige-einschaetzung-der-google-entscheidung-des-eugh/. Accessed 28 July 2021.
Milanovic M (2021) The Grand Normalization of Mass Surveillance: ECtHR Grand Chamber Judgments in Big Brother Watch and Centrum för rättvisa. EJIL:Talk! https://www.ejiltalk.org/the-grand-normalization-of-mass-surveillance-ecthr-grand-chamber-judgments-in-big-brother-watch-and-centrum-for-rattvisa/. Accessed 28 July 2021.
Møller Pedersen A, Udsen H, Sandfeld Jakobsen S (2018) Data retention in Europe – the Tele2 case and beyond. IDPL 8:160-–174.
Mysegades J (2019) Rechtsstaat sticht Software. Verfassungsblog. https://verfassungsblog.de/rechtsstaat-sticht-software/. Accessed 28 July 2021.
Nettesheim M (2014) § 9 Privatleben und Privatsphäre [Private Life and Privacy]. In: Grabenwarter C (ed) Enzyklopädie Europarecht [Encyclopedia of European Law] Band 2: Europäischer Grundrechteschutz. Nomos, Baden-Baden, pp. 387–415.
Nettesheim M (2015) The CJEU's decision on the Data Retention Directive. In: Hess B, Mariottini C (eds) Protecting Privacy in Private International and Procedural Law and by Data Protection. Nomos, Baden-Baden, pp. 57–69.
Ojanen T (2014) Privacy Is More Than Just a Seven-Letter Word: The Court of Justice of the European Union Sets Constitutional Limits on Mass Surveillance. EuConst 10:528–541.
Ojanen T (2016) Making the Essence of Fundamental Rights Real: The Court of Justice of the European Union Clarifies the Structure of Fundamental Rights under the Charter [Case Note]. EuConst 12:318–329.
Pechstein M (2011) EU-Prozessrecht [EU Procedural Law], 4th edn. Mohr Siebeck, Tübingen.
Petri T (2009) EuGH: Rechtsgrundlage der EG-Richtlinie zur Vorratsdatenspeicherung [ECJ: Legal Basis of the EC Directive on Data Retention]. EuZW 214 et seq.
Röben V (2013) Grundrechtsberechtigte und -verpflichtete, Grundrechtsgeltung [Subjects and Addressees of Fundamental Rights, Application of Fundamental Rights]. In: Dörr O, Grote R, Marauhn T (eds) EMRK/GG Konkordanzkommentar [ECHR/Basic Law Commentary] 2nd edn, Band 1. Mohr Siebeck, Tübingen, pp. 253–286.
Roßnagel A (2014) Neue Maßstäbe für den Datenschutz in Europa – Folgerungen aus dem EuGH-Urteil zur Vorratsdatenspeicherung [New Standards for Data Protection in Europe – Consequences from the ECJ Judgment on Bulk Data Retention]. MMR 372–377.
Sajfert J (2020) Bulk data interception/retention judgments of the CJEU – A victory and a defeat for privacy. European Law Blog. https://europeanlawblog.eu/2020/10/26/bulk-data-interception-retention-judgments-of-the-cjeu-a-victory-and-a-defeat-for-privacy/. Accessed 28 July 2021.
Sandhu A (2017) Die Tele2-Entscheidung des EuGH zur Vorratsdatenspeicherung in den Mitgliedstaaten und ihre Auswirkungen auf die Rechtslage in Deutschland und in der Europäischen Union [The Tele2 Decision of the ECJ on the Bulk Data Retention Regimes in the Member States and its Consequences for the German and European Union's Legal Orders]. EuR 453–470.
Siemen B (2004) Grundrechtsschutz durch Richtlinien / Die Fälle Österreichischer Rundfunk u.a. und Lindqvist [Fundamental Rights Protection Through Directives / The Cases of Österreichischer Rundfunk and Others and Lindqvist]. EuR 306–321.
Siemen B (2006) Datenschutz als europäisches Grundrecht [Data Protection as European Fundamental Right]. Duncker & Humblot, Berlin.
Simitis S (2009) Der EuGH und die Vorratsdatenspeicherung oder die verfehlte Kehrtwende bei der Kompetenzregelung [The ECJ and Bulk Data Retention or the Misguided Turnaround in the Allocation of Jurisdiction]. NJW 1782–1786.
Spindler G (2014) Durchbruch für ein Recht auf Vergessen(werden)? – Die Entscheidung des EuGH in Sachen Google Spain und ihre Auswirkungen auf das Datenschutz- und Zivilrecht [Breakthrough for a Right to be Forgotten? – The ECJ Decision in the Google Spain Case and its Consequences for Data Protection and Civil Law]. JZ 981–991.
Streinz R (2018) EU-Grundrechte-Charta [EU Fundamental Rights Charter] 2000 Artikel 8. In: Streinz R (ed) Kommentar EUV/AEUV [Commentary TEU/TFEU], 3rd edn. C.H. Beck, Munich.

Terhechte J P (2009) Rechtsangleichung zwischen Gemeinschafts- und Unionsrecht – die Richtlinie über die Vorratsdatenspeicherung vor dem EuGH [Approximation of Laws between Community and Union Law – the Directive on Bulk Data Retention before the ECJ]. EuZW 199–204.
Tracol X (2015) Back to basics: The European Court of Justice further defined the concept of personal data and the scope of the right of data subjects to access it. CLSLR 31:112–119.
Tracol X (2016) "Invalidator" strikes back: The harbour has never been safe. CLSLR 32:345–362.
Tridimas T, Gentile G (2019) The Essence of Rights: An Unreliable Boundary? GLJ 20:794–816.
Van Alsenoy B, Koekkoek M (2015) Internet and jurisdiction after Google Spain. IDPL 5:105–120.
van der Sloot B (2017) Legal Fundamentalism: Is Data Protection Really a Fundamental Right? In: Leenes R, van Brakel R, Gutwirth S, De Hert P (eds) Data Protection and Privacy: (In)visibilities and Infrastructures. Springer, Cham, pp. 3–30.
Varju M (2014) European Union Human Rights Law. Edward Elgar, Cheltenham.
Vedaschi A (2018) Privacy and data protection versus national security in transnational flights: the EU–Canada PNR agreement. IDPL 8:124–139.
Vogiatzoglou P (2019) Mass Surveillance, Predictive Policing and the Implementation of the CJEU and ECtHR Requirement of Objectivity. EJLT 10.
Vogiatzoglou P (2020) One more time with feeling: the latest AG Opinions on data retention and national security. CiTiP Blog. https://www.law.kuleuven.be/citip/blog/one-more-time-with-feeling-the-latest-ag-opinions-on-data-retention-and-national-security/. Accessed 28 July 2021.
Vogiatzoglou P, Fantin S (2019) National and Public Security Within and Beyond the Police Directive. In: Veddor A, Schroers J, Ducuing C, Valcke P (eds) Security and Law. Legal and Ethical Aspects of Public Security, Cyber Security and Critical Infrastructure Security. Intersentia, Cambridge/Antwerp/Chicago, pp. 27–61.
von Danwitz T (2015) Die Grundrechte auf Achtung der Privatsphäre und auf Schutz personenbezogener Daten [The Fundamental Rights to the Protection of Privacy and of Personal Data]. DuD 581–585.
Wagner L-J (2013) Assoziative Anmerkungen zu den Schlussanträgen von Generalanwalt Villalón in Sachen Vorratsdatenspeicherung [Associate Remarks on the Opinion of Advocate General Villalón in the Case on Bulk Data Retention]. JuWissBlog. http://www.juwiss.de/127-2013/. Accessed 28 July 2021.
Wagner L-J (2015) Der Datenschutz in der Europäischen Union [Data Protection in the European Union]. Jan Sramek Verlag, Vienna.
Woods L (2017) Transferring personal data outside the EU. EU Law Analysis. https://eulawanalysis.blogspot.com/2017/08/transferring-personal-data-outside-eu.html. Accessed 28 July 2021.
Woods L (2019) The AG Opinion in Schrems II: Facebook, national security and data protection law. EU Law Analysis. http://eulawanalysis.blogspot.com/2019/12/the-ag-opinion-in-schrems-ii-facebook.html. Accessed 27 July 2021.
Zalnieriute M (2021) Procedural Fetishism and Mass Surveillance under the ECHR. Verfassungsblog. https://verfassungsblog.de/big-b-v-uk/. Accessed 28 July 2021.
Zanfir-Fortuna G (2016) Analysis of the AG Opinion in the "PNR Canada" Case: unlocking an "unprecedented and delicate" matter. pdpEcho. https://pdpecho.com/2016/09/12/analysis-of-the-ag-opinion-in-the-pnr-canada-case-unlocking-an-unprecedented-and-delicate-matter/. Accessed 28 July 2021.

Table of Cases: Council of Europe

ECtHR, Leander v. Sweden, App. No. 9248/81, Judgment of 26 March 1987.
ECtHR [GC], Amann v. Switzerland, App. No. 27798/95, Judgment of 16 February 2000.
ECtHR [GC], Rotaru v. Romania, App. No. 28341/95, Judgment of 4 May 2000.
ECtHR, Peck v. the United Kingdom, App. No. 44647/98, Judgment of 28 January 2003.

ECtHR, Weber and Saravia v. Germany, App. No. 54934/00, Decision of 29 June 2006.
ECtHR [GC], S. and Marper v. the United Kingdom, App. Nos. 30562/04 and 30566/04, Judgment of 4 December 2008.
ECtHR [GC], Von Hannover v. Germany (No. 2), App. Nos. 40660/08 and 60641/08, Judgment of 7 February 2012.
ECtHR [GC], Roman Zakharov v. Russia, App. No. 47143/06, Judgment of 4 December 2015.
ECtHR, Szabó and Vissy v. Hungary, App. No. 37138/14, Judgment of 12 January 2016.
ECtHR, Big Brother Watch and Others v. the United Kingdom, App. Nos. 58170/13, 62322/14 and 24960/15, Judgment of 13 September 2018.
ECtHR [GC], Big Brother Watch and Others v. the United Kingdom, App. Nos. 58170/13, 62322/14 and 24960/15, Judgment of 25 May 2021.

Table of Cases: EU

ECJ, Case 29/69 Stauder v Stadt Ulm, Judgment of 12 November 1969, ECLI:EU:C:1969:57.
ECJ, Case 136/79 National Panasonic (UK) Limited v Commission of the European Communities, Judgment of 26 June 1980, ECLI:EU:C:1980:169.
ECJ, Case 145/83 Stanley George Adams v Commission of the European Communities, Judgment of 7 November 1985, ECLI:EU:C:1985:448.
ECJ, Case 140/86 Gisela Strack v Commission of the European Communities, Judgment of 7 October 1987, ECLI:EU:C:1987:427.
ECJ, Case C-260/89 Elliniki Radiophonia Tiléorassi AE and Panellinia Omospondia Syllogon Prossopikou v Dimotiki Etairia Pliroforissis and Sotirios Kouvelas and Nicolaos Avdellas and Others, Judgment of 18 June 1991, ECLI:EU:C:1991:254.
ECJ, Case C-159/90 The Society for the Protection of Unborn Children Ireland Ltd v Stephen Grogan and Others, Judgment of 4 October 1991, ECLI:EU:C:1991:378.
ECJ, Case C-155/91 Commission of the European Communities v Council of the European Communities – Framework Directive on Waste, Judgment of 17 March 1993, ECLI:EU:C:1993:98.
ECJ, Case C-280/91 Finanzamt Kassel-Goethestrasse v Viessmann KG, Judgment of 18 March 1993, ECLI:EU:C:1993:103.
ECJ, Case C-404/92 P X v Commission of the European Communities, Judgment of 5 October 1994, ECLI:EU:C:1994:361.
ECJ, Case C-404/92 P X v Commission of the European Communities, Opinion of AG Gerven of 5 October 1994, ECLI:EU:C:1994:172.
ECJ, Case C-334/95 Krüger GmbH & Co. KG v Hauptzollamt Hamburg-Jonas, Judgment of 17 July 1997, ECLI:EU:C:1997:378.
ECJ, Case C-369/98 The Queen and Minister of Agriculture, Fisheries and Food, ex parte Trevor Robert Fisher and Penny Fisher, Opinion of AG Alber of 10 February 2000, ECLI:EU:C:2000:79.
ECJ, Case C-369/98 The Queen and Minister of Agriculture, Fisheries and Food, ex parte Trevor Robert Fisher and Penny Fisher, Judgment of 14 September 2000, ECLI:EU:C:2000:443.
ECJ, Case C-101/01 Criminal proceedings against Bodil Lindqvist, Opinion of AG Tizzano of 19 September 2002, ECLI:EU:C:2002:513.
ECJ, Joined Cases C-465/00, C-138/01 and C-139/01 Rechnungshof (C-465/00) v Österreichischer Rundfunk and Others and Christa Neukomm (C-138/01) and Joseph Lauermann (C-139/01) v Österreichischer Rundfunk, Opinion of AG Tizzano of 14 November 2002, ECLI:EU:C:2002:662.
ECJ, Case C-101/01 Criminal proceedings against Bodil Lindqvist, Judgment of 6 November 2003, ECLI:EU:C:2003:596.

ECJ, Joined Cases C-465/00, C-138/01 and C-139/01 Rechnungshof (C-465/00) v Österreichischer Rundfunk and Others and Christa Neukomm (C-138/01) and Joseph Lauermann (C-139/01) v Österreichischer Rundfunk, Judgment of 20 May 2003, ECLI:EU:C:2003:294.
ECJ, Joined Cases C-317/04 and C-318/04 European Parliament v Council of the European Union (C-317/04) and Commission of the European Communities (C-318/04) – PNR, Opinion of AG Léger of 22 November 2005, ECLI:EU:C:2005:710.
ECJ, Joined Cases C-317/04 and C-318/04 European Parliament v Council of the European Union (C-317/04) and Commission of the European Communities (C-318/04) – PNR, Judgment of 30 May 2006, ECLI:EU:C:2006:346.
ECJ, Case C-438/05 International Transport Workers' Federation and Finnish Seamen's Union v Viking Line ABP and OÜ Viking Line Eesti, Judgment of 11 December 2007, ECLI:EU:C:2007:772.
ECJ, Case C-275/06 Productores de Música de España (Promusicae) v Telefónica de España SAU Opinion of AG Kokott of 18 July 2007, ECLI:EU:C:2007:454.
ECJ, Case C-524/06 Heinz Huber v Bundesrepublik Deutschland, Judgment of 16 December 2008, ECLI:EU:C:2008:724.
ECJ, Case C-524/06 Heinz Huber v Bundesrepublik Deutschland, Opinion of AG Poiares Maduro of 3 April 2008, ECLI:EU:C:2008:194.
ECJ, Case C-301/06 Ireland v European Parliament and Council of the European Union, Opinion of AG Bot of 14 October 2008, ECLI:EU:C:2008:558.
ECJ, Case C-275/06 Productores de Música de España (Promusicae) v Telefónica de España SAU Judgment of 29 January 2008, ECLI:EU:C:2008:54.
ECJ, Case C-73/07 Tietosuojavaltuutettu v Satakunnan Markkinapörssi Oy and Satamedia Oy, Opinion of AG Kokott of 8 May 2008, ECLI:EU:C:2008:266.
ECJ, Case C-73/07 Tietosuojavaltuutettu v Satakunnan Markkinapörssi Oy and Satamedia Oy, Judgment of 16 December 2008, ECLI:EU:C:2008:727.
ECJ, Case C-553/07 College van burgemeester en wethouders van Rotterdam v M. E. E. Rijkeboer, Opinion of AG Ruiz-Jarabo Colomer of 22 December 2008, ECLI:EU:C:2008:773.
ECJ, Case C-553/07 College van burgemeester en wethouders van Rotterdam v M. E. E. Rijkeboer, Judgment of 7 May 2009, ECLI:EU:C:2010:662.
ECJ, Case C-28/08 P European Commission v The Bavarian Lager Co. Ltd., Opinion of AG Sharpston of 15 October 2009, ECLI:EU:C:2009:624.
ECJ, Case C-518/07 European Commission v Federal Republic of Germany, Opinion of AG Mazàk of 22 October 2009, ECLI:EU:C:2009:694.
ECJ, Case C-301/06 Ireland v European Parliament and Council of the European Union, Judgment of 10 February 2009, ECI:EU:C:2009:68.
ECJ, Case C-557/07 LSG-Gesellschaft zur Wahrnehmung von Leistungsschutzrechten GmbH v Tele2 Telecommunication GmbH, Order of 19 February 2009, ECLI:EU:C:2009:107.
ECJ, Case C-518/07 European Commission v Federal Republic of Germany, Judgment of 9 March 2010, ECLI:EU:C:2010:125.
ECJ, Case C-28/08 P European Commission v The Bavarian Lager Co. Ltd., Judgment of 29 June 2010, ECLI:EU:C:2010:378.
ECJ, Joined Cases C-92/09 and C-93/09 Volker und Markus Schecke GbR (C-92/09) and Hartmut Eifert (C-93/09) v Land Hessen, Judgment of 9 November 2010, ECLI:EU:C:2010:662.
ECJ, Joined Cases C-92/09 and C-93/09 Volker und Markus Schecke GbR (C-92/09) and Hartmut Eifert (C-93/09) v Land Hessen, Opinion of AG Sharpston of 17 June 2010, ECLI:EU:C:2010:353.
ECJ, Joined Cases C-468/10 and C-469/10 Asociación Nacional de Establecimientos Financieros de Crédito (ASNEF) (C-468/10) and Federación de Comercio Electrónico y Marketing Directo (FECEMD) (C-469/10) v Administración del Estado, Judgment of 24 November 2011, ECLI:EU:C:2011:777.
ECJ, Case C-461/10 Bonnier Audio AB and Others v Perfect Communication Sweden AB, Opinion of AG Jääskinen of 17 November 2011, ECLI:EU:C:2011:753.

ECJ, Case C-534/09 Deutsche Telekom AG v Bundesrepublik Deutschland, Judgment of 5 May 2011, ECLI:EU:C:2011:279.

ECJ, Case C-70/10 Scarlet Extended SA v Société belge des auteurs, compositeurs et éditeurs SCRL (SABAM), Judgment of 24 November 2011, ECLI:EU:C:2011:771.

ECJ, Case C-70/10 Scarlet Extended SA v Société belge des auteurs, compositeurs et éditeurs SCRL (SABAM), Opinion of AG Cruz Villalón of 14 April 2011, ECLI:EU:C:2011:255.

ECJ, Case C-360/10 Belgische Vereniging van Auteurs, Componisten en Uitgevers CVBA (SABAM) v Netlog NV, Judgment of 16 February 2012, ECLI:EU:C:2012:85.

ECJ, Case C-461/10 Bonnier Audio AB and Others v Perfect Communication Sweden AB, Judgment of 19 April 2012, ECLI:EU:C:2012:219.

ECJ, Case C-614/10 European Commission v Republic of Austria, Opinion of AG Mazàk of 3 July 2012, ECLI:EU:C:2012:406.

ECJ, Case C-614/10 European Commission v Republic of Austria, Judgment of 16 October 2012, ECLI:EU:C:2012:631.

ECJ, Case C-617/10 Åklagaren v Hans Åkerberg Fransson, Judgment of 26 February 2013, ECLI:EU:C:2013:105.

ECJ, Joined Cases C-293/12 and C-594/12 Digital Rights Ireland Ltd (C-293/12) v Minister for Communications, Marine and Natural Resources and Others and Kärntner Landesregierung (C-594/12) and Others, Opinion of AG Cruz Villalón of 12 December 2013, ECLI:EU:C:2013:845.

ECJ, Case C-288/12 European Commission v Hungary, Opinion of AG Wathelet of 10 December 2013, ECLI:EU:C:2013:816.

ECJ, Case C-131/12 Google Spain SL and Google Inc. v Agencia Española de Protección de Datos (AEPD) and Mario Costeja González, Opinion of AG Jääskinen of 13 April 2014, ECLI:EU:C:2013:424.

ECJ, Case C-473/12 Institut professionnel des agents immobiliers (IPI) v Geoffrey Englebert and Others, Judgment of 7 November 2013, ECLI:EU:C:2013:715.

ECJ, Case C-291/12 Michael Schwarz v Stadt Bochum, Judgment of 17 October 2013, ECLI:EU:C:2013:670.

ECJ, Case C-291/12 Michael Schwarz v Stadt Bochum, Opinion of AG Mengozzi of 13 June 2013, ECLI:EU:C:2013:401.

ECJ, Joined Cases C-141/12 and C-372/12 YS (C-141/12) v Minister voor Immigratie, Integratie en Asiel and Minister voor Immigratie, Integratie en Asiel (C-372/12) v M and S, Opinion of AG Sharpston of 12 December 2013, ECLI:EU:C:2013:838.

ECJ, Joined Cases C-293/12 and C-594/12 Digital Rights Ireland Ltd (C-293/12) v Minister for Communications, Marine and Natural Resources and Others and Kärntner Landesregierung (C-594/12) and Others, Judgment of 8 April 2014, ECLI:EU:C:2014:238.

ECJ, Case C-288/12 European Commission v Hungary, Judgment of 8 April 2014, ECLI:EU:C:2014:237.

ECJ, Case C-212/13 František Ryneš v Úřad pro ochranu osobních údajů, Judgment of 11 December 2014, ECLI:EU:C:2014:2428.

ECJ, Case C-212/13 František Ryneš v Úřad pro ochranu osobních údajů, Opinion of AG Jääskinen of 10 July 2014, ECLI:EU:C:2014:2072.

ECJ, Case C-131/12 Google Spain SL and Google Inc. v Agencia Española de Protección de Datos (AEPD) and Mario Costeja González, Judgment of 13 April 2014, ECLI:EU:C:2014:317.

ECJ, Joined Cases C-141/12 and C-372/12 YS (C-141/12) v Minister voor Immigratie, Integratie en Asiel and Minister voor Immigratie, Integratie en Asiel (C-372/12) v M and S, Judgment of 17 July 2014, ECLI:EU:C:2014:2081.

ECJ, Case C-580/13 Coty Germany v Stadtsparkasse Magdeburg, Opinion of AG Cruz Villalón of 16 April 2015, ECLI:EU:C:2015:485.

ECJ, Case C-580/13 Coty Germany v Stadtsparkasse Magdeburg, Judgment of 16 July 2015, ECLI:EU:C:2015:485.

ECJ, Case C-362/14 Maximillian Schrems v Data Protection Commissioner, Judgment of 6 October 2015, ECLI:EU:C:2015:650.

ECJ, Case C-362/14 Maximillian Schrems v Data Protection Commissioner, Opinion of AG Bot of 23 September 2015, ECLI:EU:C:2015:627.
ECJ, Joined Cases C-446 to C-449/12 W. P. Willems and Others v Burgemeester van Nuth and Others, Judgment of 16 April 2015, ECLI:EU:C:2015:238.
ECJ, Avis 1/15, Opinion of AG Mengozzi of 8 September 2016, ECLI:EU:C:2016:656.
ECJ, Case C-15/15 New Valmar BVBA v Global Pharmacies Partner Health Srl, Judgment of 21 June 2016, ECLI:EU:C:2016:464.
ECJ, Joined Cases C-203/15 and C-698/15 Tele2 Sverige v Post- och telestyrelsen (C-203/15) and Secretary of State for the Home Department v Tom Watson, Peter Brice and Geoffrey Lewis (C-698/15), Judgment of 21 December 2016, ECLI:EU:C:2016:970.
ECJ, Joined Cases C-203/15 and C-698/15 Tele2 Sverige v Post- och telestyrelsen (C-203/15) and Secretary of State for the Home Department v Tom Watson, Peter Brice and Geoffrey Lewis (C-698/15), Opinion of AG Saugmandsgaard Øe of 19 July 2016, ECLI:EU:C:2016:572.
ECJ, Case C-484/14 Tobias Mc Fadden v Sony Music Entertainment Germany GmbH, Judgment of 15 September 2016, ECLI:EU:C:2016:689.
ECJ, Avis 1/15, Opinion of 26 July 2017, ECLI:EU:C:2017:592.
ECJ, Case C-434/16 Peter Nowak v Data Protection Commissioner, Judgment of 20 December 2017, ECLI:EU:C:2017:994.
ECJ, Case C-434/16 Peter Nowak v Data Protection Commissioner, Opinion of AG Kokott of 20 July 2017, ECLI:EU:C:2017:582.
ECJ, Case C-73/16 Peter Puškár v Finančné riadite'stvo Slovenskej republiky and Kriminálny úrad finančnej správy, Judgment of 27 September 2017, ECLI:EU:C:2017:725.
ECJ, Case C-210/16 Unabhängiges Landeszentrum für Datenschutz Schleswig-Holstein v Wirtschaftsakademie Schleswig-Holstein GmbH, Opinion of AG Bot of 24 October 2017, ECLI:EU:C:2017:796.
ECJ, Case C-207/16 Ministerio Fiscal, Judgment of 2 October 2018, ECLI:EU:C:2018:788.
ECJ, Case C-207/16 Ministerio Fiscal, Opinion of AG Saugmandsgaard Øe of 3 May 2018, ECLI:EU:C:2018:300.
ECJ, Case C-210/16 Unabhängiges Landeszentrum für Datenschutz Schleswig-Holstein v Wirtschaftsakademie Schleswig-Holstein GmbH, Judgment of 5 June 2018, ECLI:EU:C:2018:388.
ECJ, C-311/18 Data Protection Commissioner v Facebook Ireland Ltd. and Maximillian Schrems – Schrems II, Opinion of AG Saugmansgaard Øe of 19 December 2019, ECLI:EU:C:2019:1145.
ECJ, Case C-496/17 Deutsche Post AG v Hauptzollamt Köln, Judgment of 16 January 2019, ECLI:EU:C:2019:26.
ECJ, Case C-18/18 Eva Glawischnig-Piesczek v Facebook Ireland Limited, Judgment of 3 October 2019, ECLI:EU:C:2019:821.
ECJ, Case C-507/17 Google LLC v Commission nationale de l'informatique et des libertés (CNIL), Judgment of 24 September 2019, ECLI:EU:C:2019:772.
ECJ, Case C-354/17 Sergejs Buivids, Judgment of 14 February 2019, ECLI:EU:C:2019:122.
ECJ, Case C-354/17 Sergejs Buivids, Opinion of AG Sharpston of 27 September 2018, ECLI:EU:C:2018:780.
ECJ, Case C-746/18 Criminal proceedings against H. K. – Prokuratuur, Opinion of AG Pitruzzella of 21 January 2020, ECLI:EU:C:2020:18.
ECJ, C-311/18 Data Protection Commissioner v Facebook Ireland Ltd. and Maximillian Schrems – Schrems II, Judgment of 16 July 2020, ECLI:EU:C:2020:559.
ECJ, Joined Cases C-511/18, C-512/18 and C-520/18 La Quadature du Net and Others v Premier ministre and Others, Opinion of AG Campos Sànchez-Bordona of 15 January 2020, ECLI:EU:C:2020:6.
ECJ, Joined Cases C-511/18, C-512/18 and C-520/18 La Quadature du Net and Others v Premier ministre and Others, Judgment of 6 October 2020, ECLI:EU:C:2020:791.
ECJ, Case C-520/18 Ordre des barreaux francophones and germanophone and Others, Opinion of AG Campos Sànchez-Bordona of 15 January 2020, ECLI:EU:C:2020:7.

ECJ, C-623/17 Privacy International v Secretary of State for Foreign and Commonwealth Affairs and Others, Opinion of AG Campos Sànchez-Bordona of 15 January 2020, ECLI:EU:C:2020:5.
ECJ, C-623/17 Privacy International v Secretary of State for Foreign and Commonwealth Affairs and Others, Judgment of 6 October 2020, ECLI:EU:C:2020:790.
ECJ, Case C-746/18 Criminal proceedings against H. K. – Prokuratuur, Judgment of 2 March 2021, ECLI:EU:C:2021:152.
ECJ, Case C-645/19 Facebook Ireland Limited and Others v Gegevensbeschermingsautoriteit, Opinion of AG Bobek of 13 January 2021, ECLI:EU:C:2021:5.
ECJ, Case C-645/19 Facebook Ireland Limited and Others v Gegevensbeschermingsautoriteit, Judgment of 15 June 2021, ECLI:EU:C:2021:483.
ECJ, Case C-401/19 Poland v Parliament and Council, Opinion of AG Saugmandsgaard Øe of 15 July 2021, ECLI:EU:C:2021:613.
ECJ, Case C-401/19 Poland v Parliament and Council, pending.
CFI, Case T-194/04 The Bavarian Lager Co. Ltd v Commission of the European Communities, Judgment of 8 November 2007, ECLI:EU:T:2007:334.
GC, Case T-738/16 La Quadrature du Net and Others v European Commission, Order of 14 December 2020, ECLI:EU:T:2020:638.

Table of Cases: National

Bundesverfassungsgericht, BVerfGE 65, pp. 1–71 – Volkszählung, Judgment of 15 December 1983.
Verfassungsgerichtshof, KR 1/00-33 Rechnungshof v Österreichischer Rundfunk, Judgment of 28 November 2003.

Other Documents: EU

Article 29 Working Party Opinion 15/2011 on the definition of consent of 13 July 2011. WP 187.
Article 29 Working Party Opinion 06/2014 on the notion of legitimate interests of the data controller under Article 7 of Directive 95/46/EC of 9 April 2014. WP 217.

Chapter 4
The Right to Data Protection: The Current Doctrinal Discourse

Contents

Abstract This chapter considers the current doctrinal discourse on the right to data protection in the EU. I analyse seven distinct approaches considering data protection law from various different perspectives: The transparency-focused approach considers data protection as a means to protect privacy, but also highlights the procedural safeguards data protection provides. The narrow self-determination approach understands data protection as an intermediate value to further privacy, but provides an early analysis of the power structures entailed by data processing practices. In opposition to this approach, the commodification approach aims to enable data subjects to market and monetize their data subject rights, while failing to consider the very power structures at work. According to the privacy approach, the right to data protection can only be applied in individual cases in conjunction with the

© T.M.C. ASSER PRESS and the author 2022

F. Bieker, *The Right to Data Protection*, Information Technology and Law Series 34,
https://doi.org/10.1007/978-94-6265-503-4_4

right to privacy and otherwise merely obliges the legislator to create some form of data protection provisions. The individualistic approach considers privacy as the core of the right to data protection and finds that the EU data protection legislation aims to guarantee data subjects' control over their data, while the top-down approach argues for the separate interpretation of the EU data protection legislation on the level of the primary and secondary law and restricts the scope of the former by focusing exclusively on the verbatim of Article 8 CFR. Lastly, the checks and balances approach considers the structural implications of the data protection rules and places an emphasis on the technical and organisational measures.

Keywords Transparency · Self-Determination · Commodification · Monetization of Data · Privacy · Control · Data Subject · Checks and Balances · Rationale of Data Protection · Scope of Data Protection · Interference · Violation · Justification · Essence of Rights · Horizontal Application

4.1 Introduction

In the analysis of the CJEU's case law, I have illustrated how the right to data protection evolved in its jurisprudence. I concluded that it has not yet been defined with regard to its distinct function in the system of EU fundamental rights and its rationale as well as what differentiates it from the right to the protection of private life, i.e. the right to privacy. Even when the Court awards the right to data protection a separate scope, it does so only on a superficial level and does not engage comprehensively with the specific instruments and characteristics of the secondary EU data protection legislation.

Many current conceptions of the right to data protection in the doctrine define this right through recourse to the debate in the US, which has its own understanding of privacy and the rationale for its protection. However, the US debate has a very different focus and constitutional background. Due to these differences, I will not examine this debate in order to achieve my aim of defining the rationale and the distinct content of the EU fundamental right to data protection.[1]

Furthermore, several current doctrinal approaches anchor the right to data protection, at least partly, in privacy, as it has been defined by the ECtHR. In this regard, it must be borne in mind that the ECHR has no direct legal effect, as the EU has not acceded to the ECHR.[2] However, Article 52(3) CFR states that the rights of the Charter, which correspond to the ECHR, must be interpreted in accordance with the

[1] For a comprehensive history of the debate on data protection in general, cf. Pohle 2018, pp. 9–230; for an extensive overview of various international data protection regulations cf. Bygrave 2002, pp. 29–169; cf. also Gellert 2015, pp. 4–6, who demonstrates that some of the structural issues, such as due process, the separation of power and the linking of databases, and risks, for instance preemptive decision-making and chilling effects, identified in the German debate, were also discussed in the US.

[2] In light of the express obligation of the Union to accede to the ECHR according to Article 6(3) TEU, one might be tempted to qualify this statement with a "yet", however, this seems unwarranted

ECHR and, as the Explanations clarify, also the case law of the ECtHR.[3] Nevertheless, the Charter may award greater protection. This is true for the interpretation of Article 7 CFR, which, clearly corresponds with Article 8 ECHR.[4] This right is thus, at least to some extent, bound to the interpretation of the ECtHR, which considers certain aspects of data protection with Article 8 ECHR.

However, as Article 8 CFR does not have a corresponding provision in the ECHR in the sense of Article 52(3) CFR,[5] it can be interpreted more freely and requires that data protection is considered in its own right, rather than from a perspective of privacy. The fundamental right to data protection, therefore, in this expressly codified form as a free-standing right is a novelty of EU law.

The case law of the Court has been subject to varied criticisms in the doctrinal discourse, where alternate rationales for and conceptualisations of data protection were developed. With regard to the shortcomings of the Court's approach, I will analyse these current conceptualisations of data protection in the following in order to assess whether they can remedy the lack of a substantive engagement with the right to data protection, independent of the right to privacy and with the structural requirements needed to ensure comprehensive protection.

In order to achieve my aim to provide a comprehensive conceptualisation of the right to data protection in EU law, where possible, I will consider how the current doctrinal approaches define the rationale and content of the right to data protection. I will further analyse how the current approaches conceptualise the horizontal application of this right and how they suggest to differentiate it from the right to privacy.

I have identified seven distinct approaches, which consider data protection and the right to data protection in detail and with regard specifically to EU law. I will firstly consider the transparency-focused approach (Sect. 4.2), which considers data protection as means to protect privacy, before, secondly, introducing the narrow self-determination approach (Sect. 4.3), which positions itself as opposed to the former approach, but ultimately also links data protection to privacy.

Thirdly, I will analyse the commodification approach (Sect. 4.4), which is based on a reductive notion of self-determination and aims to market the data subject's rights along the lines of a right to property. Fourthly, I will consider the privacy approach (Sect. 4.5), under which data protection is expressly seen as part of privacy, before turning to the individualistic approach (Sect. 4.6) according to which, much like under the top-down approach (Sect. 4.7), data protection is seen as an intermediate value ultimately serving to protect privacy. Lastly, I will analyse the checks and balances approach (Sect. 4.8), which provides a relatively comprehensive assessment

in light of the many reservations voiced by the Court in ECJ, Avis 2/13, Opinion of 18 December 2014, ECLI:EU:C:2014:2454.

[3] Explanations Relating to the Charter of Fundamental Rights. OJ C 303 of 14 December 2007, pp. 17–35, Explanation on Article 52, subpara 4.

[4] Also cf. ibid., Explanation on Article 52, para 1, fifth indent.

[5] Cf. also ECJ, Joined Cases C-203/15 and C-698/15 Tele2 Sverige v Post-och telestyrelsen (C-203/15) and Secretary of State for the Home Department v Tom Watson, Peter Brice and Geoffrey Lewis (C-698/15), Judgment of 21 December 2016, ECLI:EU:C:2016:970, para 129.

of data protection, including its structural dimension, but fails to provide protection equivalent, and much less extending beyond, the scope provided by the ECJ.

4.2 The Transparency-Focused Approach

An early specifically European interpretation of data protection in relation to privacy was developed by Paul De Hert and Serge Gutwirth. In order to differentiate between privacy and data protection, the authors categorise them as opacity and transparency tools, respectively.[6] Opacity tools, under their conception, protect the individual against the State and thus guarantee non-interference.[7] They base this non-interference on the negative function of human rights, which defend individuals against the State as well as—although the authors do not supplement this with any argument—against other societal actors. According to De Hert and Gutwirth this creates space for autonomy or self-determination as a leading principle behind opacity tools.[8]

The authors then argue that privacy assumes a negative role and is intended to limit power relationships, while ensuring the autonomy of individuals. However, they contend that privacy also has a positive role in guaranteeing self-determination and autonomy including alternative behaviour against the pressure of powerful actors.[9]

De Hert and Gutwirth juxtapose this with transparency tools, which, according to their conceptualisation, apply to legitimate uses of power. Under these auspices, transparency tools allow the exercise of power to be controlled and those exercising it to be held accountable.[10] The authors anchor these tools in human rights in their positive function of empowering individuals to participate in the political system,[11] the rule of law, which makes the government accountable and thus transparent—which also relates to the principle of democracy—and the separation of powers.[12]

With this distinction, the authors find that the rationale behind data protection is mainly to provide procedural safeguards to protect the privacy of individuals and hold the government or private actors accountable.[13] Here, it can already be seen that their approach does not actually differentiate data protection from privacy, as the former is only a means to ensure the latter.

Further, they contend that the rationale of data protection laws is not to prohibit data processing, but rather to ensure accountability and empower data subjects to

[6] De Hert and Gutwirth 2006.

[7] Ibid., pp. 67–69.

[8] Ibid., pp. 63 et seq.

[9] Ibid., pp. 71–74.

[10] Ibid., pp. 69–70.

[11] Ibid., pp. 64 et seq.

[12] Ibid., pp. 65 et seq.

[13] Ibid., p. 77.

contest illegitimate practices.[14] As data protection thus channels the exercise of power, they see it as transparency tool.[15]

In order to substantiate their argument, De Hert and Gutwirth refer to data protection principles such as fairness, openness and accountability, which they see as more procedural than normative and thus as transparency tools.[16] However, as I already discussed in Chap. 2, this assertion neglects the principle of lawfulness and its general ban of data processing included in both generations of the EU data protection legislation.[17] Furthermore, the principles of data minimisation, accuracy and purpose limitation are clearly normative, as they prescribe the scope and extent of processing operations.

However, with regard to opacity tools and data protection, De Hert and Gutwirth find that Article 8 DPD (now Article 9 GDPR) on the processing of special categories of data, which introduces additional requirements for the legal bases,[18] and the right of data subjects not to be subject of automated decision-making under Article 15 DPD (now Article 22 GDPR) are prohibitive rules.[19] Yet, the authors point to the exceptions provided by these rules, to discount their prohibitive nature.[20] However, as I have already found with regard to the principle of lawfulness,[21] which contains a general ban on processing, while including many derogations, the fact that a rule contains exceptions does not change its nature.

Lastly, the authors identify the purpose limitation principle as another opacity tool, designed to limit interference with the rights of data subjects by generally prohibiting processing for purposes other than the initial purpose, i.e. when the data were initially collected.[22] However, the authors argue that Article 6(1)(b) DPD (now Articles 5(1)(b) and 6(4) GDPR) also includes more exceptions than the previous, national provisions and thus argue that here as well the focus had, regrettably, shifted to transparency. Accordingly, it seems that the authors submit that the principle of purpose limitation in the EU data protection legislation also has no prohibitive content. However, even if there are exceptions to the rule of purpose limitation, the general rule still stands.

It thus follows that two major concepts of data protection, the principles of lawfulness and purpose limitation, in De Hert and Gutwirth's terms, must be regarded as opacity tools. The juxtaposition between privacy and data protection as opacity and transparency tools, respectively, then does not deliver its own promise of differentiating the two concepts.

---

[14] Ibid.

[15] Ibid., p. 78.

[16] Ibid.

[17] Cf. Chap. 2, Sect. 2.3.2.1.

[18] De Hert and Gutwirth 2006, p. 79.

[19] Ibid.

[20] Ibid.

[21] Cf. already Chap. 2, Sect. 2.3.2.1.

[22] De Hert and Gutwirth 2006, p. 79.

With regard to the core of privacy, De Hert and Gutwirth suggest that it should protect against harmful processing operations and, as an opacity tool, prohibit them, for instance through provisions of criminal law.[23] Consequently, they consider that privacy covers the private sanctuary of individuals—within their home, but even in a virtual domain—and the protection of other fundamental rights, such as the protection of correspondence and the content of communications.[24]

Regular processing operations—a term not further defined under this approach—and their negative consequences, De Hert and Gutwirth find, can then be addressed with the transparency tool of data protection.[25] Thus, the authors conclude that data protection's primary aim is to ensure fair processing by public authorities and private entities, while privacy parses desirable from undesirable processing activities and bans the latter from being carried out, as they interfere with individual rights to an extent that cannot be mitigated by transparency provisions.[26]

Ultimately, this approach reduces data protection to an add-on to privacy. It finds that only harmful processing operations require a ban and thus cements the level of protection already achieved with the right to privacy. However, the authors do not provide any criteria, which allow for the determination of the harmfulness of a processing operation. Their approach thus falls behind the level of protection already offered by the ECJ, which disposed of the haphazardly determined nexus to the private life of individuals. Hence, the transparency-focused approach does not consider the independent value of data protection, as it is interpreted in a reductive manner, and thereby renders data protection dependent on the right to privacy.[27]

Perhaps, the approach of De Hert and Gutwirth should rather be read as a critique of the data protection legislation and the case law of the ECtHR. In giving the controllers broad discretionary powers in balancing their own interests with the rights of data subjects, the authors see the principle of lawfulness diminished and, with the rules concerning subsequent use of data as an exception from the principle of purpose limitation, the normative core of data protection undermined.[28] They further find that the ECtHR is overly focused on the transparency-related quality of the law test, which is linked to a proceduralisation of the substantive right of Article 8 ECHR in combination with the due process rule of Article 6 ECHR, the right to an effective remedy under Article 13 ECHR and establishing very detailed conditions to enable investigations.[29] According to the authors, the ECtHR should rather engage in the opacity-focused "necessary in a democratic society" requirement and in that assessment define, which processing may be regarded as lawful and, if they are, how they can be implemented in a transparent manner in order to properly control the power relations. This critique can also be extended to the ECJ's case law on bulk data

[23] Ibid., p. 98.

[24] Ibid., p. 101.

[25] Ibid., p. 98.

[26] Ibid., p. 104.

[27] Tzanou 2017, pp. 36 et seq.

[28] De Hert and Gutwirth 2006, pp. 80 and 82–96.

[29] Ibid., pp. 85–89.

retention, which shows no general opposition to this far-reaching measure of mass-surveillance and instead focusses on how it can be implemented. In this context, De Hert and Gutwirth's finding that "[t]ransparency seems to have replaced legitimacy as the core value of data protection. Whatever processing has been rendered transparent is legitimate"[30] remains timely.

4.3 The Narrow Self-determination Approach

Antoinette Rouvroy and Yves Poullet take the right to informational self-determination developed by the BVerfG in its 1983 census judgment[31] as a basis and argue that the court rightly based this right under the German constitution on both, the right to human dignity and the right to self-development, and that privacy as a right should be construed as an instrument to promote autonomy of individuals to enable them to participate in the democratic process.[32]

However, this argument misses the fact that the combination of Article 2(1) and Article 1(1) Basic Law forms the general personality right according to the jurisprudence of the BVerfG, which covers the personal sphere of individuals and their free self-determination. Just like for the right to privacy under Article 7 CFR and Article 8 ECHR, there is no conclusive definition of this general personality right: rather it contains various rights, such as the right to the protection of personal honour or the right to legal gender recognition as well as the right to informational self-determination.[33]

Rouvroy and Poullet only see an intermediate value in data protection and criticise the transparency-focused approach and, more generally, the constitutionalisation of data protection as an individual right in Article 8 CFR. They argue that the wording of Article 8(2) CFR overemphasised consent as a legal basis, which they fear could easily be undermined and used to commodify the right to data protection, especially in an online environment, where the conditions of meaningful, informed and free consent are often not met.[34] Thus, they submit that individual consent should not be sufficient to render all kinds of processing operations, considered useful by a controller, lawful.[35] While they note that purpose limitation also applies to such cases, they argue that this cannot remedy the information asymmetry and power imbalance facing the data subject.[36]

---

[30] Ibid., p. 80.

[31] Bundesverfassungsgericht, BVerfGE 65, pp. 1–71—Volkszählung, Judgment of 15 December 1983.

[32] Rouvroy and Poullet 2009, p. 46.

[33] Di Fabio 2018, MN. 147 et seq.

[34] Rouvroy and Poullet 2009, pp. 71–73.

[35] Ibid., p. 74.

[36] Ibid., p. 73.

Yet, the authors suggest that these weaknesses of consent could be remedied by adopting measures of consumer protection, such as enhanced information rights, and class action suits in order to reduce these asymmetries, which, according to them, renders the processing more transparent.[37] This seems somewhat ironic given that De Hert and Gutwirth criticise exactly this tendency to overemphasise transparency.[38] Especially when engaging with platform providers with a (quasi-)monopoly, it can be doubted that data subjects use these services due to a lack of understanding of how the service provider uses their data. Rather, it should be noted that data subjects are faced with a lack of data protection-friendly alternatives.[39] Furthermore, class action suits are only retroactive remedies, which cannot undermine the asymmetry in power between the controller and data subject at the time of the collection of the relevant data.

More essentially, however, Rouvroy and Poullet shy away from the consequences of their critique and accept consent rather than, following their own arguments, calling for its repeal.

Furthermore, the authors hold that enshrining data protection as a fundamental right obscured the relationship of data protection and privacy.[40] They argue that a conception of data protection as final value in empowering individuals with regard to the processing of their data could be taken as a commodification of this right and allow or even induce individuals to waive its protection.[41] This would lead to a loss of its intermediate value to promote the individual's autonomy.[42] Thus, the link to human dignity, as established by the BVerfG was crucial to ensure that the inalienability of personal data was upheld.[43]

According to this narrow self-determination approach, data protection must be seen as an iteration of privacy and encompasses seclusion and control over information.[44] Data protection relates to the risks to individual self-determination caused by information technology, which leads to an increasing power asymmetry between controllers and data subjects, as there are no limits to the amount of data collected, no limits to the scope of analysis of this data and no limits to the period of storage and processing.[45] Thus, controllers were able to take decisions based on an individual's

---

37 Ibid., p. 74.

38 De Hert and Gutwirth 2006, p. 80.

39 Nocun 2018, pp. 53–55.

40 Rouvroy and Poullet 2009, pp. 50, 71 and 74; even though, as Tzanou highlights, their approach is ultimately similar to that of De Hert and Gutwirth, as both see data protection ultimately only as a means for ensuring privacy, cf. Tzanou 2017, p. 35.

41 Rouvroy and Poullet 2009, pp. 50 et seq., 72 et seq. and 74.

42 Ibid., p. 50.

43 Ibid., p. 52.

44 Ibid., pp. 61 et seq. and 70.

45 Ibid., p. 68.

data without their knowledge.[46] Data protection, according to Rouvroy and Poullet, aims to balance this "informational power".[47]

They further argue that this insight leads to an extension in the protection of data from covering only intimate or sensitive data to all personal data and contend that the ECtHR had acknowledged that Article 8 ECHR also covered informational privacy.[48] However, the authors thereby overlook the fact, that the ECtHR has, in fact, not drawn this consequence for Article 8 ECHR, but rather continues to require a link to the private life of applicants.

Therefore, they argue that privacy, conceptualized as informational self-determination, is not concerned with control of the individual over their personal data as an exercise of self-determination, but rather that the individual's control is a necessary precondition for any kind of self-determination.[49] Conversely, Anne de Hingh argues that the commodification of personal data in violation of human dignity is furthered by reliance on the subjective side of human dignity, i.e. self-determination and autonomy. Rather, in order to prevent not only the commodification, but also false assurances of control, which individuals, in practice, cannot exercise, the objective dimension of human dignity, including constraint and collective responsibility, had to be emphasised.[50] In this regard, Rouvroy and Poullet find that privacy and data protection serve not only the interest of individuals, but also the collective interest in a free and democratic society.[51] However, they connect it to what they refer to as the imperative nature of privacy, as the democratic deliberation process presupposed that individuals felt and were free to express themselves without fear of consequences.[52] While the State could not provide the final values of autonomy and self-determination for its citizens, it had to enable citizens to pursue them through privacy.[53]

While this approach of self-determination provides an analysis of the power structures at play when controllers process personal data, its conclusions fall too short and render it narrow. Rouvroy and Poullet do not demonstrate how the ultimately slight amendments to data protection legislation, which they suggest, could upend the power structures, which they found prevalent in their analysis.

Furthermore, this approach neglects to account for the State's own interest in processing personal data, which renders it a threat to the very rights at issue. Finally, the narrow self-determination approach, even though it sets out to offer a different account of data protection from the transparency-focused approach, ultimately also considers data protection merely an aspect of privacy, rather than an independent means and end. It, therefore, does not award any higher level of protection. Instead, it limits the issue of data processing to aspects of privacy.

---

[46] Ibid.

[47] Ibid., p. 69.

[48] Ibid., p. 69 et seq.

[49] Ibid., p. 51.

[50] de Hingh 2018, pp. 1286 et seq.

[51] Rouvroy and Poullet 2009, pp. 55 and 57.

[52] Ibid., pp. 55 and 61.

[53] Ibid., pp. 59 et seq.

4.4 The Commodification Approach

The commodification approach, advocated by Nadezhda Purtova, takes the right to informational self-determination, which she argues required that the individual had the capacity to decide how their data are used, as a starting point.[54] In order to implement this rule—which Purtova considers a principle of data protection, mostly based on an underlying, but not explicated, notion of individual control—she argues that consent as a legal basis should be awarded precedent over other legal bases and become the default rule.[55] In analogy to English land law, individuals would receive the broadest property right, including a right to sell data.[56]

However, data subjects would be limited in the exercise of this right in so far as they would not be able to waive data protection guarantees.[57] Of all the data protection guarantees, the commodification approach here, tellingly, only mentions consent, rather than any substantive safeguards such as technical and organisational measures. This creates the impression that the commodification approach focuses on the perspective of those processing data, rather than the needs of data subjects. This impression is affirmed when the author suggests that the legislator might choose to secure the "investment" of the data industry, which has collected personal data in their databases and protects these against data breaches and other losses of confidentiality by awarding them licences enabling trade with these data.[58] When engaging this idea from the point of view of the current EU data protection legislation, the protection of databases against risks is a basic requirement for controllers to be allowed to process data in the first place. This suggestion turns this idea around and regards simple measures of IT security as cause for a financial reward, when the controller is already creating revenue from the processing of the collected data.

On a fundamental level, the commodification approach is based on a reductive interpretation of the right to informational self-determination, which only takes its individual dimension into account. The BVerfG in its first judgment on the right to informational self-determination in 1983 already emphasised that it did not confer an absolute right over "their" data to the individual.[59] Purtova acknowledges this issue and then argues that this property right would have to be accompanied by further regulation similar to the existing data protection legislation.[60] However, this begs the question of whether the commodification of personal data offers benefits over the current regime. The narrow self-determination approach, which I discussed in the previous section, may be susceptible to various criticisms, however, Rouvroy

[54] Purtova 2012, pp. 246 et seq.

[55] Ibid., pp. 247 et seq.

[56] Ibid., pp. 248 et seq.

[57] Ibid., p. 249.

[58] Ibid., pp. 249 et seq.

[59] Bundesverfassungsgericht, BVerfGE 65, pp. 1–71—Volkszählung, Judgment of 15 December 1983, pp. 43 et seq. On this common misconception of the BVerfG's jurisprudence cf. also Marsch 2018, pp. 99–103.

[60] Purtova 2012, p. 256.

and Poullet's analysis of the issues with regard to consent and the supposedly free choices of data subjects is sound. The commodification approach does not address these concerns. Instead, it builds on the assumption that data subjects engage with controllers on a level playing field, which, ironically, ignores the real-life market conditions.

Purtova argues that data subjects already have to deal with controllers on a daily basis and could be assisted by use of technology, referring generically to privacy and transparency enhancing technologies.[61] However, the commodification of data would have the opposite effect; it would aggravate the possibilities of data subjects to counter controllers' strategies of monetizing personal data.

This leads to the other problematic side of commodification: its economic aspect. Data subjects are supposed to trade their personal data. This, however, confronts them with the issue of the value of their personal data. This will be particularly hard for an individual to determine and incentivises the sharing of personal data for individuals under economic duress. This would be exacerbated by Purtova's further suggestion that while data subjects would be free to withdraw their consent at any time—a right they already have under the current rules—this might entail "some sort of compensation to be paid to the relevant data processing actor".[62] This would put data subjects in a precarious position, where they would have to repurchase data and would, again, introduce an economical aspect to data protection legislation, which is prone to discriminate persons already under economic pressures.

The commodification of personal data would, according to Purtova, award the data protection rights erga omnes effect, i.e. an exclusive right of the owner, enforceable against anyone, as for other types of property.[63] This erga omnes effect would, according to Purtova, create a negative obligation not to process data unless explicitly authorised.[64] However, as I have demonstrated in Chap. 2, such a general ban on data processing already exists in the EU data protection legislation.[65]

Furthermore, the author argues that data subjects would not need to identify the source of a violation of personal data, but could enforce their rights directly against the entity they face.[66] Thereby the differentiation between controllers, processors and other entities, which purportedly created a lack of accountability, could be replaced.[67] Purtova argues that when, for instance, a processor violated their data protection obligations, the data subject could not enforce any rights vis-à-vis the processor. However, under the current data protection legislation, the controller is responsible for how a data subject's data are processed.[68] This is irrespective of whether they

[61] Ibid., p. 259.

[62] Ibid., p. 258.

[63] Ibid., pp. 250 et seq.

[64] Ibid., pp. 250–252 and 256 et seq.

[65] Cf. Chap. 2, Sect. 2.3.2.1.

[66] Purtova 2012, pp. 250–252.

[67] Ibid.

[68] According to Article 24 GDPR, Article 26 DPR-EU and Article 19 LED; also cf. Chap. 2, Sect. 2.3.3.3.

use a processor for certain processing operations or transfer data to other entities. Responsibility is thus squarely placed on the controller. Furthermore, this issue has also been addressed under the second generation of EU data protection legislation: as I introduced in Chap. 2, processors have certain obligations with regard to data protection and data subjects must have a right to an effective judicial remedy against controllers as well as processors.[69]

Ultimately, the commodification approach does not solve existing, but rather creates new issues concerning data practices, which have already been recognised as detrimental to the rights of individuals. Due to its inherent economic component, it turns personal data into commodities of a free market, detached from the person they represent.[70] This process entails the "datafication, commodification and commercialization of individuals",[71] where ultimately humans become tradeable objects and sources of profit, which encroaches on their human dignity.[72] While the commodification approach offers a concept of data protection, which is detached from the notion of privacy, it does not yield answers to the question of how the issue of data processing can be remedied in order to award comprehensive protection for data subjects.

4.5 The Privacy Approach

While the other approaches set out to offer a meaningful differentiation between data protection and privacy, the privacy approach, advanced by Nikolaus Marsch, aims to integrate data protection into the framework of privacy.

4.5.1 A Combined Right of Article 8 in Conjunction with Article 7 CFR

Marsch argues that the right to data protection, as an individual right, could only be used in its negative function, to defend individuals against the processing of their data, in combination with Article 7 CFR.[73] His argument builds on the preliminary observations of the Court in the *Schecke and Eifert* judgment, which I discussed in Chap. 3.[74] Marsch holds that this combined right offers pre-emptive protection

[69] Cf. Chap. 2, Sect. 2.3.3.3.

[70] Already sceptical of such approaches: Podlech 1988, p. 122.

[71] de Hingh 2018, p. 1278.

[72] Ibid.

[73] While he suggests that it may also be combined with other fundamental rights, Marsch only mentions Article 7 CFR, cf. Marsch 2018, pp. 203–205.

[74] Cf. Chap. 3, Sect. 3.2.6.

to individuals, before a violation of privacy rights occurs.[75] However, when there was an interference with the right to privacy or other fundamental rights, these took precedence over the combined right of Article 7 in conjunction with Article 8 CFR.[76]

Marsch's argument departs from AG Cruz Villalón's differentiation between personal data as such, which, the AG argued, are neutral, and personal data, which were more than personal and related, for instance, to the personal sphere, even though the AG based his argument on an independent right to data protection under Article 8 CFR.[77] According to Marsch, this differentiation in spheres is useful due to its "intuitive plausibility".[78] In his conception, not every processing of personal data comes within the scope of Article 7 in conjunction with Article 8 CFR, as a broader scope of the right would restrict the potential for innovation as well as the legislator's discretion in regulating data in the secondary law.[79]

Marsch as well as Bart van der Sloot argue that processing operations below a certain—though undefined—threshold of danger should rather be addressed by the lower standards of the secondary legislation.[80] In this regard Marsch merely offers broad categories as threshold: a connection to the private life of individuals, data processing by security or intelligence services or the processing of special categories of data according to Article 9 GDPR.[81] Accordingly, under the privacy approach, the processing of personal data can only be an interference with the right of Article 7 in conjunction with Article 8 CFR, when the data falls within one of these categories, linking it back to privacy.

It appears that the privacy approach is primarily aimed at curtailing the right to data protection, especially by introducing a de minimis approach as standard of interference. This is done in the name of innovation, which is unspecified and without consideration of the importance of understanding the risks, which may be inherent in new technology. Marsch only generically refers to big data analysis, which, however, is known to entail various risks to individuals, especially with regard to discrimination due to biases inherent in the data and processing operations.[82] It is therefore not a flawed premise to regulate such innovations through the principles of data protection, rather than embracing any technology for the sake of purported, obscure progress.

The combination of Article 8 CFR with Article 7 CFR restricts the scope of the right to data protection and ties it to the right to privacy, thereby reducing its scope to a fraction, which is then determined from the perspective of the right to privacy. When Marsch argues that—what he deems—trivial data should not be included in the scope of the right to data protection, he does not provide any indication of when this would

[75] Marsch 2018, p. 206.

[76] Ibid.

[77] Cf. Chap. 3, Sect. 3.2.8.2.

[78] Marsch 2018, p. 207.

[79] Ibid., pp. 209–211.

[80] Ibid., pp. 211 et seq. Cf. also van der Sloot 2017, p. 21.

[81] Marsch 2018, pp. 214 et seq. The latter is also emphasized by van der Sloot 2017, p. 20.

[82] Vogiatzoglou 2019, at 3.2.1 and 3.2.2.

be the case and only points to very broad categories.[83] Furthermore, he contends repeatedly that such data should not require any of the technical and organisational measures foreseen in data protection.[84] This would impose yet another considerable restriction to the EU data protection legislation de lege lata, especially the principles of integrity and confidentiality, which I introduced in Chap. 2.[85] Further, it would leave aside the risks to the rights to the rights and freedoms of natural persons, which, under the current legislation, are considered to exist for any type of processing operation and are the reason, why the rules on the responsibilities of controllers and processors are not scalable.[86] Thus, the privacy approach resolves the issue of finding a way to differentiate between the right to data protection and the right to privacy by dissolving data protection with its broader protections for individuals in the right to privacy.

4.5.2 *Article 8 CFR as Right to Data Protection Legislation*

Marsch argues that Article 8(1) CFR as an independent right only requires appropriate legislation, as it is a "right to protection" addressing the legislator rather than an individual right to data protection.[87] Article 8(2) CFR in clause 1 provides principles of data protection, which, according to him, limit the broad discretion of the legislator together with the principle of proportionality.[88] However, Marsch contends that the legislator should also be awarded the discretion to restrict the principles of lawfulness, purpose limitation and fairness as contained in Article 8(2) CFR in order to allow for innovation, such as big data analysis, which would be limited by these principles.[89]

Further, he argues that Article 8(2) CFR in clause 2 contains a directly effective data subject right to information and rectification as well as a right to erasure via Article 7 in conjunction with Article 8(1) CFR,[90] while Article 8(3) CFR contains organisational requirements with regard to data protection authorities.[91]

In this regard, however, the privacy approach focuses too narrowly on the verbatim of the provision and does not pay due consideration to the telos and system of the data protection legislation, when the Explanations explicitly point to the secondary legislation.[92] Instead, Marsch argues that only a few hand-picked concepts from the secondary legislation, such as consent or processing, should be considered in

[83] Marsch 2018, pp. 211–215.

[84] Ibid., pp. 187 et seq. and 204.

[85] Cf. Chap. 2, Sect. 2.3.2.8.

[86] Cf. Chap. 2, Sect. 2.3.3.3.

[87] Marsch 2018, p. 130.

[88] Ibid., p. 138.

[89] Ibid., pp. 140 et seq. and 191 et seq.

[90] Ibid., pp. 227–237.

[91] Ibid., pp. 237–247.

[92] Explanations Relating to the Charter of Fundamental Rights, Explanation on Article 8, clause 4.

the interpretation of the primary law, while others should be interpreted more or less strictly, depending on the circumstances.[93] Furthermore, he advances the idea that the primary law, if at all, must only be interpreted in accordance with the DPD, but not the second generation of secondary EU data protection legislation, as the former was the framework the legislator considered when signing the Treaty of Lisbon.[94] However, these arguments—essentially adopting an originalist position—would mean that the interpretation of data protection on the level of primary and secondary law would be different even though both recur to the same notions and concepts. Thus, the privacy approach does not contribute to the interpretation of an independent right to data protection and the definition of its rationale and content.

4.5.3 Horizontal Application of Article 8 CFR

According to Marsch, Article 8 CFR as an independent right requires both, the legislator and courts to protect individuals from private actors processing data by taking it into account when interpreting secondary law, while, in his conception, the combined right of Article 7 in conjunction with Article 8 CFR does not impose such an obligation.[95]

Marsch argues that a direct horizontal effect would counter the general notion that private individuals can rely on fundamental rights, but are not bound by them.[96] However, the Charter rights entailed positive obligations for the State to protect individuals from third parties.[97] He then finds that, as the data protection legislation also regulates the processing by private parties, this obligation is fulfilled.[98] Marsch thus concludes that since the Court interprets the secondary law in light of the fundamental right to data protection and thus awards it indirect horizontal effect, this was sufficient for the protection of individuals.[99]

4.6 The Individualistic Approach

A further elaboration of the right to data protection as an independent right is provided by Orla Lynskey.[100] Her individualistic approach focuses on control, which is to be exercised by individual data subjects.

---

[93] Marsch 2018, p. 145.

[94] Ibid.

[95] Ibid., pp. 261–263 and 268.

[96] Ibid., pp. 248 et seq.

[97] Ibid., p. 249.

[98] Ibid., pp. 249 et seq.

[99] Ibid., pp. 250 et seq.

[100] Lynskey 2015.

4.6.1 The Rationale of Data Protection

Lynskey argues that individual control is the rationale of data protection.[101] Accordingly, she considers data protection as an independent right, which protects privacy but goes beyond it.[102]

As opposed to privacy with its focus on intimacy-based rules,[103] data protection awarded the data subjects more rights, i.e. the data subject rights, over more kinds of data than privacy, i.e. all personal data, and thus offered enhanced control for individuals.[104] By virtue of these rights and the focus on consent, which the data subject could decide to grant or withdraw freely, Lynskey finds that the scales were tilted in favour of the data subjects who were thus equipped to enforce data protection law themselves.[105] Lynskey therefore concludes that the aim of maximising individual control, through the strengthening of the data subject rights, is the key to the interpretation of the EU data protection rules.[106]

While Lynskey briefly notes that there is a power imbalance inherent in data processing when she states that data protection needs to rebalance power asymmetries between controllers and data subjects, she finds that this can be achieved by simply granting individuals more control.[107] However, this assertion neglects the fact that individuals, especially when there is an inherent power imbalance, are not simply able to overcome this structure. Rather than exercising their rights, individuals may feel like they have no choice but to accept the terms of the more powerful party.[108] In that case, the empowerment, which Lynskey associates with giving data subjects control, leaves them without protection.[109]

Lynskey also refers to the Simitis Report,[110] which she finds supports her argument, as it already called for a right to determine the use of data.[111] However, the Simitis Report is focused on fundamental rights more generally and mentions data protection only in passing to point out the inconsistencies in protection arising under the pre-Lisbon pillar structure, in what appears to be a call for a guarantee of data

[101] Ibid., p. 131.

[102] Ibid., p. 90.

[103] Ibid., p. 103; based on De Hert and Gutwirth 2009, p. 10.

[104] Lynskey 2015, pp. 90 and 179 et seq.

[105] Ibid., pp. 181–187 and 192.

[106] Ibid., pp. 227 et seq. and 255.

[107] Ibid., p. 105.

[108] This issue is often framed as the so-called privacy paradox, however, when data subjects see no viable alternatives, accepting the risks they associate with certain behaviours can hardly be found to be paradoxical, cf. Matzner et al. 2016.

[109] Lazaro and Le Métayer 2015; Hartzog 2018.

[110] Expert Group on Fundamental Rights, Affirming Fundamental Rights in the European Union—Time to Act (Simitis Report) (1999). ftp.infoeuropa.eurocid.pt/database/000038001-000039000/000038827.pdf. Accessed 28 July 2021.

[111] Lynskey 2015, p. 103.

protection inspired by the German right to informational self-determination.[112] In that regard, the report hardly supports any specific reading of the right to data protection in EU law.

4.6.2 *The Essence of the Right to Data Protection and its Balance with Other Rights*

Concerning the balancing of the right to data protection with other rights, Lynskey submits that privacy should be seen as the essence of data protection.[113] She argues that in cases of conflicts between rights, other rights should prevail over data protection, if privacy is not breached.[114]

Accordingly, she criticises the Court's approach in *Digital Rights Ireland*, where it referred to the core principles of data protection and, prominently, the technical and organisational measures required by the secondary legislation,[115] which she dismisses as "technocratic principles" and asserts that the Court failed to delineate the right to data protection from the right to privacy.[116] Christopher Kuner, similarly, concludes that "[l]ike any fundamental right, data protection cannot be reduced to a set of formalistic or bureaucratic procedures."[117] It is certainly true that procedural rules must not be implemented for their own sake, as he also states they must be effective in practice.[118] The procedural rules of data protection pursue the aim of protecting individuals from the risks inherent in the processing of personal data. They must indeed not be reduced to formalisms, but rather be implemented with due regard to their aim.

Lynskey argues that instead of focusing on safeguards, the right to data protection should be divided into its core aspects, or essence, and peripheral aspects.[119] While the former, under her approach, cannot be balanced and must prevail vis-à-vis other rights, the core aspects of other rights trump the latter when they collide.[120] Lynskey briefly mentions Alexy's theory on the balancing of fundamental rights, but does not

---

[112] Expert Group on Fundamental Rights, Affirming Fundamental Rights in the European Union—Time to Act (Simitis Report) (1999), pp. 8 and 12, as well as included in the list of rights 'detailing and complementing the ECHR', p. 16.

[113] Lynskey 2015, pp. 161, 175 and 271.

[114] Ibid., p. 161.

[115] ECJ, Joined Cases C-293/12 and C-594/12 Digital Rights Ireland Ltd (C-293/12) v Minister for Communications, Marine and Natural Resources and Others and Kärntner Landesregierung (C-594/12) and Others, Judgment of 8 April 2014, ECLI:EU:C:2014:238, paras 40 and 67.

[116] Lynskey 2015, p. 172.

[117] Kuner 2017, p. 911.

[118] Ibid., pp. 911–913.

[119] Lynskey 2015, p. 175.

[120] Ibid.

employ it to resolve the balancing issue fully.[121] In Alexy's theory, the balancing of rights does not lead to a trumping or prevailing of one of the respective rights, but must rather strive to adhere to both to the greatest extent possible, achieving practical concordance (*praktische Konkordanz*).[122]

Furthermore, with regard to the collision of rights, Lynskey does not consider the two other possible constellations in her approach, which actually call for a balancing between data protection and the other right, i.e. when either the core aspects of data protection and another right or the peripheral aspects of both rights collide. Thus, it becomes evident that the differentiation between core and peripheral aspects in the way Lynskey proposes does not alleviate the burden of balancing two colliding rights.

Furthermore, Lynskey's definition of the essence of the right to data protection as privacy, ultimately, like the previous conceptualisations, ties data protection to privacy and therefore does not allow for a delimitation between these different rights. At least once other fundamental rights are concerned, the right to data protection would be reduced to privacy harms, as under Lynskey's approach the other rights would simply prevail over the right to data protection, where they do not concern the essence of the right. As I have demonstrated in Chap. 3,[123] in the case law of the Court an interference with the essence is exceptional and has so far only been found to exist in vertical relations between the individual and the State. Thus, under the individualistic approach, the right to data protection would not provide protection beyond that granted by the right to privacy in most horizontal relations, i.e. between individuals.

4.7 The Top-Down Approach

While Maria Tzanou contends that privacy is the most prevalent value that data protection aims to protect,[124] she argues that the transparency-focused and the narrow self-determination approach fall short in uncovering this added value, because they consider the right to data protection only by virtue of the right to privacy.[125] Tzanou argues that the fundamental right to data protection should be awarded a scope independent of the secondary legislation.[126] For the interpretation of the right to data protection she consequently derives six principles from Article 8 CFR: fair processing, purpose specification, a legitimate basis for the processing, a right to

[121] Ibid., pp. 134 and 174.

[122] Alexy 1994, p. 152; building on the term developed by Hesse 1999, MN. 317 et seq.

[123] Cf. Chap. 3, especially Sect. 3.2.9.

[124] Tzanou 2017, pp. 24 et seq.

[125] Ibid., pp. 35–37.

[126] Ibid., pp. 38–40.

access and rectification rights as well as independent supervision.[127] With this top-down approach, which is based foremost on the verbatim of Article 8 CFR, the scope of data protection is reduced considerably.

However, such a limited interpretation of data protection is reductive of the very purpose of the fundamental right. In that regard, the separation of the right to data protection from the EU data protection legislation appears a flawed premise. This is not only underscored by the references to the secondary law contained in the Explanations,[128] but also by the fact that Tzanou finds herself in a bind, as she acknowledges, when she argues that the concepts of the right to data protection should have an autonomous scope, while relying on the definitions of personal data or processing of data as defined in the secondary law.[129] While there is then a danger that the level of protection could be lowered via the secondary law, Tzanou does not provide a standard, which could be used to determine when recourse to the secondary law can be taken and when the right to data protection would have to be interpreted autonomously.

4.7.1 Interferences with the Right to Data Protection

With regard to interferences with Article 8 CFR, Tzanou finds that these only occur when one of the six principles was violated, as, according to her approach, establishing an interference with the right to data protection whenever data are processed was counter-intuitive, due to the fact that this also brought lawful processing operations within review.[130] However, this argument does not consider, that the lawfulness is contingent on the legitimacy and proportionality of the specific processing operation. Therefore, whether an interference, i.e. the processing of personal data, is a violation of this right, can only be determined after the assessment of its justification. The approach pursued by Tzanou therefore does not consider the justification stage of the fundamental right assessment.

4.7.2 The Essence of the Right to Data Protection

Tzanou finds that the basis for the determination of the essence should be the six data protection principles she identifies in Article 8 CFR.[131] As she finds an interference

[127] Ibid., pp. 39 et seq.

[128] Explanations Relating to the Charter of Fundamental Rights, Explanation on Article 8, clause 4.

[129] Tzanou 2017, p. 40.

[130] Ibid.

[131] Ibid., p. 43.

only to occur where a principle has been violated, she finds that a processing operation, which interferes with several of these principles, should be regarded as a grave interference.[132] The essence of the right to data protection was only concerned when the "hard core" of the purpose specification and limitation principle was concerned in a way that would threaten the core of the principle of non-discrimination or the right individual self-determination.[133] As the principles of data protection have been strengthened in the second generation of data protection law,[134] it is sensible to consider them for the determination of the essence of the right to data protection. Yet, Tzanou does not provide a reason why the core of data protection should be reduced to only concern the principle of purpose limitation. Instead, she establishes a nexus between the essences of several rights. Tzanou herself points out that the essence of a right can be hard to determine, which makes it seem doubtful whether making the essence of one right contingent on the essence of another right is helpful in this exercise. Rather, it could add a layer of complexity and ultimately diminish the content and thus the contribution of the right to data protection to the canon of existing fundamental rights, as then the right to non-discrimination[135] could just as well fulfil the function of the right to data protection.

4.8 The Checks and Balances Approach

The most elaborate conception of data protection yet, has been advanced by a group of authors, who consider data protection a system of checks and balances.

4.8.1 The Rationale of Data Protection

Peter Hustinx submits that the goal of data protection is not to prevent the processing of data or the use of certain technology, but rather to protect individuals against inappropriate uses of IT for the processing of personal data.[136] Thus, safeguards were required to protect the rights and interests of individuals, which were at the core of data protection.[137]

Pointing out that IT changed substantively since the inception of data protection and continues to do so, Hustinx argues that data protection is threatened by public authorities collecting data on a mass-scale as well as by private parties engaging

[132] Ibid.

[133] Ibid., p. 44.

[134] Cf. Chap. 2, Sect. 2.3.2.

[135] Or apparently also the right to informational self-determination, which she adopts from the narrow self-determination approach, Tzanou 2017, p. 44.

[136] Hustinx 2017, p. 123.

[137] Ibid.

in business practices centred on monitoring the behaviour of individuals.[138] Thus, the issue of data protection since the DPC had been considered "a matter of great structural importance for a modern society".[139]

Hustinx finds that both, the right privacy and the right to data protection, represented the need to prevent undue interferences with an individual's private affairs and the need to ensure adequate control for individuals over matters that potentially affect them.[140] However, he argues that the right to data protection is conceived as a proactive protection.[141] The right to data protection was thus independent of the right to the protection of private life and not a mere addition or expansion, which is intended to provide structural protection to individuals vis-à-vis public authorities as well as private entities.[142]

According to Hustinx and Herke Kranenborg, data protection is thus intended as a system of checks and balances.[143] This system of checks and balances consists of substantive conditions, individual rights, procedural provisions and independent supervision, which thus constitute the "main elements" of data protection.[144] Hustinx elaborates that these central principles of data protection, which were mostly already contained in the DPC and its Additional Protocol as well as the DPD,[145] were lawfulness, purpose limitation, necessity/data minimisation, proportionality—i.e. data must be adequate, relevant and not excessive in relation to the purpose—accuracy, the increased protection for special categories of personal data, appropriate security measures and safeguards for data subjects, as well as independent supervision.[146] With regard to the rights of individuals, Hustinx affirms that effective control for data subjects is an important objective of data protection, but concludes that this does not lead to a formal right to informational self-determination.[147]

---

[138] Ibid., p. 124.

[139] Ibid., p. 128.

[140] Ibid., p. 124.

[141] Which especially concerns the controller, who is charged with the deployment of adequate data management throughout the life cycle of the processing operation, ibid., p. 154; as Hustinx later points out, a "risk is inherent to any data processing", ibid., p. 159. This essential argument also motivates the shift in the burden of proof to the controller, who creates a risk to the rights and freedoms of individuals (and an interference with their fundamental rights) by processing their data and is thus responsible to minimize any adverse effects, cf. also Chap. 2, Sect. 2.3.3.3 and Chap. 5, Sect. 5.3.1.1.

[142] Simitis 2014, MN. 16 and 25; Hustinx 2017, p. 139.

[143] Hustinx 2017, p. 139; Kranenborg 2014, MN. 08.25 et seq.; also cf. Docksey 2015, who echoes this approach.

[144] Hustinx 2017, pp. 139 and 171.

[145] Ibid., pp. 127 et seq.

[146] Ibid.; most of these are also highlighted by Kranenborg 2014, MN. 08.100-08.151.

[147] Hustinx 2017, p. 153.

4.8.2 The Scope of the Right to Data Protection

According to Juliane Kokott and Christoph Sobotta the personal scope of the right to data protection under Article 8 CFR is more limited than that of Article 7 CFR as it, much like the DPD, does not apply to legal persons, whereas this was the case for the right to privacy.[148]

However, under this conceptualisation, the substantive scope of data protection is broader, as it covers all information on an identified or identifiable person according to Article 2(b) DPD (now Article 4(2) GDPR) and the DPC, while privacy requires a nexus to the private life of individuals, at least in the case law of the ECtHR.[149] Kokott and Sobotta state that the ECJ "has not yet added these potential qualifications".[150] As I have shown above, the ECJ never adopted this nexus required by the ECtHR throughout its jurisprudence, even though it referred directly to the ECtHR's case law.[151] Instead, the ECJ found an interference with the right to private life when personal data were processed, even when it was still framing its fundamental rights analysis in terms of the ECHR.

However, now that the ECJ is assessing the Charter and therefore has to consider an independent right to data protection, the ECJ could adopt the ECtHR's approach for the right to private life in order to differentiate between Articles 7 and 8 CFR. This would also be supported by Article 52(3) CFR, which states that rights of the Charter corresponding to rights of the ECHR have the same meaning and scope and, according to the Explanations,[152] Article 7 CFR corresponds to Article 8 ECHR.

As Hustinx notes, even though the scope of private life has been extended significantly, the notion of private life itself remains unclear.[153] While the ECtHR had expanded it inter alia to professional life and the individual's conduct in the public, it had never found that Article 8 ECHR extended to all processing of personal data, but continued to cover data processing only depending on the specific nature and context, thus limiting the Convention to a mere additional source of standards.[154] Accordingly, Hustinx criticizes the Court's joint reading of Articles 7 and 8 CFR, which he finds to prevent the latter from reaching its full potential.[155]

According to Hustinx, data protection is broader than privacy in another sense, as it also concerns other fundamental rights and freedoms.[156] He concludes from these

[148] Kokott and Sobotta 2014, pp. 89 et seq.; Cf. also Hustinx 2017, p. 127.

[149] Kokott and Sobotta 2014, pp. 86 and 89; Kranenborg 2014, MN. 08.83-08.88 and 08.96, who simply argues that Article 8 is defined by the secondary legislation at ibid., MN. 08.75. Critical of this nexus De Hert and Gutwirth 2009, pp. 25 et seq.

[150] Kokott and Sobotta 2014, p. 87.

[151] Cf. Chap. 3, Sect. 3.2.2.

[152] Explanations Relating to the Charter of Fundamental Rights, Explanation on Article 52, para 1, fifth indent.

[153] Hustinx 2017, p. 129. Also cf. Chap. 5, Sect. 5.2.1.

[154] Ibid., pp. 129 et seq.; also pointed out by Kranenborg 2014, MN. 08.52-08.55.

[155] Hustinx 2017, p. 140.

[156] Ibid., p. 127.

points that the objective of the DPC is to protect individuals, in their roles as citizens, consumers and employees among others, against unjustified processing.[157] This, he finds, requires that it is ensured that individuals can participate in social relations, be they public or private, have their freedom of expression protected against surveillance, that unfair discrimination is prevented and "fair play" in decision-making processes promoted.[158]

4.8.3 Interferences with the Right to Data Protection

The checks and balances approach is highly critical of the Court's standard of interference with Article 8 CFR,[159] even though Hustinx agrees that every processing operation poses a risk.[160] Hustinx and Kranenborg build a narrative from the first international regulation on data protection with the DPC to the interpretation of Article 8 CFR: the DPC's approach was not based on a general ban of processing personal data, but rather stipulated that every processing had to adhere to the substantive rules of data protection, such as purpose limitation and necessity, identified as the main elements.[161]

This approach, Kranenborg and Hustinx argue, had to be differentiated from the BVerfG's approach regarding the German right to informational self-determination.[162] The BVerfG does indeed find that any processing of personal data interferes with the right to informational self-determination.[163]

Hustinx argues that, since the European Convention discussed the inclusion of a right to informational self-determination, but ultimately rejected it in favour of the more encompassing notion of data protection,[164] the approach of the BVerfG should not be adopted.

---

157 Ibid.

158 Ibid.; the Commission had also considered making a distinction between public authorities and private entities, but did not pursue this option, as Hustinx points out at ibid., p. 152; cf. Chapters II and III of the Commission's proposal, Commission of the European Communities, 13 September 1990 CELEX no. 51990DC0314, Commission Communication on the Protection of Individuals in Relation to the Processing of Personal Data in the Community and Information Society. COM(90) 314 final—SYN 287 and 288, pp. 53–57.

159 Hustinx 2017, pp. 144–146.

160 Ibid., p. 159.

161 Ibid., p. 128; Article 29 Working Party, Opinion 06/2014 on the notion of legitimate interests of the data controller under Article 7 of Directive 95/46/EC of 9 April 2014. WP 217, pp. 6 et seq.

162 Kranenborg 2014, MN. 08.32, 08.1159 and 08.23; Hustinx 2017, p. 130.

163 Cf., for instance, Bundesverfassungsgericht, NJW 2019, pp. 827–842—Automatisierte Kennzeichenerfassung, Order of 18 December 2018, p. 829, para 43.

164 Hustinx 2017, p. 140; unfortunately, Hustinx, does not provide any references; however, Lynskey 2015, p. 100, provides two specific draft documents supporting this claim, CHARTE 4284/00 of 5 May 2000, p. 14 and CHARTE 4360/00 of 14 June 2000, p. 25.

Kranenborg defines informational self-determination as being based predominantly on consent, which, he argues, is different from the CoE and EU level, where consent is only one of the legal bases allowing for the processing of data.[165] However, as I pointed out above,[166] the BVerfG in its seminal census decision already described something rather different from what Kranenborg depicts. The court made clear that while the right to informational self-determination encompasses the individual's right to determine for themselves how personal data are shared, this does not imply that the individual has an absolute right to "their" data.[167] As the case concerned the census law, consent was never mentioned in the case. Rather, the BVerfG found that the right to informational self-determination could be interfered with in the public interest, where this was based on a legitimate legal basis, which was accessible and transparent to individuals and conformed to the principle of proportionality.[168] Furthermore, the court has also emphasised the strong nexus between the right to informational self-determination and the proper functioning of a democratic society.[169] Reducing this right to being concerned predominantly with the consent of data subjects is therefore a mischaracterisation.

However, Hustinx contrasts this flawed understanding[170] of the BVerfG's jurisprudence with the DPC and argues that the DPC's approach was not that every processing is an interference with right to privacy. Rather, every processing had to adhere to the substantive rules of data protection, such as purpose limitation and necessity.[171] There, however, lies a subtle shift in argument that is not acknowledged: the DPC and DPD refer to the right to privacy, where it can be argued, based on the jurisprudence of the ECtHR, that not every processing of data results in an interference. Yet, the DPC and DPD did not yet refer to the right to data protection of Article 8 CFR, as the second generation of EU data protection legislation now does. Thus, they do not have any impact on the question of when an interference with the right to data protection occurs.

Even though Hustinx points out that the DPD "includes six criteria for legitimacy of processing which are not specified in the [DPC]" and states that data may only be processed if one of them is applicable, he only finds a "prohibition with certain exceptions" for Article 9 DPD, much like the transparency-focused approach.[172] The checks and balances approach, in its overstated reliance on the DPC, thereby overlooks a crucial difference between the DPC and the DPD: while the DPC indeed

[165] Kranenborg 2014, MN. 08.25.

[166] Cf. above Sect. 4.4.

[167] Bundesverfassungsgericht, BVerfGE 65, pp. 1–71—Volkszählung, Judgment of 15 December 1983, pp. 43 et seq.

[168] Ibid.

[169] Ibid., p. 43; Bundesverfassungsgericht, BVerfGE 113, pp. 29–63—Anwaltsdaten, Judgment of 12 April 2005, p. 46.

[170] Cf. also Marsch 2018, pp. 99–103.

[171] Hustinx 2017, p. 128; Article 29 Working Party, Opinion 06/2014 on the notion of legitimate interests of the data controller under Article 7 of Directive 95/46/EC of 9 April 2014, pp. 6 et seq.

[172] Hustinx 2017, p. 132. This argument mirrors the transparency-focused approach discussed above, cf. Sect. 4.2.

only sets out principles for data protection in its Chapter II and merely states in Article 5(a) that data are to be obtained and processed lawfully, Article 6 DPD explicitly states that the processing of personal data is only legitimate, i.e. lawful in the sense of Article 6(1)(a) DPD,[173] when it is based on an express legal basis. This interpretation is supported by the Article 29 Working Party, which states that this was a major shift from the DPC as well as the OECD guidelines to the DPD.[174]

This argument is further reinforced by Article 6(1) GDPR, which explicitly states that the "[p]rocessing shall be lawful only if and to the extent that" it is based on one of the exhaustively listed legal bases. Even though, as De Hert and Gutwirth rightly assert, these legal bases have been painfully broad under the DPD[175] and continue to be so under the GDPR, it is clear that the EU data protection legislation has evolved from the approach of the DPC and includes a general ban on the processing of personal data.[176]

Concerning Article 8 CFR Hustinx contends that since Article 8(2) and (3) CFR import the main elements of data protection, this suggests that an interference only arises when the main elements of data protection are not respected.[177] While the scope of Article 8 CFR extended to any processing of personal data, this should not be confused with an interference.[178] Rather, Article 8(2) CFR laid down conditions for legitimate processing.[179]

However, this argument, like the top-down approach conflates the notion of interference with the finding of a violation of a fundamental right.[180] When drawing this important distinction, the Court's approach appears rather systematic in that it first finds an interference with the right to data protection and then, as Article 52(1) CFR demands, assesses whether that interference is justified. If it is justified, i.e. is provided for by law, respects the essence of the right, and is proportionate according to Article 52(1) CFR, then there is no violation. If one of these requirements is not fulfilled, then there is a violation. The Court has generally followed this approach since *Schecke and Eifert*.[181] Yet, Kokott and Sobotta argue that in that case the ECJ found that, just like Hustinx and Kranenborg suggest, there was no interference with Article 8 CFR as the conditions for legitimate processing under Article 8(2) CFR had been met.[182] However, they only cite the preliminary observations given by the

---

173 Cf. also Article 29 Working Party, Opinion 06/2014 on the notion of legitimate interests of the data controller under Article 7 of Directive 95/46/EC of 9 April 2014, p. 4.

174 Ibid., p. 7.

175 De Hert and Gutwirth 2006, pp. 78 et seq. Also cf. above Sect. 4.2.

176 Cf. on this issue already Chap. 2, Sect. 2.3.2.1.

177 Hustinx 2017, p. 140.

178 Ibid.

179 Ibid., pp. 140 et seq.; Kokott and Sobotta 2014, p. 91.

180 Cf. above Sect. 4.7.1.

181 Cf. Chap. 3, Sect. 3.2.9.

182 Kokott and Sobotta 2014, p. 91; citing ECJ, Joined Cases C-92/09 and C-93/09 Volker und Markus Schecke GbR (C-92/09) and Hartmut Eifert (C-93/09) v Land Hessen, Judgment of 9 November 2010, ECLI:EU:C:2010:662, para 49.

Court, rather than the substantive assessment of the right to data protection.[183] As I have pointed out in Chap. 3, the Court, after its preliminary observations, went on to assess the interference with Article 8 CFR[184] and found that the processing of personal data falls under Article 8(2) CFR and thus there was an interference.[185] The Court stated unequivocally when assessing the justification that "[…] the interference aris[es] from the publication on a website of data by name relating to the beneficiaries concerned".[186]

4.8.4 Justifications for Interferences

Kranenborg argues that data protection as a system of checks and balances encompasses several rights as well as their limitations under Article 8(2) CFR.[187] Again reducing the right to informational self-determination to the processing of data only with the consent of a data subject, he finds that the application of the general justifications clause of Article 52(1) CFR would disregard the differences between the right in Article 8 CFR and the right to privacy of Article 7 CFR, while correctly pointing out that Article 8 ECHR provides no guidance for the interpretation of Article 8 CFR.[188] He consequently finds that the Court's assessment of Article 52(1) CFR as limitations clause is flawed and asserts that in examining the justification of an interference, the Court should refer to the secondary legislation, as it elaborated the specificities of the rights contained in Article 8 CFR.[189]

Kokott and Sobotta argue that a yardstick for the assessment of the justification of a measure under Article 52(1) CFR, for instance in a criminal investigation, could be the ECtHR's *M.M.*[190] case, where it held that with the amount and sensitivity of data, the requirements for appropriate safeguards were raised.[191] This allowed taking the specific risks of data processing into account.[192] While it should be pointed out that the right to data protection must not be linked back to the right to privacy and thereby make privacy the yardstick for data protection, the authors essentially argue

183 Cf. ECJ, Joined Cases C-92/09 and C-93/09 Volker und Markus Schecke and Eifert, Judgment of 9 November 2010, paras 43–52.

184 Ibid., paras 56–64.

185 Ibid., paras 60 and 64.

186 Ibid., para 66.

187 Kranenborg 2014, MN. 08.152 et seq.

188 Ibid., MN. 08.154 et seq.

189 Ibid., MN. 08.159 et seq.

190 ECtHR, M.M. v. the United Kingdom, App. No. 24029/07, Judgment of 13 November 2012, para 200.

191 Kokott and Sobotta 2014, p. 92.

192 Ibid.

for a variable degree of scrutiny, depending on the gravity of the interference.[193] In its recent case law, the Court has taken to asserting beforehand, what standard of review it is applying for the justification of the interference in the case at hand.[194]

4.8.5 *Horizontal Application of the Right to Data Protection*

Kokott and Sobotta also touch upon the horizontal application of data protection, which includes responsibilities of private entities,[195] as Article 2(d) DPD as well as Article 4(7) GDPR do not differentiate whether a controller is a public authority or private entity. However, they find that this cannot apply to either Article 7 or Article 8 CFR, as the rights of the Charter according to Article 51(1) CFR only addressed public authorities and thus neither the right to privacy nor data protection could be applied horizontally.[196] However, they refer to the ECtHR's concept of positive obligations to justify the regulation of private actors with regard to the extensive data processing carried out by them, for instance, as employers, service providers or advertisers.[197]

4.8.6 *Conclusions on the Checks and Balances Approach*

The checks and balances approach provides many insightful points with regard to the right to data protection. It is the only current doctrinal approach to data protection, which acknowledges its structural dimension. Yet, it does not draw the necessary conclusions from this finding, when it restricts itself to finding that the inappropriate use of IT could cause harm or inconvenience to individuals. It thereby neglects the further societal implications of the processing of personal data, which extend beyond the individual.

Furthermore, the checks and balances approach, in its critique of the jurisprudence of the Court, especially with regard to the assessment of the interference, falls short in providing more comprehensive protection to individuals with regard to the issue

---

[193] This notion of risk to rights of individuals has also been taken up in the GDPR of course, where Articles 25, 32 and 35 explicitly refer to the risks to rights of individuals in order to determine appropriate safeguards.

[194] ECJ, Joined Cases C-293/12 and C-594/12 Digital Rights Ireland and Seitlinger and Others, Judgment of 8 April 2014, para 48; ECJ, Case C-362/14 Maximillian Schrems v Data Protection Commissioner, Judgment of 6 October 2015, ECLI:EU:C:2015:650, para 78; more implicitly in ECJ, Joined Cases C-203/15 and C-698/15 Tele 2 Sverige, Judgment of 21 December 2016, para 116; ECJ, Case C-207/16 Ministerio Fiscal, Judgment of 2 October 2018, ECLI:EU:C:2018:788, paras 54–56.

[195] Kokott and Sobotta 2014, p. 90.

[196] Ibid.

[197] Ibid.

posed by data processing. The authors overstate the relevance of the DPC for the interpretation of Article 8 CFR and neglect the differences between the DPC and the secondary EU data protection legislation. They thereby fail to take account of the improvements which had already been achieved in the first generation of EU data protection legislation.

4.9 Conclusions on the Current Doctrinal Discourse

In this analysis of the current conceptualisations of data protection I have argued that none of them offer a comprehensive understanding of the right to data protection, which would allow for the concise differentiation between this right and the right to privacy.

Under the transparency-focused approach, data protection is a means to protect privacy and concerns procedural safeguards, which enhance the transparency of processing operations. Privacy protects against harmful processing by prohibiting it, while data protection concerns the conditions of the processing and renders it fair. However, this approach reduces the scope of data protection by tying it to privacy and an undefined notion of harmful processing operations.

The narrow self-determination approach considers privacy in the vein of a reductive interpretation of the German constitutional right to informational self-determination, as concerning only the autonomy of individuals. The authors consider the information asymmetry and power imbalance between controller and data subject and accurately analyse and criticise the notion of consent under these conditions. However, the narrow self-determination approach fails to consider appropriate remedies for this power imbalance and reduces its critique to calls for enhanced transparency. Rouvroy and Poullet only see an intermediate value in data protection, which sought to give individuals control over their data, so that they could act self-determinedly with regard to their privacy. Yet, the narrow self-determination approach provides an early analysis of power relations in data processing and connects data protection to the collective interest in a free and democratic society.

The commodification approach then takes the right to self-determination as starting point to argue that under an implicit notion of control, consent should become the primary legal basis of data processing, just as the narrow self-determination approach cautions against. While the commodification approach conceives of data protection independently of privacy, it paves the way to cement the existing power structures and allow data subjects to surrender their rights without substantive procedural or organisational safeguards, in analogy to a property right.

Especially from an economic perspective such a commodification would entail the risk that data subjects come under economic pressure to market their data or cannot revoke consent, as this would entail an obligation of compensation on their part. On the flipside, the positive effects of an erga omnes effect, which the commodification approach would impart on the data subject rights, in practice do not go beyond the current scope of protection.

The privacy approach considers data protection expressly only in terms of the right to privacy and argues that not every processing of data should be awarded protection. However, it does not define, which processing operations are seen as worthy of protection, but only offers vague categories. On its own terms, this approach argues, data protection merely required the legislator to adopt appropriate laws, which included only the principles contained in the verbatim of Article 8 CFR, while still allowing the legislator to curtail even these in order to enable controllers to adopt new data processing practices without any restrictions. This approach ultimately aims to curtail data protection in order to promote a diffuse notion of innovation, devoid of any specific rationale.

The individualistic approach focuses on control, exercised by individual data subjects. To this end, data protection awarded data subject individual rights, which, it argues, along with the requirement of consent, allows them to overcome the power imbalance of data processing. However, this approach neglects the fact that having to enforce various different rights against controllers places a considerable burden on data subjects, which are the structurally weaker party. The individualistic approach further considers privacy to be the essence of data protection and thereby, ultimately, also links these two rights together, while dismissing the structural safeguards provided by technical and organisational measures. Under this conception, privacy remains at the very core of the right to data protection and thus hampers its independent scope.

The top-down approach advocates for the separate interpretation of data protection in the Charter and in the secondary legislation. It restricts the right to data protection to the principles included in the verbatim of Article 8 CFR and thereby reduces its scope considerably, as it does not consider the broader telos and system of the EU data protection legislation. However, the top-down approach does recur to the definitions of the secondary legislation in some instances, without providing any standard to determine, when such recourse should be taken. While it links the interferences with the principles contained in Article 8 CFR, which is a novelty, the top-down approach asserts that only unlawful processing operations should be brought under its scope. Yet, this neglects the fact that in order to examine whether a processing operation is lawful, it must first be reviewed and thus fall under the scope of the right in order to examine whether that interference is justified. Under this approach, the essence of data protection is considered to only consist of the principle of purpose limitation, without providing any reason for such a reduced scope of the essence.

Under the checks and balances approach, data protection is considered a system of checks and balances, which provides structural safeguards in order to protect individuals against inappropriate uses of technology to process personal data. This system consists of the individual rights, procedural provisions and independent supervision mechanism provided by the EU data protection legislation.

The checks and balances approach also criticises the unclear scope of the right to private life as well as the joint reading of Articles 7 and 8 CFR, as carried out partly by the ECJ and advocated in an even more restrictive manner by the privacy approach. However, the checks and balances approach argues for a restrictive interpretation of interferences with the right to data protection, which is based on a reductive interpretation of the right to informational self-determination as being focused only on consent: under this approach, interferences only occur when the main elements of data protection are not respected. This is based essentially on the DPC, which does not include a general ban of data processing. Yet, this interpretation neglects the fact that this is the case under the secondary EU data protection legislation, which is the appropriate standard to assess interferences with the EU fundamental right to data protection. Furthermore, the checks and balances approach, with this limited standard, just like the top-down approach, conflates the finding of an interference with that of a violation. However, a processing operation must be reviewed as to its justification, only then can it be ascertained whether there is a violation.

As I have illustrated, almost all of the current doctrinal approaches ultimately rely on some notion of privacy to define data protection and thereby cannot offer an advanced understanding of this right. While the checks and balances approach offers a comparatively comprehensive understanding of data protection in its own right, it also restricts the protection offered by Article 8 CFR when it limits the interference to cases where the 'main elements of data protection' are concerned. This restriction, in practice, means that many processing operations fall outside the scope of review. The checks and balances approach thereby limits the effects of data protection and fails to consider the inherent risks of any such processing.

However, as González Fuster has concluded after analysing the genesis of the right to data protection in the EU and several Member States: "It is a misconception, thus, to claim that the protection of personal data derives, generally speaking, from privacy."[198]Rather, she argues, the notions of privacy and data protection had to be disentangled.[199] As this is not achieved to an appropriate degree by the conceptualisations of the current doctrinal discourse, they cannot provide a coherent framework for the right to data protection. The current conceptualisations thus cannot help to overcome the shortcomings of the Court's jurisprudence.

In order to achieve a comprehensive understanding of data protection, I will develop a framework to analyse the EU data protection legislation in the following chapter, in order to uncover the aspects that are fundamental to this legislation. These aspects will form the foundations of a right to data protection, which defines data protection in its own right and thereby disentangles data protection from privacy to uncover its full potential as an independent right.

References

Articles, Books and Chapters in Books

Alexy R (1994) Theorie der Grundrechte [A Theory of Fundamental Rights]. Suhrkamp Taschenbuch, Frankfurt am Main.

[198] González Fuster 2014, p. 268.

[199] Ibid., pp. 268–271.

Bygrave L A (2002) Data Protection Law—Approaching its Rationale, Logic and Limits. Kluwer Law, The Hague.
De Hert P, Gutwirth S (2006) Privacy, Data Protection and Law Enforcement. Opacity of the Individual and Transparency of Power. In: Claes E, Duff A, Gutwirth S (eds) Privacy and the Criminal Law. Intersentia, Antwerp/Oxford, pp. 61–104.
De Hert P, Gutwirth S (2009) Data Protection in the Case Law of Strasbourg and Luxemburg: Constitutionalisation in Action. In: Gutwirth S, Poullet Y, De Hert P, de Terwangne C, Nouwt S (eds) Reinventing Data Protection? Springer, Dordrecht, pp. 3–44.
de Hingh A (2018) Some Reflections on Dignity as an Alternative Legal Concept in Data Protection Regulation. GLJ 19:1269–1290.
Di Fabio U (2018) GG Art. 2 Abs. 1. In: Herzog R, Scholz R, Herdegen M, Klein H H (eds) Grundgesetz Kommentar [Basic Law Commentary], 84th EL. C.H. Beck, Munich.
Docksey C (2015) Articles 7 and 8 of the EU Charter: Two Distinct Fundamental Rights. In: Grosjean A (ed) Enjeux Européens et Mondiaux de la Protection des Données Personelles. Larcier, Brussels, pp. 71–97.
Gellert R (2015) Understanding Data Protection as Risk Regulation. Journal of Internet Law 3–16.
González Fuster G (2014) The Emergence of Personal Data Protection as a Fundamental Right of the EU. Springer, Cham/Heidelberg/New York/Dordrecht/London.
Hartzog W (2018) The Case Against Idealising Control. EDPL 4:423–432.
Hesse K (1999) Grundzüge des Verfassungsrechts der Bundesrepublik Deutschland [Tenets of the Constitutional Law of the Federal Republic of Germany], 20th edn. C.F. Müller, Heidelberg.
Hustinx P (2017) EU Data Protection Law: The Review of Directive 95/46/EC and the General Data Protection Regulation. In: Cremona M (ed) New Technologies and EU Law. OUP, Oxford, pp. 123–173.
Kokott J, Sobotta C (2014) The Distinction between Privacy and Data Protection in the Jurisprudence of the CJEU and the ECtHR. In: Hijmans H, Kranenborg H (eds) Data Protection 2014: How to Restore Trust? Contributions in Honour of Peter Hustinx. Intersentia, Cambridge, pp. 83–95.
Kranenborg H (2014) Article 8. In: Peers S, Hervey T, Kenner J, Ward A (eds) The EU Charter of Fundamental Rights—A Commentary. Hart Publishing, Oxford.
Kuner C (2017) Reality and Illusion in EU Data Transfer Regulation Post Schrems. GLJ 18:881–918.
Lazaro C, Le Métayer D (2015) Control over Personal Data: True Remedy or Fairy Tale? SCRIPTed 12:3–34.
Lynskey O (2015) The Foundations of EU Data Protection Law. OUP, Oxford.
Marsch N (2018) Das europäische Datenschutzgrundrecht [The European Fundamental Right to Data Protection]. Mohr Siebeck, Tübingen.
Matzner T, Masur P, Ochs C, von Pape T (2016) Do-It-Yourself Data Protection—Empowerment or Burden? In: Gutwirth S, De Hert P, Leenes R (eds) Data Protection on the Move. Springer, Dordrecht, pp. 277–305.
Nocun K (2018) Datenschutz unter Druck [Data Protection Under Pressure]. In: Roßnagel A, Friedewald M, Hansen M (eds) Die Fortentwicklung des Datenschutzes [The Development of Data Protection]. Springer Fachmedien, Wiesbaden, pp. 39–58.
Podlech A (1988) Unter welchen Bedingungen sind neue Informationssysteme gesellschaftlich akzeptabel? [Under Which Conditions Are New Information Systems Socially Acceptable?]. In: Steinmüller W (ed) Verdatet und Vernetzt [Registered and Networked]. Fischer Taschenbuch, Frankfurt am Main, pp. 118–126.
Pohle J (2018) Datenschutz und Technikgestaltung [Data Protection and Technology Design]. Berlin. https://edoc.hu-berlin.de/bitstream/handle/18452/19886/dissertation_pohle_joerg.pdf. Accessed 28 July 2021.
Purtova N (2012) Property Rights in Personal Data. Wolters Kluwer, Alphen aan den Rijn.
Rouvroy A, Poullet Y (2009) The Right to Informational Self-Determination and the Value of Self-Development: Reassessing the Importance of Privacy for Democracy. In: Gutwirth S, Poullet Y, De Hert P, de Terwangne C, Nouwt S (eds) Reinventing Data Protection? Springer, Dordrecht, pp. 45–76.

Simitis S (2014) Einleitung [Introduction]. In: Simitis S (ed) Bundesdatenschutzgesetz [Federal Data Protection Act] 8th edn. Nomos, Baden-Baden.
Tzanou M (2017) The Fundamental Right to Data Protection. Hart, Oxford/Portland, OR, USA.
van der Sloot B (2017) Legal Fundamentalism: Is Data Protection Really a Fundamental Right? In: Leenes R, van Brakel R, Gutwirth S, De Hert P (eds) Data Protection and Privacy: (In)visibilities and Infrastructures. Springer, Cham, pp. 3–30.
Vogiatzoglou P (2019) Mass Surveillance, Predictive Policing and the Implementation of the CJEU and ECtHR Requirement of Objectivity. EJLT 10.

Table of Cases: Council of Europe

ECtHR, M.M. v. the United Kingdom, App. No. 24029/07, Judgment of 13 November 2012.

Table of Cases: EU

ECJ, Joined Cases C-92/09 and C-93/09 Volker und Markus Schecke GbR (C-92/09) and Hartmut Eifert (C-93/09) v Land Hessen, Judgment of 9 November 2010, ECLI:EU:C:2010:662.
ECJ, Joined Cases C-293/12 and C-594/12 Digital Rights Ireland Ltd (C-293/12) v Minister for Communications, Marine and Natural Resources and Others and Kärntner Landesregierung (C-594/12) and Others, Judgment of 8 April 2014, ECLI:EU:C:2014:238.
ECJ, Case C-362/14 Maximillian Schrems v Data Protection Commissioner, Judgment of 6 October 2015, ECLI:EU:C:2015:650.
ECJ, Joined Cases C-203/15 and C-698/15 Tele2 Sverige v Post- och telestyrelsen (C-203/15) and Secretary of State for the Home Department v Tom Watson, Peter Brice and Geoffrey Lewis (C-698/15), Judgment of 21 December 2016, ECLI:EU:C:2016:970.
ECJ, Case C-207/16 Ministerio Fiscal, Judgment of 2 October 2018, ECLI:EU:C:2018:788.

Table of Cases: National

Bundesverfassungsgericht, BVerfGE 65, pp. 1–71—Volkszählung, Judgment of 15 December 1983.
Bundesverfassungsgericht, BVerfGE 113, pp. 29–63—Anwaltsdaten, Judgment of 12 April 2005.
Bundesverfassungsgericht, NJW 2019, pp. 827–842—Automatisierte Kennzeichenerfassung, Order of 18 December 2018.

Other Documents: EU

Article 29 Working Party Opinion 06/2014 on the notion of legitimate interests of the data controller under Article 7 of Directive 95/46/EC of 9 April 2014. WP 217.
Expert Group on Fundamental Rights Affirming Fundamental Rights in the European Union—Time to Act (Simitis Report) (1999). ftp.infoeuropa.eurocid.pt/database/000038001-000039000/000038827.pdf. Accessed 28 July 2021.

Chapter 5
The Right to Data Protection: The Dualistic Approach

Contents

Abstract This final chapter introduces the dualistic approach to data protection. The framework for this approach builds on a historic debate, which emancipated data protection from privacy and will be introduced in the first part of this chapter. The discourse at the time had already identified many of the issues of modern data processing and can be transferred to the provisions of EU data protection law, as will be achieved in the second part of the chapter. Firstly, the dualistic approach will be applied to the secondary EU data protection law by considering the dual rationale of data protection: addressing the risks to the rights of individuals as well as mitigating the power imbalance inherent in data processing. Secondly, by reference to this frame, the fundamental principles of EU data protection law will be derived, which reflect the entirety of the rules of the secondary EU data protection law.

© T.M.C. ASSER PRESS and the author 2022
F. Bieker, *The Right to Data Protection*, Information Technology and Law Series 34,
https://doi.org/10.1007/978-94-6265-503-4_5

These fundamental principles are comprised of lawfulness, separation, integrity, availability, confidentiality, transparency and control. Particular regard will be paid to the structural dimension of data protection law, which extends beyond its individual dimension and considers the democratic society as a whole. Thirdly, the dualistic approach is applied to the primary EU data protection law in order to define the rationale and content of the right to data protection. This right of EU law also includes the structural dimension of data protection law and both dimensions as well as the fundamental principles of EU data protection law inform its interpretation. Lastly, this chapter considers how the right to privacy can be differentiated clearly from the right to data protection, with the distinct rationales, scopes and essences of these rights.

Keywords Data Processing · Individual Data Protection · Structural Data Protection · Dualistic Approach · Data Protection Principles · Lawfulness · Purpose Limitation · Necessity · Data Minimisation · Storage Limitation · Separation · Integrity · Availability · Confidentiality · Transparency · Control · Accountability · Risk to Rights · Risk-Based Approach · Risk Management · Bias · Rationale of Data Protection · Scope of Data Protection · Material Scope · Personal Scope · Interference · Violation · Justification · Essence of Rights · Horizontal Application

5.1 Introduction

In the conclusions of the previous two chapters, I have argued that there is no comprehensive approach to the fundamental right to data protection, which is based on data protection as a distinct issue. In that sense, while the constitutional legislator, as González Fuster put it, "un-coupl[ed]"[1] the right to data protection from the right to privacy in the Charter[2] and the legislator continued this process in the second generation of EU data protection legislation, by including a reference to the right to data protection, rather than privacy in the respective provisions,[3] the process of disentanglement has not yet been completed. The right to data protection, under all current conceptualisations, whether provided by the Court or the academic discourse, is not based on a notion that is truly independent of privacy.

In this final chapter, I will show an avenue to complete the disentanglement of the right to data protection. In order to achieve this, I will firstly develop my own framework in order to explicate the dualistic nature of EU data protection law, i.e. its individual and structural dimension (Sect. 5.2). As I have illustrated in Chap. 2, the right to data protection has been reverse-engineered in the sense that it was modelled after the pre-existing secondary EU law,[4] i.e. the first generation of EU data protection

[1] González Fuster 2014, pp. 269 et seq.

[2] Cf. Chap. 2, Sect. 2.2.1.

[3] Article 1(2) GDPR and DPR-EU, Article 1(2)(a) LED.

[4] Cf. Chap. 2, Sect. 2.2.1.

legislation, comprised of the DPD, DPR-EC and ePD.[5] Therefore, the interpretation of the right to data protection is contingent on the secondary law; the fundamental right to data protection must be reflective of the telos and system of the secondary EU data protection law.

My approach builds on a discourse between German scholars, which—as I will demonstrate throughout the following sections—can be applied to the EU level. As this framework considers the dualities of data protection—the differentiation between individual and structural data protection, I briefly introduced in Chap. 1,[6] and its dual rationale—I will refer to it as the dualistic approach.

In the third section of this chapter, I will use the concepts developed in the German historic discourse and apply the dualistic approach to the secondary EU data protection legislation—the body of EU law labelled data protection, which does not exclusively regulate data protection, but also covers other, related fields—in order to uncover the secondary EU data protection law, i.e. the body of EU legislation labelled data protection that specifically addresses the issue of data processing (Sect. 5.3). In this process, I will develop my argument that the dual rationale of EU data protection law is to protect the individual from the risks of data processing and its inherent power imbalance. From this rationale and the uncovered secondary EU data protection law, I will derive the fundamental principles of EU data protection law.

In the fourth section of this chapter, I will apply the dualistic approach and, specifically, its dual rationale and the fundamental principles of EU data protection law, to the primary EU data protection legislation, in order to uncover the fundamental right to data protection as part of EU data protection law (Sect. 5.4). I will demonstrate that EU law addresses the issue of data processing expansively, albeit not comprehensively, as the structural dimension of data protection law, which is already implicitly included in many of the rules of EU data protection legislation, must be awarded more prominence in order to achieve a comprehensive remedy for the issues posed by the processing of personal data. After showing that the right to data protection, due to its distinct rationale and scope, can be clearly separated from the right to privacy, I will draw general conclusions on the fundamental right to data protection in EU law.

My argument throughout this chapter will build on the rules of the EU data protection legislation I introduced in Chap. 2, the interpretation of the fundamental right to data protection as it evolved, but has not yet been fully developed in the jurisprudence of the Court, analysed in Chap. 3, as well as, where appropriate, the current conceptualisations of data protection in the doctrine and their shortcomings, discussed in Chap. 4.

---

[5] Cf. Chap. 1, Sect. 1.2.

[6] Cf. Chap. 1, Sects. 1.2 and 1.6.

5.2 The Dualistic Approach: Data Protection Law as Answer to the Issue of Data Processing

The framework I employ for this book builds on a theory of data protection conceptualised in discourse by German scholars Wilhelm Steinmüller, Adalbert Podlech and others between the 1970s and 1980s, especially a report prepared for the German Federal Ministry of the Interior and published in 1971.[7] At this time, the German State and private companies explored the then new possibilities of data processing through databases and the thus conceivable linkage of what seemed like vast amounts of data.[8] It was also the time when the first German data protection legislation was debated and passed in the state of Hesse.[9] The debate, therefore, had not been formed under the influence of any specific regulation, as it took place before the first data protection legislations were passed. Rather, it built more generally on the fundamental rights of individuals and constitutional principles, such as democracy, the rule of law and the separation of powers.

The discussions departed from a critical stance on privacy as a remedy for the processing of personal data (Sect. 5.2.1). The authors were adamant that data protection had to be differentiated from privacy and already identified many of the chances, challenges and risks of modern data processing. Rather than engage with the concept of privacy, Steinmüller, Podlech and others developed the notion of data protection in its own right (Sect. 5.2.2). In order to allow for a more nuanced debate, they introduced a differentiation between individual and structural data protection law (Sect. 5.2.3), which I have already briefly introduced in Chap. 1.[10]

5.2.1 *Critique of Privacy and Need for Data Protection*

In their report, Steinmüller et al. argued that the notion of privacy as an area where the individual can make autonomous decisions and is protected against encroachment by the State or other private parties, is not useful for the protection of individuals with regard to the processing of their data.[11] Abstract definitions of a right to share and to withhold information or a right to be let alone, they found, did not allow a precise definition of when the privacy of an individual is violated, as this would depend on the meaning each individual attaches to their privacy.[12] Yet, a casuistic determination would either require the legislator to lay down an exhaustive, but static set of violations, likely limited to the most severe violations in order to circumvent

---

[7] Steinmüller et al. 1971.

[8] Also cf. Mayer-Schönberger 1997, p. 221 et seq.

[9] Land Hessen, Datenschutzgesetz [Data Protection Act], 7 October 1970, Gesetz- und Verordnungsblatt für das Land Hessen (GVBl.) Part I, Issue 41 of 12 October 1970, pp. 425–427.

[10] Cf. Chap. 1, Sect. 1.2.

[11] Steinmüller et al. 1971, p. 48.

[12] Ibid., pp. 50 et seq.

the relativity of privacy and allow for such a definitive list, or include a general clause, which would then require further elaboration by the judiciary.[13]

Establishing different groups of typical violations, based on various spheres, was no more helpful to determine the scope of privacy, as there were constant interferences with, for instance, spatial privacy, some of which were deemed justified, while others were seen as violations.[14] While the interference with a certain type of privacy was thus indeterminate for establishing a violation, it was actually crucial to consider whether there was a legal basis for the interference, which shifted the issue fundamentally from defining specific groups of privacy to finding a legal basis that could justify an interference.[15]

Therefore, the notion of privacy, due to its broad, yet undefined and undefinable scope was not useful to determine more than the most basic and egregious violations of individuals through data processing.[16] Privacy, the authors argued, does not engage with the risks posed by the processing of personal data,[17] but rather reduces the issue to one of "private spaces".[18] The individual spheres, or spaces, to which privacy refers, Jochen Schneider pointed out, can also not be implemented on the technical level, due to the relativity of data depending on context.[19]

While it may seem counterintuitive to assume that all personal data warrant protection,[20] this finding was necessitated by the central shortcoming of privacy: there are no clear criteria to delimit the instances where the integrity of the privacy of an individual is encroached.[21] As the true content of information is dependent on the context, and seemingly innocuous data can be highly compromising in certain situations, the protection of all personal data is the only way to ensure that such gaps in protection are averted.[22]

On the level of EU law, the ECJ has already acknowledged the importance of context for information in its case law on mass-surveillance, which I introduced above,[23] and especially so in the case law since *Tele2 Sverige*,[24] where the Court noted that electronic communications metadata, which relates "only" to the date,

[13] Ibid., p. 52.

[14] Ibid., pp. 52 et seq.

[15] Ibid., p. 53.

[16] Ibid.

[17] I will consider these specific risks in more detail below, cf. Sect. 5.3.1.1.

[18] Steinmüller et al. 1971, p. 53.

[19] Schneider 1973, p. 229.

[20] Also cf. De Hert and Gutwirth 2009, p. 25.

[21] Simitis 1971, p. 680.

[22] Ibid.

[23] Cf. Chap. 3, Sect. 3.2.

[24] Discussed in detail in Chap. 3, Sect. 3.2.8.9.

time, a location and/or an interlocutor and excludes the contents of a communication, may serve to profile individuals intimately.[25]

Due to this relativity of privacy, the report by Steinmüller et al. concluded that, as a positive definition of privacy is not possible, the concept allows only to find the lowest common denominator.[26] As the legal notion of privacy could not adjust to the rapid social change brought about by automated data processing, it had to make way for a new concept, which was rooted in the actual process of data processing: the notion of data protection.[27]

5.2.2 The Development of the Notion of Data Protection by Steinmüller, Podlech and Others

As the ideas from this discourse build the frame of reference for my analysis of the EU data protection legislation in the following subsection (Sect. 5.2.3), I will introduce the main lines of the debate in the following.

On a foundational level, the report by Steinmüller, Podlech and others differentiates between data protection and data protection law.[28] As data protection, in their understanding, is the specific answer to the societal issue posed by data processing, it is the flipside of the processing of personal data.[29] Jörg Pohle points out that this means that the issue of data protection cannot be "solved", but must rather be negotiated constantly within society.[30]

Accordingly, the purpose of data protection, as opposed to privacy, is not to allow residual areas of alleged retreat for individuals;[31] data protection aims essentially to protect individuals *from* the processing of data by means of individual rights and structural guarantees.[32] The report defines data protection as comprising the measures that prevent undesirable outcomes of the processing of personal data,[33] which is also the basis of the checks and balances approach.[34] According to Steinmüller et al., an outcome is seen as undesirable when it runs counter to fundamental constitutional goals, such as the protection of individuals and groups, especially minorities as

[25] ECJ, Joined Cases C-203/15 and C-698/15 Tele2 Sverige v Post- och telestyrelsen (C-203/15) and Secretary of State for the Home Department v Tom Watson, Peter Brice and Geoffrey Lewis (C-698/15), Judgment of 21 December 2016, ECLI:EU:C:2016:970, paras 98 et seq., and cf. Chap. 3, Sect. 3.2.8.9.

[26] Steinmüller et al. 1971, p. 53.

[27] Ibid., pp. 54 and 60.

[28] As I briefly introduced in Chap. 1, Sect. 1.2.

[29] Steinmüller et al. 1971, p. 44.

[30] Pohle 2014, pp. 47 et seq.

[31] Lenk 1973, p. 20.

[32] Schneider 1971, p. 27. And as I briefly mentioned in Chap. 1, Sect. 1.2 and Chap. 5, Sect. 5.2.2.

[33] Steinmüller et al. 1971, p. 44.

[34] As I discussed in Chap. 4, Sect. 4.8.1.

particularly vulnerable groups, in a democratic society under the rule of law.[35] This is the case when the processing itself is undesirable as well as when the processing is legitimate, but leads indirectly to undesired results.[36]

These undesired outcomes relate to the individual, but also society as a whole.[37] Therefore, data protection can, on a very fundamental level, be separated into two dimensions:[38] individual data protection (*Individualdatenschutz*), which aims to protect individuals and (minority) groups,[39] and structural data protection (*Systemdatenschutz*[40]), which aims to protect the democratic State and its institutions.[41]

Individual data protection aims to protect the individual against damage, which may result from risks to the rights of individuals inherent in the processing of personal data.[42] However, as data protection, according to the report, also protects the democratic society under the rule of law as a whole,[43] including its institutions and their constitutional position,[44] it is not merely an issue of the individual, which could be remedied on the legal level, for instance by awarding the individual exclusive rights, as the commodification approach purports.[45] Rather, it concerns the issue of securing the communication structure of a democratic society.[46] Even though Podlech held that data processing was not currently a threat to fundamental rights, he found that it would, once it was adopted more widely, and thus data protection had to be implemented in the structure of any information system.[47] Individual measures were not sufficient, as each individual measure could be circumvented and thus required an effective combination of multiple safeguards.[48] In that sense, structural data protection covers aspects, which are not directly related to the individual,

---

[35] Steinmüller et al. 1971, p. 44.

[36] Ibid.; cf., with regard to the GDPR, Konferenz der unabhängigen Datenschutzaufsichtsbehörden des Bundes und der Länder 2018, p. 1. I will discuss this in further detail below in Sect. 5.4.2.1.

[37] Geiger 1973, p. 174. Cf. also recital 4 clause 1 GDPR.

[38] As I briefly introduced in Chap. 1, Sect. 1.2.

[39] Steinmüller et al. 1971, p. 82.

[40] In keeping with the meaning of the report by Steinmüller et al., I have translated the term *Systemdatenschutz* as structural data protection, to clarify that it relates to the structural aspects of a democratic society under the rule of law. The term—which directly translates to system data protection—has, after the report, been used in the context of what Steinmüller initially described as application protection (*Programmschutz*). This concept relates to built-in protection mechanisms for (IT) system design, which allow for the supervision and accountability of the users of these systems. The term *Systemdatenschutz* has also been misunderstood as focusing only on technical data protection, cf. Steinmüller 1972b, p. 461; Steinmüller 1973, pp. 71 et seq.; Podlech 1982; overview in Dix 2003, pp. 364–369, esp. MN. 13.

[41] Schneider 1971, p. 27; cf. also Rouvroy and Poullet 2009, pp. 55 and 57, discussed in Chap. 4, Sect. 4.3.

[42] Steinmüller et al. 1971, p. 82. Cf. also recital 75 and Articles 24, 32–35 GDPR.

[43] Cf. recitals 73, 153 and Article 23(1) GDPR.

[44] Schneider 1971, p. 27.

[45] Cf. Chap. 4, Sect. 4.4.

[46] Simitis 2014, MN. 26. Also cf. recital 49 GDPR.

[47] Podlech 1973b, p. 7; Podlech 1973a, pp. 37 et seq.

[48] Podlech 1973b, p. 8; Podlech 1973a, p. 38.

but rather extend to the systemic aspects of data protection, such as institutional guarantees and organisational requirements.[49]

Therefore, Steinmüller et al. argued that it would not be sufficient to anchor data protection only at the individual level; it also had to be safeguarded on an institutional level,[50] in order to comprehensively remedy the risks emanating from data processing.[51] While institutions can serve to protect individuals against shifts of societal power, for instance through the separation of powers, institutions, in turn, must be protected against negative shifts in power caused by data processing.[52]

The two dimensions of data protection complement each other: individual data protection would be moot, if not combined with rules on the structure and organisation of the State's institutions. Conversely, undesirable effects of data processing on the organisation of the State cannot be prevented effectively without individual data protection.[53]

While the term data protection thus concerns the issues posed by data processing, the term data protection law refers specifically to the legal regime on the processing of personal data, which is concerned with control and supervision of the processing of personal data[54] and has the objective of addressing the issue of data protection.[55]

Data protection law also has the two dimensions of individual and structural data protection law.[56] This further differentiation, which I have already introduced in Chap. 1,[57] allows for a more nuanced answer to the issues posed by the processing of personal data, as the answer to this issue is not exclusively within the realm of the law. Rather, it requires interdisciplinary approaches in order to fully grasp these issues.[58] This requires a continued critical analysis of the current legal system and then allows to discuss alternative approaches.[59]

Based on the consideration that access to an information system is a source of considerable power,[60] Podlech had initially introduced the notion of informational separation of powers by suggesting that the access to databases for public authorities should be distributed to an entity that was not the controller.[61] He argued that data protection expanded the constitutional principle of separation of powers to the

---

[49] Podlech 1982, p. 451.

[50] Steinmüller 1975, p. 78.

[51] On these cf. below in Sect. 5.3.1.1 and, more specifically, in Sect. 5.4.2.1.

[52] Steinmüller 1975, p. 79.

[53] Steinmüller et al. 1971, p. 44.

[54] Kilian 1973, p. 289.

[55] Cf. already in Chap. 1, Sect. 1.2.

[56] Steinmüller et al. 1971, p. 44.

[57] Cf. Chap. 1, Sect. 1.2.

[58] Steinmüller 1972a, pp. 237 et seq.; Pohle 2018, pp. 7 et seq.

[59] Steinmüller 1972a, pp. 284 et seq.

[60] Podlech 1970, pp. 473 et seq.; I analyse the issue of data processing as exercise of power under EU law in-depth below in Sect. 5.3.1.1.

[61] Ibid.

principle of system differentiation (*Systemdifferenzierung*), which separates parts of integrated data systems within the branches of government.[62]

Furthermore, he introduced the principle of competing partial public systems (*Konkurrenz der staatlichen Teilsysteme*), which serves to protect the individual's fundamental rights by ensuring that any public authority is able to check another authority's access to its data and ensure that this access is lawful.[63] This can be illustrated with the example of the postal service or nowadays perhaps an electronic communications service provider ensuring that intelligence services cannot access its data without going through a formal process, so that the postal service can confirm that a request for information is grounded on a proper legal basis and is proportionate.[64] Podlech considered that such measures guarantee that there will be proper supervision and control of data processing, as individuals are no longer able to gain access to data on their own and the controllers of the data would otherwise tend to undermine rules, which led Podlech to a general presumption of non-compliant behaviour of uncontrolled social systems.[65] Data protection, in this understanding, strives to control social systems concerned with the processing of information.[66]

Concerning the processing of personal data by private entities, the report concluded that there must be a weighing of interests between the private entities and the data subjects, which has to take into account the risks of information systems.[67] From this, the report drew one of its seminal conclusions, which is that the processing of information must generally be prohibited.[68] An exception could only be made, if information was publicly available or there was a legal basis, i.e. contractual obligations between the parties or consent of the individual.

With regard specifically to individual data protection, Steinmüller, in what can be described as an early iteration of the principle of data minimisation, found that the principle of competence-based processing (*kompetenzorientierte Datenverarbeitung*) required that only a minimum of legitimate users could process a minimum of legitimate data—in conformity to the principle of proportionality—to protect the individual from unnecessary interference.[69]

However, Steinmüller argued that necessity cannot be the only criterion for processing by public authorities. Rather, it had to be supported by a competence to process the data in question. This could be ensured through application protection (*Programmschutz*), where applications, from an integrated pool of information, grant each authority access only to the data within its competence and deny access

---

[62] Podlech 1973b, p. 9; Podlech 1973a, p. 39.

[63] Podlech 1973b, p. 10; Podlech 1973a, p. 40.

[64] Podlech 1973b, p. 10; Podlech 1973a, p. 40.

[65] Podlech 1973b, p. 11; Podlech 1973a, p. 41.

[66] Steinmüller 1975, p. 82.

[67] Steinmüller et al. 1971, p. 142.

[68] Ibid.

[69] Steinmüller 1975, p. 84. Also cf. already Steinmüller et al. 1971, p. 99; Podlech 1973b, p. 11; Podlech 1973a, p. 42.

to all other data.[70] This was to be accompanied by measures ensuring that the application used could be revised and supervised, but only by authorised users and while ensuring verification through measures such as logging or rights and roles concepts.[71] Aside from this internal oversight, external supervision had to be ensured and data subjects had to have enforceable rights to information, notification, rectification and compensation.[72]

Podlech had identified several principles of structural data protection law:[73] under the principle of transparency data subjects had to be able to know which entities processed their data for which purposes and to whom these data were disclosed.[74] According to the principle of necessity, the controller had to describe which data where necessary to achieve a certain, pre-defined task. In this, he argued, it is paramount that the description extends beyond naming the task and elaborates the contingency of processing of the specific data in question to the achievement of the purpose.[75] Any change of the task or the data processed had to be accounted for and documented.[76] These two principles, according to Podlech, could be combined to form a third principle: the prohibition of hyper complex processing operations.[77] If it was not possible to process personal data in a manner transparent to data subjects or if the task was so expansive or the data processing so complicated that the necessity of processing could not be described comprehensively, a processing operation was hyper complex.[78] Such a hyper complex processing operation could not be reconciled with the rule of law and was thus prohibited.[79]

Furthermore, under the requirement of validity, data could only be processed when their accuracy could be assured with a socially and individually acceptable likelihood.[80] This likelihood was dependant on how the data were collected. For instance, whether they were collected from the data subject or a database of a public authority and whether they were verified.[81] However, as the validity of information was contingent on the specific context in which they were processed, the requirement of validity had to be accompanied by the prohibition of context changes.[82] By coupling information with their social context, it had to be guaranteed that the

---

[70] Steinmüller 1972b, p. 461; Steinmüller 1973, pp. 71 et seq.

[71] Steinmüller 1975, pp. 83–85.

[72] Ibid., pp. 88–91.

[73] Podlech 1982, p. 454, albeit without claiming comprehensiveness.

[74] Ibid., p. 455. While this principle, for the purposes of structural data protection law, is phrased in oddly individualistic terms, the structural dimension of transparency will be elaborated further below, cf. Sect. 5.3.2.7.

[75] Ibid., pp. 455 et seq.

[76] Ibid., p. 456.

[77] Ibid.

[78] Ibid.

[79] Ibid.

[80] Ibid., p. 458.

[81] Ibid.

[82] Ibid., p. 459.

information did not change their meaning and undermined the rights and interests of data subjects.[83] This could, inter alia, be achieved by ensuring that information could be processed only for as long as was necessary to achieve the purpose of the processing operation and by defining deletion periods.[84]

Structural data protection further required the protection of the legal position of data subjects.[85] Information systems had to be designed and built in a way that ensured that data subjects could exercise their rights, have access to evidence in order to pursue legal remedies and not be undermined in their position by superior knowledge of the controller.[86]

As can be seen from these principles, the original debate engaged with both, individual and structural data protection. The extent of Steinmüller's reasoning also demonstrates that the argument that this early debate on data protection was focused only on the structural side of data protection, is not accurate.[87] With regard to this point raised by Meyer-Schönberger it could perhaps rather be argued that the early laws on data protection did not sufficiently link the issue of data processing to the relevant fundamental rights,[88] which were, however, in the focus of the debate. The report by Steinmüller et al. successfully called for the inclusion of data subject rights in data protection legislation[89] and was well aware of the need to protect the individual through fundamental rights.[90]

With regard to the current conceptualisations of data protection I discussed in Chap. 4, the engagement with the structural side of data protection is a distinct advantage of this discourse. Even the checks and balances approach, which is the only current approach to acknowledge that data protection should have structural implications, does not draw any further consequences from this assessment with regard to the substantive guarantees of a right to data protection.[91] Instead, it advances a very narrow definition for the interferences with the right to data protection, which

---

[83] Ibid., pp. 459 et seq.

[84] Ibid., p. 460.

[85] Ibid., pp. 460 et seq.

[86] Ibid.

[87] Mayer-Schönberger 1997, pp. 223–225 and with a caveat concerning data subject rights, p. 226. However, Mayer-Schönberger argues on ibid., pp. 226–228 that the data subject rights only concerned information on the processing or the rectification of data and no substantive "say" such as consent or rights to lodge complaints. However, § 3 BDSG 1977 as well as § 7 para 2 of the 1970 Hessian data protection law contained provisions on consent and § 21 BDSG 1977 as well as § 11 of the Hessian data protection law gave any individual a right to file a complaint with the respective supervisory authority.

[88] This was, however, accomplished in the first generation of EU data protection legislation, cf. Article 1(1) and recital 2 DPD and, subsequently, Article 1(1) DPR-EC, Article 1(1) ePD and even Article 1(1) Council Framework Decision 2008/977/JHA of 27 November 2008 on the protection of personal data processed in the framework of police and judicial cooperation in criminal matters, OJ L 350 of 30 December 2008, pp. 118–129.

[89] Cf. for instance § 4 BDSG and § 8 HDSG.

[90] Steinmüller et al. 1971.

[91] Cf. Chap. 4, Sect. 4.8.1.

renders it much less effective.[92] The discourse between Steinmüller, Podlech and others took the structural dimension and its implications seriously and therefore awarded it the same prominence as the individual dimension.

5.2.3 *The Duality of EU Data Protection Law: Individual and Structural Data Protection Law*

In the following, I will show that the findings of this discourse can be utilized with regard to the EU data protection legislation in order to identify the rules, which, under the conception of Steinmüller, Podlech and others, can be considered data protection law, i.e. the legal rules concerning the issue of data processing. While my approach thus builds on theory from a German discourse, I will link it to the secondary EU data protection legislation in the following. In the course of this, the principles defined by Steinmüller, Podlech and others, will serve as points of reference, as they had identified core issues of data protection. However, I will apply those principles only insofar as the secondary EU data protection legislation allows.

Steinmüller et al. emphasised the duality of data protection law, which had to include an individual (Sect. 5.2.3.1) as well as a structural dimension (Sect. 5.2.3.2) in order to comprehensively address the issue of data processing. Furthermore, I will briefly consider the potential of group rights in the context of data protection law, which Steinmüller et al. highlighted as an important remedy (Sect. 5.2.3.3), before concluding that a dualistic approach must be adopted in order to uncover the EU data protection law (Sect. 5.2.4), i.e. the rules of EU law concerned exclusively with the issue of data processing. Throughout this subsection, I will refer to the secondary EU data protection legislation to demonstrate that the findings of Steinmüller et al. can be transferred to the level of EU law and thereby adapt the discourse into a framework for the further analysis of the EU data protection legislation.

5.2.3.1 Individual Data Protection Law

Individual data protection law encompasses the norms of data protection law, which serve to protect the individual or a group.[93] While it is, of course, the stated mission of EU data protection law as a whole to protect individuals and their fundamental rights[94] and all provisions must be interpreted in light of this rationale, this dimension concerns the provisions that aim to safeguard the interests of data subjects and/or award them specific enforceable rights.[95] The obvious example of such individual

---

[92] Cf. Chap. 4, Sect. 4.8.3.

[93] Steinmüller et al. 1971, p. 44.

[94] Cf. Article 1(2) GDPR, Article 1(1) DPD, Article 1(1) ePD, Article 1(2)(a) LED, Article 1(1) DPR-EC, Article 1(2) DPR-EU.

[95] Podlech 1982, pp. 451 et seq.

rights are the data subject rights.[96] These are accompanied by procedural rights, which give individuals access to legal remedies in order to enforce their rights.[97]

However, individual data protection law is not restricted to those rights. Many other provisions serve to safeguard the interests of individuals, sometimes very specifically, for instance in Article 6(1)(f) GDPR, where they can override the interests of controllers. Sometimes the individual dimension is more implicit, e.g. in the rules on the transfer of personal data to third countries or international organisations. These provisions aim to ensure that the level of protection for data subjects, achieved under the EU data protection legislation, is not undermined by the transfer of the data to a third country with lower standards.[98]

5.2.3.2 Structural Data Protection Law

Structural data protection law includes legal rules, which go beyond the specific rights in the interest of individuals to further include normative and institutional requirements for the organisation of the State as well as private entities when processing personal data.[99] It encompasses the legal rules on the processing of personal data, which, irrespective of whether a certain individual is concerned, ensure that the processing has no adverse effects on society.[100] In protecting society as a whole, they also benefit the individual, but are not contingent on enforcement by a specific data subject.

The rules of structural data protection law are derived from the rule of law, which is a foundational value of the EU according to Article 2 TEU, and are based specifically on the principles of legality, proportionality and the separation of powers.[101] The rule of law also obliges the State to regulate the exercise of power by the private sector to render it socially acceptable and ensure the well-being of its citizens, as information technology has reduced the difference between the public and private sector with regard to the processing of the data of individuals.[102]

---

[96] As I have introduced in Chap. 2, Sect. 2.3.3.2.

[97] Cf. Chap. 2, Sect. 2.3.3.2.

[98] Cf. already Chap. 2, Sect. 2.3.3.4; Article 44 and recitals 101 and 107 GDPR; Articles 46 and 94(1) as well as recital 63 DPR-EU; Article 35(3) and recitals 70–73 LED.

[99] Steinmüller et al. 1971, p. 44; this aspect was covered explicitly in § 1 para 2 of the Hessian Data Protection Act, cf. Land Hessen, Hessisches Datenschutzgesetz (HDSG) [Hessian Data Protection Act], 10 November 1998, Gesetz- und Verordnungsblatt für das Land Hessen (GVBl.) Part I, Issue 4 of 19 February 1999, pp. 98–111 which was in force until 24 May 2018.

[100] Podlech 1982, p. 452.

[101] Cf. already Steinmüller et al. 1971, p. 82; Brouwer 2011, pp. 275 et seq.; De Hert also notes the similarities between the principles of data protection law and administrative procedural law, but argues that the latter could replace the former as they included power considerations, aspects of democracy and checks and balances. However, this focus obscures that data protection law itself, through structural data protection law, addresses the issues he identifies, De Hert 2017, pp. 178 et seq.

[102] Podlech 1988, pp. 122 et seq.; and cf. in more detail below in Sect. 5.4.4

The secondary EU data protection law, through structural rules, expands the application of these general principles beyond public authorities to also encompass private entities, when they process personal data. For instance, the obligation to carry out a DPIA under the conditions of Article 35 GDPR[103] is intended to ensure that the controller is aware of the risks, which the envisaged processing operation poses and able to take appropriate safeguards according to Article 32 GDPR in order to mitigate these risks. Furthermore, the appointment of a Data Protection Officer according to Articles 37–39 GDPR[104] is a measure which aims to provide an additional layer of oversight within the organisation processing the personal data.

However, structural data protection law is not limited to the secondary law. Under Article 16 TFEU, primary EU law also enshrines data protection as an organisational and structural principle of EU law.[105] From this principle it follows, that the EU must ensure that the right to data protection is fulfilled not only in an individualistic sense, but also in its own organisation and structure.[106]

5.2.3.3 Collective Rights

However, individual data protection law as specifically legal answer to the issue of data processing, in order to holistically address the issues entailed by data processing, also has to consider groups, especially minorities, who may be particularly affected by adverse effects.[107] Collective rights of groups are an important factor in order to counter issues arising from the processing of personal data on a large scale, especially when using these data to create personality profiles.

Yet, as often as it has been observed that data protection law should include group rights, it has been observed that this was not currently the case.[108] The factual focus on individual rights is highly incentivized by the Western conceptualization of fundamental rights as a remedy against intrusions on the individual. Pursuing this conventional approach opens—in the sense of Sara Ahmed[109]—a path well-trodden and promises swift implementation, whereas the notion of collective rights for groups is much less developed in the current legal system. Following such a concept would imply that the traditional system of rights protection would have to be changed, along with the EU primary law, which appears a utopian endeavour at this time.[110]

---

[103] Also cf. Articles 39 and 89 DPR-EU as well as Article 27 LED.

[104] Also cf. Articles 43–45 DPR-EU and Articles 32–34 LED.

[105] Cf. Chap. 2, Sect. 2.2.2.

[106] I will elaborate below in how far Article 8 CFR also engages the structural dimension, cf. Sect. 5.4.1. However, at a very basic level, Article 8(3) CFR evidently contains a structural element, cf. Chap. 2, Sect. 2.3.3.5 and Chap. 3, Sect. 3.3.

[107] Steinmüller et al. 1971, p. 40.

[108] Pohle 2018, p. 251; Mantelero 2016.

[109] Ahmed 2006, p. 16.

[110] And yet, such endeavours may well be worth pursuing, as pointed out by Theilen et al. 2017, pp. 330 et seq.

However, the fact that, with a model of a group based on data collected from multiple individuals, a controller can infer information about other individuals is not a recent development of big data analytics. Rather, this insight had already been gained at a time, when big data was still referred to simply as databases.[111]

Groups especially can be rendered transparent by the use of automated data processing: by collecting information about members of marginalized groups, for instance, they can be discriminated even though there is no information on one specific individual.[112] This information can, however, be used to reliably influence or screen entire populations.[113]

A recent example of this is the use of an algorithm by the Austrian employment office, which found women's chances to integrate in the job market worse than men's and therefore downgraded the prospects of any unemployed women.[114] This illustrates how the data on an individual data subject—in the example, the employment prospects of an individual—does not have to be accurate in order to discriminate against group members by virtue of data derived about other individuals.[115] Thus, especially in the context of discrimination, there is a grave risk for individuals, as they may be discriminated as part of an already marginalized group.[116] However, in this context it might be a valuable addition, if the right of the individual not to be discriminated was accompanied by a collective claim of the group, which can organise more effectively. Such a right would serve to reduce the burden placed on the individual, who is already marginalized.

Individual EU data protection law de lege lata, can counter this problem only on the individual level: a data subject has a right to be informed of the processing of their personal data, irrespective of whether the data have been collected from them directly or through a third-party, according to Articles 13 and 14 GDPR. If the controller bases the processing on the legitimate interest clause of Article 6(1)(f) GDPR, the interests and fundamental rights of data subjects may override the legitimate interests of the controller. In instances of discriminatory practices, the individual will generally have a claim under Articles 21 or 23 CFR and thereby override the interest of the controller.[117]

If the data are not accurate, the data subject may demand rectification according to Article 16 GDPR and to temporarily restrict the processing under Article 18(1)(a) GDPR. If the data are, in fact, inaccurate, they have been processed unlawfully and the data subject has a right to erasure of the data according to Article 17(1)(d)

[111] Steinmüller et al. 1971, p. 40.

[112] Steinmüller 1975, p. 78.

[113] Steinmüller 1971, p. 7.

[114] Fröhlich and Spiecker gen. Döhmann 2018.

[115] Steinmüller 1975, p. 78.

[116] Steinmüller 1993, p. 673.

[117] Even though the notion of legitimacy under Article 6(1)(e) GDPR allows any legally protected interest, a processing operation aiming to directly or indirectly discriminate individuals based on one of the criteria in Articles 21 or 23 CFR would not pass this test, cf. Robrahn and Bremert 2018, pp. 291 et seq.

GDPR. Furthermore, the data subject may object to the processing of their data on grounds relating to their particular situation according to Article 21(1) GDPR, if the processing is based on the public or legitimate interest clauses of Article 6(1)(e) or (f) GDPR. This is particularly relevant for instances of profiling, which is often linked to discrimination and may be based on information inferred from other data subjects' data. If the data subject can demonstrate a specific, individual ground beyond the interests and fundamental rights taken into consideration under Article 6(1)(f) GDPR[118] or the weighing of interests carried out by the legislator for Article 6(1)(e) GDPR, the controller then has to demonstrate a compelling legitimate ground, which overrides the interests and individual rights of the data subject. In cases of direct marketing purposes, the data subject has an unconditional right to object to the processing under Article 21(2) GDPR.

If the processing entails automated individual decision-making with legal or similar effects, for instance, the offer of certain discounts or products based on a profile of the data subject in an e-commerce setting, the data subject has a right to object to such processing where it is not necessary for entering into or performance of a contract, is not laid down by specific regulation or is not based on the data subject's explicit consent according to Article 22 GDPR.[119] It can thus be seen that the protection awarded to the individual in these instances is very much contingent on their own resources and actions.

In EU data protection law de lege lata,[120] it is only possible for non-profit organisations conforming to certain requirements to represent data subjects and to exercise their procedural rights.[121] Yet, this is contingent on a mandate by an individual data subject and while it thus enables collective action in principle, it does not amount to a collective right of a group in the sense I am discussing here, and is not guaranteed on a constitutional level.

In the debate, the lack of group or collective rights is often attributed to the definition of personal data as information relating to an identified or identifiable natural person,[122] however, this would not per se stop an individual from enforcing data subject rights with regard to the processing of the data of other individuals. Pohle finds that it is baffling that data protection legislation recognises that there is an issue when Alice's rights are restricted due to the processing of her data, while it is not recognised that there is also an issue when Alice's rights are restricted due to the processing of Bob's personal data.[123]

[118] Cf. ibid., p. 296.

[119] Also cf. Article 11 LED. For an in-depth analysis of Article 22 GDPR and Article 11 LED, cf. Brkan 2019a.

[120] According to Article 80 GDPR, Article 55 LED and Article 76 DPR-EU.

[121] For a detailed analysis of collective redress in EU law generally as well as the provisions of the GDPR and the upcoming ePR, cf. Jančiūtė 2019.

[122] Cf. Schmitz 2018. Also cf. Pohle 2018, pp. 251–253.

[123] Pohle 2018, pp. 251 et seq.

However, this example is in fact covered by the data subject rights. The legal definition of Article 4(1) GDPR[124] states that a data subject is an identified or identifiable natural person. This does not necessarily exclude the possibility that a data subject could rely on data from a different data subject. The verbatim of the data subject rights states that data subjects have rights with regard to personal data, which concern[125] them.[126] The interpretation of the term "concern" is crucial in this regard. It could be defined narrowly as only meaning data *about* the data subject or more broadly as referring to data, which *affect* the data subject.

If, for instance, Alice were denied a loan, because Bob—who has the same post code as her—has not repaid his loan, the data which relate to Bob also *affect* Alice. In this simplified case of profiling based on residence, Alice is denied her loan, due to the processing of Bob's personal data. In that regard, the data on Bob, which are used to profile Alice, would also concern her. This is confirmed by the wording of Article 22 GDPR, which, with regard to automated decision-making, stipulates that "[t]he data subject shall have the right not to be subject to a decision based solely on automated processing, including profiling, which produces legal effects concerning [them] or similarly significantly affects [them]." This shows that, with regard to an automated decision, Alice already has a claim against the controller under the current EU data protection legislation. Yet, this may not be equipped to handle other issues, which come with artificial intelligence systems: if a controller uses the image of one person for training such a system, this may not harm that individual, but it may be used to harm other, already marginalized individuals, who may not be recognised by that system.[127]

Yet, de lege ferenda the EU data protection law, through a reform of the legal definition of data subject to include one or more identified or identifiable individuals, could be extended to also allow groups to enforce data subject rights collectively. A collective right, as I envision it here, would award an individual belonging to a marginalized group as well as the group itself a claim to enforce the rules, which ban the data processing operation.[128]

For the implementation of such a group right, I suggest to draw a parallel to the ECtHR's case law on whether an applicant can claim to be the victim, in the sense of Article 34 ECHR, of secret surveillance measures, when they cannot prove that they have been affected by this measure. In these instances, the ECtHR has consistently held that this proof may well be impossible for the applicant due to the very nature of

[124] Also cf. Article 3(1) DPR-EU and Article 3(1) LED.

[125] From a cursory comparison, it appears that this term is used consistently in different language versions: EN: "concerning"; FR: "concernant"; ES: "conciernen"; DE/NL: "betreffende".

[126] Cf., for instance, Article 15 GDPR: "The data subject shall have the right to obtain [...] confirmation as to whether or not personal data *concerning him or her* are being processed [...]" (emphasis added). Also cf. Articles 16–21 and especially 22 GDPR.

[127] Benjamin 2021. On artificial intelligence systems not identifying black women correctly, cf. Buolamwini and Gebru 2018. For a critical approach to consequences to be drawn from this, cf. Hassein 2017.

[128] For an Afrofuturist imagination of the data subject as a collective, cf. Kadiri 2021.

such surveillance measures.[129] In a Grand Chamber judgment, the ECtHR held that it would consider whether the applicant, in principle, can be affected by the measure, because they belong to a group targeted under the relevant legislation authorising the surveillance.[130]

This jurisprudence can be applied mutatis mutandis to marginalized groups: they would not have to establish that a specific individual's data are being processed—for instance, to train a discriminatory artificial intelligence system. Instead, it would be assumed that the relevant individual, as member of a group that is being discriminated against by a specific processing operation, as well as the group itself have a claim to stop that processing operation. This claim would apply vis-à-vis both, the controller as well as the competent supervisory authority.

However, de lege lata, there is also another possible avenue to address these issues: it should be borne in mind that the law on access to documents[131] can be employed to enable control of processing activities of public authorities. These rules can be used to enable individuals to exercise control in order to ensure that such technology is not used to discriminate against certain groups.[132] The right of access to documents or information is enshrined in Article 42 CFR as well as Article 15(3) TFEU and is not limited to personal data, but relates to any information held by public authorities and serves the transparency and accountability of public action.

5.2.4 Interim Conclusions: A Dualistic Approach to Data Protection

In the preceding subsections, I have illustrated that data protection can well be defined on its own terms, as relating to the issue posed by data processing. Data protection thus requires the protection of individuals *from* the processing of personal data. In order to achieve this protection, the issue of data processing must be considered on the individual as well as the structural level.

When comparing the basic principles of data protection law, as introduced by Steinmüller, Podlech and others to those of the EU data protection legislation, which I introduced in Chap. 2, it can be seen that principles such as transparency, or necessity, have remained relevant throughout the evolution of data protection in EU

[129] Cf. ECtHR, Klass and Others v. Germany, App. No. 5029/71, Judgment of 6 September 1978, para 34; ECtHR, Iordachi and Others v. Moldova, App. No. 25198/02, Judgment of 10 February 2009, para 30; ECtHR, Kennedy v. the United Kingdom, App. No. 26839/05, Judgment of 18 May 2010, para 124; ECtHR, Szabó and Vissy v. Hungary, App. No. 37138/14, Judgment of 12 January 2016, paras 32–37.

[130] ECtHR [GC], Roman Zakharov v. Russia, App. No. 47143/06, Judgment of 4 December 2015, para 171.

[131] It also addresses the power asymmetry based on superior knowledge and information in the executive branch and can therefore be considered data protection law in the sense of Steinmüller et al., as pointed out by Pohle 2018, pp. 272 et seq.

[132] Bieker et al. 2018b.

law.[133] Other principles, like competence-based processing, separation, the prohibition of hyper-complex processing activities or validity, have been incorporated in the principles under different headings, such as data minimisation, purpose and storage limitation, control[134] or accuracy. Overall, several requirements of these principles are closely connected to the general legal principle of proportionality, which requires measures to have a legal basis, pursue a legitimate aim, be necessary and proportionate.[135]

Furthermore, the differentiation between data protection and data protection law allows the conceptual clarity required to identify the content and scope of the fundamental right to data protection as a part of data protection law. The further differentiation between individual and structural data protection law is of particular importance, as it showcases that individual control—unlike the individualistic approach suggests[136]—is an important, albeit not the only, rationale of data protection.[137]

Under the EU data protection law, the structural dimension of data protection law must to be considered in more detail in order to provide safeguards for the democratic society under the rule of law and thereby also protect individuals. Essentially, structural data protection law ensures that data protection works, even when the individual is not looking. Due to the ubiquity of data processing and its inherent risks, it cannot be left at the exclusive disposal of the individual.[138] Rather, there must be rules in place which ensure that the rule of law-based, democratic society persists and which do not put this burden on an individual already faced with the data power of controllers.

Thus, I have described a dualistic approach to the issue posed by data processing, which takes due account of the individual as well as structural dimensions of the specific answer to this issue, i.e. data protection, and engages the risks and power structures in a comprehensive manner.

However, I have also shown that the debate of Steinmüller, Podlech et al. has not found answers to all problems inherent in data processing activities. While they saw the need for a collective right for groups, they did not explore its potential in detail and rather relegated it to a side note.[139]

---

[133] Cf. Chap. 2, Sect. 2.3.

[134] While not included in the principles of Article 5 GDPR, Articles 4 and 71 DPR-EU as well as Article 4 LED, the principle that the controller has to be in control of the processing and has able to intervene in it, is not only inherent in the concept of controller, but also the obligations of controllers that I introduced in Chap. 2, Sect. 2.3.3.3.

[135] Cf. for instance Sobotta 2017, MN. 8; and already Steinmüller et al. 1971, p. 115; stating that the requirement of data minimisation/necessity substantiates the general principle of proportionality, also cf. Chap. 2, Sect. 2.3.2.5 and below in Sect. 5.3.2.3.

[136] Cf. Chap. 4, Sect. 4.6.

[137] Also cf. Pohle 2018, pp. 237 et seq.

[138] Cf. also de Hingh 2018, who links data protection with human dignity.

[139] I will pick up on this notion of collective rights below in Sect. 5.4.3.1.

5.3 The Application of the Dualistic Approach to the Secondary EU Data Protection Legislation: Uncovering the Secondary EU Data Protection Law

With the dualistic approach—considering the individual as well as the structural dimension of data protection law—set out in the previous section, I will now apply this framework to the secondary EU data protection legislation, i.e. the body of EU secondary law labelled as data protection, which does not exclusively regulate data protection, but also covers other, related fields, in order to uncover the secondary EU data protection law, viz. the body of EU legislation labelled data protection that specifically addresses the issue of data protection.

To achieve this goal of uncovering the secondary EU data protection law, I will analyse the secondary EU data protection legislation in order to identify the rationales it serves as a first step in parsing the actual content of EU data protection law from the secondary EU data protection legislation (Sect. 5.3.1).

In the second step of parsing the content of EU data protection law from the secondary EU data protection legislation, I will analyse the principles of the secondary EU data protection legislation,[140] —which fail to cover the entirety of the rules contained in the secondary EU data legislation itself[141]—as introduced in Chap. 2, with reference to my framework and the rationales of EU data protection law in order to derive the *fundamental principles* of EU data protection law. These *fundamental principles*, unlike the principles expressly included in the current secondary EU data protection legislation, form an abstract general part of EU data protection law, which is reflective of the entirety of the norms (Sect. 5.3.2). I will also argue that both, the individual and structural dimensions of data protection law, are included in the provisions of EU data protection law.

I will conclude this section with the seven fundamental principles of EU data protection law (Sect. 5.3.3). These fundamental principles are lawfulness, separation, transparency, control, confidentiality, integrity and availability and they are representative of the material content of the secondary EU data protection law.

5.3.1 Rationales of the Secondary EU Data Protection Legislation: Data Protection Law and Beyond

Under the conception of Steinmüller, Podlech and others, data protection aims to protect individuals from the processing of personal data and the potential damage this may cause them or society as a whole. As I have argued above,[142] data protection

[140] Article 5 GDPR, Articles 4 and 71 DPR-EU as well as Article 4 LED, as introduced in Chap. 2, Sect. 2.3.2.

[141] Cf. Chap. 2, Sects. 2.3.3.6 and 2.4.

[142] Cf. above in Sect. 5.2.2.

must engage the risks that the processing of personal data creates for individuals and the persistent power structures.

5.3.1.1 Rationales of the Secondary EU Data Protection Law

In the following, I will link these two aspects of risks and power structures back to the secondary EU data protection legislation and argue that the rationale of EU data protection law is to mitigate the risks to the rights and freedoms of individuals and to address the inherent exercise of power. I will then turn to rationales, which are present in the secondary EU data protection legislation, but extend beyond these rationales of data protection law. There, I will point to aspects of the secondary EU data protection legislation, which do not pursue the goals of data protection and can therefore not be considered part of EU data protection law.

Data Processing as Risk to the Rights of Individuals

In data protection it is crucial to prevent misuse, rather than focus protection on post-factum remedies, such as civil law damages, as illegitimate use is hardly detectable, especially for data subjects.[143] Thus, waiting idly for the materialisation of the identifiable risks of data processing may pose an even greater danger, as these risks occur in thousands of cases simultaneously and such developments are reversible only with great difficulty or not at all.[144]

The secondary EU data protection legislation, in its aim to protect fundamental rights of individuals according to Article 1(2) GDPR[145] and to ensure a high level of protection according to recitals 6 and 10 GDPR, adopts the concept of risks to the rights and freedoms of natural persons. These risks must be addressed and mitigated through the implementation of appropriate technical and organisational measures.[146]

In the following, I will, firstly, introduce the concept of risk included in the secondary EU data protection legislation and its function as an instrument which provides scalability of technical and organisational measures.[147] Secondly, I will define the notion of risk to the rights and freedoms of natural persons, which is specific to the secondary EU data protection legislation.

The secondary EU data protection legislation refers to the notion of risk to the rights and freedoms of natural persons. In the first generation of EU data protection legislation, recital 53 DPD already mentioned “risks to the rights and freedoms of data subjects”, which were based in the nature, scope or purposes of a processing operation and listed the risk of “excluding individuals from a right, benefit or a

---

143 Schneider 1973, p. 225.

144 Kilian 1973, p. 305.

145 Cf. also Article 1(2) DPR-EU and Article 1(2)(a) LED.

146 Cf. Articles 35(7)(d), 32(1), 24(1), 25(1) GDPR, Articles 39(7)(d), 27(1), 33(1), 89(2), 85(1), 91(1) and (2) DPR-EU as well as Articles 27, 29(1), 19(1), 20(1) LED.

147 In a second step, I will identify the kinds of risks the processing of personal data poses with regard to the right to data protection according to Article 8 CFR below, cf. Sect. 5.4.2.1.

contract" as well as risks emanating from the use of new technologies. The DPD further noted in recital 54 that such specific risks should be limited.

This restriction has not been included in the GDPR; instead the system of prior notification under Article 20 DPD has been replaced by the records of processing activities according to Article 30 GDPR and the more comprehensive DPIA according to Article 35 GDPR, showing that the legislator found that the risks to the rights and freedoms of natural persons have to be mitigated.

Even though the second generation of secondary EU data protection legislation has become applicable only recently, there has already been much debate on its concept of risk.[148] Gellert, for instance, juxtaposes a risk-based and a rights-based approach and finds that these are similar, yet different practices.[149] Allegedly, the secondary EU data protection legislation, following the rights-based approach, does not allow scaling the measures and instead requires the same safeguards for every processing.[150] However, as he also points out,[151] the GDPR itself does not proclaim to subscribe either to a risk-based or a rights-based approach as defined by Gellert.[152]

The provisions on the responsibility of the controller, data protection by design and the security of the processing operation are the most prominent rules that refer to this notion of risk.[153] According to these provisions, the controller has to implement technical and organisational measures in order to protect individuals against the risks of processing personal data. In the DPD, this had been linked only to the principle of proportionality, where Article 17 DPD required appropriate technical and organisational measures, albeit without further qualifying the term risk.[154]

Similarly, but with the qualification that the risks relate to the rights and freedoms of natural persons, the extent of the technical and organisational measures is determined, among other factors, by this specific risk under the GDPR, DPR-EU and LED.[155] Therefore, the provisions allow controllers to scale their technical and organisational measures in a way that ensures that the principles and the rights of individuals are safeguarded appropriately. Macenaite thus fittingly labels the notion of risk an "obligation adjuster".[156]

However, it must be pointed out that while the extent of the measures to be taken is scalable, technical and organisational measures, under the current EU data

[148] Quelle 2017; Macenaite 2017; Böröcz 2016; Gellert 2016; Gellert 2015; Rost 2018b.

[149] Gellert 2016, unfortunately, he does not identify any specific risks to the rights of individuals.

[150] Ibid., p. 489.

[151] Ibid., p. 483.

[152] Perhaps that is why he concludes that there is not much value in pitting these two approaches against one another, cf. ibid., p. 492.

[153] Articles 24(1), 25(1) and 32(1) and (2) GDPR; Articles 26(1), 27(1), 33(1), 85(1), 91(1) and (2) DPR-EU as well as Articles 19(1), 20(1) and 29(1) and (2) LED

[154] The relation of the risk to the rights of individuals to the principle of proportionality is also rightly pointed out by Gellert 2016, p. 492.

[155] Cf. Chap. 2, Sect. 2.3.3.3.

[156] Macenaite 2017, p. 522.

protection legislation, cannot be omitted for a processing operation,[157] as submitted by the privacy approach.[158] It must also be noted that even though the mitigation of risks is a rationale of EU data protection law generally, the concept of risk as a yardstick for the scope of technical and organisational measures is limited to these provisions. Other obligations, such as the data subject rights or the general rules on the transfer to third countries, do not refer to the risks for the rights and freedoms of natural persons, because they cannot be scaled.[159] Controllers always have to fully comply with these requirements.[160]

Furthermore, it must be borne in mind that just because the notion of risk is relevant for an obligation, this does not necessarily make it scalable. This concerns for instance the obligation to perform a DPIA when it is likely that the processing operation will entail a high risk to the rights and freedoms of individuals. With regard to any processing operation, it is the responsibility of the controller to ascertain whether a high risk is likely under Article 35(1) GDPR. However, this is not surprising, as the risk to the rights of individuals already has to be ascertained under Articles 24(1) and 32(1) GDPR. If that risk is high, a DPIA is required. Yet, the obligation to perform the DPIA is triggered once a high risk is likely. The process of the DPIA itself, which then has to be carried out, also cannot be scaled according to how high the risk seems. Rather, scalability only concerns the question, which measures to take in order to mitigate the identified risks.[161]

However—and with this, I turn to the second part on the notion of risk to the rights and freedoms—what the debate has been lacking so far is an appropriate engagement with how the notion of rights and freedoms relates to the notion of risk and how these terms must be defined.[162] The phrase rights and freedoms, which comes from the French legal tradition, is based on Article 52(1) CFR and recurs back to the ECHR. It encompasses all European fundamental rights of individuals.[163] I will therefore refer to it as risk to the rights of individuals in the following.

The notion of risk to the rights of an individual covers potential material and non-material damages according to recital 75 GDPR. This includes interferences with fundamental rights of individuals, as referred to in recital 94 clause 2 GDPR.[164] However, from this recital it should not be inferred that any interference is damage, but rather that the interference with a fundamental right, logically, poses a risk to

[157] Cf. also ibid., p. 525.

[158] Marsch 2018, pp. 187 et seq. and 204. Cf. also Chap. 4, Sect. 4.5.2.

[159] Except for the narrow clauses of Article 23(2)(g) and Article 49(1)(a) GDPR; ultimately similarly Quelle 2017, p. 59.

[160] Cf. also Macenaite 2017, p. 525.

[161] More ambiguous but ultimately arguing about the scalability of technical and organisational measures Quelle 2017, p. 44.

[162] Hallinan and Martin 2020; Gellert, for instance, asserts that the right to data protection had no substance, without advancing any further arguments, cf. Gellert 2015, p. 12.

[163] Borowsky 2014, MN. 19.

[164] Bieker 2018, p. 29.

the rights of an individual. This risk materialises, when the interference with the fundamental right is not justified according to Article 52(1) CFR.[165]

Thus, the potential damage to be taken into consideration necessarily includes unjustified interference with the rights of individuals, which can manifest in both material and non-material damage.[166] The perspective of individual rights is crucial in the determination of which measures should be taken. Quelle, who does not define the notion of rights and freedoms of individuals, finds that a controller is not obliged "to take all imaginable measure to address the possibility that biases in algorithmic systems will have discriminatory effects."[167] However, where a controller uses an algorithm that discriminates against certain groups, the risk for the rights of these individuals will be high and the controller will have to ensure that these risks are reduced to an acceptable level. In this case, a DPIA is required and if the residual risk for the rights of individuals remains high, the controller may decide on their own not to carry out the processing operation in question or, if they still want do to so, must trigger the prior consultation mechanism according to Article 36 GDPR, which may lead the supervisory authority to impose a limitation on or ban of the processing operation under Article 58(2)(f) GDPR.[168]

The GDPR provides some examples of potential damage in recital 75, which I mentioned in Chap. 2.[169] While it seems rather unstructured at first glance, it lists potential damage resulting from processing operations in its first half and goes on to list certain processing operations, which the legislator deems prone to entail higher risks. The first part thus relates to subsequent damages, which may occur where a processing operation does not conform to the rules of data protection law. This includes discrimination, identity theft or fraud, financial or reputational damage,[170] loss of confidentiality or any other significant economic or societal disadvantage, which relate to various fundamental rights, such as the right to non-discrimination according to Article 21 CFR, the right to privacy under Article 7 CFR as well as the right to data protection of Article 8 CFR. Furthermore, the deprivation of rights and the loss of control explicitly relate to the principle of control and thus Article 8 CFR.

The broad scope of the EU data protection legislation can be seen in the reference to the processing of special categories of data under Articles 9 and 10 GDPR, which relate to the right to privacy,[171] as well as the right to non-discrimination, as these categories are particularly prone to be used for discriminating against specific groups. Recital 75 finds further risks in the evaluation of aspects of the personality and the

---

[165] Ibid.

[166] Ibid.; Konferenz der unabhängigen Datenschutzaufsichtsbehörden des Bundes und der Länder 2018, pp. 1–3; Cf. also Böröcz 2016, pp. 474 and 479, who, unfortunately, does not elaborate on any specific risks to the rights of individuals.

[167] Quelle 2017, p. 45.

[168] Friedewald et al. 2017, p. 35.

[169] Cf. Chap. 2, Sect. 2.3.3.3.

[170] Lenk 1973, pp. 16 et seq. had already identified these risks of data processing, i.e. loss of employment, reputational damage, financial loss or targeted advertising.

[171] Cf. below in Sect. 5.3.1.2.

analysis or prediction of behaviour in order to create profiles, which relates to the right to data protection and the right to privacy, as well as the processing of large amounts of data or data subjects. However, these are mere examples of risks to the rights of individuals. In order to safeguard the rights of data subjects, the controller has to identify, evaluate and address the risks to the rights of individuals, which emanate from their specific processing operation.[172]

Hence, it emerges that the scope of the secondary EU data protection legislation is not limited to the fundamental right to data protection. The secondary EU data protection legislation expressly includes other fundamental rights, which relate to the risks posed by data processing.[173] However, this only explicates the legislator's obligation to adhere to all fundamental rights.[174] As I have demonstrated, rights such as privacy, the freedom of expression and information or non-discrimination have to be considered where the processing of personal data might interfere with them. In order to identify risks to these rights in practice, the individual risks should be analysed with regard to how, and in which stage of a processing operation, this might lead to damage for the individual, i.e. a violation of fundamental rights.[175]

However, it should be noted that, in theory, no additional risks would be identified in an analysis taking other rights into consideration, as the right to data protection already covers any instance of processing personal data.[176] Of course, in practice, such an identification of risks is a necessary corrective measure.[177] Analysing a processing operation under the angle of a different, specific right, and especially from the perspective of an oppressed group in the context of non-discrimination,[178] is a crucial exercise in order to ensure that a processing operation does not only comply with legal obligations in a majority of cases or for a majority of persons.[179]

Data Processing as Exercise of Power

As the controller, by processing personal data, exposes the data subject as well as the democratic society to risks, which I have demonstrated in the previous subsection, the controller thereby exercises power. The power of the controller is that through

---

[172] A method for this kind of risk analysis, which is explicitly based on the notion of risk to the rights of individuals is provided by Friedewald et al. 2017.

[173] Cf. Article 1(2) GDPR, Article 1(2) DPR-EU and Article 1(2)(a) LED.

[174] To this effect cf. the affirmation in recital 4 GDPR.

[175] Bieker and Bremert 2020.

[176] Cf. below in Sect. 5.4.2.1. Also cf. ibid.

[177] Ibid.

[178] While the voices of the marginalized persons who identify these risks are then, in practice, often ignored, as pointed out by Hicks 2021, p. 15. Cf. also, for instance, Noble 2021, pp. 200–204; Ni Loideain and Adams 2019, pp. 22 et seq.; Lawrence 2021. Another example is the automated discrimination of LGBTIQ content on YouTube, cf. Alexander 2019, The Verge. https://www.theverge.com/2019/9/30/20887614/youtube-moderation-lgbtq-demonetization-terms-words-nerd-city-investigation. Accessed 28 July 2021. With regard to data processing in the area of criminal law and its specific risks with a focus on discrimination cf. Golla 2019.

[179] Bieker and Bremert 2020; as already stated in Steinmüller et al. 1971, p. 40.

their action they create a risk for others, which may lead to damages, which these others have to bear, while the controller experiences a gain or profit.

Steinmüller argued that information technology allows for the industrial production and distribution of power as a non-material good.[180] As information, i.e. knowledge and decisions or non-material images of other things and processes, allow for planning and management, they allow control over those that are depicted in the information and grant the controller power over them.[181] Information systems amplify this power, as they multiply and intensify the means of control.[182] The control over the depicted objects on the scale of an entire society allows for control of all citizens or workers and employees.[183] The narrow self-determination approach also refers to these power constellations entailed by data processing.[184]

At the heart of the power imbalance is that the data subject, once their personal data are collected, is not in a position to stop the continued processing, due to the nature of information. The data subject thus experiences a loss of control. Furthermore, data subjects are hardly able to register illegitimate use of their data, for instance when the controller expands the purpose of the processing illegitimately.[185] The controller can supplement their data with data collected from other sources and use them to render individuals or groups transparent and predictable.[186]

The more data is available, the more accurate the controller's profile becomes and might ultimately form a model of an entire group of people.[187] The personal data then "have become *proxies* for persons", as Rouvroy and Poullet put it.[188] Whoever has access to an information system with such a kind of model, has tremendous power to acquire information,[189] which can be used to influence individuals in many different directions or to single out certain groups.[190]

---

180 Steinmüller 1981, p. 166.

181 Ibid., pp. 166 et seq.

182 Ibid., p. 167.

183 Ibid., p. 172.

184 Cf. Chap. 4, Sect. 4.3 and Rouvroy and Poullet 2009, p. 68.

185 Which also illustrates a specific risk to the principle of purpose limitation which I will identify along with other specific risks to the right to data protection below, cf. Sect. 5.4.2.1.

186 Steinmüller et al. 1971, p. 40.

187 Ibid.

188 Rouvroy and Poullet 2009, p. 51, emphasis in original.

189 Even if the data is not fully reliable, the controller can base assumptions and decisions on the model's data and thereby limit the choice of data subjects, even if the data on some individuals are inaccurate.

190 Steinmüller et al. 1971, p. 40 and hence their focus on the importance of effective protections for groups and especially minorities, as discussed below, cf. Sect. 5.2.3.3; Lynskey also picks this up with regard to profiling and discrimination, cf. Lynskey 2018, pp. 177–179; for a practical example of such a practice, cf. Facebook's sharing of personal data with Cambridge Analytica, Tufekci 2018, The New York Times. https://www.nytimes.com/2018/03/19/opinion/facebook-cambridge-analytica.html. Accessed 28 July 2021.

Such information systems—and through them the controller—reduce the data subjects to an object that is being processed and merely feeds data into databases.[191] The industrially produced planning, management and control capacity over persons, things and structures then shifts the existing information and power structures between the various competing groups and institutions of society.[192] The informational divide thus opens in favour of big enterprises and the executive branch.[193]

Podlech coined the phrase, that the individual must know, which of their data are processed by which entity for what purpose.[194] If the individual can no longer ascertain these questions, an organisation, be it private or public, exercises power over the individual through the superior knowledge gathered in the information system.[195] In both the public and private sector, the use of physical force and economic power could thus easily be replaced by the use of superior knowledge based on the processing of personal data.[196]

When the controller, without the knowledge of the data subject, has access to information, for instance, on their personal preferences, interests, finances or medical conditions, the individual faces an entity they cannot actually perceive: the concentrated power of the information system, which remains opaque to the individual.[197] The information system then amplifies the power of controllers.[198] The individual is thus confronted with a power deficit, which has to be compensated.[199]

Data protection provides tools and mechanisms to lay bare the power structures and to expose the power asymmetry between organisations and individuals.[200] However, as the previous analysis of the wider structures already indicates,[201] this cannot be solved on an individual basis,[202]—for instance, by discounting the power structures and simply granting data subjects more rights, which they must enforce on their own, as suggested by the individualistic approach[203]—but must also duly consider the wider implications for a democratic society.[204]

---

[191] Steinmüller et al. 1971, p. 137; de Hingh 2018, esp. p. 1287.

[192] Steinmüller 1981, p. 173.

[193] Ibid.

[194] Podlech 1982, p. 455; which was famously adopted by the Bundesverfassungsgericht, BVerfGE 65, pp. 1–71—Volkszählung, Judgment of 15 December 1983; although the fact of this adoption has largely gone unnoticed, cf. Steinmüller 2007, p. 160.

[195] Podlech 1987, p. 21; Podlech 1988, p. 123.

[196] Podlech 1988, p. 123.

[197] Steinmüller 1981, pp. 175 et seq.

[198] Pohle 2018, p. 261.

[199] Steinmüller 1981, p. 176; Fröhlich and Spiecker gen. Döhmann 2018.

[200] Rost 2018b, p. 84.

[201] Cf. above in Sect. 5.2.3.

[202] Steinmüller 1981, pp. 176 et seq.; Steinmüller here refers back to the solutions already discussed in the early 1970s.

[203] Cf. Chap. 4, Sect. 4.6.

[204] Rost 2018b, p. 84.

It transpires that the ability to store, not to store, change, use or delete data concerning individuals is a form of power.[205] This describes the fundamental asymmetry in power between controllers and data subjects and is at the core of the societal need for data protection: the controller wields data power (*Datenmacht*[206]).[207] Rendering this power imbalance visible and addressing it is therefore also the rationale of data protection. It is deeply entwined with the other rationale of addressing the risks to the rights of individuals, as the controller's ability to set those risks for individuals as well as society at large is a more specific iteration of this inherent power imbalance and thus exemplifies their data power.

5.3.1.2 Rationales Beyond EU Data Protection Law

As is frequently the case with any kind of regulation, the secondary EU data protection legislation does not exclusively regulate the specific issue of data protection in all instances. In passing this legislation—which in the first generation was linked with the right to privacy,[208] as a specific fundamental right to data protection did not yet exist—the legislator also pursued other objectives: a recent example for this is the new data subject right of data portability, where the legislator engaged in an indirect form of market regulation.[209] It enables data subjects to acquire data, which they have previously provided to the controller. Such data must, subject to several caveats,[210] either be provided to the data subject in a machine-readable format or transferred by the controller directly to another controller. While Article 20 GDPR also strengthens the control of users[211] and can be seen as a more elaborate right to access of personal information,[212] there is also an underlying market rationale: in order to undermine mono- and oligopolies by avoiding lock-in effects[213] the right enables individuals to migrate their personal data from one controller to another with greater ease[214] and thereby strives to foster competition.[215]

---

205 Podlech 1988, p. 123.

206 von Lewinski 2009, p. 200.

207 Pohle 2018, p. 261.

208 Cf. above in Sect. 5.2.1.

209 Lynskey also notes that data portability seems to be at odds with the goals of data protection, cf. Lynskey 2015b, pp. 99 and 129.

210 For a detailed discussion of the restricted scope of Article 20 GDPR, cf. Ursic 2018, pp. 50–58.

211 Cf. recital 68 and Article 29 Working Party, Guidelines on the right to data portability of 13 December 2016. WP 242 rev.01, p. 4; Ursic 2018, pp. 58–67.

212 Hustinx 2017, p. 153.

213 Hornung 2012, p. 74.

214 As explicitly acknowledged by the Article 29 Working Party, Guidelines on the right to data portability of 13 December 2016, p. 4.

215 Almunia, Competition and personal data protection—Speech delivered by the Vice President of the European Commission at the Privacy Platform event on 26 November 2012. SPEECH/12/860. http://europa.eu/rapid/press-release_SPEECH-12-860_en.htm. Accessed 28 July 2021; Dix 2014, MN. 105; Scudiero 2017, p. 119.

The rules concerning special categories of data according to Article 9 GDPR are another example: they serve to protect the privacy of individuals.[216] The rules on these special categories of data operate on the premise that some data require more protection than others, even though it is often hard to differentiate, which data should fall into this category.[217]

Nevertheless, the specific norms all include a definite list of data that are awarded special protection.[218] While most include religion, race and political opinions, other categories differ widely and there are no discernible objective criteria that explain these differences.[219] Instead, the content of these rules show a specific political and societal view on the processing of personal data and its implications.[220] Thus, it can be seen that the special categories of data are dependent on a subjective notion of which data should be awarded special protection[221] in order to offer the individual a residual space of freedom from intrusion. They are thus linked to privacy and encounter the same issues that come with this concept, such as its broad but undefined scope, which I have discussed above.[222] Most notably, the relativity of information depending on the context does not allow for a generally valid list of exclusions.[223]

Excluding the special categories of data from the scope of data protection law may seem counterintuitive, as these are a longstanding part of the EU, as well as international data protection legislation.[224] However, as I have argued above,[225] data protection assumes that all personal data can potentially damage individuals, depending on the specific context. The introduction of special categories of data runs counter to this very notion.

Thus, the focus on special categories is not helpful to answer the specific issue posed by the processing of personal data and—while generally some categories of data may be more prone to be used in a discriminatory manner[226]—may even be harmful to remedying the issue of data protection, as it includes the notion that other data require less or no protection, as purported by the privacy approach,[227] even though the same negative consequences for the rights of individuals can occur with

---

[216] Which I have already mentioned briefly above in Sect. 5.3.1.1. Also cf. De Hert and Gutwirth 2006, p. 101.

[217] Simitis 1990, p. 470; who provides a good overview of various regulations.

[218] Ibid., p. 471.

[219] Ibid., pp. 471–473.

[220] Ibid., pp. 474 et seq.

[221] Ibid., pp. 482 et seq.

[222] Cf. above in Sect. 5.2.1.

[223] Steinmüller et al. 1971, p. 144.

[224] Bygrave 2014, pp. 165–167.

[225] Cf. above in Sect. 5.2.1.

[226] Yet, Article 9 GDPR fails to take into account other data which are often used to discriminate and mentioned inter alia in Article 22 CFR, such as sex, social origin, membership of a national minority, age or disability; cf. also Petri 2019, MN. 10; Weichert 2018a, MN. 15 and 21.

[227] Cf. Chap. 4, Sect. 4.5.

data of any variety, depending on the context of the processing.[228] However, under the current secondary EU data protection legislation, the responsibility of controllers[229] as well as the requirement for technical and organisation measures to ensure an appropriate level of protection[230] are not limited to special categories of data, but rather apply to all kinds of data and their specific inherent risks.

Furthermore, the principle of fairness under the second generation of secondary EU data protection legislation, as I have elaborated in Chap. 2, incorporates ethical considerations and goals of consumer protection into the GDPR.[231] However, with regard to the right to data protection under Article 8 CFR, the notion of fair processing included in Article 8(2) CFR—which, in its wording, is based on the first generation of secondary EU data protection law, in force when the European Convention discussed the right—is linked to the transparency of the processing for data subjects. This interpretation conforms to the telos of Article 8 CFR, as interpreted with regard to the second generation of secondary EU data protection legislation, and is confirmed by a historical interpretation: at the time of the drafting of the Charter, the first generation of secondary EU data protection legislation served as frame of reference, which also understood fairness as referring to the transparency of the processing.[232]

This is not to exclude the interest of consumer protection from the GDPR, but rather to achieve conceptual clarity with regard to the fundamental right to data protection and its aim to address the issue of data protection: while it is perfectly reasonable to include other rationales in legislation like the GDPR, for a delimitation of the right to data protection, it is crucial to identify those concepts that directly serve to promote its aims.

The right to be forgotten, in its dimension as a right to delisting from internet search engines, as developed by the ECJ[233] and, according to the Court, now anchored in Article 17 GDPR,[234] is another instrument that is based on the secondary EU data protection legislation,[235] even though it does not serve to mitigate the issue of data processing. While the initial question of whether the processing of data is still necessary[236] relates to the principles of purpose and storage limitation, the answer

[228] Simitis 1990, pp. 483 et seq.; Pohle 2018, p. 242; Schneider 2017, p. 304.

[229] Article 24 GDPR, Article 26 DPR-EU and Article 19 LED.

[230] Article 32 GDPR, Articles 33 and 91 DPR-EU as well as Article 29 LED.

[231] Cf. Chap. 2, Sect. 2.3.2.2.

[232] Cf. Chap. 2, Sect. 2.3.2.2.

[233] ECJ, Case C-131/12 Google Spain SL and Google Inc. v Agencia Española de Protección de Datos (AEPD) and Mario Costeja González, Judgment of 13 April 2014, ECLI:EU:C:2014:317, and as discussed above, cf. Chap. 3, Sect. 3.2.8.3.

[234] ECJ, Case C-507/17 Google LLC v Commission nationale de l'informatique et des libertés (CNIL), Judgment of 24 September 2019, ECLI:EU:C:2019:772, paras 46 et seq.

[235] The Court interpreted the data subject rights of Articles 12 and 14 DPD in the light of Articles 7 and 8 CFR to grant this right to be forgotten, cf. ECJ, Case C-131/12 Google Spain and Google, Judgment of 13 April 2014, paras 88 and 99.

[236] Cf. ibid., para 93.

to this question cannot be provided by recourse to the concepts of data protection.[237] Rather, this right to be forgotten concerns the privacy of the individual, which in this case collides with the right to freedom of expression and information of internet users relying on search engines.[238] The conflict is thus similar to the cases concerning media reports on the private lives of individuals,[239] which the secondary EU data protection legislation according to Article 85 GDPR, explicitly removes from its ambit, as these cases require a balancing of the conflicting fundamental rights. In order to answer the question whether the processing is still necessary, the conflict between these rights must be resolved. However, providing this answer is not within the rationale of data protection.

From all of the above, I conclude that the special categories of data, the principle of fairness, when understood to extend beyond transparency, the right to be forgotten and, partially, the right to data portability do not address the issue of data protection. Rather, they serve other interests, such as privacy or consumer protection, that are not useful to determine the content of EU data protection law in general and the EU fundamental right to data protection specifically. Removing these extraneous rationales from the EU legislation, uncovers the content of EU data protection law. I will therefore not consider these notions, when deriving the fundamental principles from the remaining provisions, which form the body of the secondary EU data protection law, in the following.

5.3.2 *Deriving the Fundamental Principles from the Secondary EU Data Protection Law*

After having set out the dual rationale of data protection law, I will now derive the fundamental principles of EU data protection law, i.e. the principles which stem from the entirety of the rules of secondary EU data protection law and which are therefore truly reflective of its material content.[240]

In order to achieve this, I will analyse the secondary EU data protection law, structured along the lines of the principles of the EU secondary legislation, while taking into account that these principles—in their current form, as I concluded in Chap. 2[241]—are not fully reflective of the rules contained in the EU data protection legislation itself. Hence, I will also take those further provisions of the secondary

---

[237] Also cf. Lynskey 2015a, pp. 528–531, who argues, however, that the right to be forgotten is part of the right to data protection.

[238] ECJ, Case C-131/12 Google Spain and Google, Judgment of 13 April 2014, para 81.

[239] Cf. ECtHR [GC], Von Hannover v. Germany (No. 2), App. Nos. 40660/08 and 60641/08, Judgment of 7 February 2012.

[240] Cf. already ECJ, Case C-275/06 Productores de Música de España (Promusicae) v Telefónica de España SAU Opinion of AG Kokott of 18 July 2007, ECLI:EU:C:2007:454, para 51.

[241] Cf. Chap. 2, Sects. 2.3.3.6 and 2.4.

EU data protection legislation, which I have introduced in Chap. 2,[242] and which pursue the rationales of EU data protection law into consideration. These further provisions are relevant in order to derive a comprehensive set of fundamental principles, which are representative of the system and characteristics of the secondary EU data protection law, such as the data subject and procedural rights, the responsibility of controllers or the independence of the supervisory authorities.[243]

As I already illustrated in Chap. 2 that the principle of fairness does not conform to the dual rationale of data protection,[244] I will not consider it in the following. I will restructure and systematise the remaining principles and I will also link them to general principles of EU law, such as proportionality, legality or the rule of law. My argument, therefore, will be both, inductive with regard to the principles of the secondary EU data protection legislation, and deductive as concerns the general principles of EU law.

In deriving the fundamental principles of EU data protection law, I will explore their individual and structural dimensions, which, as I will demonstrate in the following subsections, are inherent in all of the fundamental principles. As the principles of the secondary EU data protection legislation are generally interpreted with regard to their individual dimension in the current debate, I will place an emphasis on the structural dimension of each fundamental principle, in order to demonstrate that their understanding, and thereby the protection from the processing of personal data, offered to the individual as well as the democratic society as a whole, can thus be improved.

5.3.2.1 Lawfulness

For the public sector, the fundamental principle of lawfulness is a specific iteration of the general principle of the rule of law and the legality principle, under which public authority may only be exercised when there is a legitimate legal basis and the task lies within the competence and jurisdiction of the authority in question.[245] With regard to the private sector, the fundamental principle of lawfulness extends this general principle to private entities processing personal data, due to the risks associated with the processing of personal data, which are, in most instances, the same as for public administration.[246]

By obliging controllers to recur to a legal basis before processing any personal data, the fundamental principle of lawfulness, anchored in the general principle of the rule of law and the principle of legality, has a strong structural dimension. Due to the risks to the rights of individuals[247] associated with the processing of personal

[242] Cf. Chap. 2, Sect. 2.3.3.

[243] Cf. Chap. 2, Sect. 2.3.3.6 and also Roßnagel 2019, MN. 29.

[244] Cf. above in Sect. 5.3.1.2.

[245] Steinmüller et al. 1971; Podlech 1973b, p. 11; Podlech 1973a, p. 42.

[246] On the rationale of this extension cf. above in Sects. 5.3.1.1 and 5.4.4.

[247] As introduced above, cf. Chap. 2, Sect. 2.3.3.3 and Sect. 5.3.1.1.

data, the imposition of such a general ban on processing is a preliminary step to ensure that the question whether data should be processed at all, is regulated.

However, the fundamental principle of lawfulness, as expressed in Article 6 GDPR,[248] by requiring a legal basis for any processing operation also protects the individual from overreach of controllers and the loss of control and autonomy with regard to the processing of their data by ensuring that controllers must justify their actions through recourse to a legal basis before commencing the processing.[249] This can also be seen in the rules on transfers to third countries and international organisations under Chapters V GDPR, DPR-EU and LED, which require a particular additional legal basis in order to ensure that data subjects' rights and interests are safeguarded against the additional risks posed by such a transfer.[250] Correspondingly, the data subject has the right to be informed of such a transfer and the safeguards taken by the controller.[251] The fundamental principle of lawfulness thereby also serves the individual dimension of data protection law.

The fulfilment of the fundamental principle of lawfulness is a necessary prerequisite, as it addresses the issue whether data may be processed, but is itself not sufficient to render a processing operation legal,[252] as can be seen by reference the other principles. While the fundamental principle of lawfulness concerns the issue if data may be processed, the other principles concern the question of how the processing is carried out. Lawfulness is also closely related to the principle of purpose limitation, as the legal basis may provide a justification for the processing of personal data only for specified purposes.

5.3.2.2 Purpose Limitation

For public authorities, the requirement of legitimacy of the purpose adapts the first step of the proportionality test according to Article 52(1) CFR—under which any measure of a public authority has to serve a legitimate aim—to the principles of EU data protection law. The GDPR extends this general requirement of EU law to private entities processing data, due to the inherent risks of such processing to the rights of individuals and in order to address the power imbalance between controllers[253] and data subjects.[254]

---

[248] Cf. also Articles 5 and 72 DPR-EU as well as Article 8 LED.

[249] Karg 2013, pp. 77 et seq.

[250] Cf. Chap. 2, Sect. 2.3.3.4. While the rules on special categories of data cannot be considered data protection law in the sense of this framework, cf. above in Sect. 5.3.1.2, they employ a similar regulatory approach here, where they also demand a particular additional legal basis in order to render the processing of certain data lawful, cf. Article 9 GDPR, Articles 10 and 76 DPR-EU as well as Article 10 LED.

[251] Article 15(1)(c) and (2) GDPR, Article 17(1)(c) and (2) and Article 80(c) DPR-EU as well as Article 14(c) LED.

[252] Podlech 1982, p. 461.

[253] Cf. below in Sect. 5.3.3.

[254] Cf. above in Sect. 5.3.1.1 and below in Sect. 5.4.4.

Simitis has argued that the debate on the legitimacy of purposes[255] should take into focus the question of the desirability of data processing generally in some contexts and explore its limits, rather than restrict itself to accepting all forms of automation and merely mitigating its adverse effects.[256] Just as the rule of law limits the exercise of public power monopolized by the State, data protection law regulates the processing of personal data, in order to render it socially acceptable.[257] With the provisions of EU data protection law, in particular Article 5(1)(b) GDPR[258] requiring that data are collected for legitimate purposes, the legislator has set limits for the processing of personal data that is deemed acceptable. This means that the purpose of any processing operation must be compatible with and adhere to the framework of EU data protection law. When a private entity, for instance, operates under a business model, which is in opposition to the very foundations of data protection law, the purposes of its processing activities are illegitimate.

In instances where the data subject can actually make a free and informed choice whether to conclude a contract with the controller according to Article 6(1)(b) GDPR[259] or to consent[260] to a processing operation under Articles 6(1)(d) and 7 GDPR,[261] the specified purpose and the thereby defined objective of the processing is the determinative factor in their decision. In this regard, the specification of the purpose[262] is a prerequisite for transparency and illustrates the importance of purpose limitation for individual data protection, as without it, the level of transparency would be lower and the choices of data subjects less informed. This assessment is confirmed by the corresponding requirements and data subject rights of, inter alia, Articles 13–15 GDPR[263] on information to be provided to data subjects upon the collection of data and their right of access. Furthermore, it allows the individual a degree of control, as they can refer to the specified purpose as a benchmark to check the activities of the controller, at least in as far as these activities are accessible to them.

At the same time, the requirement of purpose limitation restricts the processing activities of controllers. By virtue of this obligation, controllers are required to explain themselves to data subjects[264] and supervisory authorities[265] and to justify their processing activities.

---

[255] Cf. Chap. 2, Sect. 2.3.2.4.

[256] Simitis 1973, p. 141, fn. 12.

[257] Podlech 1987, p. 23.

[258] Cf. also Articles 4(1)(b) and 71(1)(b) DPR-EU as well as Article 4(1)(b) LED.

[259] Cf. also Article 5(1)(b) DPR-EU.

[260] Cf. especially Kamp and Rost 2013; de Hingh 2018, pp. 1279–1281, arguing that consent commodifies the individual through their data and thus violates the principle of non-commercialisation as part of human dignity; also already Rouvroy and Poullet 2009, pp. 73 et seq; Pohle 2018, pp. 226 et seq. with further references.

[261] Cf. also Articles 5(1)(d) and 7 DPR-EU.

[262] Cf. Chap. 2, Sect. 2.3.2.4.

[263] Cf. also Articles 15–17 DPR-EU.

[264] Hence the obligations to inform data subjects according to Article 12–14 GDPR, Articles 15 et seq. and 79 DPR-EU as well as Articles 12 et seq. LED.

[265] Cf. Articles 58(1) GDPR and DPR-EU as well as Article 47(1) LED.

However, the requirement of purpose specification transcends the immediate concerns of the individual. Whether an individual data subject checks the purposes of a given processing operation or not, purpose limitation restrains controllers by limiting their activities to a pre-defined and specified purposes and limiting subsequent use of those data.[266] Purpose limitation thus also has a structural aspect to it, which connects it to the principle of accountability: the organisation, as controller, has to limit itself and thereby act against its own interests in administrative procedural efficiency.[267]

That the inherent restriction of the controller in this principle is not limited to control by data subjects is even more evident with regard to the requirement of a legitimate purpose: it allows for a substantive review of controllers' activities. This limitation of the controllers' data power and their ability to process individuals as objects embodies the structural side of the requirement of purpose limitation.

The purpose of a processing operation is highly relevant for the determination of which data may be collected under the requirement of data minimisation[268] as well as the start and end points of the processing operation, i.e. whether the purpose has been attained, which relates to the requirements of necessity and storage limitation.[269]

5.3.2.3 Necessity and Data Minimisation

The question whether the processed data are necessary to attain the specified purpose is at the core of data minimisation and a paramount rule of data protection law: it ensures that the processing of personal data is restricted, as required by EU primary law.[270] In this regard, the requirement of data minimisation sets limits on which specific data can be processed, for a specified purpose in a specific context. It contextualises and further defines the principle of lawfulness and the requirement of purpose limitation in substance and thereby imposes organisational and institutional requirements on controllers. These requirements are, for instance, featured prominently in the obligation to implement data protection by design according to Article 25(1) GDPR[271]—which requires controllers to implement technical and organisational measures before as well as during the processing operation and thus demands a

---

[266] Article 29 Working Party, Opinion 03/2013 on purpose limitation of 2 April 2013. WP 203, p. 15; which has not been endorsed by the EDPB, as it concerned the DPD, rather than the GDPR. Nevertheless, Article 5(1)(b) clause 1 GDPR has the exact same wording as Article 6(1)(b) clause 1 DPD.

[267] Steinmüller 1975, p. 75; Podlech 1982, p. 452; cf. also Simitis et al. 2019, MN. 13 and 45.

[268] Cf. Chap. 2, Sect. 2.3.2.5.

[269] Cf. below in Sect. 5.3.3.

[270] Cf. Chap. 2, Sect. 2.2.

[271] Cf. also Articles 27(1) and 85(1) DPR-EU as well as Article 20(1) LED.

holistic approach for the entirety of the processing operation[272]—and data protection by default according to Article 25(2) GDPR,[273] which requires that by default, only data that are necessary are processed and thus explicitly refers to the requirement of necessity. Necessity and data minimisation, like purpose limitation, are thus also a structural requirement aimed at curtailing the data power of controllers.

Yet, necessity and data minimisation are also the basis for the exercise of data subject rights. This can be seen for instance in the data subject right to erasure or restriction of processing or blocking, when the data are no longer necessary.[274] It thus also concerns the protection of data subjects and therefore has an individual dimension.

5.3.2.4 Storage Limitation

By introducing storage limitation in Article 5(1)(e) GDPR,[275] EU data protection law prima facie explicates an aspect of purpose limitation and necessity, which is logically already included in those requirements: when personal data have been processed and the purpose of this processing has been attained or can definitely no longer be attained, the personal data are no longer necessary and have to be deleted.[276]

However, by stating that the personal data should be pseudo- or anonymised as soon as possible, storage limitation is an addition to purpose limitation. It can be seen as a combination of data minimisation, i.e. necessity, and purpose limitation: if specific personal data are necessary in order to achieve a purpose, they must be processed pseudo- or anonymously whenever identification is not necessary. This also applies to the clause on archiving purposes, which requires appropriate technical and organisational measures to safeguard the rights of data subjects.

The pseudonymisation of personal data is one of the examples for technical and organisational measures to ensure the security of the processing, listed expressly in Article 32(1)(a) GDPR.[277] While additional measures will be required, this strong link to pseudonymisation whenever the identification of data subjects is not necessary, shows that storage limitation, by requiring data to be processed in a way that minimises the identification of data subjects, adds an additional layer of protection to the requirements of purpose limitation and necessity.

Just as the requirements of data minimisation define the limits of the processing operation with regard to the purpose, the requirement of storage limitation thus combines purpose limitation and necessity in order to further define the limits of

---

[272] Cf. in-depth Hansen 2019a, MN. 15-18 and 66.

[273] Cf. also Articles 27(2) and 85(2) DPR-EU as well as Article 20(2) LED.

[274] Articles 17(1)(a) and 18(1)(c) GDPR as well as Articles 19(1)(a) and 20(1)(c) DPR-EU.

[275] Cf. also Articles 4(1)(e) and 71(1)(e) DPR-EU as well as Article 4(1)(e) LED.

[276] The deletion of data is a technical and organisational measure aiming to implement the principles of purpose limitation and data minimisation, cf. Konferenz der unabhängigen Datenschutzaufsichtsbehörden des Bundes und der Länder 2020, p. 17.

[277] Cf. also Article 33(1)(a) DPR-EU.

processing personal data, by reducing the identifiability of individuals. This obligation is also included in the provision on data protection by default, which extends to all stages of a processing operation according to Article 25(2) GDPR.[278] It is therefore, ultimately, a structural rule and concerns individual data protection only insofar as the requirements of purpose limitation and necessity cover them, for instance with regard to the right to erasure.

5.3.2.5 Separation

From the requirements of purpose limitation, necessity and data minimisation as well as storage limitation, as I discussed in the preceding subsections, the common theme of separation emerges. This is further substantiated by the requirement of data protection by design, which refers to the principles contained in Article 5 GDPR:[279] as the obligation of data protection by design requires controllers to already incorporate the principles in the design of a processing operation, i.e. when determining the means for processing, and thus well before any personal data are processed, the mere retrospective addition of technical and organisational measures to an already existing system[280] is not sufficient.[281] This is true both where a controller develops their own system or relies on systems or components supplied by third parties.[282] Thus, the obligation extends to the entire lifecycle of a processing operation.[283]

While the processing of personal data, may, according to Article 5(1)(b) GDPR,[284] explicitly be permissible for multiple purposes, it must be ensured that "only the personal data which are necessary for each specific purpose of the processing are processed" according to the requirement of data protection by default,[285] which mirrors the requirements of data minimisation. In order to implement purpose limitation in practice, collected data should—bearing in mind the obligation of data protection by design—already be stored separately according to their different purposes.[286]

When the data are processed separately for each specific purpose, they should also be processed, both on the system and the organisational side, in a way that

[278] Cf. also Articles 27(2) and 85(2) DPR-EU as well as Article 20(2) LED.

[279] Cf. also Articles 4 and 71 DPR-EU as well as Article 4 LED.

[280] Regardless whether this concerns an IT or organisational, viz. procedural, system.

[281] Hansen 2019a, MN. 17.

[282] While manufacturers and producers of products are not regulated by the EU data protection legislation, controllers are responsible to adhere to all data protection norms when they employ such products; ibid., MN. 18.

[283] Ibid., MN. 32.

[284] Cf. also Articles 4(1)(b) DPR-EU and LED.

[285] According to Article 25(2) GDPR, Articles 27(2) and 85(2) DPR-EU as well as Article 20(2) LED.

[286] Hansen 2019a, MN. 65.

reduces the ability to link the separated sets of data.[287] On the system side, this can be achieved, for instance, by using different and non-inferable identifiers or by pseudonymisation of the data according to the requirement of storage limitation.[288] On the organisational side, data must be separated when they are stored, which can be organised in a decentralised manner[289] implementing the informational separation of powers[290] within the entity processing the data and thereby ensuring through technical and organisational measures that the data are separated.[291]

Furthermore, under Article 24 GDPR,[292] the controller has to ensure that within their own organisation only competent personnel can process the specific data that are required for the completion of a specific task, which also entails an aspect of organisational separation. This can be achieved, inter alia, by closing ports and interfaces of processes and components, rights and roles concepts with differentiated access rights or the distribution of competences across different departments.[293] With regard to the latter measure especially, it must be pointed out that the public sector is not one unit, but rather purposefully separated into different entities,[294] which provides an element of checks and balances within the administration.[295]

The use of pseudonymisation in the GDPR and DPR-EU[296] as an example can also be read as a case where the legislator considers that data should be separated, especially when taking into account the obligation of storage limitation concerning the removal of data identifying an individual. According to the legal definition,[297] the pseudonymisation of data must be accompanied by further technical and organisational measures to ensure that the additional information which allow the re-identification of individuals are not available.[298] This includes, in particular, the separation of data.[299]

Recital 28 GDPR explicitly states, however, that the example of pseudonymisation is not intended to preclude other measures. This use of pseudonymisation where the legislator intends for the separation of data can be observed in Article 25(1)

---

[287] Konferenz der unabhängigen Datenschutzaufsichtsbehörden des Bundes und der Länder 2020, p. 27.

[288] Hansen 2019a, MN. 65 et seq.

[289] Ibid., MN. 65.

[290] While Podlech initially introduced this notion, cf. above in Sect. 5.2.2, I have adapted it to fit EU data protection law, i.e. purpose limitation.

[291] Roßnagel 2019, MN. 169.

[292] Cf. also Article 26 DPR-EU and Article 19 LED.

[293] Weichert 2018b, MN. 30; Konferenz der unabhängigen Datenschutzaufsichtsbehörden des Bundes und der Länder 2020, p. 33.

[294] Weichert 2018b, MN. 30; as already included in Steinmüller 1975, p. 84; also cf. Simitis 1986, p. 2800.

[295] Steinmüller 1981, p. 173; von Berg et al. 1972, p. 3.

[296] As well as, albeit to a lesser degree, in recital 53 and Article 20 LED.

[297] Article 4(5) GDPR, Article 3(6) DPR-EU and Article 3(5) LED.

[298] Hansen 2019b, MN. 34.

[299] Ibid.

GDPR,[300] where it serves as an example for technical and organisational measures taken to implement the principles of the EU data protection legislation, and Article 32(1)(a) GDPR,[301] where it is listed as one of the measures to improve the security of the processing operation.

Even when the limitation of data processing to a specific purpose is reduced for compatible purposes, such as scientific research according to Article 5(1)(b) GDPR,[302] this further processing requires appropriate safeguards according to recital 156 and Articles 6(4)(e), 89(1) GDPR,[303] such as pseudonymisation. This is sensible when one considers that in these cases, the requirements of data minimisation, especially necessity and storage limitation still apply.

The example of an online store, as introduced in Chap. 2,[304] which offers a range of services—ranging from buying items, shipping them to customers, to personalised recommendations—and may rely on a contract encompassing several purposes as legal basis, can again be illustrative here. By default, the controller has to process only those data necessary for each specific purpose. The purposes of the processing may be expanded by additional services, which will require an additional legal basis, such as consent or a separate contract. The linking of the separate datasets is not allowed, unless it is necessary to achieve a different specific task, which itself must fulfil the requirements of the principles.

In order to implement data protection by design with regard to purpose limitation, it must be ensured that data cannot be combined after collection for other than the initial purposes by preventing the linking by the same or derivable identifiers.[305] However, for the completion of the different tasks, such as sale and shipping, it is not necessary to link the data for these individual purposes. Instead, the data can be separated through technical and organisational measures, such as pseudonymisation.

On a higher level, of course, the separation of informational powers could be achieved through identity infrastructures built on anonymous communication infrastructures that only allow for the processing of the personal data necessary in a specific context.[306] This exemplifies the paramount importance of structural data protection with regard to infrastructures: if the communication infrastructure is not designed in conformity to the rules of data protection, it cannot contribute to answering the issue posed by the processing of personal data, but rather exacerbates this issue. However, even where such infrastructures are not available, controllers are not absolved of their responsibility. Rather, EU data protection law requires them to implement the principles in as far as possible.[307]

---

300 Cf. also Articles 27(1) and 85(1) DPR-EU as well as Article 20(1) LED.

301 Cf. also Article 33(1)(a) DPR-EU.

302 Cf. also Articles 4(1)(b) and 71(3) DPR-EU as well as Article 4(3) LED.

303 Cf. also Articles 6(e) and 13 DPR-EU.

304 Cf. Chap. 2, Sect. 2.3.2.4.

305 Hansen 2019a, MN. 64.

306 Hansen and Thomsen 2010, pp. 287 et seq.

307 I will address how this can be achieved practically for all fundamental principles by considering them optimisation requirements below in Sect. 5.3.3.

In conclusion, the combined requirements of purpose limitation, data minimisation and storage limitation can be unified under the fundamental principle of separation, which extends to the data themselves, but also includes the systems and procedures. This ensures that the manifold interconnections between purpose limitation, data minimisation and storage limitations are taken into account. This fundamental principle encompasses the provisions of the EU data protection legislation, which aim to ensure that personal data is not subject to the controller's unfettered power to combine and link sets of data collected for various purposes, in a single set in order to pursue illegitimate or unlawful purposes.[308] It thereby represents both the individual as well as the structural side of data protection law: the individual is awarded rights which ensure that they can enforce their interests with regard to purpose limitation and data minimisation, while the structural side of the principle guarantees that the controller's power is checked by safeguards on the system and organisational side.

5.3.2.6 Confidentiality, Integrity and Availability

The fundamental principles of confidentiality, integrity and availability are independent principles with separate scopes. The principle of confidentiality,[309] which aims to ensure that only authorised persons or entities have access to personal data, protects the individual against the unauthorised disclosure of their data. In that regard, the confidentiality of data is also protected by the fundamental principles of lawfulness and separation, which allow data subjects to require the deletion of data according to Article 17 GDPR[310] when they were processed unlawfully or when they were processed for an illegitimate purpose. From the perspective of structural data protection law, the fundamental principle of confidentiality ensures that the distribution of personal data is limited.

The requirement of the principle of integrity[311] that data are qualitatively intact and quantitatively complete, also has an individual as well as a structural dimension. In the EU data protection legislation, the individual dimension is covered by accuracy, which requires that data are accurate and kept up to date and thus relates to both the quantitative and qualitative aspect of integrity[312] in order to protect the data subject against the processing of inaccurate data.

The structural dimension of integrity is visible in the provision on the security of the processing in Article 32 GDPR,[313] which requires technical and organisational

[308] It is therefore very closely related to the Standard Data Protection Model's data protection goal of unlinkability, cf. Konferenz der unabhängigen Datenschutzaufsichtsbehörden des Bundes und der Länder 2020, p. 27.

[309] Article 5(1)(f) GDPR, Articles 4(1)(f) and 71(1)(f) DPR-EU as well as Article 4(1)(f) LED.

[310] Cf. also Articles 19 and 82 DPR-EU.

[311] Article 5(1)(f) GDPR, Articles 4(1)(f) and 71(1)(f) DPR-EU as well as Article 4(1)(f) LED.

[312] Konferenz der unabhängigen Datenschutzaufsichtsbehörden des Bundes und der Länder 2020, p. 26; also cf. Hansen 2019b, MN. 13.

[313] Cf. also Articles 33 and 91 DPR-EU as well as Article 29 LED.

measures in order to ensure the integrity of data, regardless of the interests of a specific individual, but rather, more generally, due to the risks that the processing of inaccurate data poses for individuals.

Concerning these measures and their implementation, the lists of Article 32(1) GDPR and Article 33(1) DPR-EU are rather generic. However, Article 91(2) DPR-EU and Article 29(2) LED contain more detailed provisions, including, inter alia, equipment and media access, storage, user and communication control as well as recovery, reliability and integrity. While the former measures relate to confidentiality as well as integrity and reliability—i.e. ensuring the system functions are performed and that errors are reported—the latter is a part of integrity: recovery relates to the availability of data, i.e. the ability to restore data that are not currently—or no longer—available. In turn, Article 32(2) GDPR refers to the specific risks of accidental or unlawful destruction, loss, alteration, unauthorised disclosure of or access to processed data, which corresponds to the measures of Article 32(1) GDPR and, in litera b, lists the protection of the integrity, availability and confidentiality of processing systems and services.[314]

The availability of data relates to the risks of destruction and loss specifically mentioned in Article 32(2) GDPR[315] and requires that data can be used as intended.[316] Hence, data must be retrievable, accessible and interpretable.[317] While availability has not been included expressly in the principles of the EU data protection legislation, availability is also a fundamental principle. When data is not available, this ultimately has the same effect as if the data were not collected at all.[318] For instance, if the key to encrypted data is not available, the integrity and confidentiality of these data are ensured on a very high level. However, they can ultimately not be used, as without the key they are unreadable and cannot be processed. This example illustrates that availability adds an important aspect that is separate from the fundamental principles of integrity and confidentiality.

The example further illustrates that availability relates to both, the individual and structural dimension of data protection. If data are not available in order to achieve the desired purpose, this puts the individual at risk, as they might depend on the data being processed, for instance, when these data relate to their social security benefits.

When data are not available on a massive scale, this is a severe issue for society as a whole, viz. the cases where hospitals were affected by ransomware, which encrypted

[314] Article 32(1)(b) GDPR also mentions resilience, however, it is a more general aspect of several principles: it aims to achieve sustained control of a processing operation by ensuring that the system can withstand disturbances, is structurally robust and agile, cf. Gonscherowski et al. 2018, pp. 442 et seq. and 445 et seq.; also cf. Hansen 2019b, MN. 42–45.

[315] Also mentioned in Article 33(2) DPR-EU and referred to in Article 91(2)(i) DPR-EU as well as Article 29(2)(i) LED.

[316] Bishop 2004, p. 3.

[317] Konferenz der unabhängigen Datenschutzaufsichtsbehörden des Bundes und der Länder 2020, p. 26.

[318] Cf. Bishop 2004, p. 3.

their data.[319] Thus, availability must be considered a fundamental principle, as the specific risks of loss or destruction, which are expressly mentioned in the secondary law,[320] illustrate its importance.[321]

As I have pointed out in Chap. 2, the triad of confidentiality, integrity and availability originally stems from the field of information security.[322] However, data protection and information security pursue different aims[323] and not every measure of information security conforms to the principles and requirements of data protection law.[324] An information security measure may further the aims of one principle, but undermine another—for instance when the integrity of a filing cabinet is ensured by video monitoring, which can undermine confidentiality—and thus requires a balancing exercise.[325] From this it follows, that information security brings its own risks for data protection, when IT security measures are not implemented in a way that conforms to the requirements of data protection law or runs counter to fundamental rights of data subjects.[326]

In order to maintain confidentiality, integrity, and availability, it is necessary that the controller continuously monitors the technical and organisational measures and assesses the risks to the rights of individuals posed by the processing operation.[327]

The fundamental principle of separation as well as its requirement of storage limitation via pseudo- and anonymisation also serve to increase the confidentiality of a processing operation, as measures serving both reduce the likelihood of a breach of confidentiality. For instance, personnel tasked with processing personal data will only have access to a specific subset of the data or not be able to link the data to a data subject, as they have no access to the assignment function.[328]

---

[319] Hern 2017, The Guardian. https://www.theguardian.com/technology/2017/dec/30/wannacry-petya-notpetya-ransomware. Accessed 28 July 2021; Winton 2016, Los Angeles Times. https://www.latimes.com/business/technology/la-me-ln-hollywood-hospital-bitcoin-20160217-story.html. Accessed 28 July 2021.

[320] They are included both in Article 32 GDPR/Articles 33/91 DPR-EU/Article 29 LED and Article 5(1)(f) GDPR/Articles 4(1)(f)/71(1)(f) DPR-EU/Article 4(1)(f) LED.

[321] Hansen 2019b, MN. 12.

[322] Cf. Chap. 2, Sect. 2.3.2.8.

[323] Bieker et al. 2018a, p. 492; also Roßnagel 2019, MN. 169.

[324] Hansen 2019b, MN. 11.

[325] The SDM of the Conference of German Supervisory Authorities aims to achieve this balance, cf. Konferenz der unabhängigen Datenschutzaufsichtsbehörden des Bundes und der Länder 2020, p. 9.

[326] Rost 2018b, p. 87.

[327] Hansen 2019a, MN. 68; Hansen 2019b, MN. 18 and 36.

[328] Cf. Chap. 2, Sect. 2.3.2.7.

5.3.2.7 Transparency

As I have argued in Chap. 2,[329] the current understanding of transparency focusses on the individual side of the principle. While transparency, also from a rule of law perspective, is required so as to render the exercise of power transparent to the individual—i.e. the competences and purposes of the controller and how they exercise them must be predictable for the individual[330]—there is a substantive side of transparency beyond this formal aspect. It relates to the controller/processor and is the basis for their actions with regard to their responsibility and accountability, as I have elaborated in Chap. 2:[331] transparency is also relevant for the controller to implement appropriate technical and organisational measures under the provisions on the responsibility of the controller, data protection by design and by default and on the security of the processing according to Articles 24, 25 and 32 GDPR[332] and for the supervision by the competent authorities, which have the power to access all relevant information according to Article 58(1)(a) and (b) GDPR.[333]

Before controllers can provide the required information to data subjects, they must first, of course, gather this information. While this may sound rather obvious, in practice, this can be an issue, as a controller, for a specific processing operation, may use software provided and maintained by processors on the hardware of yet another party, which is only one of many in the processing activities of that controller. This illustrates how transparency further extends to all aspects of the processing: It serves as a vehicle to answer the substantive questions of who (responsibility) processes which categories of data (formats, interfaces) for what purpose (purpose limitation) by what means (hardware, software, infrastructure and processes) and for how long (necessity and storage limitation).[334]

Hence, transparency must be understood as reaching beyond the interests of individuals and requires that the controller, processor as well as the supervisory authority, to differentiated degrees, must have knowledge of all relevant circumstances and factors regarding the processing of personal data.[335] Thereby, the fundamental principle of transparency effectively limits the complexity of information systems, as mentioned in recital 58 GDPR, as well as infrastructure relating to these systems, such as communication infrastructures.[336]

---

[329] Cf. Chap. 2, Sect. 2.3.2.3.

[330] Podlech 1988, p. 124.

[331] Cf. Chap. 2, Sect. 2.3.3.3.

[332] Cf. also Articles 26, 27, 33, 85 and 91 DPR-EU as well as Articles 19, 20 and 29 LED.

[333] Cf. also Article 58(1)(a) and (b) DPR-EU as well as Article 47(1) LED.

[334] Cf. also recital 58 GDPR; similarly Weichert 2018b, MN. 24 and 26; briefly Roßnagel 2019, MN. 57; partly based on Konferenz der unabhängigen Datenschutzaufsichtsbehörden des Bundes und der Länder 2020, p. 31; already argued by Podlech 1982, pp. 454 et seq., as I have introduced above in Sect. 5.2.2.

[335] Konferenz der unabhängigen Datenschutzaufsichtsbehörden des Bundes und der Länder 2020, p. 27.

[336] Podlech 1988, p. 125 et seq. That the controller must also be able to change and amend processing operations then relates to the principle of control, which I identify below in Sect. 5.3.2.8.

With regard to controllers' responsibility for the processing operation under Article 24 GDPR,[337] the fundamental principle of transparency requires that controllers understand the functionality of the system they use and bars them from relying on components that are essentially black boxes and thus removed from their influence.[338] Furthermore, the aspect of transparency that relates to the internal side of the controller is one of the preconditions for adherence to the principle of accountability[339] according to Article 5(2) GDPR,[340] which concerns the external side of transparency. As recital 82 GDPR emphasises, transparency is not limited to the data subject, but also serves the controller and the supervisory authority to fulfil their respective obligations. This demonstrates that the fundamental principle of transparency must also be recognised in its structural dimension.

5.3.2.8 Control

When juxtaposing the principles of the EU data protection legislation with its further provisions,[341] which relate to EU data protection law for the purposes of this chapter,[342] I have argued that they do not comprehensively address the rules on the responsibility of controllers—beyond ensuring confidentiality and integrity—the data subject[343] and procedural rights as well as the role of the independent supervisory authorities. In the following, I will show that all of these rules relate to a common theme, which is not yet covered by the principles identified so far, but also serves the individual and structural dimension of data protection law, and which must thus be regarded as a fundamental principle.

When considering the dual rationale of data protection law—to mitigate risks to individuals and address the processing of personal data as an exercise of power over these individuals—a remedy, which has often been identified is control, for instance, in both, the commodification as well as the individualistic approach.[344] However, these current conceptualisations fail to consider the pervasiveness of power relations and tend to overly rely on the capabilities of the weaker party, i.e. data subjects.[345] Lynskey, for instance, argues that individual control of data subjects is achieved by requiring their consent and by granting them rights, which allow them to access their

[337] Cf. also Article 26 DPR-EU.

[338] Cf. Bieker et al. 2018b.

[339] The other one is control, cf. the following subsection below in Sect. 5.3.2.8.

[340] Cf. also Articles 4(2) and 71(4) DPR-EU as well as Article 4(4) LED.

[341] Cf. Chap. 2, Sect. 2.4.

[342] Cf. above in Sect. 5.3.1.2.

[343] Including the right to data portability as a means of control for data subjects, rather than read as a tool for market regulation, as I discussed above in Sect. 5.3.1.2.

[344] Cf. Lynskey 2015b, pp. 227 et seq. and 255; Purtova 2012, pp. 247 et seq.

[345] Cf. Lazaro and Le Métayer 2015, p. 33; also, although not differentiating between privacy and data protection, cf. Hartzog 2018.

data.[346] However, granting rights to individuals, just like asking for their consent, does not remedy the power relation between data subjects and controllers. Data subjects must be in a position to actually exercise these instruments and be able to rely on their enforcement when a controller is not compliant.

Data subjects may refrain from exercising their rights, especially when a controller is the only provider of a certain service or good and would otherwise refuse service.[347] Even when data subjects exercise their rights, controllers do not always conform to their legitimate requests.[348] The competent supervisory authority might refuse to take effective remedial action[349] or the courts fail to interpret EU law correctly, without initiating the preliminary reference procedure before the ECJ.[350]

In order to avoid the pitfalls of previous approaches, the fundamental principle of control I envisage here, does not purport to achieve full control of the individual. Rather, the fundamental principle of control introduces measures of control. There are two aspects, which have to be introduced: firstly, the fundamental principle of control is not limited to data subjects, it also extends to controllers and the supervisory authorities: both must exercise—different degrees of—control[351] over processing activities. Through this extension it, secondly, becomes clear that the fundamental principle of control cannot be limited to the individual dimension, but further encompasses the structural dimension of data protection law.

The data subject rights illustrate that, under EU data protection law, there must be a possibility for individuals to intervene in the processing of their personal data,[352] which is not provided sufficiently by the fundamental principle of transparency.[353] In order to protect the individual, oversight by public authorities is not sufficient on its own, instead, the individual must be given rights to control the processing,

[346] Lynskey 2015b, pp. 181–187, 192, 227 et seq. and 255. Also cf. above in Sect. 5.3.1.1.

[347] Matzner et al. 2016, p. 289.

[348] ECJ, Case C-131/12 Google Spain and Google, Judgment of 13 April 2014; Andrejevic 2014, p. 1682; European Parliament 2019, European Parliament Multimedia Centre. https://multimedia.europarl.europa.eu/en/hearing-of-margrethe-vestager-executive-vice-president-designate-europe-fit-for-the-digital-age-questions--answers-part-5_I178254-V_rv. Accessed 28 July 2021.

[349] ECJ, Case C-362/14 Maximillian Schrems v Data Protection Commissioner, Judgment of 6 October 2015, ECLI:EU:C:2015:650, paras 28 et seq.

[350] Especially clear in ECJ, Case C-210/16 Unabhängiges Landeszentrum für Datenschutz Schleswig-Holstein v Wirtschaftsakademie Schleswig-Holstein GmbH, Opinion of AG Bot of 24 October 2017, ECLI:EU:C:2017:796, para 27; while lower courts according to Article 267 subparagraphs 1 and 2 TFEU are not under an obligation to refer to the ECJ, this can prolong proceedings considerably, which, especially when a court rules against the interests of data subjects, can leave them without any protection vis-à-vis powerful controllers.

[351] Interestingly, while the English term controller relates directly to control, which occurs in recitals 7, 68, 75, 85 GDPR concerning control of individuals over their data or control over supervisory authorities, which would be counter to independence in recital 118 and Article 52(6) GDPR, the German term for controller, *Verantwortlicher*, has responsibility as word stem.

[352] It thus resembles the principle of intervenability, cf. Konferenz der unabhängigen Datenschutzaufsichtsbehörden des Bundes und der Länder 2020, p. 28.

[353] Cf. the previous subsection above Sect. 5.3.2.7.

which go beyond a mere right to information.[354] If, for instance, data changes and it is necessary for the achievement of the purpose to keep this data up to date as the requirement of accuracy[355] demands, it must be possible for the controller to update the data, at least at the request of the data subject under Article 16 GDPR.[356] A simple example for this is a change in address, which must be possible to ensure that goods are delivered to data subjects as customers.

While these rights serve the implementation of individual data protection, the ability to intervene[357] must also be guaranteed on a structural level: as the information system must be capable of safeguarding the rights and interests of individuals, the controller has to ensure that data subjects can exercise their rights effectively, have access to relevant evidence and their position is not undermined by the superior knowledge of the controller.[358] In that sense, the exercise of control by the controller is a prerequisite for transparency.

The controller, thus, must have the possibility to intervene in the processing, as, firstly, if the controller could not intervene in the processing, they could not conform to the intervention requests of individuals. Secondly, the controller is responsible for the processing, which means they must determine the means and purposes of the processing and hence, by definition,[359] be able to change and amend it. As is the case for the fundamental principle of transparency, this requirement limits the complexity of processing operations and is directly related to the responsibility and accountability of controllers.[360] Here, the focus shifts from the direct benefit of a specific individual to the benefit of society more generally, as a requirement for the controller to be in control of their processing activities serves to ensure that the fundamental principles of a democratic society under the rule of law are safeguarded. It thus relates to the structural dimension of data protection.

However, it also transpires that the fundamental principle of control and any intervention by the controller, can come in conflict with the integrity of the personal data. With regard to evidence required by data subjects in order to take remedial action against controllers, for instance in cases of unlawful processing, an intervention by the controller to permanently delete their data would undermine their position. Thus, a balance has to be achieved with regard to these two fundamental principles.[361]

Furthermore, infrastructures, especially in the structural dimension, are an essential part of control. The State must, under the obligation to implement data protection

---

[354] Simitis 1970, pp. T 42 et seq.

[355] Cf. Chap. 2, Sect. 2.3.2.6.

[356] Cf. also Article 18 and 82 DPR-EU as well as Article 16 LED.

[357] Concerning the above example of an address change, the controller also is under an obligation to keep processed data up to date under the requirement of accuracy according to Article 5(1)(d) GDPR, Articles 4(1)(d) and 71(1)(d) DPR-EU as well as Article 4(1)(d) LED.

[358] Podlech 1982, pp. 460 et seq.

[359] Article 4(7) GDPR, Article 3(8) DPR-EU and Article 3(8) LED.

[360] Cf. above in Sect. 5.3.2.7 and below in Sect. 5.3.2.9.

[361] Cf. below in Sect. 5.3.3.

by design according to Article 25(1) GDPR,[362] build infrastructures in a way that incorporates data protection from the very beginning.[363] However, this does not only concern the State, but also private entities providing infrastructure as well as manufacturers and producers of hard- and software. While calls to include these as addressees of the EU data protection legislation have been voiced repeatedly,[364] they were not included in the second generation of EU data protection legislation, aside from an appeal to the Member States to encourage producers to offer data protection-friendly products and services in recital 78 GDPR.[365] Under this status quo, it remains unnecessarily challenging for the controller to implement their obligations,[366] especially with regard to their own obligation to implement data protection by design.[367]

Lastly, the supervisory authorities must also be enabled to exercise control. As I have demonstrated in Chaps. 2 and 3,[368] the requirements the Court derived from Article 8(3) CFR with regard to their independence have now largely been incorporated into the second generation of EU data protection legislation. They must be free from direct or indirect influence from public or private entities, so that they can independently enforce the high level of protection required under EU data protection law. However, the provisions on control by the supervisory authorities are not restricted to organisational requirements. The Court has emphasised that data subjects have a right to lodge complaints with the supervisory authorities under Article 8(1) and (3) CFR, which then must conduct effective investigations.

With regard to actions of the supervisory authorities as well as the Board, the judiciary exercises oversight. While natural and legal persons may sue the Board under the same conditions as the supervisory authorities under Article 263 TFEU, Article 78 GDPR[369] requires that data subjects must have effective judicial remedies against decisions of the supervisory authorities. Even though this procedural right supports the legal position of individuals in specific circumstances and thus has an individual dimension, the system of judicial remedies generally serves the structural dimension of data protection law and the rule of law.

---

[362] Cf. also Articles 27(1) and 85(1) DPR-EU as well as Article 20(1) LED and especially with regard to public tenders, cf. recital 78 GDPR and recital 48 DPR-EU.

[363] Hansen and Thomsen 2010, pp. 285 et seq.

[364] Dix 2003, MN. 40 et seq.

[365] Bieker and Hansen 2017, p. 286.

[366] Dix 2003, MN. 19–21.

[367] Cf. Chap. 2, Sect. 2.3.3.3.

[368] Cf. Chap. 2, Sect. 2.3.3.5. and Chap. 3, Sect. 3.3.

[369] Cf. also Article 64 DPR-EU and Article 53 LED.

5.3.2.9 Accountability

The long list of provisions related to the requirement of accountability, I provided in Chap. 2,[370] demonstrates that the requirement of accountability is indeed far-reaching. However, as it intends to ensure the proper implementation of the principles of EU data protection legislation,[371] this necessarily has to be the case. Accountability therefore is a keystone for ensuring both the formal and substantive aspects of transparency, ensuring that controllers are in control of the processing operation and ensuring measures of control by data subjects as well as independent oversight by supervisory authorities.

However, while it is helpful to explicate these aspects with regard to the individual as well as structural dimension, the requirement of accountability does not amount to a fundamental principle. It has no content that could be seen as distinct from the fundamental principles of transparency and control.

5.3.3 The Fundamental Principles of EU Data Protection Law

I have thus illustrated how the rules of the second generation of the EU data protection legislation, as far as they relate to the issue of data protection, can be incorporated into seven fundamental principles. These fundamental principles are lawfulness, separation, transparency, control, confidentiality, integrity and availability.

I have set these fundamental principles and the requirements they include in relation in the figure below (see Fig. 5.1). They reflect the material content of EU data protection law and comprise the legal requirements on the processing of personal data. Each principle thus represents a set of different rules on the processing of personal data contained in EU data protection law.

Further, I have argued that EU data protection law goes well beyond awarding individuals specific rights to enforce and also addresses controllers as well as processors, albeit not manufacturers, directly with specific obligations serving the protection of the rights and interests of individuals. The EU data protection law thus aims to ensure that the processing of personal data is carried out in a way that protects individuals "out of the box".[372]

The fundamental principle of lawfulness has a central role, as it concerns the question of whether a given data processing operation is permissible. Only after

---

[370] Cf. Chap. 2, Sect. 2.3.2.9.

[371] As, for instance, called for by the Article 29 Working Party, due to the difficulties of controllers to implement the principles in practice, cf. Article 29 Working Party, Opinion 3/2010 on the principle of accountability. WP 173, pp. 4 et seq.

[372] As manifested particularly in the requirements of data protection by design and by default in Article 25 GDPR, Articles 27 and 85 DPR-EU as well as Article 20 LED, which oblige controllers to consider the requirements EU data protection legislation from the very inception of a processing operation and to protect the rights of individuals already in the standard configuration.

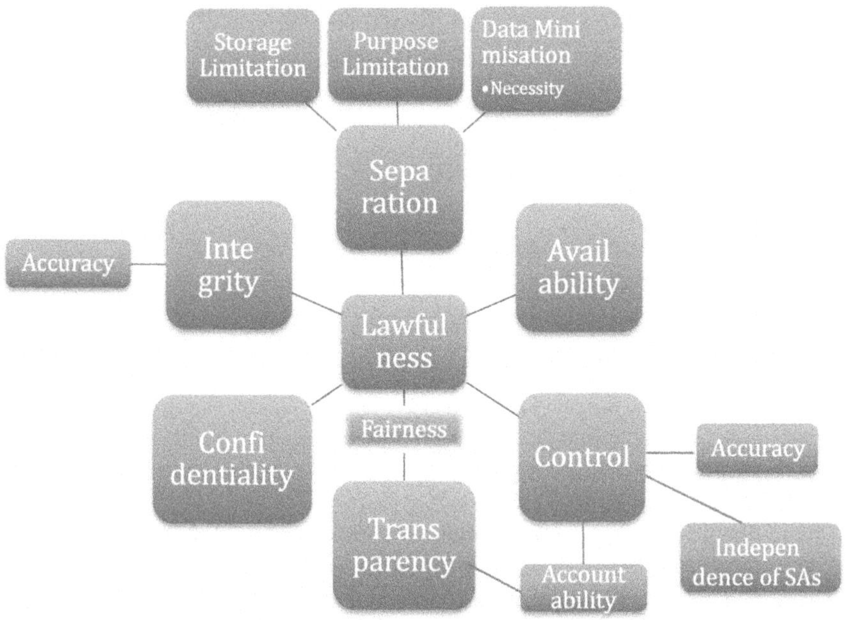

Fig. 5.1. The fundamental principles of EU data protection law in relation to one another *Source* The author

this preliminary question has been answered, the question of how the processing may be carried out comes into play. Yet, lawfulness is not isolated from the other principles: especially with regard to the principle of separation, the definition of a legitimate purpose also concerns the lawfulness of a processing operation. This can be seen particularly clearly when the processing is based on legitimate interests of controllers under Article 6(1)(f) GDPR, which requires a balancing of the purpose of the processing with the interests and fundamental rights of data subjects[373] and where the lawfulness of the processing operation depends on the proportionality of this balancing exercise.[374]

The remaining six fundamental principles interact with one another on several levels and further requirements can be derived from a principle or from two principles read in conjunction, as I have illustrated in Fig. 5.1. These fundamental principles substantiate Articles 1 GDPR/DPR-EU/LED and, in conjunction with Article 8 CFR,

373 Cf. for an in-depth analysis Robrahn and Bremert 2018. Also cf. above in Sect. 5.2.3.3.

374 Which, in turn, may be dependent on the implementation of specific technical and organisational measures in order to mitigate risks to the rights and freedoms of the data subjects: a processing operation, which would normally entail a high risk and therefore could not be based on legitimate interests of the controller—as it would be outweighed by the interests and fundamental rights of data subjects—may be lawful if technical and organisational measures are implemented that mitigate the specific risks.

contain the normative foundations of the EU data protection law.[375] The fundamental principles thus inform the interpretation of EU data protection law generally.

When taken together, two fundamental principles can emphasise an aspect, which relates to both of these principles. Transparency can serve as an example here: while it is never an end in itself, from the perspective of control, it requires that the controller must be able to demonstrate compliance to both, data subjects—via the information and data subject rights—and to supervisory authorities, carrying out their task of enforcing the data protection legislation.

However, two fundamental principles may also be in opposition to one another. As can be seen in Fig. 5.1. above, opposing pairs of fundamental principles have inherent tensions and opposing aims, which must be resolved: for instance, the principle of integrity demands that data are unchanged, while the principle of control may require that data are kept up to date and might therefore necessitate a change in the data. By logging changes to a dataset, a balance can be achieved between the two principles, as the changes can be traced, which also benefits the transparency of the processing operation.

There may also be tensions with regard to neighbouring fundamental principles: in the example from the preceding paragraph, extensive logging may raise issues with regard to the fundamental principles of separation and confidentiality, which can be mitigated by restricting the scope of the logging, by use of pseudonyms and by restricting access to the log files to certain parties. This underlines the multiple dimensions of the fundamental principles, which can create tensions between principles in some scenarios, while creating coherence in others.[376]

The fundamental principles are principles in an Alexyian sense and thus optimisation requirements (*Optimierungsgebote*): one principle does not take precedence over another.[377] Rather, they have to be implemented in a way that achieves an optimal balance between the different principles.[378] Thus, the fundamental principles lay down objectives for the design and implementation of data processing operations, which can be achieved to certain, varying,[379] degrees.[380]

These fundamental principles of EU data protection law, in some regards and especially in their structure, are similar to the data protection goals of the Standard

---

[375] The fact that the violation of a principle can incur the highest tier of administrative fine under Article 83(5)(a) GDPR emphasises the intent of the legislator as to the normative, prescriptive character of these provisions.

[376] Cf., with regard to the protection goals of the SDM, Rost 2018a, pp. 14 et seq.

[377] Alexy 1994, pp. 75 et seq. and 78 et seq.

[378] Robrahn and Bock 2018.

[379] While the adherence to the principle of lawfulness in cases, especially when there is no legal basis, can generally be enforced without much ado, the degree of adherence to the principle of data minimisation will depend on the specific purposes set by the controller and thus leaves more leverage.

[380] Roßnagel 2019, MN. 22.

Data Protection Model (SDM),[381] as could be seen throughout the previous subsection.[382] While both approaches arrive at similar results, they depart from different premises. With the dualistic approach, I have derived the fundamental principles of EU data protection law from the secondary EU data protection legislation, as I have demonstrated in this chapter. The Standard Data Protection Model uses the predefined data protection goals, which it links to the relevant data protection provisions, in order to operationalise the legal requirements and facilitate the implementation of the technical and organisational measures by providing standardised catalogues of such measures.[383] This approach of standardised catalogues of measures has been adopted from information security and redefined with regard to the specific rationales of data protection law.[384] These standardised protection measures are a helpful tool to mitigate the risks of a processing operation.

5.4 The Application of the Dualistic Approach to the Primary EU Data Protection Legislation: Uncovering the EU Fundamental Right to Data Protection

After having identified the dual rationale and the fundamental principles of EU data protection law and demonstrating that they serve both individual data protection law and structural data protection law, I will now apply the dualistic approach to the primary EU data protection legislation. Thereby, I will comprehensively define the rationale and content of the EU fundamental right to data protection as part of EU data protection law, before addressing the horizontal application of this right and how it can be differentiated from the right to privacy.

In the first subsection, I will argue that the structural dimension of data protection law, which aims to protect the democratic society under the rule of law, is also covered by the fundamental right to data protection, as fundamental rights in general are part of a value system that aims to guarantee precisely these structures (Sect. 5.4.1).

Taking recourse to the dual rationale of EU data protection law in the second subsection of this section, I will identify the dual rationale of the fundamental right to data protection (Sect. 5.4.2): to mitigate the risks of data processing (Sect. 5.4.2.1)—which I assess comprehensively on a generic level through recourse to the fundamental principles of EU data protection law—and to address the processing of data as instrument of power (Sect. 5.4.2.2).

As I move on to consider the content of the fundamental right to data protection (Sect. 5.4.3), I will firstly address its material and personal scope (Sect. 5.4.3.1). I

---

[381] Konferenz der unabhängigen Datenschutzaufsichtsbehörden des Bundes und der Länder 2020.

[382] Cf. for instance above in Sect. 5.3.2.5.

[383] Konferenz der unabhängigen Datenschutzaufsichtsbehörden des Bundes und der Länder 2020, pp. 6 et seq.

[384] Pointedly Rost 2017.

argue that the scope must be interpreted broadly and with regard to the secondary EU data protection law, in order to allow for the review of all data processing activities. The same applies to interferences with the right to data protection (Sect. 5.4.3.2), as the focus of the assessment lies in the justification stage (Sect. 5.4.3.3). Mirroring the broad scope of the fundamental right to data protection, there are also extensive possibilities to justify interferences and to achieve a balance with other fundamental rights. At the justification stage, I will consider the previously derived generic risks to the fundamental principles of EU data protection law again, as they can be used to systematise the interferences with the fundamental right to data protection, which facilitates the assessment and selection of appropriate technical and organisational measures.

For the determination of the essence of the fundamental right, I will argue that the fundamental principles offer a systematisation, which ensures that the gravest interferences with Article 8 CFR can be identified (Sect. 5.4.3.4). Lastly, I will consider how it can be ensured that individuals are protected from the adverse effects of processing personal data in situations, where such processing is carried out by private entities, i.e. the horizontal application of the right to data protection (Sect. 5.4.4). In the last subsection of this chapter, I will then demonstrate that the right to data protection, due to its dual rationale and distinct scope, can be differentiated clearly from the right to privacy (Sect. 5.4.5), as it pursues different rationales (Sect. 5.4.5.1), has a distinct scope (Sect. 5.4.5.2) and essence (Sect. 5.4.5.3).

5.4.1 The Right to Data Protection as Part of a Value System

As the fundamental right to data protection must be interpreted in coherence with the secondary EU data protection law,[385] it includes both of its dimensions, i.e. individual and structural data protection law, and enables the individual to enforce both of them. The report by Steinmüller and others, in light of the totalitarian rule of the Nazi regime, argued that one of the goals of data protection law is to protect the individual and marginalized groups in a democracy and thus also the democratic society under the rule of law.[386] Simits elaborates this point, arguing that data protection is not merely an issue of the individual, but rather aims to preserve the communication structure, which is paramount to a democratic society.[387] In this understanding data protection is a foundational requirement of a democratic society.[388] Furthermore, the rule of law, especially its aspects of proportionality and the separation of powers, are inherent in fundamental rules of data protection, such as lawfulness, necessity and purpose limitation, as argued by Steinmüller et al.[389]

---

385 Cf. Chap. 2, Sect. 2.2.1.

386 Steinmüller et al. 1971, p. 44.

387 Simitis 2014, MN. 26.

388 Simitis 1971, p. 682.

389 Cf. Chap. 2, Sects. 2.3.2.1, 2.3.2.4 and 2.3.2.5 as well as Sects. 5.2.2 and 5.2.3.2.

This early discourse on data protection in the 1970s and 1980s, in lieu of pre-existing data protection legislation, recurred in many ways to more general consideration of constitutional rights and principles. Steinmüller et al. were well aware of the case law of the BVerfG, which had already in 1958 declared that the German constitution with its rules and especially the guarantee of fundamental rights formed an objective value system (*objektive Wertordnung*), which enhanced the binding force of these fundamental rights,[390] when drafting their report for the Ministry of the Interior. This notion of a value system, the BVerfG held, was a foundational constitutional decision, which affected the entire legal order.[391]

Under German constitutional law, the positive obligations of the State are based on this concept of fundamental rights as an objective value system, which extends the merely individualistic aspect of fundamental rights—as rights against the State—to an obligation of the State to adhere to certain organisational and procedural standards.[392] The objective element of a fundamental right can further extend to institutional guarantees. It can, for instance, extend to ensuring certain public institutions, such as religious education in public schools or the constitutional protection of the existence of private schools.[393] The requirement of data protection supervisory authorities in Article 8(3) CFR could thus be seen as a similar institutional guarantee.

However, while German constitutional law informed the German discourse in the 1970s and 1980s and hence the conceptualisation of Steinmüller, Podlech and others, to which I recur in this book, it cannot alone provide the rationale for guaranteeing structural elements of EU fundamental rights, which belong to an autonomous legal order.[394] However, this can be achieved by considering the ECHR, which is a point of reference for EU fundamental rights protection.[395]

The ECHR itself was a counter-project to totalitarianism and has, from its inception, been regarded as a collective guarantee to preserve democracy.[396] The system established under the convention was perceived as a means with the end of protecting the democratic society.[397] Under the ECHR, a measure may be justified, when it is "necessary in a democratic society",[398] a standard, to which the ECJ still recurs,

---

[390] Bundesverfassungsgericht, BVerfGE 7, pp. 198–230—Lüth, Judgment of 15 January 1958, para 27.

[391] Ibid.

[392] Herdegen 2019, MN. 21.

[393] Cf. Article 7(4)(1) and (2)(1) Basic Law, respectively; ibid., MN. 19.

[394] ECJ, Case 26/62 Van Gend en Loos v Administratie der Belastingen, Judgment of 5 February 1963, ECLI:EU:C:1963:1, p. 12.

[395] Cf. Article 6 TEU, Articles 52(3) and 53 CFR.

[396] Marks 1995, pp. 210 et seq.

[397] Zysset 2016, p. 17.

[398] Cf. for instance Articles 6(1), 8(2)-11(2) ECHR.

although generally, it is now phrased merely as "necessity" within the proportionality test.[399] Thus, according to Marks, the entire body of the ECHR can "be seen as articulating the scope and limits of democracy."[400]

This is further substantiated in the jurisprudence of the ECtHR. Zysset has found that the ECtHR's case law shows a particular focus on procedural and substantive aspects of democracy, especially when it considers a right's rationale and scope or balances it with other rights.[401]

The ECtHR has also discussed the separation of powers as a facet of the democratic principle[402] and held that democracy does not imply that the majoritarian view must be strictly upheld, but rather that it was a hallmark of the democratic society that "a balance must be achieved, which ensures the fair and proper treatment of minorities".[403] This case law illustrates that the issues concerning the processing of personal data, as raised by Steinmüller, Podlech and others go beyond the German discourse and are also rooted at the European level.

The considerations on the ECHR can be transferred to the EU level, where Article 2 TEU explicitly proclaims that the Union is founded on values such as respect for democracy, the rule of law and human rights. According to Article 3(1) TEU, it is the aim of the EU to promote these values. With these provisions of primary law and the elevated status of the Charter according to Article 6(1) TEU, the EU fundamental rights contain elements, which also constitute an objective value system.[404] The Charter especially contains maxims and directives for the State, similar to structural guarantees and principles.[405] Therefore, EU fundamental rights inherently protect objective legal or structural aspects along with their subjective or individualistic legal dimension, especially with regard to the democratic society under the rule of law.

However, while individuals can thus also enforce the structural alongside the individual dimension of data protection law, this does not imply that they have a right to specific technical and organisational measures. Rather they have a right that their data are processed in a way that safeguards their interests, including technical and organisational measures that are appropriate to the risks, which the processing operation poses to their rights.

---

[399] Cf. Chap. 3, Sect. 3.2.8.

[400] Marks 1995, p. 211.

[401] Zysset 2016, p. 36.

[402] ECtHR [GC], Regner v. the Czech Republic, App. No. 35289/11, Judgment of 19 September 2017, Partly Dissenting Opinion of Judge Serghides, para 106; ECtHR [GC], Karácsony and Others v. Hungary, App. Nos. 42461/13 and 44357/13, Judgment of 17 May 2016, paras 138 and 157; ECtHR [GC], Baka v. Hungary, App. No. 20261/12, Judgment of 23 June 2016, para 165; ECtHR, Klass and Others, App. No. 5029/71, Judgment of 6 September 1978, p. 30.

[403] ECtHR, Young, James and Webster v. the United Kingdom, App. Nos. 7601/76 and 7806/77, Judgment of 13 August 1981, para 63; ECtHR [GC], Chassagnou and Others v. France, App. Nos. 25088/94, 28331/95 and 28443/95, Judgment of 29 April 1999, para 112; ECtHR [GC], Sørensen and Rasmussen v. Denmark, App. Nos. 52562/99 and 52620/99, Judgment of 11 January 2006, para 58.

[404] Cf. also, albeit a bit more reluctantly, Schorkopf 2014, MN. 35.

[405] Frenz 2009, MN. 355.

5.4.2 *The Rationale of the Right to Data Protection*

The rationale of the right to data protection is intrinsically linked with the aim of data protection itself: to protect individuals *from* the processing of their data and to protect the democratic society under the rule of law from adverse, undesirable effects of data processing. The fundamental right to data protection, as part of an objective value system in general,[406] therefore relates to both, the individual as well as the structural dimension of data protection law. Accordingly, just like the secondary EU data protection law,[407] the fundamental right follows a dual rationale and aims to mitigate the risks of data processing (Sect. 5.4.2.1) as well as to address the processing of data as an instrument of power (Sect. 5.4.2.2).

5.4.2.1 Mitigating the Risks of Data Processing

In order to prevent damage to individuals, it is crucial to consider the inherent risks of data processing before and throughout any processing operation, as I have argued in the previous subsection.[408] The general risk to the right to data protection according to Article 8 CFR, in the terms of fundamental rights, is that the gravity of the interference,[409] which comes with any form of processing personal data,[410] is not justified by proportionate and legitimate objectives of general interest, so as to appropriately protect the rights of individuals, and thus a violation.[411] In short, this means that the risk to a fundamental right is that it may be a violated.

When expressed in terms of risk to the rights of individuals this means that the likelihood and severity of potential damage (i.e. the interference that may not be justified) are not mitigated sufficiently (i.e. not justified by legitimate objectives of general interest, which meet the requirements of proportionality) to minimise the realisation of the risk to an appropriate level (i.e. to ensure there is no violation).[412]

There are various avenues to define such risks. One approach is to find examples of specific risks, which can illustrate risks in various areas. The legislator, for instance, followed that approach in recital 75 GDPR, where it referred to several different kinds of risks, as I discussed above.[413] While the drawing up of checklists of risks to the rights of individuals is commendable, it is likely to overlook some current and especially future challenges for any given processing operation.[414] Furthermore, such an exercise can lead to the same issues that have been encountered with regard

---

[406] Cf. the preceding subsection above Sect. 5.4.1.

[407] Cf. above in Sect. 5.3.1.1.

[408] Cf. above in Sect. 5.3.1.1.

[409] Or limitation in the wording of Article 52(1) CFR.

[410] As rightly found by the Court in its jurisprudence, cf. Chap. 3, Sect. 3.2.9.

[411] Bieker 2018, p. 29.

[412] Ibid.

[413] Cf. above in Sect. 5.3.1.1 as well as Chap. 2, Sect. 2.3.3.3.

[414] Rost 2018b, p. 82.

to the right to privacy and its undefined scope: the reduction of the fundamental right to specific (privacy) harms, which are open-ended and to be determined only haphazardly through case law,[415] as also advocated by the privacy approach.[416]

In order to avoid the pitfalls of overly specific checklists, which are prone to overlooking crucial risks, I will take a more general approach and employ the fundamental principles derived in the previous section as basis for my analysis.[417] They are the starting point to systematically derive generic risks[418] to the rights of individuals, which can be achieved on different levels of generality.[419]

Accordingly, the specific risk to the right to data protection under Article 8 CFR, to put it abstractly, lies in the violation of the fundamental principles of EU data protection law.[420] Rather than defining various specific risks and risking missing crucial risks, I will keep this section on a more abstract level and identify generic risks to the rights of individuals by examining the individual fundamental principles, which reflect the material content of EU data protection law. This will provide an overview, which can be used for the analysis of a specific processing operation as to its specific risks.

In the following, I will firstly identify potential risk sources, which is crucial to then determine the generic risks to the individual fundamental principles of EU data protection law. These risks follow from the negation of a fundamental principle, i.e. I will deduce them by assuming that the opposite of what the fundamental principle aims to ensure will happen. From these risks, I will draw the interim conclusions that the identified risks illustrate the adverse effects of data processing and must be mitigated in order to protect individuals as well as the democratic society as a whole.

Risk Sources

From the perspective of data protection, the authorised legitimate user of the system is the greatest source of risks for the rights of an individual. Unlike in information

---

[415] Cf. above in Sect. 5.2.1.

[416] Cf. Chap. 4, Sect. 4.5.1.

[417] Cf. above in Sect. 5.3.3.

[418] This approach can also be generalised and used to identify risks to other fundamental rights beyond Article 8 CFR, which may be relevant in a processing operation, cf. Bieker and Bremert 2020.

[419] While this book engages with these risks on a more theoretical and hence generic level, in practice, the fundamental principles of EU data protection law will have to be considered with regard to a processing operation long before it is carried out, in order to conform to the requirement of data protection by design and ensure that the controller can fulfil their responsibilities. As a processing operation will become more defined and redefined in this process, its scope and data flows will become clearer and ultimately allow to identify specific risks to the rights of individuals. This is the reason why any risk evaluation, whether in the context of a DPIA or as a separate exercise, is an iterative process, cf. Friedewald et al. 2017, p. 37; Konferenz der unabhängigen Datenschutzaufsichtsbehörden des Bundes und der Länder 2018, p. 6.

[420] Cf. above in Sect. 5.3.3; also cf. similarly already Bieker 2018, p. 29; as well as, albeit limited to the principles of Article 5 GDPR, Rost 2018b, p. 86; Gellert also notes that the data protection principles determine which processing operations pose a risk to the rights of individuals: Gellert 2015, p. 8.

security, in data protection, the controller is the greatest risk source, not third parties. The controller, who exercises data power and thus creates these risks, can misuse the data by circumventing necessary data protection measures in order to achieve a higher degree of efficiency.[421]

Therefore, the focus must be on the activities of the entity processing the personal data.[422] The marketing division, management or individual employees, for instance, who use collected data for incompatible purposes are sources of risks to the rights of individuals.

However, in order to comprehensively evaluate all potential risk sources, it must be taken into account that risks can also emanate from authorised or unauthorised third parties, such as processors, contractors, manufacturers, hackers or public authorities, pursuing vested interests. With regard to public authorities, law enforcement agencies are a considerable risk source, as they may access the vast amounts of data stored by private entities with warrants. Further, technical malfunctions and external factors, such as force majeure, also have to be taken into account.[423]

Risks to Lawfulness

Concerning the fundamental principle of lawfulness, which requires a legitimate legal basis, the most obvious risk is that no legal basis is provided or invoked at all. Furthermore, there is the risk that a legal basis does not cover the extent of a processing operation, i.e. that the chosen legal basis or bases are not sufficient to justify the scope or the entirety of a processing activity, which consists of several processing operations.[424]

However, the issue becomes subtler, when considering that the legal basis must be legitimate,[425] as also required by Article 8(2) CFR and Article 52(1) CFR. This requirement extends to both, legal provisions, which—as any law—must be proportionate, and the interpretation of the other legal bases, especially contracts and consent.

In Article 7 GDPR, the legislator has regulated consent more substantively than it had in the first generation of EU data protection legislation,[426] but contracts as legal basis under Article 6(1)(b) GDPR still leave considerable leeway for the controller. The EU data protection legislation does not include any specific rules on contracts as legal basis, but they are subject to review under the national law and relevant EU

---

[421] Steinmüller 1975, p. 75; more pointedly Steinmüller 1993, pp. 477 et seq.

[422] Rost 2018b, pp. 85 et seq.

[423] Konferenz der unabhängigen Datenschutzaufsichtsbehörden des Bundes und der Länder 2018, p. 4.

[424] Cf. Article 6(1) GDPR and Article 5(1) DPR-EU: "Processing shall be lawful only if and *to the extent* that at least one of the following applies […]" (emphasis added); Article 72(1) DPR-EU: "Processing of operational personal data shall be lawful only if and *to the extent* that processing is necessary" (emphasis added); Article 8 LED: "Member States shall provide for processing to be lawful only if and *to the extent* that processing is necessary […]" (emphasis added).

[425] Rost 2018b, p. 85.

[426] Article 2(h) DPD.

legislation for the protection of consumers.[427] Especially in relations where the data subject depends on the use of services offered by the controller, where the controller has a monopoly or the market is dominated by an oligopoly, which does not offer services implementing data protection rules, the data subject has a considerable disadvantage, which effectively hampers their freedom of entering into a contract. This limitation on data subjects, which is based on the data and market power of controllers, creates a risk to the individual, which must be considered in the analysis of a data processing operation.

Risks to Separation

As the legal bases of data protection law regulate individual processing operations, it can be overlooked that the accumulation of processing operations creates its own risks. For instance through the linking or integration of individual, lawful processing operations, which can be accessed by other entities or are accessed repeatedly and on a massive scale by the same entity.[428] These risks are addressed under the fundamental principle of separation, which requires that data must only be processed according to their specific purpose and must not be linked beyond that purpose.

The possibility of linking data leads to a tendency—rather than an actual practical constraint—to integrate separate systems, while maintaining the organisational separation of an entity on all except the informational level.[429] In the public sector this concentration of informational power can dismantle the functional differentiation between different authorities' competences and jurisdictions, which are aimed precisely at curtailing their power and creating areas of freedom for the individual.[430] The centralisation of data in order to increase the efficiency of data flows is a risk, as the separation of powers[431] is severed and can no longer attain its objective to protect the individual and society as a whole from the overreach of controllers.[432]

A related risk concerning separation is the conflation of various roles. In everyday life an individual may encounter a public authority or private entity in various different roles, corresponding to the various functions and purposes of the interaction. This is true especially for the State, which bears the monopoly on the use of force, but also acts as an employer, credit agent, etc.[433] This example, of course, applies to the private sector, as well: for instance a bank, which also operates as insurance company or a search engine website, which also operates a vast online advertising network.[434]

---

[427] For instance, the respective national rules implementing Council Directive 93/13/EEC of 5 April 1993 on unfair terms in consumer contracts, OJ L 95 of 21 April 1993, pp. 29–34.

[428] Podlech 1982, p. 452.

[429] Steinmüller 1975, p. 76.

[430] von Berg et al. 1972, pp. 3 et seq.; a point also raised by Simitis 1970, p. T 38; Simitis 1971, pp. 675 et seq.

[431] Lenk 1973, p. 24; referring to Podlech 1973b, p. 9.

[432] Lenk 1973, pp. 21–28; Brouwer 2011, pp. 280 and 291 et seq.

[433] Lenk 1973, p. 20.

[434] Another example is a single sign on service, which offers users authentication for various different services through one account. However, these service providers process data from the

Through the introduction of integrated forms of data processing, there is the risk that the separation of the individual's data in multiple, separated roles is lifted.[435] This risk relates to the requirements of necessity, as the data that are being processed, are not necessary to attain the specific purpose, which is pursued in the role assumed by the data subject. It also relates to the requirement of storage limitation, as the various roles, under this requirement, should be separated. This can be achieved, for instance, by using different pseudonyms for each role.

The integration of different processing operations could lead to a situation, where, e.g., a controller could make the rendering of services contingent on consent to other processing operations.[436] While Article 7(4) GDPR aims to prevent such practices, its application is limited.[437] Furthermore, the more integrated different sets of data from various contexts are, the higher the risk of surveillance becomes for the individual, which has further implications for a democratic society.[438]

The requirement of purpose limitation is a crucial aspect of the principle of separation. A primary risk in data protection is that the purpose of a processing operation is not sufficiently defined in advance. As the purpose is a central benchmark to assess the scope, extent and context of the processing operation and justifies the processing operation,[439] it is a watershed, which can lead to a myriad of risks to the rights of individuals. This concerns the risk that the purpose of the processing is not predefined, but rather defined and expanded as the controller sees fit.

However, even when the purpose is defined in advance, there is always the risk of intentional or undeliberate extensions of the purpose. In that sense, purpose limitation also aims to prevent the risk of function creep, i.e. the retroactive expansion of the uses of collected data.[440] Once a public authority or private entity has acquired data, it may identify other purposes it might wish to attain. Some of these purposes might even actually, and not just purportedly, be in the interest of the data subject, but might not be covered by the legal basis invoked.

The separation of data according to the specific task they serve and the limitation of its use to a specific public authority is not only sanctioned by the requirement of storage limitation, but is particularly important with regard to surveillance. As Lenk accurately predicted, once public authorities process certain data, there will always be calls to use them, inter alia, in order to combat crime.[441] However, the retroactive expansion of purposes can also be observed in the private sector, where data, once

various services prolifically in order to profile their users and create revenue by selling these profiles. This is offered by Google and Facebook, but also a new German service, which apparently follows this approach, cf. Bröckling 2018, netzpolitik.org. https://netzpolitik.org/2018/eine-identitaet-fuer-alles-das-schwierige-geschaeftsmodell-von-verimi/. Accessed 28 July 2021.

435 Lenk 1973, pp. 20 et seq.

436 Cf. ibid., p. 26; also cf. de Hingh 2018, p. 1279.

437 Engeler 2018a.

438 Foundationally Lyon 2003. Also cf. Adams and Purtova 2016.

439 Cf. above in Sect. 5.3.2.2 as well as Chap. 2, Sect. 2.3.2.4.

440 For an excellent case study on Google's privacy policy update in 2012, cf. Rauhofer 2015.

441 Lenk 1973, p. 30; Brouwer identifies several legal rules on the EU level, which undermine the principle of purpose limitation, cf. Brouwer 2011, pp. 281–284.

they are collected from data subjects, are used for other purposes. For instance, when data subjects buy items in an online shop, their data are often used for purposes, such as marketing or advertising products and thus to profile them.

Public authorities, in turn can access these data with warrants.[442] The surveillance of individuals on a large scale, whether by public authorities or private entities, is a risk not only for those individuals, but also society as a whole.

In that regard, the collection of more data than necessary to achieve a purpose is another risk, which concerns the requirements of necessity and data minimisation. Where the controller does not predefine the purpose in a sufficiently precise manner, data, which is not necessary, but perhaps desirable to acquire, is collected and thus creates an incentive to overextend the purpose of a processing operation. This can also manifest in the storage of data, which are no longer necessary, as the purpose has been attained. Due to the lack of control of the data subject over the data, there is a risk that such data are not deleted, but rather kept in case that they are required again for a different, unspecified purpose at a later—and uncertain—time. A related risk is that, perhaps in combination with an overly broad purpose, no deletion periods are set for the processed data.

These risks are ultimately another iteration of the argument of increasing the efficiency of a processing operation, which is a matter of convenience for the controller, but undermines the position of the individual. This convenience of the controller can, for instance, lead to the creation of shadow profiles or swaths of retained data. These data may be of interest to law enforcement authorities, which can obtain existing data from controllers, even when there was no legal basis for their collection or continued storage.

Furthermore, new technology, which increases the volume of, access to and ease of use of data processing, offers the ability to reproduce data without geographical constraints and increases their availability. This creates its own risks as especially physical separation can easily be lifted.[443] This comes with an increased potential for misuse[444] and hence creates a risk with regard to the principle of separation and its requirement of purpose limitation.

As technology is only neutral in a vacuum, it is, in reality, a tool for humans and is thus created for specific purposes.[445] These purposes create a specific context, from which the data must not be removed.[446] Information systems, hence, serve the planning, regulation and control purposes of their controller.[447] This further connects to the issue of misappropriation of technology for extraneous purposes: as the models created through information systems are built to serve a specific purpose, the same system cannot be employed in a different context for a different purpose without creating great risks. An example of this is if the police were granted access to a

---

[442] Cf. also de Hingh 2018, pp. 1282 et seq. with further references.

[443] Lenk 1973, p. 17.

[444] Kilian 1973, pp. 293 et seq.

[445] Also cf. Fröhlich and Spiecker gen. Döhmann 2018.

[446] Steinmüller 1981, p. 182.

[447] Ibid., p. 183.

hospital's information system,[448] which further demonstrates the extent, to which the proper and comprehensive identification of risks depends on the specific context of the processing operation.

Another risk to the principle of separation is the processing of personal data for an illegitimate purpose. As the processing of personal data has to be justified under EU data protection law, such a justification can necessarily be provided only by a legitimate purpose. However, the risk that the legislator passes laws that are disproportionate can be observed in real-time, especially with regard to legislation concerning surveillance.[449]

The requirement of a legitimate purpose also applies to private entities processing personal data. Hence, the risk of illegitimate purposes also persists in the private sector, especially where the business model of a controller is not in conformity to the rules of EU data protection law.[450]

Risks to Confidentiality

Concerning the fundamental principle of confidentiality, which aims to ensure that only authorised persons or entities have access to personal data, there is the risk of unauthorised disclosure. The data may be disclosed by the controller to a third party unlawfully, unnecessarily or even unintentionally. The latter is the case, when a malicious third party intrudes on the processing operation or when a third party happens to become aware of certain information by chance, for instance by simply overhearing a conversation. However, an unauthorised disclosure can also occur within the organisation of the controller: whenever data are accessible to personnel who are not authorised to access a specific date, there is a risk of unauthorised disclosure.

Risks to Integrity

Any form of unauthorised alteration of data is a risk to the fundamental principle of integrity, i.e. the qualitative intactness and quantitative completeness of personal data. Just as the unauthorised disclosure, this risk is posed by actors internal as well as external to the controller.

While the risk of hackers intruding the systems of a controller concerns this external dimension and is also covered by information or data security measures, the risk posed by the controller is even more relevant to data protection. For instance, the

---

[448] Ibid., p. 184; this example also illustrates how the "sensitivity" of data is not an inherent quality of data, but rather depends on their use: public authorities have different competences and roles and the same data that might be innocuous in the hands of one authority could be a risk to the rights of an individual if used by another, cf. Lenk 1973, p. 25; also cf. Steinmüller 1993, pp. 678 et seq.

[449] This has, in fact, produced considerable case law from the ECJ alone, cf., for instance, ECJ, Joined Cases C-293/12 and C-594/12 Digital Rights Ireland Ltd (C-293/12) v Minister for Communications, Marine and Natural Resources and Others and Kärntner Landesregierung (C-594/12) and Others, Judgment of 8 April 2014, ECLI:EU:C:2014:238; ECJ, Case C-362/14 Schrems, Judgment of 6 October 2015; ECJ, Joined Cases C-203/15 and C-698/15 Tele 2 Sverige, Judgment of 21 December 2016; ECJ, Avis 1/15, Opinion of 26 July 2017, ECLI:EU:C:2017:592.

[450] Cf. above in Sect. 5.3.2.2.

migration of data to a new system or a new application can compromise the integrity of data. Further, there is the risk that employees may deliberately or unintentionally alter or manipulate datasets.

However, beyond these risks concerning particularly the accuracy of data, the fundamental principle of integrity also concerns risks of manipulation. Especially with regard to integrated information systems, which include profiles of individuals, there is a risk that the controller can use these profiles to manipulate individuals by presenting information in a certain manner.[451]

Risks to Availability

With regard to the fundamental principle of availability, which aims to ensure that data are retrievable, accessible and interpretable, there is a risk that data are removed or deleted. Again, this risk can be caused at the hands of third parties, for instance through ransomware,[452] as well as by the controller. The latter risk is particularly high when the data may be comprising for the controller, for instance, when they or their mere existence in the system of the controller document a violation of laws or individual rights.[453]

Risks to Transparency

Concerning the fundamental principle of transparency, which aims to ensure that controllers, supervisory authorities and data subjects understand the functioning and implications of a data processing operation, there is a twofold risk with regard to data subjects. On the one hand, there is the risk that data subjects are not provided sufficient information on how their data are processed.[454]

On the other hand, controllers can intentionally drown data subjects in information, which is not relevant for the specific decision the data subject has to make and therefore not suited for the situation.[455] In line with the controller's obligation to implement data protection by default,[456] basic use has to be enabled as a standard and can, if the data subject requires further functionality, be expanded at a later

[451] This can be used to manipulate data subjects emotionally, cf. Booth 2014, The Guardian. https://www.theguardian.com/technology/2014/jun/29/facebook-users-emotions-news-feeds. Accessed 28 July 2021; but may apparently also influence whole elections Rosenberg et al. 2018, The New York Times. https://www.nytimes.com/2018/03/17/us/politics/cambridge-analytica-trump-campaign.html. Accessed 28 July 2021.

[452] Cf. for one of many examples Gayle et al. 2017, The Guardian. https://www.theguardian.com/society/2017/may/12/hospitals-across-england-hit-by-large-scale-cyber-attack? Accessed 28 July 2021.

[453] Hence, Article 18(1)(c) GDPR, Article 16(3)(b) LED and Articles 20(1)(c) and 82(3)(b) DPR-EU give the data subject a right to restrict the processing of certain data, in order to ensure that they are available as evidence.

[454] When individuals are unable to foresee how their data are processed, this may also produce chilling effects with regard to the exercise of other fundamental rights, such as the freedom of expression or assembly of Articles 11 et seq. CFR, cf. Bieker and Bremert 2020.

[455] Roßnagel 2019, MN. 60 et seq.

[456] Article 25(2) GDPR, Articles 27(2) and 85(2) DPR-EU as well as Article 20(2) LED.

point.[457] However, if that is not the case, there is a risk of information overload, which obfuscates the processing operation rather than rendering it understandable for the data subject.

Furthermore, with regard to the controllers themselves, there is the risk that they do not understand the processing operations involved in their own processing activities entirely. Due to the complexity of processing operations—even when they should be rather simple, but in fact incorporate various third-party hardware and software components or products—this can be challenging for controllers. In many instances this complexity is not necessary, but rather used to obscure other processing operations, which a service provider, product manufacturer or other third party may run in the background to achieve their own, not necessarily legitimate, purposes. For instance, on the very basic level of the operating system[458] or seemingly simple word processing software,[459] some manufacturers implement non-transparent data flows through backchannels, which are not fully disclosed or documented and may also pose risks to control with regard to the transfer of data to third countries and the protection of employees using such products.

This problem is aggravated in complex processing operations, where there is a tendency to rely on third parties in order to achieve certain results, for instance in order to profile or score data subjects. Often this leads controllers to introduce black boxes into their processing operations, which they do not fully understand. According to the myth of humanly unattainable objectivity and neutrality, the machine—or nowadays "the algorithm"—delivers results seemingly beyond reproach.[460]

The complexity of processing activities also entails the risk that the supervisory authorities cannot exercise their tasks sufficiently. The supervision of such complex processing activities requires considerable know how[461] as well as financial resources and personnel.[462] Yet, when large service providers or manufacturers focus

---

[457] Cf. the examples in ENISA, Recommendations on shaping technology according to GDPR provisions (2018), pp. 24 et seq. and 27. https://www.enisa.europa.eu/publications/recommendations-on-shaping-technology-according-to-gdpr-provisions-part-2/at_download/fullReport. Accessed 28 July 2021; the extension of functionality brings the risk that the controller, after one click of the data subject, introduces sweeping purposes, which would, of course, contravene other principles, such as separation or integrity, cf. Hansen 2019a, MN. 56.

[458] Autoriteit Persoonsgegevens, Summary of Investigation Report on Microsoft Windows 10 Home and Pro (2017). https://autoriteitpersoonsgegevens.nl/sites/default/files/atoms/files/public_version_dutch_dpa_informal_translation_summary_of_investigation_report.pdf. Accessed 28 July 2021.

[459] Nas and Roosendaal 2018.

[460] Simitis 1971, p. 676; Noble 2021, p. 205; Gillespie 2014; Hassein 2017; Fröhlich and Spiecker gen. Döhmann 2018; however, the knowledge of the fallibility of such automated decision-making has now explicitly been used to regulate it, inter alia in Article 22 GDPR. On this provision cf. Brkan 2019a.

[461] Also cf. Rost 2018b, p. 88, who further points out that the investigations carried out by supervisory authorities must also conform to the data protection principles, especially with regard to transparency.

[462] For a study on the resources needed by the German supervisory authorities for the implementation of the GDPR cf. Roßnagel 2017.

their efforts on stalling, delaying or obstructing investigations, time also becomes an important resource.[463] If the supervisory authority cannot gain a verified understanding of how a given software or hardware operates, this is a great risk to the rights of individuals, as it does not allow for the enforcement of the very rules that aim to protect these individuals.

Risks to Control

The fundamental principle of control, in extension of the fundamental principle of transparency, aims to ensure that data subjects, controllers and supervisory authorities exercise their respective measures of oversight over the processing operation. Data subjects, in practice, are dependent on the controller to exercise their data subject rights—which aim to provide them with some measure of control—as the controller controls the processing operation.

If the controller cannot or does not implement measures to allow for the meaningful exercise of these rights on an operational level, for instance by ensuring that they can retrieve information about the processing or rectify data that are processed by an information system, the data subjects experience a further loss of control.[464]

However, the assumption that a controller is fully in control of a processing operation illustrates another risk to the principle of control. Building on the risk to individuals that comes with processing operations that are obscure to controllers,[465] this can further extend to the control of controllers when they have to rely on third-party software or hardware. When manufacturers exercise great market power, for instance, because there are few alternatives to their product, the control the controller exercises over their processing operation may be severely restricted. However, individuals, whose data are processed by fully or partly automated decision-making systems, face risks of serious discrimination,[466] in processing operations in which neither they nor the controller can intervene and thus lose control.[467]

---

[463] Frenkel et al. 2018, The New York Times. https://www.nytimes.com/2018/11/14/technology/facebook-data-russia-election-racism.html. Accessed 28 July 2021; Hern 2018, The Guardian. https://www.theguardian.com/technology/2018/nov/19/mark-zuckerberg-faces-more-calls-to-attend-facebook-misinformation-hearing. Accessed 28 July 2021; Nakashima 2018, Associated Press. https://www.apnews.com/828aefab64d4411bac257a07c1af0ecb. Accessed 28 July 2021; Privacy International 2018, Press Release. https://privacyinternational.org/press-release/2424/press-release-privacy-international-files-complaints-against-seven-companies. Accessed 21 June 2021.

[464] The initial loss of control for data subjects is that, factually, they cannot prevent the processing of their data, cf. above in Sect. 5.3.1.1.

[465] Cf. the previous subsection above in Sect. 5.4.2.1.

[466] European Union Agency for Fundamental Rights 2018, #BigData: Discrimination in data-supported decision making. Vienna. https://fra.europa.eu/sites/default/files/fra_uploads/fra-2018-focus-big-data_en.pdf. Accessed 28 July 2021; Simonite 2018, Wired. https://www.wired.com/story/when-it-comes-to-gorillas-google-photos-remains-blind/. Accessed 28 July 2021; Hassein 2017.

[467] Bieker et al. 2018b.

A further risk concerning the fundamental principle of control, which builds on risks concerning transparency,[468] persists when supervisory authorities are not able to fulfil their tasks and exercise their powers effectively. This concerns the issue of resources relating to both finance and qualified personnel. As I have shown in Chap. 3, the ECJ has encountered this risk as well in its jurisprudence on Article 8(3) CFR.[469] EU data protection law now explicitly requires the allocation of sufficient resources in a separate budget for supervisory authorities in Article 52(4)-(6) GDPR and a transparent procedure to appoint qualified members of supervisory authorities according to Article 53 GDPR. While it will have to be seen how Member States carry out these obligations in practice,[470] the measures of control awarded to data subjects as well as the structural dimension of data protection, based on the rule of law aspect, are weakened when supervisory authorities are not fulfilling their functions effectively.

Interim Conclusions on Risks of Data Processing
Considering these risks, the fundamental right to data protection is required as remedy to substantively protect the individual as well as the structures of a democratic, rule of law-based society against the inherent risks of data processing. However, while EU data protection law addresses many of these risks, they cannot be resolved by the law alone. These risks exist due to the fact that, in practice, processing operations do not necessarily conform to the law. The risks can therefore only be mitigated, with the aim of minimising the damage when they materialise. In the conceptualisation of Steinmüller, Podlech et al.,[471] these risks are what renders a processing operation undesirable, i.e. runs counter to the fundamental goals of the constitution.

5.4.2.2 Addressing Data Processing as Instrument of Power

The fundamental right to data protection, just like data protection law in general, further has the rationale of addressing the processing of personal data as an instrument of power. As the controller exposes individuals and the democratic society to the risks elaborated in the previous section, this exposure and the ability to process personal data must be recognised as an instrument of power. In order to address the risks, individual and structural data protection law offer various safeguards, which aim to mitigate this power asymmetry. However, beyond these substantive rules, the fundamental right to data protection renders the power structures, which tilt the scales in favour of controllers, visible. The fundamental right to data protection therefore is a tool, which facilitates the analysis of the risks which are the consequence of the inherent power imbalance of data processing.

---

[468] Cf. the previous subsection above Sect. 5.4.2.1.

[469] Cf. Chap. 3, Sect. 3.3.

[470] Cf. the criticism of the 2018 election of the German Federal Data Protection Commissioner by Engeler 2018b.

[471] Cf. above in Sect. 5.2.2.

5.4.3 *The Content of the Right to Data Protection*

The fundamental right to data protection is the legal answer to the issue posed by the processing of personal data and is aimed at curtailing the power of controllers to create risks for individuals. In that regard, the content of the fundamental right to data protection follows from its twofold rationale to mitigate the risks to individuals and address the power asymmetry between them and controllers.

In the following, I will firstly address the scope of protection (Sect. 5.4.2.1), which, as Steinmüller et al. already found in 1975 and as confirmed by the jurisprudence of the ECJ,[472] with regard to the rationale of data protection law, must be wide to cover a broad range of interferences. I will then turn to the extent of protection, i.e. interferences (Sect. 5.4.2.2) and their justifications (Sect. 5.4.2.3), which, as Steinmüller argued, allow for more differentiation with regard to individual processing operations.[473] Lastly, I will turn to the essence of the right to data protection (Sect. 5.4.2.4), which I will define through recourse to the fundamental principles of EU data protection law.

5.4.3.1 The Scope of Protection of the Right to Data Protection

Due to the inherent risks of data processing, which I have considered in the previous subsection,[474] the scope of the fundamental right to data protection, in line with the jurisprudence of the Court[475] and the secondary EU data protection law, must be interpreted broadly. In the following, I will consider the material as well as the personal scope of the right to data protection.

The Material Scope

Concerning the material scope, data protection law does not allow for a differentiation between different kinds of personal data[476] and must thus apply to all personal data, i.e. any information that renders an individual identifiable. This broad definition is anchored in the secondary EU data protection law, to which the fundamental right to data protection is tied. This broad definition of personal data is also necessary with regard to the rationale of data protection law, and the right to data protection more specifically, to address the issue of data processing. It ensures that any data processing operation falls within the scope of the fundamental right to data protection and thus under the review of the Court.[477]

---

[472] Cf. Chap. 3, Sect. 3.2.9.

[473] Steinmüller 1975, p. 78.

[474] Cf. above in Sect. 5.4.2.1.

[475] Cf. Chap. 3, Sect. 3.4.

[476] Cf. already above in Sect. 5.3.1.2 and further, with regard to the right to privacy, below in Sect. 5.4.5.

[477] Cf. Chap. 3, Sect. 3.2.9.

Accordingly, it is not necessary to extend the scope to include any information. The definition of personal data in the EU data protection law ensures that whenever a date either by itself or, most likely, through linking with other data, enables the identification of an individual, data protection law applies. Steinmüller et al., even though they relied on the term information,[478] argued in their report that it was not necessary that data protection covered purely factual information, which could not be attributed to an individual.[479] For instance, the mere information that at a certain time the weather was sunny at a certain location or the information contained in a manual for assembling furniture, do not render an individual identifiable and are an example of purely factual information, in the sense of the report.

However, Steinmüller et al. sensibly argued that due to the power asymmetry between data subject and controller, which is based on the superior knowledge about how their information system—which is opaque to the individual—processes data, there should be a rebuttable presumption for cases of doubt. In such cases, where it is not clear, whether any given information renders an individual identifiable, the controller would have to rebut the presumption that this is the case.[480] With regard to the scope of the right to data protection, the adoption of such a presumption is a way to mediate the power structures, which favour controllers and which data protection aims to address.[481]

The broad scope of the right to data protection, therefore, can be derived from its twofold rationale of addressing the power imbalance as well as the risks inherent in data processing. It is a prerequisite to ensure that the inherent risks of data processing operations[482] are not dismissed or ignored, but rather analysed appropriately in order to mitigate them in accordance with the general obligations of controllers. At the same time, this exercise of analysis and mitigation according to the general obligations of controllers is an instrument to curtail the data power exercised by controllers and to address data processing as instrument of power.[483] As a powerful actor, the controller must be subject to close scrutiny.

The Personal Scope

The personal scope of the fundamental right to data protection is limited to natural persons, i.e. individuals. As the risks, which are inherent in the processing of personal data are limited to individuals, the personal scope extends accordingly.

There have been various proposals to include legal persons within the scope of data protection, in order to offer them protection. The Article 29 Working Party has argued that certain data protection rules might apply indirectly.[484] An important

---

[478] Steinmüller et al. 1971, p. 43.

[479] Ibid., p. 56.

[480] Ibid., pp. 56 et seq.

[481] Cf. above in Sect. 5.4.2.2.

[482] As I elaborated in the previous subsection, cf. above in Sect. 5.4.2.1.

[483] Cf. above in Sect. 5.4.2.2.

[484] Article 29 Working Party, Opinion 4/2007 on the concept of personal data of 20 June 2007. WP 136, pp. 23 et seq.

aspect to highlight, for instance, is that of corporate email accounts linked to individual employees by name.[485] However, this is a matter of labour law protections and, data protection in the employment sector, rather than awarding a right to the employer, who might be a legal person. The Court has rightly limited the personal scope to individuals and clarified that it does not generally extend to legal persons.[486]

The only exception the Court allowed is the case of legal persons, which, through their name, identify one or more specific individuals.[487] Yet, it must be noted that in this case, the natural person standing behind the legal person, i.e. the individual is associated with its name, is protected and not the legal person as such.

There have also been proposals to allow legal persons access to some data subject rights, while excluding others, or by awarding a lower level of protection.[488] However, the general rule that legal persons are not covered by the right to data protection is confirmed by the secondary EU data protection law, which already only addresses the rights of natural persons in the respective official titles,[489] in the provision on its subject matter and objectives[490] and expressly states that it does not cover the processing of data concerning legal persons in the recitals.[491]

Furthermore, when discussing the personal scope of the right to data protection, it is crucial to take into account that this is not defined arbitrarily. Rather, the scope of the right follows the rationale of the right to data protection to protect individuals and the democratic society from the processing of personal data. Legal persons are not affected by the risks inherent in data processing in the way that individuals are. Profiling can serve as an example here: even though the behaviour of legal persons can also be monitored, it does not entail the same risk of the creation of personality profiles, as legal persons simply do not have a personality. Therefore, the limitation of the personal scope of the right to data protection to individuals, rather than including legal persons, is sensible.

However, in order to offer full protection for individuals from the inherent risks of data processing, the personal scope of the right, de lege ferenda, must be extended in order to enable groups of individuals to enforce this right collectively. Especially with regard to risks of discrimination arising from profiling—where certain aspects relating to an individual are evaluated to inter alia predict the individual's behaviour[492]—and the processing of data of some individuals to infer information

[485] Ibid., p. 23.

[486] ECJ, Joined Cases C-92/09 and C-93/09 Volker und Markus Schecke GbR (C-92/09) and Hartmut Eifert (C-93/09) v Land Hessen, Judgment of 9 November 2010, ECLI:EU:C:2010:662, para 53. Also cf. Chap. 3, Sect. 3.2.6.

[487] Ibid.

[488] Cf. van der Sloot 2015; also cf. Korff 1998.

[489] "Regulation (EU) 2016/679 [...] on the protection of natural persons [...]"; "Directive (EU) 2016/680 [...] on the protection of natural persons [...]"; "Regulation (EU) 2018/1725[...] on the protection of natural persons [...]".

[490] Articles 1(2) GDPR, LED and DPR-EU.

[491] Recital 14 GDPR and recital 6 DPR-EU.

[492] As defined in Article 4(4) GDPR, Article 3(5) DPR-EU and Article 3(4) LED.

about other individuals, there currently is a gap in protection, especially with regard to groups who are already vulnerable.[493]

Particularly in the area of profiling, which entails a high risk for the individual due to the severe damage that can result from discrimination, the outcome of such a process is determined by the group, to which the data subject is assigned. However, there is currently no right, which gives a marginalized group or an individual belonging to such a group, who cannot prove that their data are processed in the specific processing operation in question, a claim against the controller or a claim vis-à-vis the supervisory authority, not to be discriminated against, even though the secondary EU data protection law explicitly refers to such a risk.[494]

This lack of protection is not remedied by the right to non-discrimination of Article 21 CFR, which also offers no collective dimension. Even though aspects of discrimination are addressed under Article 21 CFR, the secondary EU data protection law specifically aims to protect all relevant fundamental rights with regard to the processing of personal data according to Article 1(2) GDPR.[495] While an analysis of a data processing operation from the perspective of other fundamental rights is a sensible corrective measure to ensure that all relevant risks to the rights of individuals are identified, the right to data protection has to address any risk, which arises from the processing of personal data.[496]

However, as I have argued in the first subsection of this chapter, with regard to the EU data protection law on the level of primary and secondary EU law, this current lacuna of protection can be alleviated through the reform of the legal definition of the term data subject, to relate to one or more individuals.[497] Furthermore, a collective right could be enforced by an individual or a group, where, in recourse to the ECtHR's case law on measures of secret surveillance,[498] they demonstrate that a given processing operation generally discriminates against members of this group, rather than having to demonstrate first that their data are being processed by the relevant processing operation.[499]

---

[493] Cf. above in Sect. 5.2.3.3.

[494] Cf. already Chap. 2, Sect. 2.3.3.3 and below in Sect. 5.3.1.1. Also cf. recital 75 GDPR and recital 46 DPR-EU.

[495] Cf. also Article 1(2) DPR-EU and Article 1(2)(a) LED.

[496] Bieker and Bremert 2020.

[497] Cf. above in Sect. 5.2.3.3.

[498] Cf. especially ECtHR [GC], Roman Zakharov, App. No. 47143/06, Judgment of 4 December 2015, para 171; also cf. ECtHR, Klass and Others, App. No. 5029/71, Judgment of 6 September 1978, para 34; ECtHR, Szabó and Vissy, App. No. 37138/14, Judgment of 12 January 2016, paras 32–37.

[499] Cf. as I suggested in more detail above in Sect. 5.2.3.3.

5.4.3.2 Interferences with the Right to Data Protection

Due to the risks of data processing, I have identified above,[500] the power of controllers to create such risks has to be restricted. Article 8 CFR achieves this on two levels. Article 8(1) and (2) CFR addresses the processing of personal data, which, as a default, has to be justified. Article 8(1) and (3) CFR guarantees the individual the right of complaint to independent supervisory authorities, which are tasked with enforcing the EU data protection law.

Interferences with Article 8(1) and (2) CFR

Requiring controllers to justify any processing of personal data, rather than just allowing it, imposes a first level of protection for individuals as well as society as a whole. Consequently, whenever any personal data are processed, there is an interference with the right to data protection, as the ECJ has held in its jurisprudence.[501] This standard is necessary in order to ensure that any processing operation is analysed with regard to its specific inherent risks. The interference mirrors the broad scope of the right to data protection, which also aims to ensure that any processing operation comes under scrutiny.[502] This standard then ensures that the assessment of the interference takes due account of the inherent risks and power structures of data processing.

The standard of interference with the right to data protection also sets out the scope of the secondary EU data protection law: it requires the general ban of the processing of personal data that I already discussed in Chap. 2.[503] In this regard, the current doctrinal discourse on data protection, which I have analysed in the previous chapter,[504] falls short. All of the current conceptualisations of data protection law and more explicitly, the right to data protection, argue that the finding of an interference had to be restricted and limited to only the gravest violations.[505] Therefore the current approaches undermine the comprehensive protection established by the secondary EU data protection law. Under the current approaches, the level of scrutiny is drastically reduced, as only processing operations, which prima facie pose considerable risks—a standard, which is not even defined, but rather left to the discretion of practitioners—are even reviewed. However, with such an approach, it cannot be ensured that, in practice, the risks entailed by a processing operation are taken into consideration, before this process is carried out.

Interferences with Article 8(1) and (3) CFR

A different kind of interference with the right to data protection occurs, when the individual's right to lodge a complaint with an independent supervisory authority is

[500] Cf. above in Sect. 5.4.2.1.

[501] Cf. Chap. 3, Sect. 3.2.9.

[502] Cf. above in Sect. 5.4.3.1.

[503] Cf. Chap. 2, Sect. 2.3.2.1.

[504] Cf. Chap. 4.

[505] Cf. especially the privacy approach, Chap. 4, Sect. 4.5.1, and the checks and balances approach Chap. 4, Sect. 4.8.3.

limited. In this regard the right to data protection supplements the right to an effective remedy under Article 47 CFR and provides another remedy to data subjects, below the level of judicial proceedings, for instances when controllers do not conform to the rules of EU data protection law.

In the individual dimension of Article 8(1) and (3) CFR, there is an interference with the individual's right to lodge a complaint with an independent supervisory authority, when the legislator limits the competent supervisory authority's powers in a way that encroaches on its independence. The independence of supervisory authorities, as I have shown in Chap. 3,[506] has been interpreted by the Court in the sense that they must be free from any direct or indirect influence. The fundamental principle of control includes this notion of independence of the supervisory authorities, as it is a prerequisite for them to exercise their powers.[507]

It is also an interference with the individual's right to data protection under Article 8(1) and (3) CFR, when a supervisory authority does not consider the complaint of an individual in a meaningful way. At the same time, the right to data protection does not award the data subject a right that the supervisory authority takes a particular action or exercises a specific power. Yet, it would be reductive to argue that this was entailed by their independence. It is the very purpose of the supervisory authorities to protect individuals and especially data subjects. The notion of independence therefore applies vis-à-vis those entities the supervisory authorities supervise and cannot be used against those it is tasked to protect. With regard to individuals, supervisory authorities, under the fundamental principles of transparency and control, must be accountable and justify their actions or inaction in a comprehensible manner. The position of individuals is further secured by Article 47 CFR: if they find that the actions taken by a supervisory authority are insufficient, they can seek a judicial remedy, as with any other public authority.[508]

Furthermore, Article 8(3) CFR illustrates the structural side of the right to data protection. The supervisory authorities, as actors independent from other powerful entities, are institutions tasked specifically with the protection of individuals *from* the processing of data. However, they are not restricted to only consider complaints by individuals. The supervisory authorities also have original powers and competences to monitor and control data processing operations. This demonstrates that they are not intended to be institutions which exclusively serve the interests of specific individuals. Rather, the supervisory authorities themselves are an institutional safeguard for the democratic society under the rule of law.

---

[506] Cf. Chap. 3, Sect. 3.3.

[507] Cf. above in Sect. 5.3.2.8 and Sect. 5.4.2.1.

[508] As I have discussed in Chap. 3, Sect. 3.3. Also cf. ECJ, Case C-362/14 Schrems, Judgment of 6 October 2015, paras 57 et seq. and 62–64.

5.4.3.3 Justifications for Interferences with the Right to Data Protection

According to Article 52(1) CFR, and as the Court often reaffirms with reference to *Schmidberger*,[509] the fundamental rights of EU law are not absolute and an interference can be justified when it does not violate the essence of the right and is based on a legal basis, which fulfils the criteria of the proportionality test. I will firstly elaborate on the justifications for interferences with the right to data protection more generally in the following, before considering the violation of the essence separately below (Sect. 5.4.3.4).

As the extent of protection awarded by the right to data protection can be different for each specific processing operation, which will have its own specific requirements, depending on the particular circumstances of the case, there are numerous exceptions to the general ban of data processing, which allow for the processing of personal data, when there are a legitimate aim and legal basis, as also laid down by Article 8(2) CFR. Hence, the fundamental principle of lawfulness extends beyond pure formalism, as the legal basis—as well as the specified purpose of the processing operation—must be legitimate.[510]

With regard to the broad exceptions to that general ban in the form of the various legal bases, which ultimately allow the processing, if there are appropriate safeguards in place, the broad definition of the interference with the right to data protection ensures that any legitimate processing activity falls within the ambit of the rules on how the processing is carried out.[511] This can already be seen in the jurisprudence of the ECJ, which allows a wide variety of legitimate aims to be pursued by processing activities and has established that the EU data protection law includes mechanisms to balance the rights and interests of all involved parties through appropriate safeguards.[512]

The other fundamental principles, as opposing pairs,[513] are also present in Article 8(2) CFR, which includes fairness and purpose limitation and thereby refers to the fundamental principles of transparency and separation. Further, it specifically refers to the right to rectification, which concerns the fundamental principle of integrity, and to the right to access, which relates to the fundamental principles of availability and confidentiality. The provision also mentions the data subject rights, which are an important part of the fundamental principle of control. This principle is also at

[509] Cf., inter alia, ECJ, Avis 1/15, Opinion of 26 July 2017, para 136; ECJ, Case C-291/12 Michael Schwarz v Stadt Bochum, Judgment of 17 October 2013, ECLI:EU:C:2013:670, para 33; ECJ, Joined Cases C-92/09 and C-93/09 Volker und Markus Schecke and Eifert, Judgment of 9 November 2010, para 48.

[510] Here again, data protection law extends a general rule, which the rule of law imposes on the democratic State, i.e. the legitimacy and proportionality of the law, onto private entities through the requirement of a legitimate purpose.

[511] Chapters IV GDPR, DPR-EU and LED.

[512] Cf. Chap. 3, Sect. 3.4 and especially ECJ, Case C-101/01 Criminal proceedings against Bodil Lindqvist, Judgment of 6 November 2003, ECLI:EU:C:2003:596, para 79.

[513] Cf. above Fig. 5.1 and in Sect. 5.3.3.

the heart of Article 8(3) CFR, which guarantees a right to complain to and oversight by an independent supervisory authority.

The broad definitions of scope and interference thus aim to ensure that any processing activity can be scrutinised at the justification stage with regard to its inherent risks and power imbalance. As any processing operation concerning personal data is within the scope and constitutes an interference with the right to data protection, it follows that the main focus in the assessment of Article 8 CFR has to be on the justification stage. With regard to the right under Article 8(1) and (2) CFR, this can also be seen in the structure of the Charter, where the legislator introduced Article 8(2) CFR, which lays out additional requirements beyond the general justification clause of Article 52(1) CFR.

As I have argued in the preceding paragraphs, Article 8(2) and Article 8(3) CFR introduce the fundamental principles of EU data protection law as an additional layer to assess the specific technical and organisational measures required to render a processing operation proportionate.

On a general level, the risk to the right of data protection, as I elaborated above,[514] is that the gravity of an interference is not sufficiently mitigated and therefore the interference is not justified and violates the right. It follows, hence, that the risks to the right of data protection I set out in the previous subsection,[515] are examples for interferences with this very right, as they all concern the processing of personal data. The damage to individuals that may materialise from these risks, which also constitute interferences, is the violation of the right to data protection.[516] Thus, if one or multiple of the risks concerning the fundamental principles of EU data protection law—i.e. an interference with the right to data protection—is not appropriately mitigated—i.e. justified—the inherent damage materialises and there is a violation of the fundamental right to data protection.

The mitigation of risks has two levels: the *if* and the *how* of processing. As I have shown above, the fundamental principle of lawfulness concerns the *if* of a processing operation, i.e. whether it is based on a legitimate legal basis.[517] The other level is the *how*, which concerns the practical selection of technical and organisational measures and other safeguards, which help to mitigate the risks and thereby limit the gravity of the interference to a proportionate extent. This means that a processing operation based on a legitimate legal basis, which amounts to a grave interference with the right to data protection, can be justified, if there are appropriate technical and organisational measures in place, which mitigate the gravity of the interference. However, if the legal basis is not legitimate, there is no need to further assess technical

514 Cf. above in Sect. 5.4.2.1.

515 Cf. above in Sect. 5.4.2.1.

516 Cf. also Konferenz der unabhängigen Datenschutzaufsichtsbehörden des Bundes und der Länder 2018, pp. 1 et seq.

517 Cf. above in Sect. 5.3.2.1 as well as already in Chap. 2, Sect. 2.3.2.1. This also builds on an idea by Maria Tzanou, who proposes to use principles of data protection law in order to determine the violation of the essence of the right to data protection, which I have introduced in Chap. 4, Sect. 4.7.2.

and organisational measures, as this alone already renders the processing operation disproportionate.

The fundamental principles, which are representative of the system and characteristic provisions of EU data protection law,[518] also allow for a systematisation of the interferences with the right to data protection, which is useful at the justification stage, especially when considering which technical and organisational measures to implement.

Accordingly, the interferences with the right to data protection can be categorised into seven different types, which correspond to the risks to each of the fundamental principles of EU data protection law:[519] interferences with the right to data protection, which concern the lack of a sufficient or legitimate legal basis relate to the fundamental principle of lawfulness. When data are linked or datasets are integrated, differentiated roles merged or conflated, purposes illegitimate, undefined or retroactively expanded or data not deleted when the purpose of their collection has been attained, a processing operation concerns the fundamental principle of separation. When data are disclosed, altered or removed/deleted without authorisation, this relates to the fundamental principles of confidentiality, integrity and availability, respectively. If there is a lack of information about or understanding of the processing operation on the level of the controller, data subject or supervisory authority, this pertains to the fundamental principle of transparency. And lastly, when there is a lack of oversight on any of these levels, this concerns the fundamental principle of control.

With regard to interferences with Article 8(1) and (3) CFR, it follows from this enumeration and the three different levels where transparency and control must be established—i.e. controller, data subject and supervisory authority—that any interference will relate either to the principle of transparency or the principle of control.[520]

An interference with the right to data protection is thus always linked to a fundamental principle, which is relevant at the justification stage, where the fundamental principles must be balanced. As the fundamental principles have various dimensions and interact with each other—which may also lead to tensions between them, especially when they are opposing principles[521]—the degree of implementation of each of the principles will depend on the particular processing operations.

The fundamental principles must thus be balanced in order to achieve practical concordance between them. It is possible to justify a lower standard for one of the fundamental principles with a legitimate and proportionate benefit to another fundamental principle. An example can be a processing operation, which allows for the broad disclosure of data and therefore undermines the fundamental principle of confidentiality. In order to justify the processing operation,[522] the technical and

---

[518] As I have introduced above in Sect. 5.3.3.

[519] As exemplified above on a generic level, cf. Sect. 5.4.2.1.

[520] Cf. already above in Sect. 5.4.2.1 and Sect. 5.4.3.2.

[521] Cf. already above in Sect. 5.3.3 and Fig. 5.1.

[522] While public authorities have to justify interferences with fundamental rights, this may be different in horizontal relations. However, a private entity, as controller, has to be able to demonstrate

organisational measures will have to focus particularly on other measures to ensure confidentiality in order to mitigate the associated risks and reduce the gravity of the interference.

However, a broader disclosure of data can also, depending on the specific processing operation, be justified by increased needs of availability, as the opposing fundamental principle. The lack of confidentiality might then even be remedied on a different level, for instance by ensuring that, where personal data is published online, as was the case in the *Schecke and Eifert* judgment,[523] and therefore available to an unlimited number of persons, the data published are limited to only those strictly necessary to attain a more narrowly defined purpose, and thereby increasing the measures concerning the fundamental principle of separation.

As the ECJ noted in *Tele2 Sverige*, technical and organisational measures are the key to mitigating the gravity of an interference, which has to be assessed in order to determine the proportionality of a measure, and thereby ensure that the measure fulfils its requirements.[524] In the terms of the secondary EU data protection law and the risk to the rights of individuals, the technical and organisational measures have to mitigate the severity of the impact—i.e. the potential damage—in order to ensure an appropriate level of protection.

The implementation of technical and organisational measures to a level appropriate to the risks of the processing operation is a paramount step in order to ensure that a processing operation complies with the EU data protection law and thus ensures the protection of the individuals affected, i.e. data subjects, but also society as a whole. The processing of personal data without any technical and organisational measures—as suggested under the privacy approach[525]—is necessarily a violation of the right to data protection. In many instances, technical and organisational measures are already a default to some extent and go hand in hand with very basic information security: requiring login credentials for a computer system or locking a smartphone with a passcode fall under the notion of technical and organisational measures.

With the gravity of the interference, the measures taken to ensure the rights of individuals must be increased. Hence, the Court, for instance, demands that where communications data is stored in bulk, it must, inter alia, be protected through an elaborate rights and roles concept.[526]

Consequently, any processing operation must provide safeguards to protect individuals at the justification stage, including, on a structural level, the implementation of technical and organisational measures, which are appropriate to the risks posed by the processing operation in question. These provisions aim to curtail the power

---

compliance with the secondary EU data protection legislation in conformity to the requirements of accountability.

523 Discussed above, cf. Chap. 3, Sect. 3.2.6.

524 ECJ, Joined Cases C-203/15 and C-698/15 Tele 2 Sverige, Judgment of 21 December 2016, para 122.

525 Cf. Chap. 4, Sect. 4.5.1.

526 ECJ, Joined Cases C-293/12 and C-594/12 Digital Rights Ireland and Seitlinger and Others, Judgment of 8 April 2014, paras 60–62; similarly Classen 2014, pp. 443 et seq.

of controllers to interfere with the rights of individuals. Nevertheless, the caveat concerning the appropriateness with regard to the risks to the rights of individuals provides scalability for the measures. This scalability implies that the EU data protection law does not require specific measures for processing operations, but rather allows to tailor them individually to the processing operation in question. However, this requires a granular analysis of the processing operation with attention to the specific risks in all potential scenarios of its use. This can be achieved by introducing another level of balancing to the justification stage.

As I have argued, the fundamental principles of EU data protection law can be used to identify the areas where technical and organisational measures can best be used to mitigate the gravity of an interference. By balancing the fundamental principles of EU data protection law with one another and with regard to the particular requirements of the specific processing operation in question, a first level of protection can be achieved.

In a second step then, the general criteria of the fundamental rights assessment—the legitimate aim justifying the processing operation and its proportionality—can be assessed. This follows the requirements of Article 52(1) CFR,[527] where the standard of review depends on the gravity of the interference. When the interference has already been matched to a fundamental principle and it has already been balanced with the other fundamental principles, the assessment of the gravity can also be carried out more precisely, as any safeguards, which may already remedy certain problematic aspects of a processing operation, have already been identified.

5.4.3.4 The Essence of the Right to Data Protection

However, for certain interferences there cannot be a justification according to Article 52(1) CFR. This is the case, when an interference violates "the core content"[528] of a right, as the Court has described the essence.[529] In general, when the Court finds a violation of the essence, it assumes a violation of the right without any further

[527] For a particularly well-structured assessment by the ECJ, cf. ECJ, Joined Cases C-293/12 and C-594/12 Digital Rights Ireland and Seitlinger and Others, Judgment of 8 April 2014, paras 41–51; ECJ, Avis 1/15, Opinion of 26 July 2017, paras 139–217.

[528] ECJ, Case C-283/11 Sky Österreich GmbH v Österreichischer Rundfunk, Judgment of 22 January 2013, ECLI:EU:C:2013:28, para 49.

[529] While there is a debate on whether the essence of the right is a separate requirement or part of the assessment of proportionality—for an excellent overview of the debate cf. Brkan 2018, pp. 335–377—the Court, in its more recent jurisprudence, has examined the essence as a separate point before the assessment of proportionality cf. ECJ, Joined Cases C-293/12 and C-594/12 Digital Rights Ireland and Seitlinger and Others, Judgment of 8 April 2014, para 39; ECJ, Case C-291/12 Schwarz, Judgment of 17 October 2013, para 39; as opposed to, e.g. ECJ, Case C-408/03 Commission of the European Communities v Kingdom of Belgium, Judgment of 23 March 2006, ECLI:EU:C:2006:192, para 68.

assessment of the proportionality of the measure,[530] i.e. with regard to Article 8 CFR, the processing operation in question.[531]

The notion of such an inviolable core of a right, however, comes with practical difficulties in delimiting interferences of varying gravity[532]—which concerns the question whether a measure is only a grave interference or rather amounts to a violation of the essence—as well as the differentiation between the essence and the proportionality assessment.[533]

Brkan has suggested a very narrow interpretation of the essence: according to her, the essence would only be violated where the legislator does not provide any—valid—legitimate reasons in accordance with Article 52(1) CFR.[534] It seems difficult to determine under this approach, when there would still be an acceptable overriding interest, and when a purported interest invoked by a Member State would be regarded as not meeting this standard. Brkan takes legislation abolishing the right to vote for women, justified by the argument that women in general were a threat to democracy, as an example.[535] With this crass case, of course, it would be easy to find that the invoked argument is not valid. However, there are more subtle justifications imaginable, where it would be harder to differentiate. Yet, more importantly, an interference, which does not follow a legitimate interest, would already fail to satisfy the proportionality test, as it would not fulfil the criterion of legitimate aim under Article 52(1) CFR. Thus, the essence would, in fact, be consumed by the proportionality assessment.

Yet, the requirement that any interference must respect the essence of the right is explicitly included in Article 52(1) CFR. Under the Court's own jurisprudence, the content of protection of a right must "be seriously reduced"[536] to the point that it is rendered ineffective. With regard to the Court's case law, Lenaerts has suggested that an interference may violate the essence of a right, when it is particularly intense in gravity and broad in extent.[537]

The ECJ has demonstrated that it does not principally shy away from finding a violation of the essence: it held that when an employer was bound to a collective agreement, which they were barred from negotiating, the essence of the right to conduct a business under Article 16 CFR was violated,[538] which shows that, in the case law, the extent of the effects of an interference is less determinative than its gravity. Furthermore, the Court found that the mass-scale access to contents of

---

[530] Cf., for instance, ECJ, Case C-362/14 Schrems, Judgment of 6 October 2015, paras 94 et seq. and discussed in Chap. 3, Sect. 3.2.8.8.

[531] Cf. ibid., para 98.

[532] For an overview cf. Dawson et al. 2019, pp. 766–768. For an in-depth analysis cf. Brkan 2018.

[533] Tridimas and Gentile 2019, p. 810.

[534] Brkan 2019b, pp. 869 and 872.

[535] Ibid., p. 869.

[536] ECJ, Case C-426/11 Mark Alemo-Herron and Others v Parkwood Leisure Ltd, Judgment of 18 July 2013, ECLI:EU:C:2013:521, para 35.

[537] Lenaerts 2019, pp. 784 et seq.

[538] ECJ, Case C-426/11 Alemo-Herron and Others, Judgment of 18 July 2013, para 35.

electronic communications violated the essence of the right to private life according to Article 7 CFR and that the absence of any legal remedies for individuals in order to access their data or have them rectified, violated the essence of the right to an effective remedy and a fair trial according to Article 47 CFR in the *Schrems* case.[539]

In *Digital Rights Ireland* and *Opinion 1/15*, the only cases where the Court considered the essence of the right to data protection in substance, it held that legislation had to provide that "certain principles of data protection and data security must be respected",[540] which it further elaborated by reference to rules on purpose limitation in the latter case.[541] It had to be ensured that there are appropriate technical and organisational measures to implement the principles.[542]

The Court therefore has already tacitly begun to link the principles of the EU data protection legislation with the essence of Article 8 CFR.

Brkan has, on a more general level, argued that a Member State failing to offer any safeguards violated the essence of Article 8 CFR and also linked this to the EU secondary legislation, which, as she also emphasises, gives expression to the fundamental right.[543]

In order to implement technical and organisational measures, which cover the substantive scope of protection of the EU data protection law, in practice, recourse can be had to the fundamental principles of EU data protection law, I have derived above.[544] Under the dualistic approach, these fundamental principles represent the relevant principles of EU data protection law for Article 8 CFR, as they represent the system and characteristic provisions of EU data protection law comprehensively. With regard to the interferences with the fundamental principles, as set out in the previous subsection, and in concordance with the jurisprudence of the Court, there cannot be a processing operation, which completely negates one of these principles.[545] The fundamental principles, as they are derived from the secondary EU data protection law, form the core content of EU data protection law and hence also inform the essence of the fundamental right to data protection.

---

[539] ECJ, Case C-362/14 Schrems, Judgment of 6 October 2015, paras 94 et seq. and discussed in Chap. 3, Sect. 3.2.8.8.

[540] ECJ, Joined Cases C-293/12 and C-594/12 Digital Rights Ireland and Seitlinger and Others, Judgment of 8 April 2014, para 40. Which AG Saugmandsgaard Øe in ECJ, Joined Cases C-203/15 and C-698/15 Tele2 Sverige v Post- och telestyrelsen (C-203/15) and Secretary of State for the Home Department v Tom Watson, Peter Brice and Geoffrey Lewis (C-698/15), Opinion of AG Saugmandsgaard Øe of 19 July 2016, ECLI:EU:C:2016:572, paras 209 and 213 et seq. amended to include all principles of data protection, as I have pointed out above, cf. Chap. 3, Sect. 3.2.8.9.

[541] ECJ, Avis 1/15, Opinion of 26 July 2017, para 150.

[542] ECJ, Joined Cases C-293/12 and C-594/12 Digital Rights Ireland and Seitlinger and Others, Judgment of 8 April 2014, para 40; similarly Bock and Engeler 2016, p. 596 argue that the essence requires rules that substantively regulate the processing of personal data beyond a merely abstract permission.

[543] Brkan 2019b, p. 868.

[544] Cf. above in Sect. 5.3.3.

[545] As demonstrated by the Court's reference to rules on purpose limitation in ECJ, Avis 1/15, Opinion of 26 July 2017, para 150.

While there is a sliding scale with regard to the degree to which a principle is implemented, as I have elaborated in the previous subsection,[546] the complete negation of one of them would be a violation of the essence of the right to data protection: the fundamental principles of data protection are derived from the secondary EU data protection law and are thus anchored in it. However, the violation of one provision of secondary law does not in all instances necessarily lead to the full negation of a fundamental principle, as these principles are based on systematic and teleological considerations deduced from various provisions. A violation of the essence would rather only follow when a processing operation infringes the provisions concerning the relevant principle in a way that renders it ineffective.[547] This would, at the same time, constitute a grave violation of the secondary EU data protection law.[548]

As I elaborated in the example from the previous subsection, a processing operation may warrant a low degree of confidentiality, when the availability of the data is crucial. However, if there is no measure of confidentiality of a processing operation on any level, this will constitute not only an interference, but this interference will violate the essence of the right to data protection. It can therefore not be justified.

Similarly, Kunnert argues that in the cases concerning data retention, the Court should have found a violation of the essence of Article 8 CFR.[549] The collection of all communications data in bulk under the DRD required the collection of data, even when they are devoid of any connection with a specific crime at the time of their collection.[550] Hence, Kunnert finds that the DRD did not only violate the principle of purpose limitation, but negated it completely.[551] Under the dualistic approach, this would constitute a negation of the fundamental principle of separation and indeed be a violation of the essence of Article 8 CFR.

Another example would be a case where a Member State does not allocate resources to a supervisory authority so as to enable it to enforce the EU data protection legislation. This would negate the principle of control and thus violate the individual's right to data protection.[552]

The standard I advance for the finding of a violation of the essence does not imply that *any* interference with a fundamental principle is also a violation of the essence, as an interference is different from the negation of a principle. This can

---

[546] Cf. above in Sect. 5.4.3.3.

[547] Cf. also Article 23(1) GDPR, which states that Member States may restrict the scope of data subject rights only insofar as these restrictions respect the essence of fundamental rights.

[548] And, as a consequence, the relevant Member State or the EU itself, in order to fulfil its positive obligation, would have to ensure that an independent supervisory authority can and does take action in order to sanction and remedy this violation. Also cf. above in Sect. 5.3.2.2 with regard to a private entity operating under a business model, which is opposed to the foundations of data protection law.

[549] Kunnert 2014, p. 775.

[550] Ibid., p. 776.

[551] Ibid.

[552] This would simultaneously constitute a violation of the essence of Article 47 CFR, as this would render the right to lodge a complaint with a supervisory authority according to Article 77 GDPR, Article 63 DPR-EU and Article 52 LED ineffective, and illustrates the close connection of the right to data protection to the rule of law.

also be seen from *Digital Rights Ireland* and *Opinion 1/15*, where there would have been a negation of the principles of confidentiality and integrity, if there had been no provision at all on the security of the processing and/or a negation of purpose limitation, i.e. the principle of separation, if there had been no provisions on limiting the purposes of the transfer at all. However, the Court did not need to assess the quality of the relevant provision at the stage of the essence, as the quality of the provision with regard to the standards of purpose limitation would be a question concerning the establishment of an interference: this marks the difference between the complete absence of any safeguards and safeguards which are inadequate.[553]

5.4.4 The Horizontal Application of the Right to Data Protection

While the secondary EU data protection legislation, and hence also the secondary EU data protection law, undoubtedly applies in both vertical relations, i.e. between the individual and the State, and horizontal relations, i.e. between private parties, I will now examine whether the fundamental right to data protection according to Article 8 CFR can be applied horizontally.

The risks of processing personal data, illustrated above,[554] are the same, regardless whether the processing is carried out by public authorities or private entities. In either case, data protection is an impediment for the controller to employ more efficient processes, when all actors strive to use personal data to allow for more reliable and efficient decision-making.[555] As Simits pointedly phrased it: dismantling data protection is not a privilege of the public sector.[556]

Rost rightfully observes that the difficulty of extending the rules of data protection law from the public sector to private entities is due to the scope of law and its justifications and by no means due to any difference in the conflicts or matters regulated.[557] Therefore, it must be ensured that the right to data protection and its fundamental principles, which are essential in order to mitigate these risks, can be applied to any risk source. In light of the risks posed by powerful private actors, von Danwitz has argued that the horizontal application of Article 8 CFR was self-evident.[558]

The report by Steinmüller et al. found that while the State must adhere to fundamental rights in order to restrain its social power, the same can be true for private actors and thus the State must regulate them accordingly.[559] The authors argued

[553] Tridimas and Gentile 2019, p. 810.

[554] Cf. above in Sect. 5.4.2.1.

[555] Simitis 1971, p. 675.

[556] Ibid., p. 679.

[557] Rost 2013, p. 86, esp. fn. 6.

[558] von Danwitz 2015, pp. 584 et seq.

[559] Steinmüller et al. 1971, p. 138.

that due to the prevalent power structures, fundamental rights may not be limited to vertical relations, but must also extend horizontally, between individuals and powerful private entities.[560]

When applying fundamental rights directly horizontal, private parties are considered to have the same obligations as the State.[561] As fundamental rights often are still seen primarily as aiming to protect citizens from the State, there is a broader debate on whether such a direct application[562] in horizontal relations is feasible.[563] However, the indirectly horizontal application of fundamental rights is commonly accepted.[564] When applying fundamental rights indirectly in horizontal relations, the secondary law is interpreted in the light of fundamental rights.[565] In that sense, the content of a fundamental right "radiates across the legal system."[566] Such an indirectly horizontal application is generally supported under the current doctrinal conceptualisations of the right to data protection, especially the privacy as well as the checks and balances approach.[567]

On the level of EU fundamental rights protection, the Charter generally addresses the EU and the Member States, when they implement EU law, according to Article 51 CFR. However, the Court has observed that Article 51 CFR does not specifically exclude the horizontal application of the Charter.[568] In fact, several rights in the Charter contain guarantees without specifying that they apply only to public authorities,[569] while others explicitly refer to actions of private entities,[570] such as the prohibition of slavery and forced labour in Article 5 CFR, the right to equality between men and women of Article 23 CFR, the rights of the child according to Article 24, especially para 2 CFR, as well as the labour rights contained in Articles 27–32 CFR.

---

560 Ibid.; Pohle finds the arguments presented in favour of this not sufficient, cf. Pohle 2018, p. 46.

561 Schorkopf 2014, MN. 32–36; Ehlers 2014, MN. 81 with further references.

562 Critical of the distinction between direct and indirect effect, Leczykiewicz 2013, pp. 490 et seq.

563 Frantziou 2015; Ward 2014, MN 51.42-51.47; von Danwitz 2014, MN. 60; Kerikmäe 2014; ECJ, Case C-176/12 Association de médiation sociale v Union locale des syndicats CGT and Others, Opinion of AG Cruz Villalón of 18 July 2013, ECLI:EU:C:2013:491, paras 28–40; ECJ, Case C-282/10 Maribel Dominguez v Centre informatique du Centre Ouest Atlantique and Préfet de la région Centre, Opinion of AG Trstenjak of 8 September 2011, ECLI:EU:C:2011:559, paras 80–83.

564 Cf. already Streinz and Michl 2011, pp. 386 et seq.; more implicitly von Danwitz 2014, MN. 60.

565 Schorkopf 2014, MN. 32–36; Ehlers 2014, MN. 81 with further references; cf. also Hijmans 2016, pp. 37 et seq.

566 Frantziou 2019, p. 315, who relies on the radiating effect (*Ausstrahlungswirkung*) of fundamental rights conceptualised by Alexy 1994.

567 Cf. Chap. 4, Sects. 4.5.3 and 4.8.5.

568 Cf. ECJ, Joined Cases C-569/16 and C-570/16 Stadt Wuppertal v Maria Elisabeth Bauer and Volker Willmeroth v Martina Broßonn, Judgment of 6 November 2018, ECLI:EU:C:2018:871, paras 87–90.

569 For instance, human dignity according to Article 1 CFR or non-discrimination according to Article 21 CFR.

570 Frantziou 2015, pp. 659–661.

In a line of case law concerning the application of a diverse set of fundamental rights,[571] the Court has found that, especially where the effects of a directive aiming to protect the rights of individuals would otherwise be undermined,[572] the rights of the Charter can be applied between private parties. This is the case when they are themselves sufficient to confer rights on individuals, which can apply horizontally in a field of law covered by EU law.[573] From this jurisprudence it seems that there could only be very limited rights, if any, which would not fulfil this criterion.[574] Once it is met and the national law cannot be interpreted in conformity, the respective right[575] can be applied in vertical as well as horizontal relations.[576]

However, while private entities in these instances have to respect fundamental rights, they—unlike the State—can also rely on fundamental rights.[577] Yet, this seeming conflict can be resolved easily: where fundamental rights are in conflict, they must be balanced in order to achieve practical concordance.[578]

---

[571] The right to collective action, the right not to be discriminated on grounds of age, the right to paid annual leave and the right to non-discrimination.

[572] Cf. also von Danwitz 2014, MN. 61 et seq., who is more reluctant concerning the direct horizontal application; already, with regard to the general principles, Muir 2011, p. 60.

[573] Recently in ECJ, Case C-684/16 Max-Planck-Gesellschaft zur Förderung der Wissenschaften eV v Tetsuji Shimizu, Judgment of 6 November 2018, ECLI:EU:C:2018:874, especially paras 49–55; ECJ, Joined Cases C-569/16 and C-570/16 Bauer, Judgment of 6 November 2018, especially paras 79–86; and ECJ, Case C-414/16 Vera Egenberger v Evangelisches Werk für Diakonie und Entwicklung e.V., Judgment of 17 April 2018, ECLI:EU:C:2018:257, especially paras 76–79; also cf. ECJ, Case C-176/12 Association de médiation sociale v Union locale des syndicats CGT and Others, Judgment of 15 January 2014, ECLI:EU:C:2014:2, para 47; ECJ, Case C-282/10 Maribel Dominguez v Centre informatique du Centre Ouest Atlantique and Préfet de la région Centre, Judgment of 24 January 2012, ECLI:EU:C:2012:33; ECJ, Case C-555/07 Seda Kücükdeveci v Swedex GmbH & Co. KG, Judgment of 19 January 2010, ECLI:EU:C:2010:21; ECJ, Case C-438/05 International Transport Workers' Federation and Finnish Seamen's Union v Viking Line ABP and OÜ Viking Line Eesti, Judgment of 11 December 2007, ECLI:EU:C:2007:772; ECJ, Case C-144/04 Werner Mangold v Rüdiger Helm, Judgment of 22 November 2005, ECLI:EU:C:2005:709.

[574] Cf. von Danwitz 2014, MN. 63, who argues that the legislator has a margin of appreciation in implementing and substantiating abstract norms, especially with regard to economic and social rights; however, the Court has held that the right to paid annual leave of Article 31(2) CFR fulfilled the test for horizontal application, cf. ECJ, Joined Cases C-569/16 and C-570/16 Bauer, Judgment of 6 November 2018, paras 85 et seq. Also in favour of the general horizontal application of the Charter: Colombi Ciacchi 2019; Frantziou 2015; ECJ, Case C-176/12 Association de médiation sociale, Opinion of AG Cruz Villalón, paras 28–41.

[575] Lenaerts suggests that for certain rights, such as the right to paid annual leave under Article 31(2) CFR, only the essence is sufficiently defined to be directly effective and thus be applied horizontally, while the non-essential elements require further specification by the legislator, cf. Lenaerts 2019, pp. 788–792.

[576] Frantziou 2019, pp. 318 et seq.

[577] Pohle argues that powerful private entities should not be able to rely on fundamental rights vis-à-vis less powerful individuals, given that fundamental rights were an instrument to protect the less powerful from the exercise of power, cf. Pohle 2018, pp. 46 et seq., fn. 323.

[578] Cf. already above with regard to the fundamental principles Sect. 5.3.3; also cf. ECJ, Case C-414/16 Egenberger, Judgment of 17 April 2018, para 80.

When applying the right to data protection horizontally, the rights of controllers have to be taken into account when determining the extent of purposes of a processing operation. However, it must be borne in mind that, as elaborated above,[579] the data subject is, structurally, in a weaker position than the controller and therefore must be protected. At an initial level, the legislator has balanced these opposing positions in the secondary EU data protection law. The legislation explicitly calls for interpretation in conformity to this fundamental right.[580]

Furthermore, under data protection law, the controller has to rely on a legal basis in order to justify the processing of personal data.[581] In that sense, the EU data protection legislation can be qualified as an act of regulated horizontality: the controller, whether they are a public authority or a private entity, has to invoke a legitimate legal basis and is under an obligation to protect the fundamental rights of individuals.

The Court, in its jurisprudence on horizontality, has engaged with cases where the protection of individuals was in jeopardy due to the fact that the rights were inscribed in directives. However, with regard to the fundamental right to data protection, the second generation of EU data protection legislation has resolved this issue: as the GDPR takes the form a regulation, it is applicable directly and there can be only limited issues concerning the implementation. Although the GDPR contains several opening clauses, for instance in Chapter IX, the fundamental right to data protection according to Article 8 CFR still applies to the national legislation based on these provisions under the case law of the Court.[582] Therefore, the current situation is a decisive improvement from the DPD.

Under the DPD, individuals would be at a disadvantage where the national legislator failed to implement its provisions at all or did not do so properly. In instances where the individual faced a private entity as a controller, the individual was subject to the restriction of the horizontal application of directives vis-à-vis private entities. However, this restriction does not apply to regulations such as the GDPR or the upcoming ePR. With regard to the DPR-EU and LED, the issue of horizontality also does not affect the individual since they only apply to the processing of personal data by public authorities.[583]

Concerning the substantive protection awarded by the fundamental right to data protection under the dualistic approach, the fundamental principles showcase the

---

579 Cf. above in Sect. 5.4.2.2.

580 Article 1(2) GDPR, Article 1(2) DPR-EU and Article 1(2)(a) LED; already in Article 1(1) DPD, Article 1(1) DPR-EC and Article 1(1) ePD, however, as they were drafted before the Charter, they referred to the right to privacy.

581 In a case concerning labour law one of the arguments invoked by AG Trstenjak is that private parties could not fulfil the legality requirement of Article 52(1) CFR, which thus does not apply to data protection law, ECJ, Case C-282/10 Dominguez, Opinion of AG Trstenjak, para 83. Furthermore, the principle of purpose limitation transposes the requirement that all acts of public authority must serve a legitimate aim according to Article 52(1) CFR to private entities processing data.

582 ECJ, Case C-617/10 Åklagaren v Hans Åkerberg Fransson, Judgment of 26 February 2013, ECLI:EU:C:2013:105.

583 According to Article 2(1) in conjunction with Article 1(1) and Article 2(2) in conjunction with Article 70 DPR-EU as well as Article 2(2) in conjunction with Article 1(1) LED.

close relationship between the primary and secondary EU data protection law. I have derived the fundamental principles of the EU data protection law from the general rules of the secondary law and linked them with the primary law. However, as such, these general rules and therefore the principles already apply horizontally between private parties due to the material scope of the secondary law, i.e. as defined by Article 2 GDPR.

Therefore, regardless whether the fundamental right to data protection and its fundamental principles apply directly or indirectly between private parties, this relation is mediated through the GDPR, DPR-EU and LED. Thus, the legislator, by expressly demanding the interpretation of the EU data protection law in the light of the fundamental right to data protection, has fulfilled their positive obligation and enshrined the content of the fundamental right to data protection on the level of secondary law, which ensures that the obligations concerning data protection apply between private parties. In interpreting the first generation of EU data protection legislation and more generally, beyond the issue of data protection and with regard to other fundamental rights, the Court has already proven willing to interpret EU secondary law in the light of fundamental rights, so that there is no gap in the protection of individuals.

5.4.5 Differentiating the Right to Data Protection from the Right to Privacy

Now that I have positioned the fundamental right to data protection as part of a general value system, applied the dualistic approach to the secondary EU data protection law to uncover the fundamental principles of EU data protection law and the primary EU data protection law and identified the dual rationale as well as the distinct content of the right to data protection, I will lay out how the fundamental right to data protection under Article 8 CFR can be differentiated from the right to privacy contained in Article 7 CFR. In the following, I will build on my previous arguments regarding the specific rationale (Sect. 5.4.5.1) and the scope (Sect. 5.4.5.2) as well as the essence of the right to data protection as opposed to the right to privacy (Sect. 5.4.5.3), before concluding that the differentiation between these two rights is crucial and offers the potential for the enhanced protection of individuals (Sect. 5.4.5.4).

5.4.5.1 The Different Rationales of Data Protection and Privacy

In my understanding, based on the conceptualisation of Steinmüller, Podlech and others, data protection is the specific answer to the societal issue of data protection, which aims to protect individuals *from* the processing of personal data with its dual rationale, and is therefore the flipside of data processing.[584] This discourse, as I have

[584] Steinmüller et al. 1971, p. 44. Also cf. above in Sect. 5.2.2.

pointed out in Sect. 5.2,[585] considered privacy as unsuitable to address the issue of data processing, as it aimed to protect individuals only against the gravest, specific harms and only provided limited areas of retreat for individuals.[586]

This "failure of privacy"[587] with regard to data processing has also been encountered by the ECJ. As I demonstrated in Chap. 3, the Court chose a very pragmatic solution: it never recurred to the nexus to private life, established by the ECtHR, as a standard.[588] Instead, it is satisfied that there is an interference with the right to privacy according to Article 7 CFR whenever personal data are being processed. While this leads to an overlap concerning the interference with Article 8 CFR, the Court was apparently not convinced by the casuistic approach adopted by the ECtHR, which determines on a case-by-case basis whether it deems this connection to exist. [589] This approach of the ECtHR has also been criticised by the transparency-focused approach, as I have illustrated in Chap. 4.[590] However, the overlap between the rights of Articles 7 and 8 CFR, which the Court also considers to be independent from each other, has led to ambiguities in the case law, which blur the lines between the rights.[591]

Still, the current doctrine as well as the ECtHR consider the right to private life to be open-ended[592]—which, from the perspective of Steinmüller et al., corresponds to its indeterminacy—and as aiming to provide spaces, spheres and roles where the individual can withdraw.[593] There are also notions of privacy, which extend beyond a right to be let alone—which remains one of its facets—and aim to protect individual self-determination for the development of personal relations.[594] All of this further illustrates that privacy does not address the specific risks of data processing. Instead, it remains, from its very rationale, focussed on the individual.

Data protection, as I have argued above,[595] aims to ensure that the individual is protected from the processing of personal data, even when nobody is looking, i.e. even in instances where the individual does not notice any harm. Data protection law provides this protection through its individual as well as its structural dimension,

---

585 Cf. above in Sect. 5.2.1.

586 Cf. above in Sect. 5.2.1; Lenk 1973, p. 20.

587 Steinmüller et al. 1971, p. 53.

588 Cf. Chap. 3, Sect. 3.2.2.

589 Cf. ECtHR, Uzun v. Germany, App. No. 35623/05, Judgment of 2 September 2010, paras 51 et seq., where the court found that GPS surveillance of a car was "less likely" to interfere with Article 8(1) ECHR.

590 De Hert and Gutwirth 2009, pp. 25 et seq. Cf. also Chap. 4, Sect. 4.2.

591 Cf. Chap. 3, Sect. 3.2.9.

592 Cf. for instance ECtHR, Pretty v. the United Kingdom, App. No. 2346/02, Judgment of 29 April 2002, para 61; Burbergs 2013.

593 Nettesheim 2014, MN. 1.

594 Cf. for instance ECtHR [GC], Von Hannover, App. Nos. 40660/08 and 60641/08, Judgment of 7 February 2012, para 95; Nettesheim 2014, MN. 3; Bernsdorff 2014, MN. 19. With regard to the rationale of privacy, it must be noted that the debate in the US is very relevant and offers many insights, cf. for instance Marwick and boyd 2018; Cohen 2000; boyd 2010; Zuboff 2015.

595 Cf. above in Sect. 5.2.4.

which aim to ensure that the democratic society under the rule of law persists, and therefore goes beyond privacy in addressing the issue of data processing.[596]

5.4.5.2 The Distinct Scopes of Data Protection and Privacy

Beyond these distinct rationales of data protection and privacy, the respective scopes of the rights are different. As observed by González Fuster, disentangling data protection and privacy, as I have just demonstrated with regard to the rationale of the rights, offers the potential to consider privacy in other terms, as distinct from and unburdened by the perspective of data protection.[597] Accordingly, privacy should also be reconsidered on its own terms. With regard to its scope, the right to privacy contained in Article 7 CFR is not limited to personal data, but applies to any information that is within the personal sphere of an individual.[598] This conforms to the general function of Article 7 CFR with its intentionally broad scope,[599] to provide protection for various forms of self-expression within society.[600] The right to data protection is much narrower in this regard, as any measure that does not involve personal data, is outside its scope.

However, where personal data are at issue, the scopes of both rights overlap under the jurisprudence of the ECJ.[601] With the right to data protection to address the issue of data processing, this line of case law, which was developed before the Charter existed, could also be reconsidered.[602] The Court might introduce the nexus to private life, in line with the ECtHR's jurisprudence, after all. Even then, of course, there would still be an overlap with regard to personal data, which concern the private life of an individual, when the right to privacy is considered on its own terms. This reinterpretation along the lines of the ECtHR's jurisprudence mirrors the scope of the right to data protection as well the restrictive interpretation of interferences with Article 8 CFR, envisaged by the checks and balances approach.[603]

In a recent case on the interpretation of the ePD with regard to consent by users, the ECJ did not recur to Article 8 CFR, but instead found that the field of privacy

---

596 Cf. above in Sect. 5.2.4.

597 González Fuster 2014, p. 271.

598 In this regard cf. ECJ, Case C-673/17 Bundesverband der Verbraucherzentralen und Verbraucherverbände—Verbraucherzentrale Bundesverband e.V. v Planet49, Judgment of 1 October 2019, ECLI:EU:C:2019:801, para 70. Also cf. Bock and Engeler 2016, p. 595.

599 Cf. Chap. 3, Sect. 3.2.2; also cf. ECtHR [GC], Amann v. Switzerland, App. No. 27798/95, Judgment of 16 February 2000, para 65; ECtHR [GC], Rotaru v. Romania, App. No. 28341/95, Judgment of 4 May 2000, para 43; ECJ, Joined Cases C-465/00, C-138/01 and C-139/01 Rechnungshof (C-465/00) v Österreichischer Rundfunk and Others and Christa Neukomm (C-138/01) and Joseph Lauermann (C-139/01) v Österreichischer Rundfunk, Judgment of 20 May 2003, ECLI:EU:C:2003:294, para 73.

600 Grabenwarter and Pabel 2016, § 22 MN. 6; Marauhn and Thorn 2013, MN. 26.

601 Cf. Chap. 3, Sect. 3.2.2.

602 As I have already suggested above in Sect. 5.4.3.1.

603 Cf. above in Sect. 5.4.3.1 and Sect. 5.4.3.2.

protection of electronic communications operated under a different scope, which also concerned information stored on the device of a user, in the case at hand cookies, regardless whether this information constituted personal data or not.[604] Instead of engaging with the DPD/GDPR, the Court—following the argument of AG Szpunar—held that recital 24 and Article 5(3) ePD explicitly included even anonymous data.[605] Such information would be outside the scope of the EU data protection legislation according to Article 4(1) GDPR, as it requires that a natural person is at least identifiable, which is not the case with anonymous data. The Court, due to this reasoning, did not have to consider, whether the data in question were, in fact, personal data.

This judgment opens an interesting avenue to extend the scope of Article 7 CFR to the processing of any information, when there is a connection to the private life of an individual. In cases such as the one at hand in the judgment, the connection to private life would exist due to the fact that the information is stored on the equipment of the user. Such an interpretation could offer additional protection to individuals beyond the scope of their right to data protection. It would award individuals a right not to have information stored on their equipment. This would not be related to the risks of processing personal data, as protected by Article 8 CFR, but would extend further and perhaps incorporate general considerations of information security. Cookies are not necessarily used to identify specific users, but are also necessary to store general information, for instance, whether a user has expanded a sidebar on a website.

Nevertheless, it seems doubtful that the information stored on the user's device in the case at issue would indeed be anonymous and not somehow aim to render the user identifiable in some way. If this were the case, the data in question would be personal data and the EU data protection law applicable. While the AG argued that this was the case,[606] he also stated that any information stored on user equipment had "a privacy aspect".[607] Even the Court, in the final sentence of the relevant paragraph, argued that the relevant provisions of the ePD aim to protect users from hidden identifiers,[608] which contradicts the assumption that the relevant data would be anonymous. While the judgment in this regard is not entirely consistent, it offers a perspective on how the scope of the right to privacy could be developed, once it is disentangled from data protection.

5.4.5.3 The Distinct Essences of Data Protection and Privacy

The distinction between the right to data protection and the right to privacy is also visible in the respective essences of both rights. The essence of the right to data

---

604 ECJ, Case C-673/17 Planet49, Judgment of 1 October 2019, para 70.

605 Ibid.; based on ECJ, Case C-673/17 Bundesverband der Verbraucherzentralen und Verbraucherverbände—Verbraucherzentrale Bundesverband e.V. v Planet49, Opinion of AG Szpunar of 21 March 2019, ECLI:EU:C:2019:246, para 107.

606 ECJ, Case C-673/17 Planet49, Opinion of AG Szpunar, para 105.

607 Ibid., para 107.

608 ECJ, Case C-673/17 Planet49, Judgment of 1 October 2019, para 70.

protection is violated, when, in the words of the Court,[609] there are no rules on the principles of data protection and data security or, more comprehensively, under the dualistic approach, when a fundamental principle is negated in its entirety.[610]

With regard to the right to privacy, the Court has found a violation of its essence even in instances where it had no further information on a processing operation, such as in the *Schrems* case and thus could not rule on the essence of Article 8 CFR.[611] The focus on the content of communications for the essence of the right to privacy under Article 7 CFR[612] demonstrates that the Court indeed conceptualises the privacy of electronic communications as distinct from the issue of data protection. In its interpretation of the essence of the right to privacy, which is supported in the doctrine,[613] the Court essentially recurs to the theme of the sensitivity of information,[614] as also included in the EU data protection legislation, but which cannot be considered part of EU data protection law.[615] This illustrates the importance of a thorough differentiation between concepts of data protection and privacy.

5.4.5.4 Conclusions on the Differentiation between the Right to Data Protection and the Right to Privacy

While privacy due to its indeterminacy and relativity[616] is not useful to illuminate the notion of data protection, it should not be abandoned as value or right, as it clearly meets a societal need.[617] A legal positivist argument for this is that Article 7 CFR remains a fundamental right under the Charter and, according to Article 52(3) CFR read in conjunction with the Explanations, the right to private life must be awarded the same meaning and scope as Article 8 ECHR.[618]

More importantly, however, privacy is needed as a fundamental right with regard to the processing of personal data, precisely because it serves as protection against

[609] ECJ, Joined Cases C-293/12 and C-594/12 Digital Rights Ireland and Seitlinger and Others, Judgment of 8 April 2014, para 40.

[610] Cf. above in Sect. 5.4.3.4.

[611] ECJ, Case C-362/14 Schrems, Judgment of 6 October 2015, para 94; as also observed by Bock and Engeler 2016, p. 596.

[612] Cf. Chap. 3, Sect. 3.2.8, especially ECJ, Joined Cases C-293/12 and C-594/12 Digital Rights Ireland and Seitlinger and Others, Judgment of 8 April 2014, para 39; ECJ, Case C-362/14 Schrems, Judgment of 6 October 2015, para 94; ECJ, Joined Cases C-203/15 and C-698/15 Tele 2 Sverige, Judgment of 21 December 2016, para 101.

[613] Jarass 2016, MN. 35; Kingreen 2016, MN. 15.

[614] Particularly clear in ECJ, Joined Cases C-203/15 and C-698/15 Tele 2 Sverige, Judgment of 21 December 2016, para 99.

[615] Cf. above in Sect. 5.3.1.2.

[616] Also cf. Nettesheim 2014, MN. 1 et seq. and 14, although he also subsumes Article 8 CFR under the heading of privacy protection, which does not consider the distinctions drawn here.

[617] Steinmüller 1973, p. 67; which is taken up by Simitis 1973, p. 148.

[618] Explanations Relating to the Charter of Fundamental Rights. OJ C 303 of 14 December 2007, pp. 17–35, Explanation on Article 52, para 1, fifth indent.

the most egregious violations. The special categories of data, as enshrined in the secondary law, may be determined in a haphazard manner,[619] but they represent a baseline of categories of data, which are often processed to the detriment of individuals.[620] However, this does not have to be achieved under the right to data protection, which has a different rationale and therefore a narrower scope, focussed on the issue of data processing. While under the right to data protection, all data potentially entail the same risk to the rights of individuals, as it depends on the way the individual controller decides to use them, i.e. the specific context,[621] the right to privacy can be employed to protect against the processing of data that is particularly prone to be used for discrimination.

For data subjects, this means that the controller may violate two different fundamental rights when they process special categories of data without adhering to the stricter standards set out in the secondary legislation. Where a controller processes personal data, whether they are special categories or other data,[622] in a discriminatory way, there is also a violation of Article 21 CFR. The fact that a processing operation violates several fundamental rights is not to the detriment of the individual, but rather underlines the weight of the interference with the rights of the individual and thereby leads to a stricter standard with regard to the justification of these interferences.

Furthermore, it must be borne in mind that a right to data protection is not currently acknowledged at the universal level. As the Charter applies only to the EU and its Member States, it has a comparatively limited scope when viewed from the global plane. In order to maintain compatibility with regional and international human rights law, the right to privacy must, according to Article 53 CFR, be protected within the EU at the same level as provided by the ECHR and international human rights treaties.

Thus, while neither the notion of privacy, nor the right to privacy are suitable points of reference for the rationale or scope of the fundamental right to data protection, they are closely related to data protection, both as an issue and as a right. The right to privacy provides basic protections for individuals, much like other fundamental rights, such as the freedom of expression and information or the right to non-discrimination, which may also become relevant in instances of data processing.[623]

However, as regards the specific risks and power structure inherent in data processing, the right to data protection fills a void, which cannot be addressed in terms of privacy. It is therefore a necessary companion of any data processing operation. As I have laid out in the previous subsections, the right to data protection is a tool to analyse any data processing operation with regard to its specific inherent risks and to thereby mitigate the power structures in order to protect individuals and

[619] Cf. already Simitis 1990, esp. pp. 470–474. Cf. also above in Sect. 5.3.1.2.

[620] Cf. even Podlech 1988, p. 123.

[621] Steinmüller 1993, pp. 676–679.

[622] Notably, the protected categories of Article 21 CFR extend further than the special categories of data under the GDPR and also include inter alia property, birth, disability and age.

[623] For an overview of other relevant fundamental rights, cf. Bieker 2018, p. 28; Bieker and Bremert 2020.

the democratic society under the rule of law. This analysis can only be achieved comprehensively when the right to data protection is differentiated from the right to privacy and its distinct rationale, scope and content.

5.5 Conclusions on the Right to Data Protection in EU Law

The dualistic approach, which I have introduced in this chapter, enables a clear differentiation of the fundamental right to data protection from the related right to privacy, as envisaged in the Charter. My approach further offers a way to systematise the EU data protection legislation with regard to the dual rationale of data protection. The entirety of EU data protection law on the level of both, the primary and secondary law, follows the dual rationale of mitigating the inherent risks of all data processing operations and addressing the power imbalance, which is created by this unilateral creation of risks. The dualistic approach considers both, the individual and the structural dimensions of data protection, which are already contained in the current EU data protection law.

Due to the risks, which the processing of personal data poses for both, the individual as well as society as a whole, and the way this ability to create risks structures the power relations, the fundamental right to data protection is a paramount safeguard for individuals and society as a whole. The processing of personal data is a ubiquitous condition of modern society. Hence, data protection—as the flipside of such data processing—is a cornerstone to preserve the modern democratic State under the rule of law. The fundamental right to data protection is therefore indeed a foundational right of EU law.

Generally, the fundamental right to data protection has to be interpreted in a way that considers the extensive secondary legislation appropriately. In order to elucidate the content of the right to data protection and identify the risks of data processing, I have derived the fundamental principles of EU data protection law from the secondary EU data protection law. These fundamental principles are reflective of the telos and content of EU data protection law, which shapes the more general provisions of the primary EU data protection law. Extracting the fundamental principles of EU data protection law from the secondary law has enabled me to define the scope and content of the right to data protection comprehensively with regard to its dual rationale of mitigating the risks of data processing and addressing its inherent power imbalance.

Due to its rationale and the risks inherent in the processing of personal data, the scope of protection of the right to data protection must be wide in order to apply to any processing operation. In order to respond to the particular vulnerabilities of marginalized groups, the personal scope of the right to data protection must be further expanded in order to allow such groups to challenge data processing activities, which pose particular risks to them as a group, collectively.

In order to ensure that any processing operation is analysed and evaluated with regard to its specific inherent risks, the notion of interference with this right, just as its scope, must be wide. Therefore, any processing of personal data interferes with the right to data protection.

However, there can be various justifications for interferences. Thereby, the extent of protection can be differentiated and provides scalability, as it concerns the question of which technical and organisational measures have to be implemented in each individual case.[624] The generic risks to the fundamental principles, which I have introduced, allow to systematise the various interferences with the right to data protection: the respective risks to each fundamental principle constitute a different category of interference with the right to data protection. This becomes relevant at the justification stage, as the different categories of interferences help to identify areas, where safeguards, specifically the technical and organisational measures, must be increased in order to ensure that the risks of the specific processing operation in question are mitigated appropriately.

The fundamental principles of EU data protection law can further be used to identify violations of the essence of the right to data protection. When a fundamental principle is negated entirely, i.e. there are no safeguards to ensure adherence to one of them, then the essence is violated and the interference cannot be justified. When a processing operation negates a fundamental principle, it is also an egregious violation of the secondary EU data protection law.

While, as I have illustrated, the horizontal application of fundamental rights generally is still the subject of a broad debate, this is a less pressing issue with regard to the right to data protection, when it is interpreted in harmony with the secondary EU data protection law. As the relevant secondary law now takes the form of regulations,[625] its rules also bind private entities. This naturally also includes the provisions which are the bases of the fundamental principles of EU data protection law. Therefore, the content of the right to data protection, which is based on the secondary EU data protection law, is inherent in the provisions of the GDPR and therefore protects individuals also in horizontal relations.

Yet, as the Court has repeatedly stressed, in order to achieve the envisaged high level of protection of fundamental rights, the secondary EU data protection law has to be interpreted broadly.[626] However, I have argued that the current debate on data protection law and especially the fundamental right to data protection has addressed the duality of data protection law only insufficiently. The fundamental right to data protection, in order to realise its full potential, has to be understood as addressing both the individual as well as the structural dimension of EU data protection law. When this duality is considered appropriately, the fundamental right can be a powerful tool in order to address the inherent risks of data processing as well as the structural power imbalances grounded in such processing. Beyond the individual enforcement of such a right, its structural dimension must be considered more carefully: as fundamental

[624] Steinmüller 1975, p. 81.

[625] With the GDPR and ePR, whereas the DPR-EU and LED only apply in vertical relations.

[626] ECJ, Case C-210/16 Unabhängiges Landeszentrum für Datenschutz Schleswig-Holstein v Wirtschaftsakademie Schleswig-Holstein GmbH, Judgment of 5 June 2018, ECLI:EU:C:2018:388, paras 26 et seq.

rights are addressed to the legislator, who has to implement them in every act they take, the fundamental right to data protection lifts the secondary law to a higher level.

In that sense, everything has already been said about data protection. However, much of what has already been said and enables a coherent analysis of the issue posed by the processing of personal data, has either not been heard[627] or already been forgotten.

References

Articles, Books and Chapters in Books

Adams S, Purtova N (2016) Introducing the Special Issue "Rethinking Surveillance: Theories, Discourses, Structures, and Practices". Philosophy & Technology 30:5–7.

Ahmed S (2006) Queer Phenomenology. Duke University Press, Durham/London.

Alexy R (1994) Theorie der Grundrechte [A Theory of Fundamental Rights]. Suhrkamp Taschenbuch, Frankfurt am Main.

Andrejevic M (2014) The Big Data Divide. International Journal of Communication 8:1673-1689.

Benjamin G (2021) What we do with data: a critique of 'collection'. IPRev 10(4). https://doi.org/10.14763/2021.4.1588.

Bernsdorff N (2014) Artikel 7. In: Meyer J (ed) Charta der Grundrechte der Europäischen Union [Charter of Fundamental Rights of the European Union], 4th edn. Nomos, Baden-Baden.

Bieker F (2018) Die Risikoanalyse nach dem neuen EU-Datenschutzrecht und dem Standard-Datenschutzmodell [Risk Analysis under the New EU Data Protection Law and the Standard Data Protection Model]. DuD 27–31.

Bieker F, Bremert B (2020) Die Identifizierung von Risiken für die Grundrechte von Individuen [Identifying Risks to the Rights of Individuals]. ZD 7–14.

Bieker F, Bremert B, Hansen M (2018a) Die Risikobeurteilung nach der DSGVO [Risk Assessment under the GDPR]. DuD 492–496.

Bieker F, Bremert B, Hansen M (2018b) Verantwortlichkeit und Einsatz von Algorithmen bei öffentlichen Stellen [Responsibility for and Deployment of Algorithms by Public Authorities]. DuD 608–612.

Bieker F, Hansen M (2017) Normen des technischen Datenschutzes [Norms of Technical Data Protection]. DuD 41 285-289.

Bishop M (2004) Introduction to Computer Security. Addison-Wesley Professional, Boston, MA, USA.

Bock K, Engeler M (2016) Die verfassungsrechtliche Wesensgehaltsgarantie als absolute Schranke im Datenschutzrecht [The Essence of Fundamental Rights as Absolute Limit in Data Protection Law]. DVBl 593–599.

Böröcz I (2016) Risk to the Right to the Protection of Personal Data. EDPL 2:467-480.

Borowsky M (2014) Artikel 52. In: Meyer J (ed) Charta der Grundrechte der Europäischen Union [Charter of Fundamental Rights of the European Union], 4th edn. Nomos, Baden-Baden.

boyd d (2010) Making Sense of Privacy and Publicity. SXSW transcript. http://www.danah.org/papers/talks/2010/SXSW2010.html. Accessed 28 July 2021.

[627] Steinmüller, who ultimately changed professions, observed that many submissions to the debate on data protection were of dubious quality or driven by specific agendas, which were incompatible not only with data protection, but also fundamental rights and the rule of law generally, cf. Steinmüller 1993, p. 703.

Brkan M (2018) The concept of essence of fundamental rights in the EU legal order: peeling the onion to its core. EuConst 14:332-368.
Brkan M (2019a) Do algorithms rule the world? Algorithmic decision-making and data protection in the framework of the GDPR and beyond. IJLIT 27:91-121.
Brkan M (2019b) The Essence of the Fundamental Rights to Privacy and Data Protection: Finding the Way Through the Maze of the CJEU's Constitutional Reasoning. GLJ 20:864-883.
Brouwer E (2011) Legality and Data Protection Law: The Forgotten Purpose of Purpose Limitation. In: Besselink L, Pennings F, Prechal S (eds) The Eclipse of the Legality Principle in the European Union. Kluwer Law, Alphen aan den Rijn, pp. 273–294.
Buolamwini J, Gebru T (2018) Gender Shades: Intersectional Accuracy Disparities in Commercial Gender Classification. In: Friedler S A, Wilson C (eds) Conference on Fairness, Accountability, and Transparency. Proceedings of Machine Learning Research 81, pp. 1–15. http://proceedings.mlr.press/v81/buolamwini18a/buolamwini18a.pdf. Accessed 28 July 2021.
Burbergs M (2013) How the right to respect for private and family life, home and correspondence became the nursery in which new rights are born. In: Brems E, Gerards J (eds) Shaping rights in the ECHR: the role of the European Court of Human Rights in determining the scope of human rights. CUP, Cambridge, pp. 315-329.
Bygrave L A (2014) Data Privacy Law. OUP, Oxford.
Classen C D (2014) Datenschutz ja – aber wie? [Data Protection, yes – but how?]. EuR 441–448.
Cohen J (2000) Examined Lives: Informational Privacy and the Subject as Object. Stan. L. Rev. 52:1373-1438.
Colombi Ciacchi A (2019) The Direct Horizontal Effect of EU Fundamental Rights. EuConst 15:294-305.
Dawson M, Lynskey O, Muir E (2019) What is the Added Value of the Concept of the "Essence" of EU Fundamental Rights? GLJ 20:763-778.
De Hert P (2017) Data Protection as Bundles of Principles, General Rights, Concrete Subjective Rights and Rules. EDPL 3:160-179.
De Hert P, Gutwirth S (2006) Privacy, Data Protection and Law Enforcement. Opacity of the Individual and Transparency of Power. In: Claes E, Duff A, Gutwirth S (eds) Privacy and the Criminal Law. Intersentia, Antwerp/Oxford, pp. 61–104.
De Hert P, Gutwirth S (2009) Data Protection in the Case Law of Strasbourg and Luxemburg: Constitutionalisation in Action. In: Gutwirth S, Poullet Y, De Hert P, de Terwangne C, Nouwt S (eds) Reinventing Data Protection? Springer, Dordrecht, pp. 3-44.
de Hingh A (2018) Some Reflections on Dignity as an Alternative Legal Concept in Data Protection Regulation. GLJ 19:1269-1290.
Dix A (2003) 3.5 Konzepte des Systemdatenschutzes [Approaches to Structural Data Protection]. In: Roßnagel A (ed) Handbuch Datenschutzrecht [Handbook Data Protection Law]. C.H. Beck, Munich, pp. 363–386.
Dix A (2014) § 34. In: Simitis S (ed) Bundesdatenschutzgesetz [Federal Data Protection Act], 8th edn. Nomos, Baden-Baden.
Ehlers D (2014) § 14 Allgemeine Lehren der Unionsgrundrechte [General Principles of EU Fundamental Rights]. In: Ehlers D (ed) Europäische Grundrechte und Grundfreiheiten, 4th edn. De Gruyter, Berlin, pp. 513-579.
Engeler M (2018a) Das überschätzte Kopplungsverbot [The Overrated Prohibition of Tying-In]. ZD 55–62.
Engeler M (2018b) Die Ernennung der Beauftragten für den Datenschutz und das transparente Wahlverfahren nach Art. 53 Abs. 1 DSGVO [The Appointment of Members of Data Protection Authorities and the Transparent Voting Procedure of Art. 53(1) GDPR]. CR-online.de Blog. https://www.cr-online.de/blog/2018/08/06/die-ernennung-der-beauftragten-fuer-den-datenschutz-und-das-transparente-wahlverfahren-nach-art-53-abs-1-dsgvo/. Accessed 28 July 2021.
Frantziou E (2015) The Horizontal Effect of the Charter of Fundamental Rights of the EU: Rediscovering the Reasons for Horizontality. Eur Law J. 21:657-679.

Frantziou E (2019) (Most of) the Charter of Fundamental Rights is Horizontally Applicable. EuConst 15:306-323.
Frenz W (2009) Handbuch Europarecht [Handbook European Law], Band 4 Europäische Grundrechte. Springer, Berlin/Heidelberg.
Friedewald M, Bieker F, Obersteller H, Nebel M, Martin N, Rost M, Hansen M (2017) Datenschutz-Folgenabschätzung – Ein Werkzeug für einen besseren Datenschutz [Data Protection Impact Assessment – A Tool for Improved Data Protection], 3rd edn. https://www.forum-privatheit.de/wp-content/uploads/Forum-Privatheit-WP-DSFA-3-Auflage-2017-11-29.pdf. Accessed 28 July 2021.
Fröhlich W, Spiecker gen. Döhmann I (2018) Können Algorithmen diskriminieren? [Can Algorithms Discriminate?]. Verfassungsblog. https://www.verfassungsblog.de/koennen-algorithmen-diskriminieren/. Accessed 28 July 2021.
Geiger H (1973) Datenschutz und Gewaltenteilung [Data Protection and Separation of Powers]. In: Kilian W, Lenk K, Steinmüller W (eds) Datenschutz. [Data Protection] S. Toeche-Mittler, Darmstadt, pp. 173–185.
Gellert R (2015) Understanding Data Protection as Risk Regulation. Journal of Internet Law 3–16.
Gellert R (2016) We Have Always Managed Risks in Data Protection Law. EDPL 2:481-492.
Gillespie T (2014) The Relevance of Algorithms. In: Gillespie T, Boczkowski P J, Foot K A (eds) Media Technologies: Essays on Communication, Materiality, and Society. MIT Press, Cambridge, MA, USA, pp. 167-194.
Golla S J (2019) Der virtuelle Mr. Hyde [The Virtual Mr. Hyde]. Verfassungsblog. https://verfassungsblog.de/der-virtuelle-mr-hyde/. Accessed 28 July 2021.
Gonscherowski S, Hansen M, Rost M (2018) Resilienz – eine neue Anforderung aus der Datenschutz-Grundverordnung [Resilience – A New Requirement in the General Data Protection Regulation]. DuD 442–446.
González Fuster G (2014) The Emergence of Personal Data Protection as a Fundamental Right of the EU. Springer, Cham/Heidelberg/New York/Dordrecht/London.
Grabenwarter C, Pabel K (2016) Europäische Menschenrechtskonvention [European Convention on Human Rights], 6th edn. C.H. Beck, Munich.
Hallinan D, Martin N (2020) Fundamental Rights, the Normative Keystone of DPIA. EDPL 6:178-193.
Hansen M (2019a) Artikel 25. In: Simitis S, Hornung G, Spiecker gen. Döhmann I (eds) Datenschutzrecht [Data Protection Law]. Nomos, Baden-Baden.
Hansen M (2019b) Artikel 32. In: Simitis S, Hornung G, Spiecker gen. Döhmann I (eds) Datenschutzrecht [Data Protection Law]. Nomos, Baden-Baden.
Hansen M, Thomsen S (2010) Lebenslanger Datenschutz: Anforderungen an vertrauenswürdige Infrastrukturen [Life-long Data Protection: Requirements for Trustworthy Infrastructures]. DuD 283–288.
Hartzog W (2018) The Case Against Idealising Control. EDPL 4:423-432.
Hassein N (2017) Against Black Inclusion in Facial Recognition. Digital Talking Drum. https://digitaltalkingdrum.com/2017/08/15/against-black-inclusion-in-facial-recognition/. Accessed 28 July 2021.
Herdegen M (2019) Art. 1 Abs. 3. In: Maunz T, Dürig G (eds) Grundgesetz-Kommentar [Basic Law Commentary], 87th EL, Band 1. C.H. Beck, Munich.
Hicks M (2021) When Did the Fire Start? In: Mullaney T S, Peters B, Hicks M, Philip K (eds) Your Computer is On Fire. MIT Press, Cambridge, MA, USA, pp. 11-26.
Hijmans H (2016) The European Union as Guardian of Internet Privacy. Springer, Cham.
Hornung G (2012) A General Data Protection Regulation for Europe? SCRIPTed 9:64-81.
Hustinx P (2017) EU Data Protection Law: The Review of Directive 95/46/EC and the General Data Protection Regulation. In: Cremona M (ed) New Technologies and EU Law. OUP, Oxford, pp. 123-173.
Jančiūtė L (2019) Data protection and the construction of collective redress in Europe: exploring challenges and opportunities. IDPL 9:2-14.

Jarass H D (2016) Artikel 7. In: Charta der Grundrechte der EU [Charter of Fundamental Rights of the EU], 3rd edn. C.H. Beck, Munich.

Kadiri A P L (2021) Data and Afrofuturism – An emancipated subject? IPRev 10(4). https://doi.org/10.14763/2021.4.1597.

Kamp M, Rost M (2013) Kritik an der Einwilligung [A Critique of Consent]. DuD 80–84.

Karg M (2013) Die Renaissance des Verbotsprinzips im Datenschutz [The Renaissance of the Prohibition Principle in Data Protection]. DuD 75–79.

Kerikmäe T (2014) EU Charter: Its Nature, Innovative Character, and Horizontal Effect. In: Kerikmäe T (ed) Protecting Human Rights in the EU. Springer, Berlin/Heidelberg, pp. 5-19.

Kilian W (1973) Datenschutz in Wirtschaftsunternehmen [Data Protection in Economic Enterprises]. In: Kilian W, Lenk K, Steinmüller W (eds) Datenschutz [Data Protection]. S. Toeche-Mittler, Darmstadt, pp. 289–309.

Kingreen T (2016) EU-GRCharta [EU CFR] Art. 7. In: Calliess C, Ruffert M (eds) EUV/AEUV Kommentar [TEU/TFEU Commentary], 5th edn. C.H. Beck, Munich.

Korff D (1998) Study on the protection of the rights and interests of legal persons with regard to the processing of personal data relating to such persons. Cambridge. http://ssrn.com/abstract=1288583. Accessed 28 July 2021.

Kunnert G (2014) EuGH zur Vorratsdatenspeicherung [ECJ on Bulk Data Retention]. DuD 774–784.

Lawrence H M (2021) Siri Disciples. In: Mullaney T S, Peters B, Hicks M, Philip K (eds) Your Computer is On Fire. MIT Press, Cambridge, MA, USA, pp. 178-197.

Lazaro C, Le Métayer D (2015) Control over Personal Data: True Remedy or Fairy Tale? SCRIPTed 12:3-34.

Leczykiewicz D (2013) Horizontal Application of the Charter of Fundamental Rights. ELRev 38:479-497.

Lenaerts K (2019) Limits on Limitations: The Essence of Fundamental Rights in the EU. GLJ 20:779-793.

Lenk K (1973) Datenschutz in der öffentlichen Verwaltung [Data Protection in Public Administration]. In: Kilian W, Lenk K, Steinmüller W (eds) Datenschutz [Data Protection]. S. Toeche-Mittler, Darmstadt.

Lynskey O (2015a) Control over Personal Data in a Digital Age. MLR 78:522-548.

Lynskey O (2015b) The Foundations of EU Data Protection Law. OUP, Oxford.

Lynskey O (2018) The Power of Providence. In: Moore M, Tambini D (eds) Digital Dominance. OUP, Oxford, pp. 176-201.

Lyon D (2003) Introduction. In: Lyon D (ed) Surveillance as Social Sorting: Privacy, risk, and digital discrimination. Routledge, London/New York, NY, USA, pp. 1-8.

Macenaite M (2017) The "Riskification" of European Data Protection Law through a two-fold Shift. EJRR 8:506-540.

Mantelero A (2016) Personal data for decisional purposes in the age of analytics: From an individual to a collective dimension of data protection. CLSLR 32:238-255.

Marauhn T, Thorn J (2013) Privat- und Familienleben [Private and Family Life]. In: Dörr O, Grote R, Marauhn T (eds) EMRK/GG Konkordanzkommentar [ECHR/Basic Law Commentary] 2nd edn, Band 2. Mohr Siebeck, Tübingen, pp. 253–286.

Marks S (1995) The European Convention on Human Rights and its 'Democratic Society'. BYIL 66:209-238.

Marsch N (2018) Das europäische Datenschutzgrundrecht [The European Fundamental Right to Data Protection]. Mohr Siebeck, Tübingen.

Marwick A, boyd d (2018) Understanding Privacy at the Margins. International Journal of Communication 12:1157-1165.

Matzner T, Masur P, Ochs C, von Pape T (2016) Do-It-Yourself Data Protection — Empowerment or Burden? In: Gutwirth S, De Hert P, Leenes R (eds) Data Protection on the Move. Springer, Dordrecht, pp. 277-305.

Mayer-Schönberger V (1997) Generational Development of Data Protection in Europe. In: Agre P E, Rotenberg M (eds) Technology and Privacy: The New Landscape. MIT Press, Cambridge, MA, USA, pp. 219-241.

Muir E (2011) Of Ages in – and Edges of – EU Law. CMLRev 48:39-62.

Nas S, Roosendaal A (2018) DPIA Diagnostic Data in Microsoft Office Ministerie van Justitie en Veiligheid. https://www.rijksoverheid.nl/binaries/rijksoverheid/documenten/rapporten/2018/11/07/data-protection-impact-assessment-op-microsoft-office/DPIA+Microsoft+Office+2016+and+365+-+20191105.pdf. Accessed 28 July 2021.

Nettesheim M (2014) § 9 Privatleben und Privatsphäre [Private Life and Privacy]. In: Grabenwarter C (ed) Enzyklopädie Europarecht [Encyclopedia of European Law] Band 2: Europäischer Grundrechteschutz. Nomos, Baden-Baden, pp. 387-415.

Ni Loideain N, Adams R (2019) From Alexa to Siri and the GDPR: The Gendering of Virtual Personal Assistants and the Role of EU Data Protection Law. CILJ 241–257.

Noble S U (2021) Your Robot Isn't Neutral. In: Mullaney T S, Peters B, Hicks M, Philip K (eds) Your Computer is On Fire. MIT Press, Cambridge, MA, USA, pp. 199-212.

Petri T (2019) Artikel 9. In: Simitis S, Hornung G, Spiecker gen. Döhmann I (eds) Datenschutzrecht [Data Protection Law]. Nomos, Baden-Baden.

Podlech A (1970) Verfassungsrechtliche Probleme öffentlicher Datenbanken [Constitutional Implications of Public Databases]. DÖV 473–475.

Podlech A (1973a) Datenschutz im Bereich der öffentlichen Verwaltung [Data Protection in the Sector of Public Administration]. DVR Beiheft 1.

Podlech A (1973b) Prinzipien des Datenschutzes in der öffentlichen Verwaltung [Principles of Data Protection in Public Administration]. In: Kilian W, Lenk K, Steinmüller W (eds) Datenschutz [Data Protection]. S. Toeche-Mittler, Darmstadt, pp. 3–13.

Podlech A (1982) Individualdatenschutz – Systemdatenschutz [Individual Data Protection – Structural Data Protection]. In: Brückner K, Dalichau G (eds) Festgabe für Hans Grüner. R.S. Schulz, Percha am Starnberger See, pp. 451–462.

Podlech A (1987) Der Datenschutz und die Akzeptabilität unserer Gesellschaftsordnung [Data Protection and the Acceptability of our Societal Order]. In: Hohmann H (ed) Freiheitssicherung durch Datenschutz [Securing Political Freedom through Data Protection]. Suhrkamp, Frankfurt am Main, pp. 19–24.

Podlech A (1988) Unter welchen Bedingungen sind neue Informations systeme gesellschaftlich akzeptabel? [Under Which Conditions Are New Information Systems Socially Acceptable?]. In: Steinmüller W (ed) Verdatet und Vernetzt [Registered and Networked]. Fischer Taschenbuch, Frankfurt am Main, pp. 118–126.

Pohle J (2014) Die immer noch aktuellen Grundfragen des Datenschutzes [The Still Pressing Fundamental Questions of Data Protection]. In: Garstka H, Coy W (eds) Gedächtnisschrift für Wilhelm Steinmüller: Wovon – für wen – wozu, Systemdenken wider die Diktatur der Daten [Whereof – for Whom – Why, Systems Thinking against the Tyranny of Data]. Helmholtz-Zentrum für Kulturtechnik, Humboldt-Universität zu Berlin, Berlin, pp. 45-58.

Pohle J (2018) Datenschutz und Technikgestaltung [Data Protection and Technology Design]. Berlin. https://edoc.hu-berlin.de/bitstream/handle/18452/19886/dissertation_pohle_joerg.pdf. Accessed 28 July 2021.

Purtova N (2012) Property Rights in Personal Data. Wolters Kluwer, Alphen aan den Rijn.

Quelle C (2017) The 'risk revolution' in EU data protection law: We can't have our cake and eat it, too. In: Data Protection and Privacy: The Age of Intelligent Machines. Hart Publishing, Oxford/Portland, OR, USA, pp. 33-62.

Rauhofer J (2015) Of Men and Mice: Should the EU Data Protection Authorities' Reaction to Google's New Privacy Policy Raise Concern for the Future of the Purpose Limitation Principle? EDPL 5:5-15.

Robrahn R, Bock K (2018) Schutzziele als Optimierungsgebote [Protection Goals as Optimisation Requirements]. DuD 7–12.

Robrahn R, Bremert B (2018) Interessenskonflikte im Datenschutzrecht [Conflicts of Interest in Data Protection Law]. ZD 291–297.
Roßnagel A (2017) Datenschutzaufsicht nach der EU-Datenschutz-Grundverordnung [Enforcing the EU General Data Protection Regulation]. Springer Fachmedien, Wiesbaden.
Roßnagel A (2019) Artikel 5. In: Simitis S, Hornung G, Spiecker gen. Döhmann I (eds) Datenschutzrecht [Data Protection Law]. Nomos, Baden-Baden.
Rost M (2013) Zur Soziologie des Datenschutzes [On the Sociology of Data Protection]. DuD 85–91.
Rost M (2017) Bob, es ist Bob! [Bob, it is Bob!]. FifF-Kommunikation 4:63-66.
Rost M (2018a) Die Ordnung der Schutzziele [The System of Protection Goals]. DuD 13–17.
Rost M (2018b) Risiken im Datenschutz [Risks in Data Protection]. vorgänge 221/222:79–91.
Rouvroy A, Poullet Y (2009) The Right to Informational Self-Determination and the Value of Self-Development: Reassessing the Importance of Privacy for Democracy. In: Gutwirth S, Poullet Y, De Hert P, de Terwangne C, Nouwt S (eds) Reinventing Data Protection? Springer, Dordrecht, pp. 45-76.
Schmitz B (2018) Der Abschied vom Personenbezug [Farewell to Personal Data]. ZD 5–8.
Schneider J (1971) Datenschutz – Datensicherung [Data Protection – Data Security]. C.F. Müller, Munich.
Schneider J (1973) Technische Möglichkeiten des Datenschutzes [Technical Approaches to Data Protection]. In: Kilian W, Lenk K, Steinmüller W (eds) Datenschutz [Data Protection]. S. Toeche-Mittler, Darmstadt, pp. 223–233.
Schneider J (2017) Schließt Art. 9 DS-GVO die Zulässigkeit der Verarbeitung bei Big Data aus? [Does Art. 9 GDPR Preclude Big Data Processing?]. ZD 303–308.
Schorkopf F (2014) § 3 Grundrechtsverpflichtete [Addressees of Fundamental Rights]. In: Grabenwarter C (ed) Enzyklopädie Europarecht [Encyclopedia of European Law], Band 2: Europäischer Grundrechteschutz. Nomos, Baden-Baden, pp. 137-159.
Scudiero L (2017) Bringing Your Data Everywhere: A Legal Reading of the Right to Portability. EDPL 3:119-127.
Simitis S (1970) Konsequenzen der Datenverarbeitung für die Rechtsordnung [Consequences of Data Processing for the Legal Order]. In: Ständige Deputation des Deutschen Juristentages (ed) Verhandlungen des Achtundvierzigsten Deutschen Juristentages [Proceedings of the 48. German Lawyer Association Conference], Band 2. C.H. Beck, Munich, pp. T 35-T 43.
Simitis S (1971) Chancen und Gefahren der elektronischen Datenverarbeitung [Chances and Risks of Electronic Data Processing]. NJW 673–682.
Simitis S (1973) Datenschutz – Notwendigkeit und Voraussetzungen einer gesetzlichen Regelung [Data Protection – Exigency and Requirements of Legal Regulation]. DVR 2:138-189.
Simitis S (1986) Von der Amtshilfe zur Informationshilfe [From Administrative Assistance to Information Assistance]. NJW 2795–2805.
Simitis S (1990) "Sensitive Daten" – Zur Geschichte und Wirkung einer Fiktion ["Sensitive Data" – On the History and Effects of a Legal Fiction]. In: Brem E, Druey N J, Kramer E A, Schwander I (eds) Festschrift zum 65. Geburtstag von Mario M. Pedrazzini. Stämpfl & Cie, Bern, pp. 469–493.
Simitis S (2014) Einleitung [Introduction]. In: Simitis S (ed) Bundesdatenschutzgesetz [Federal Data Protection Act], 8th edn. Nomos, Baden-Baden.
Simitis S, Hornung G, Spiecker gen. Döhmann I (2019) Einleitung [Introduction]. In: Simitis S, Hornung G, Spiecker gen. Döhmann I (eds) Datenschutzrecht [Data Protection Law]. Nomos, Baden-Baden.
Sobotta C (2017) AEUV [TFEU] Art. 16. In: Grabitz E, Hilf M, Nettesheim M (eds) Das Recht der Europäischen Union [The Law of the European Union], 63rd EL. C.H. Beck, Munich.
Steinmüller W (1971) Rechtsinformatik [Legal Informatics]. JR 1–9.
Steinmüller W (1972a) Rechtstheorie, Rechtsinformatik und Rechtspolitik [Legal Theory, Legal Informatics and Legal Policy]. In: Albert H, Luhmann N, Maihofer W, Weinberger O (eds) Rechtstheorie als Grundlagenwissenschaft der Rechtswissenschaft [Legal Theory as Foundational Science of Jurisprudence]. Bertelsmann Universitätsverlag, Dusseldorf, pp. 373-389.

Steinmüller W (1972b) Stellenwert der EDV in der Öffentlichen Verwaltung und Prinzipien des Datenschutzrechts [The Significance of Electronic Data Processing in Public Administration and Principles of Data Protection Law]. ÖVD(11):453–462.
Steinmüller W (1973) Objektbereich "Verwaltungsautomation" und Prinzipien des Datenschutzes [Object Area "Administrative Automation" and Principles of Data Protection]. In: Kilian W, Lenk K, Steinmüller W (eds) Datenschutz [Data Protection]. S. Toeche-Mittler, Darmstadt, pp. 51–76.
Steinmüller W (1975) Datenschutz als Teilaspekt gesellschaftlicher Informationskontrolle [Data Protection as Facet of Societal Information Control]. In: Deutsche Sektion der Internationalen Juristen-Kommission (ed) Datenschutz und Datensicherung [Data Protection and Data Security]. C.F. Müller, Karlsruhe, pp. 35–95.
Steinmüller W (1981) Die Zweite industrielle Revolution hat eben begonnen [The Second Industrial Revolution Has Just Begun]. Kursbuch 66(4):152-188.
Steinmüller W (1993) Informationstechnologie und Gesellschaft [Information Technologies and Society]. Wissenschaftliche Buchgesellschaft, Darmstadt.
Steinmüller W (2007) Das informationelle Selbstbestimmungsrecht [The Right to Informational Self-Determination]. RDV(4) 158–161.
Steinmüller W, Lutterbeck B, Mallmann C, Harborth U, Gerhard K, Schneider J (1971) Grundfragen des Datenschutzes [Fundamental Questions of Data Protection], BT-Drs. VI/3826 Anlage 1, pp. 5–193.
Streinz R, Michl W (2011) Die Drittwirkung des europäischen Datenschutzgrundrechts (Art. 8 GRCh) im deutschen Privatrecht [The Horizontal Effect of the European Fundamental Right to Data Protection (Art. 8 CFR) in German Civil Law]. EuZW 384–388.
Theilen J T, Hassfurther I, Staff W (2017) Guest Editor's Introduction: Towards Utopia – Rethinking International Law. GYIL 60:315-334.
Tridimas T, Gentile G (2019) The Essence of Rights: An Unreliable Boundary? GLJ 20:794-816.
Ursic H (2018) Unfolding the New-Born Right to Data Portability: Four Gateways to Data Subject Control. SCRIPTed 15:42-69.
van der Sloot B (2015) Do privacy and data protection rules apply to legal persons and should they? A proposal for a two-tiered system. CLSLR 31:26-45.
von Berg M, Harborth U, Jarass H D, Lutterbeck B (1972) Schafft die Datenverarbeitung den modernen Leviathan? [Is Data Processing Creating the Modern Leviathan?]. ÖVD(1):3–7.
von Danwitz T (2014) § 6 Gerichtlicher Schutz der Grundrechte [Judicial Protections of Fundamental Rights]. In: Grabenwarter C (ed) Enzyklopädie Europarecht [Encylopedia on European Law], Band 2: Europäischer Grundrechteschutz. Nomos, Baden-Baden, pp. 255–301.
von Danwitz T (2015) Die Grundrechte auf Achtung der Privatsphäre und auf Schutz personenbezogener Daten [The Fundamental Rights to the Protection of Privacy and of Personal Data]. DuD 581–585.
von Lewinski K (2009) Geschichte des Datenschutzrechts von 1600 bis 1977 [History of Data Protection Law from 1600 to 1977]. In: Arndt F, Betz N, Farahat A, Goldmann M, Huber M, Keil R, Láncos P L, Schaefer J, Smrkolj M, Sucker F, Valta S (eds) Freiheit – Öffentlichkeit – Sicherheit. Nomos, Baden-Baden, pp. 196–220.
Ward A (2014) Article 51. In: Peers S, Hervey T, Kenner J, Ward A (eds) The EU Charter of Fundamental Rights – A Commentary. Hart, Oxford/Portland, OR, USA.
Weichert T (2018a) DS-GVO [GDPR] Art. 9. In: Kühling J, Buchner B (eds) Datenschutz-Grundverordnung/BDSG [General Data Protection Regulation/Federal Data Protection Act], 2nd edn. C.H. Beck, Munich.
Weichert T (2018b) DSGVO [GDPR] Art. 5. In: Däubler W, Wedde P, Weichert T, Sommer I (eds) EU-Datenschutz-Grundverordnung und BDSG-neu [EU General Data Protection Regulation and the New Federal Data Protection Act]. Bund-Verlag, Frankfurt am Main.
Zuboff S (2015) Big other: surveillance capitalism and the prospects of an information civilization. Journal of Information Technology 30:75-89.
Zysset A (2016) Searching for the Legitimacy of the European Court of Human Rights: The Neglected Role of 'Democratic Society'. Global Constitutionalism 5:16-47.

Table of Cases: Council of Europe

ECtHR, Klass and Others v. Germany, App. No. 5029/71, Judgment of 6 September 1978.
ECtHR, Young, James and Webster v. the United Kingdom, App. Nos. 7601/76 and 7806/77, Judgment of 13 August 1981.
ECtHR [GC], Chassagnou and Others v. France, App. Nos. 25088/94, 28331/95 and 28443/95, Judgment of 29 April 1999.
ECtHR [GC], Amann v. Switzerland, App. No. 27798/95, Judgment of 16 February 2000.
ECtHR [GC], Rotaru v. Romania, App. No. 28341/95, Judgment of 4 May 2000.
ECtHR, Pretty v. the United Kingdom, App. No. 2346/02, Judgment of 29 April 2002.
ECtHR [GC], Sørensen and Rasmussen v. Denmark, App. Nos. 52562/99 and 52620/99, Judgment of 11 January 2006.
ECtHR, Iordachi and Others v. Moldova, App. No. 25198/02, Judgment of 10 February 2009.
ECtHR, Kennedy v. the United Kingdom, App. No. 26839/05, Judgment of 18 May 2010.
ECtHR, Uzun v. Germany, App. No. 35623/05, Judgment of 2 September 2010.
ECtHR [GC], Von Hannover v. Germany (No. 2), App. Nos. 40660/08 and 60641/08, Judgment of 7 February 2012.
ECtHR [GC], Roman Zakharov v. Russia, App. No. 47143/06, Judgment of 4 December 2015.
ECtHR [GC], Baka v. Hungary, App. No. 20261/12, Judgment of 23 June 2016.
ECtHR [GC], Karácsony and Others v. Hungary, App. Nos. 42461/13 and 44357/13, Judgment of 17 May 2016.
ECtHR, Szabó and Vissy v. Hungary, App. No. 37138/14, Judgment of 12 January 2016.
ECtHR [GC], Regner v. the Czech Republic, App. No. 35289/11, Judgment of 19 September 2017, Partly Dissenting Opinion of Judge Serghides.

Table of Cases: EU

ECJ, Case 26/62 Van Gend en Loos v Administratie der Belastingen, Judgment of 5 February 1963, ECLI:EU:C:1963:1.
ECJ, Case C-101/01 Criminal proceedings against Bodil Lindqvist, Judgment of 6 November 2003, ECLI:EU:C:2003:596.
ECJ, Joined Cases C-465/00, C-138/01 and C-139/01 Rechnungshof (C-465/00) v Österreichischer Rundfunk and Others and Christa Neukomm (C-138/01) and Joseph Lauermann (C-139/01) v Österreichischer Rundfunk, Judgment of 20 May 2003, ECLI:EU:C:2003:294.
ECJ, Case C-144/04 Werner Mangold v Rüdiger Helm, Judgment of 22 November 2005, ECLI:EU:C:2005:709.
ECJ, Case C-408/03 Commission of the European Communities v Kingdom of Belgium, Judgment of 23 March 2006, ECLI:EU:C:2006:192.
ECJ, Case C-438/05 International Transport Workers' Federation and Finnish Seamen's Union v Viking Line ABP and OÜ Viking Line Eesti, Judgment of 11 December 2007, ECLI:EU:C:2007:772.
ECJ, Case C-275/06 Productores de Música de España (Promusicae) v Telefónica de España SAU Opinion of AG Kokott of 18 July 2007, ECLI:EU:C:2007:454.
ECJ, Case C-555/07 Seda Kücükdeveci v Swedex GmbH & Co. KG, Judgment of 19 January 2010, ECLI:EU:C:2010:21.
ECJ, Joined Cases C-92/09 and C-93/09 Volker und Markus Schecke GbR (C-92/09) and Hartmut Eifert (C-93/09) v Land Hessen, Judgment of 9 November 2010, ECLI:EU:C:2010:662.
ECJ, Case C-282/10 Maribel Dominguez v Centre informatique du Centre Ouest Atlantique and Préfet de la région Centre, Opinion of AG Trstenjak of 8 September 2011, ECLI:EU:C:2011:559.

ECJ, Case C-282/10 Maribel Dominguez v Centre informatique du Centre Ouest Atlantique and Préfet de la région Centre, Judgment of 24 January 2012, ECLI:EU:C:2012:33.
ECJ, Case C-617/10 Åklagaren v Hans Åkerberg Fransson, Judgment of 26 February 2013, ECLI:EU:C:2013:105.
ECJ, Case C-176/12 Association de médiation sociale v Union locale des syndicats CGT and Others, Opinion of AG Cruz Villalón of 18 July 2013, ECLI:EU:C:2013:491.
ECJ, Case C-426/11 Mark Alemo-Herron and Others v Parkwood Leisure Ltd, Judgment of 18 July 2013, ECLI:EU:C:2013:521.
ECJ, Case C-291/12 Michael Schwarz v Stadt Bochum, Judgment of 17 October 2013, ECLI:EU:C:2013:670.
ECJ, Case C-283/11 Sky Österreich GmbH v Österreichischer Rundfunk, Judgment of 22 January 2013, ECLI:EU:C:2013:28.
ECJ, Case C-176/12 Association de médiation sociale v Union locale des syndicats CGT and Others, Judgment of 15 January 2014, ECLI:EU:C:2014:2.
ECJ, Joined Cases C-293/12 and C-594/12 Digital Rights Ireland Ltd (C-293/12) v Minister for Communications, Marine and Natural Resources and Others and Kärntner Landesregierung (C-594/12) and Others, Judgment of 8 April 2014, ECLI:EU:C:2014:238.
ECJ, Case C-131/12 Google Spain SL and Google Inc. v Agencia Española de Protección de Datos (AEPD) and Mario Costeja González, Judgment of 13 April 2014, ECLI:EU:C:2014:317.
ECJ, Case C-362/14 Maximillian Schrems v Data Protection Commissioner, Judgment of 6 October 2015, ECLI:EU:C:2015:650.
ECJ, Joined Cases C-203/15 and C-698/15 Tele2 Sverige v Post- och telestyrelsen (C-203/15) and Secretary of State for the Home Department v Tom Watson, Peter Brice and Geoffrey Lewis (C-698/15), Opinion of AG Saugmandsgaard Øe of 19 July 2016, ECLI:EU:C:2016:572.
ECJ, Joined Cases C-203/15 and C-698/15 Tele2 Sverige v Post- och telestyrelsen (C-203/15) and Secretary of State for the Home Department v Tom Watson, Peter Brice and Geoffrey Lewis (C-698/15), Judgment of 21 December 2016, ECLI:EU:C:2016:970.
ECJ, Avis 1/15, Opinion of 26 July 2017, ECLI:EU:C:2017:592.
ECJ, Case C-210/16 Unabhängiges Landeszentrum für Datenschutz Schleswig-Holstein v Wirtschaftsakademie Schleswig-Holstein GmbH, Opinion of AG Bot of 24 October 2017, ECLI:EU:C:2017:796.
ECJ, Case C-684/16 Max-Planck-Gesellschaft zur Förderung der Wissenschaften eV v Tetsuji Shimizu, Judgment of 6 November 2018, ECLI:EU:C:2018:874.
ECJ, Joined Cases C-569/16 and C-570/16 Stadt Wuppertal v Maria Elisabeth Bauer and Volker Willmeroth v Martina Broßonn, Judgment of 6 November 2018, ECLI:EU:C:2018:871.
ECJ, Case C-210/16 Unabhängiges Landeszentrum für Datenschutz Schleswig-Holstein v Wirtschaftsakademie Schleswig-Holstein GmbH, Judgment of 5 June 2018, ECLI:EU:C:2018:388.
ECJ, Case C-414/16 Vera Egenberger v Evangelisches Werk für Diakonie und Entwicklung e.V., Judgment of 17 April 2018, ECLI:EU:C:2018:257.
ECJ, Case C-673/17 Bundesverband der Verbraucherzentralen und Verbraucherverbände - Verbraucherzentrale Bundesverband e.V. v Planet49, Judgment of 1 October 2019, ECLI:EU:C:2019:801.
ECJ, Case C-673/17 Bundesverband der Verbraucherzentralen und Verbraucherverbände - Verbraucherzentrale Bundesverband e.V. v Planet49, Opinion of AG Szpunar of 21 March 2019, ECLI:EU:C:2019:246.
ECJ, Case C-507/17 Google LLC v Commission nationale de l'informatique et des libertés (CNIL), Judgment of 24 September 2019, ECLI:EU:C:2019:772.

Table of Cases: National

Bundesverfassungsgericht, BVerfGE 7, pp. 198-230 – Lüth, Judgment of 15 January 1958.
Bundesverfassungsgericht, BVerfGE 65, pp. 1-71 – Volkszählung, Judgment of 15 December 1983.

Other Documents: EU

Article 29 Working Party Opinion 4/2007 on the concept of personal data of 20 June 2007. WP 136.
Article 29 Working Party Opinion 3/2010 on the principle of accountability. WP 173.
Article 29 Working Party Opinion 03/2013 on purpose limitation of 2 April 2013. WP 203.
Article 29 Working Party Guidelines on the right to data portability of 13 December 2016. WP 242 rev.01.
ENISA Recommendations on shaping technology according to GDPR provisions (2018). https://www.enisa.europa.eu/publications/recommendations-on-shaping-technology-according-to-gdpr-provisions-part-2/at_download/fullReport. Accessed 28 July 2021.
European Union Agency for Fundamental Rights 2018 #BigData: Discrimination in data-supported decision making. Vienna. https://fra.europa.eu/sites/default/files/fra_uploads/fra-2018-focus-big-data_en.pdf. Accessed 28 July 2021.

Other Documents: National

Autoriteit Persoonsgegevens Summary of Investigation Report on Microsoft Windows 10 Home and Pro (2017). https://autoriteitpersoonsgegevens.nl/sites/default/files/atoms/files/public_version_dutch_dpa_informal_translation_summary_of_investigation_report.pdf. Accessed 28 July 2021.
Konferenz der unabhängigen Datenschutzaufsichtsbehörden des Bundes und der Länder (2018) Kurzpapier Nr. 18 – Risiko für die Rechte und Freiheiten natürlicher Personen [Short Paper No. 18 – Risk to the Rights and Freedoms of Natural Persons]. https://www.datenschutzzentrum.de/uploads/dsgvo/kurzpapiere/DSK_KPNr_18_Risiko.pdf. Accessed 28 July 2021.
Konferenz der unabhängigen Datenschutzaufsichtsbehörden des Bundes und der Länder (2020) The Standard Data Protection Model – V.2.0b. https://www.datenschutz-mv.de/datenschutz/datenschutzmodell/. Accessed 28 July 2021.

Bibliography

Articles, Books and Chapters in Books

Adams S, Purtova N (2016) Introducing the Special Issue "Rethinking Surveillance: Theories, Discourses, Structures, and Practices". Philosophy & Technology 30:5–7.

Ahmed S (2006) Queer Phenomenology. Duke University Press, Durham/London.

Albrecht J P, Jotzo F (2017) Das neue Datenschutzrecht der EU [The New Data Protection Law of the EU]. Nomos, Baden-Baden.

Alexy R (1994) Theorie der Grundrechte [A Theory of Fundamental Rights]. Suhrkamp Taschenbuch, Frankfurt am Main.

Andrejevic M (2014) The Big Data Divide. International Journal of Communication 8:1673–1689.

Azoulai L, van der Sluis M (2016) Institutionalizing personal data protection in times of global institutional distrust: Schrems. CMLRev 53:1343–1372.

Benjamin G (2021) What we do with data: a critique of 'collection'. IPRev 10(4). https://doi.org/10.14763/2021.4.1588

von Berg M, Harborth U, Jarass H D, Lutterbeck B (1972) Schafft die Datenverarbeitung den modernen Leviathan? [Is Data Processing Creating the Modern Leviathan?]. ÖVD (1):3–7.

Bernsdorff N (2014) Artikel 7. In: Meyer J (ed) Charta der Grundrechte der Europäischen Union [Charter of Fundamental Rights of the European Union] 4th edition. Nomos, Baden-Baden.

Biber S E (2021) Machines Learning the Rule of Law: EU Proposes the World's first Artificial Intelligence Act. Verfassungsblog. https://verfassungsblog.de/ai-rol/. Accessed 28 July 2021.

Bieker F (2015) The Court of Justice of the European Union, Data Retention and the Rights to Data Protection and Privacy—Where Are We Now? In: Camenisch J, Fischer-Hübner S, Hansen M (eds) Privacy and Identity Management for the Future Internet in the Age of Globalisation. Springer, Cham/Heidelberg/New York/Dordrecht/London, pp. 73–86.

Bieker F (2016) Enforcing Data Protection Law—the Role of the Supervisory Authorities in Theory and Practice. In: Lehmann A, Whitehouse D, Fischer-Hübner S, Fritsch L, Raab C (eds) Privacy and Identity Management. Facing up to Next Steps. Springer, Cham, pp. 125–139.

Bieker F (2018) Die Risikoanalyse nach dem neuen EU-Datenschutzrecht und dem Standard-Datenschutzmodell [Risk Analysis under the New EU Data Protection Law and the Standard Data Protection Model]. DuD 27–31.

Bieker F, Bremert B (2020) Die Identifizierung von Risiken für die Grundrechte von Individuen [Identifying Risks to the Rights of Individuals]. ZD 7–14.

Bieker F, Bremert B, Hansen M (2018a) Die Risikobeurteilung nach der DSGVO [Risk Assessment under the GDPR]. DuD 492–496.

© T.M.C. ASSER PRESS and the author 2022

F. Bieker, *The Right to Data Protection*, Information Technology and Law Series 34,
https://doi.org/10.1007/978-94-6265-503-4

Bieker F, Bremert B, Hansen M (2018b) Verantwortlichkeit und Einsatz von Algorithmen bei öffentlichen Stellen [Responsibility for and Deployment of Algorithms by Public Authorities]. DuD 608–612.

Bieker F, Hansen M (2017) Normen des technischen Datenschutzes [Norms of Technical Data Protection]. DuD 41:285–289.

Bishop M (2004) Introduction to Computer Security. Addison-Wesley Professional, Boston MA, USA.

Bock K, Engeler M (2016) Die verfassungsrechtliche Wesensgehaltsgarantie als absolute Schranke im Datenschutzrecht [The Essence of Fundamental Rights as Absolute Limit in Data Protection Law]. DVBl 593–599.

Boehm F (2012) Information Sharing and Data Protection in the Area of Freedom, Security and Justice. Springer, Berlin/Heidelberg.

Boehm F, Cole M (2014) Data Retention after the Judgement of the Court of Justice of the European Union. Münster/Luxemburg. http://www.zar.kit.edu/DATA/veroeffentlichungen/237_237_Boehm_Cole-Data_Retention_Study-June_2014_1a1c2f6_9906a8c.pdf. Accessed 28 July 2021

Boehme-Neßler V (2014) Das Recht auf Vergessenwerden—Ein neues Internet-Grundrecht im Europäischen Recht [The Right to be Forgotten—A New Internet Right of European Law]. NVwZ 825–830.

Böröcz I (2016) Risk to the Right to the Protection of Personal Data. EDPL 2:467-480.

Borowsky M (2014) Artikel 52. In: Meyer J (ed) Charta der Grundrechte der Europäischen Union [Charter of Fundamental Rights of the European Union] 4th edn. Nomos, Baden-Baden.

Bossong R (2017) Passenger Name Records—from Canada back to the EU. Verfassungsblog. https://verfassungsblog.de/passenger-name-records-from-canada-back-to-the-eu/. Accessed 28 July 2021.

boyd d (2010) Making Sense of Privacy and Publicity. SXSW transcript. http://www.danah.org/papers/talks/2010/SXSW2010.html. Accessed 28 July 2021.

Breyer J (2018) Verarbeitungsgrundsätze und Rechenschaftspflicht nach Art. 5 DS-GVO [Principles of Data Processing and Accountability under Art. 5 GDPR]. DuD 311–317.

Brkan M (2018) The concept of essence of fundamental rights in the EU legal order: peeling the onion to its core. EuConst 14:332–368.

Brkan M (2019a) Do algorithms rule the world? Algorithmic decision-making and data protection in the framework of the GDPR and beyond. IJLIT 27:91–121.

Brkan M (2019b) The Essence of the Fundamental Rights to Privacy and Data Protection: Finding the Way Through the Maze of the CJEU's Constitutional Reasoning. GLJ 20:864–883.

Brouwer E (2011) Legality and Data Protection Law: The Forgotten Purpose of Purpose Limitation. In: Besselink L, Pennings F, Prechal S (eds) The Eclipse of the Legality Principle in the European Union. Kluwer Law, Alphen aan den Rijn, pp. 273–294.

Brouwer E, Zuiderveen Borgesius F (2015) Access to Personal Data and the Right to Good Governance during Asylum Procedures after the CJEU's YS. and M. and S. Judgment (C-141/12 and C-372/12). European Journal of Migration and Law 17:259–272.

Brühann U (2015) AEUV [TFEU] Art. 16. In: Groeben H v d, Schwarze J, Hatje A (eds) Europäisches Unionsrecht [European Union Law], 7th edn. Nomos, Baden-Baden.

Buolamwini J, Gebru T (2018) Gender Shades: Intersectional Accuracy Disparities in Commercial Gender Classification. In: Friedler S A, Wilson C (eds) Conference on Fairness, Accountability, and Transparency. Proceedings of Machine Learning Research 81, pp. 1–15. http://proceedings.mlr.press/v81/buolamwini18a/buolamwini18a.pdf. Accessed 28 July 2021.

Burbergs M (2013) How the right to respect for private and family life, home and correspondence became the nursery in which new rights are born. In: Brems E, Gerards J (eds) Shaping rights in the ECHR: the role of the European Court of Human Rights in determining the scope of human rights. CUP, Cambridge, pp. 315–329.

Bygrave L A (2002) Data Protection Law—Approaching its Rationale, Logic and Limits. Kluwer Law, The Hague.

Bygrave L A (2014) Data Privacy Law. OUP, Oxford.

Cameron I (2017) Balancing data protection and law enforcement needs: Tele2 Sverige and Watson. CMLRev 54:1467–1496.
Celeste E (2019) The Court of Justice and the Ban on Bulk Data Retention. EuConst 15:134–157.
Chikofsky E J, Cross J H (1990) Reverse Engineering and Design Recovery: A Taxonomy. IEEE Software 13–17.
Churches G, Zalnieriute M (2020) A Groundhog Day in Brussels. Verfassungsblog. https://verfassungsblog.de/a-groundhog-day-in-bruessels/. Accessed 28 July 2021.
Classen C D (2004) Joined Cases C-465/00, C-138/01 and C-139/01, Österreichischer Rundfunk, Judgment of 20 May 2003, Full Court, [2003] ECR I-4989 [Case Comment]. CMLRev 41:1377–1385.
Classen C D (2014) Datenschutz ja – aber wie? [Data Protection, yes – but how?]. EuR 441–448.
Cohen J (2000) Examined Lives: Informational Privacy and the Subject as Object. Stan. L. Rev. 52:1373–1438.
Cohen N (2015) The Privacy Follies: A Look Back at the CJEU's Invalidation of the EU/US Safe Harbor Framework. EDPL 3:240–244.
Cole M, Vandendriessche A (2016) From Digital Rights Ireland and Schrems in Luxembourg to Zakharov and Szabó/Vissy in Strasbourg. EDPL 1:121–129.
Colombi Ciacchi A (2019) The Direct Horizontal Effect of EU Fundamental Rights. EuConst 15:294–305.
Coudert F, Werkers E (2008) In The Aftermath of the Promusicae Case: How to Strike the Balance? IJLIT 18:50–71.
Dawson M, Lynskey O, Muir E (2019) What is the Added Value of the Concept of the "Essence" of EU Fundamental Rights? GLJ 20:763–778.
De Hert P (2017) Data Protection as Bundles of Principles, General Rights, Concrete Subjective Rights and Rules. EDPL 3:160–179.
De Hert P, Gutwirth S (2006) Privacy, Data Protection and Law Enforcement. Opacity of the Individual and Transparency of Power. In: Claes E, Duff A, Gutwirth S (eds) Privacy and the Criminal Law. Intersentia, Antwerp/Oxford, pp. 61–104.
De Hert P, Gutwirth S (2009) Data Protection in the Case Law of Strasbourg and Luxemburg: Constitutionalisation in Action. In: Gutwirth S, Poullet Y, De Hert P, de Terwangne C, Nouwt S (eds) Reinventing Data Protection? Springer, Dordrecht, pp. 3–44.
de Hingh A (2018) Some Reflections on Dignity as an Alternative Legal Concept in Data Protection Regulation. GLJ 19:1269–1290.
de S-O-l'E Lasser M (2009) Judicial Deliberations: A Comparative Analysis of Transparency and Legitimacy. OUP, Oxford.
Di Fabio U (2018) GG Art. 2 Abs. 1. In: Herzog R, Scholz R, Herdegen M, Klein H H (eds) Grundgesetz Kommentar [Basic Law Commentary], 84th EL. C.H. Beck, Munich.
Dimitropoulos G (2015) The CJEU's Decision on the Data Retention Directive: Transnational Aspects and the Push for Harmonisation. In: Hess B, Mariottini C (eds) Protecting Privacy in Private International and Procedural Law and by Data Protection. Nomos, Baden-Baden, pp. 71–79.
Dix A (2003) 3.5 Konzepte des Systemdatenschutzes [Approaches to Structural Data Protection]. In: Roßnagel A (ed) Handbuch Datenschutzrecht [Handbook Data Protection Law]. C.H. Beck, Munich, pp. 363–386.
Dix A (2014) § 34. In: Simitis S (ed) Bundesdatenschutzgesetz [Federal Data Protection Act] 8th edn. Nomos, Baden-Baden.
Docksey C (2015) Articles 7 and 8 of the EU Charter: Two Distinct Fundamental Rights. In: Grosjean A (ed) Enjeux Européens et Mondiaux de la Protection des Données Personelles. Larcier, Brussels, pp. 71–97.
Dörr O (2018) AEUV [TFEU] Art. 263. In: Grabitz E, Hilf M, Nettesheim M (eds) Das Recht der Europäischen Union [The Law of the European Union] 64th EL. C.H. Beck, Munich.
Ducuing C, Schroers J, Kindt E (2018) The Wirtschaftsakademie Fan Page Decision: A Landmark on Joint Controllership–A Challenge for Supervisory Authorities Competences. EDPL 4:547–553.

Ehlers D (2014) § 14 Allgemeine Lehren der Unionsgrundrechte [General Principles of EU Fundamental Rights]. In: Ehlers D (ed) Europäische Grundrechte und Grundfreiheiten, 4th edn. De Gruyter, Berlin, pp. 513–579.

Eichenhofer J (2016) "e-Privacy" im europäischen Grundrechtsschutz: Das "Schrems"-Urteil des EuGH [ePrivacy in European Fundamental Rights Protection: The Schrems Judgment of the ECJ]. EuR 76–89.

Engeler M (2018a) Das überschätzte Kopplungsverbot [The Overrated Prohibition of Tying-In]. ZD 55–62.

Engeler M (2018b) Die Ernennung der Beauftragten für den Datenschutz und das transparente Wahlverfahren nach Art. 53 Abs. 1 DSGVO [The Appointment of Members of Data Protection Authorities and the Transparent Voting Procedure of Art. 53(1) GDPR]. CR-online.de Blog. https://www.cr-online.de/blog/2018/08/06/die-ernennung-der-beauftragten-fuer-den-datenschutz-und-das-transparente-wahlverfahren-nach-art-53-abs-1-dsgvo/. Accessed 28 July 2021.

Frantziou E (2015) The Horizontal Effect of the Charter of Fundamental Rights of the EU: Rediscovering the Reasons for Horizontality. Eur Law J. 21:657–679.

Frantziou E (2019) (Most of) the Charter of Fundamental Rights is Horizontally Applicable. EuConst 15:306–323.

Frenz W (2009) Handbuch Europarecht [Handbook European Law], Band 4 Europäische Grundrechte. Springer, Berlin/Heidelberg.

Frenzel E M (2018) DS-GVO [GDPR] Art. 5. In: Paal B, Pauly D (eds) Kommentar Datenschutz-Grundverordnung – Bundesdatenschutzgesetz [Commentary General Data Protection Regulation – Federal Data Protection Act] 2nd edn. C.H. Beck, Munich, pp. 65–86.

Friedewald M, Bieker F, Obersteller H, Nebel M, Martin N, Rost M, Hansen M (2017) Datenschutz-Folgenabschätzung – Ein Werkzeug für einen besseren Datenschutz [Data Protection Impact Assessment – A Tool for Improved Data Protection], 3rd edn. https://www.forum-privatheit.de/wp-content/uploads/Forum-Privatheit-WP-DSFA-3-Auflage-2017-11-29.pdf. Accessed 28 July 2021.

Fröhlich W, Spiecker gen. Döhmann I (2018) Können Algorithmen diskriminieren? [Can Algorithms Discriminate?]. Verfassungsblog. https://www.verfassungsblog.de/koennen-algorithmen-diskriminieren/. Accessed 28 July 2021.

Gallie W B (1955–1956) Essentially Contested Concepts. Proceedings of the Aristotelian Society 56:167–198.

Geiger H (1973) Datenschutz und Gewaltenteilung [Data Protection and Separation of Powers]. In: Kilian W, Lenk K, Steinmüller W (eds) Datenschutz. [Data Protection] S. Toeche-Mittler, Darmstadt, [Data Protection] pp. 173–185.

Gellert R (2015) Understanding Data Protection as Risk Regulation. Journal of Internet Law 3–16.

Gellert R (2016) We Have Always Managed Risks in Data Protection Law. EDPL 2:481–492.

Giegerich T (2014) Spät kommt Ihr, doch Ihr kommt: Warum wird die Grundrechtskonformität der Vorratsdatenspeicherung erst nach acht Jahren geklärt? [You are late, but here you are: Why has the compatibility of bulk data retention with fundamental rights only been addressed after eight years?]. ZEuS 3–17.

Gillespie T (2014) The Relevance of Algorithms. In: Gillespie T, Boczkowski P J, Foot K A (eds) Media Technologies: Essays on Communication, Materiality, and Society. MIT Press, Cambridge, MA, USA, pp. 167–194.

Golla S J (2019) Der virtuelle Mr. Hyde [The Virtual Mr. Hyde]. Verfassungsblog. https://verfassungsblog.de/der-virtuelle-mr-hyde/. Accessed 28 July 2021.

Gonscherowski S, Hansen M, Rost M (2018) Resilienz – eine neue Anforderung aus der Datenschutz-Grundverordnung [Resilience – A New Requirement in the General Data Protection Regulation]. DuD 442–446.

González Fuster G (2014a) The Emergence of Personal Data Protection as a Fundamental Right of the EU. Springer, Cham/Heidelberg/New York/Dordrecht/London.

González Fuster G (2014b) Fighting for Your Right to What Exactly – The Convoluted Case Law of the EU Court of Justice on Privacy and/Or Personal Data Protection. Birkbeck Law Review 2:263–278.
González Fuster G, Gellert R (2012) The Fundamental Right of Data Protection in the European Union: in Search of an Uncharted Right. International Review of Law, Computers & Technology 26:73–82.
Grabenwarter C (2014) European Convention on Human Rights Commentary. C.H. Beck, Munich.
Grabenwarter C, Pabel K (2016) Europäische Menschenrechtskonvention [European Convention on Human Rights], 6th edn. C.H. Beck, Munich.
Hallinan D, Martin N (2020) Fundamental Rights, the Normative Keystone of DPIA. EDPL 6:178–193.
Hallinan D, Zuiderveen Borgesius F (2020) Opinions can be incorrect (in our opinion)! On data protection law's accuracy principle. IDPL 10:1–10.
Hansen M (2019a) Artikel 25. In: Simitis S, Hornung G, Spiecker gen. Döhmann I (eds) Datenschutzrecht [Data Protection Law]. Nomos, Baden-Baden.
Hansen M (2019b) Artikel 32. In: Simitis S, Hornung G, Spiecker gen. Döhmann I (eds) Datenschutzrecht [Data Protection Law]. Nomos, Baden-Baden.
Hansen M, Thomsen S (2010) Lebenslanger Datenschutz: Anforderungen an vertrauenswürdige Infrastrukturen [Life-long Data Protection: Requirements for Trustworthy Infrastructures]. DuD 283–288.
Hart H L A (1994) The Concept of Law, 2nd edn. OUP, Oxford.
Hartzog W (2018) The Case Against Idealising Control. EDPL 4:423–432.
Hassein N (2017) Against Black Inclusion in Facial Recognition. Digital Talking Drum. https://digitaltalkingdrum.com/2017/08/15/against-black-inclusion-in-facial-recognition/. Accessed 28 July 2021.
Herdegen M (2019) Art. 1 Abs. 3. In: Maunz T, Dürig G (eds) Grundgesetz-Kommentar [Basic Law Commentary], 87th EL, Band 1. C.H. Beck, Munich.
Hesse K (1999) Grundzüge des Verfassungsrechts der Bundesrepublik Deutschland [Tenets of the Constitutional Law of the Federal Republic of Germany], 20th edn. C.F. Müller, Heidelberg.
Hicks M (2021) When Did the Fire Start? In: Mullaney T S, Peters B, Hicks M, Philip K (eds) Your Computer is On Fire. MIT Press, Cambridge, MA, USA, pp. 11–26.
Hijmans H (2016) The European Union as Guardian of Internet Privacy. Springer, Cham.
Hijmans H (2017) PNR Agreement EU-Canada Scrutinised. EDPL 3:406–412.
Hörnle J (2019) Juggling more than three balls at once: multilevel jurisdictional challenges in EU Data Protection Regulation. IJLIT 27:142–170.
Hornung G (2012) A General Data Protection Regulation for Europe? SCRIPTed 9:64–81.
Hustinx P (2017) EU Data Protection Law: The Review of Directive 95/46/EC and the General Data Protection Regulation. In: Cremona M (ed) New Technologies and EU Law. OUP, Oxford, pp. 123–173.
Irion K (2020) Schrems II and Surveillance: Third Countries' National Security Powers in the Purview of EU Law. European Law Blog. https://europeanlawblog.eu/2020/07/24/schrems-ii-and-surveillance-third-countries-national-security-powers-in-the-purview-of-eu-law/. Accessed 28 July 2021.
Jančiūtė L (2019) Data protection and the construction of collective redress in Europe: exploring challenges and opportunities. IDPL 9:2–14.
Jarass H D (2016) Artikel 7. In: Charta der Grundrechte der EU [Charter of Fundamental Rights of the EU] 3rd edn. C.H. Beck, Munich.
Jozwiak M (2016) Balancing the Rights to Data Protection and Freedom of Expression and Information by the Court of Justice of the European Union. MJ 404–420.
Jung A (2018) Datenschutz-(Compliance-)Management-Systeme [Data Protection (Compliance) Management Systems]. ZD 208–213.
Kadiri A P L (2021) Data and Afrofuturism – An emancipated subject? IPRev 10(4). https://doi.org/10.14763/2021.4.1597.

Kamp M, Rost M (2013) Kritik an der Einwilligung [A Critique of Consent]. DuD 80–84.

Karg M (2013) Die Renaissance des Verbotsprinzips im Datenschutz [The Renaissance of the Prohibition Principle in Data Protection]. DuD 75–79.

Kerikmäe T (2014) EU Charter: Its Nature, Innovative Character, and Horizontal Effect. In: Kerikmäe T (ed) Protecting Human Rights in the EU. Springer, Berlin/Heidelberg, pp. 5–19.

Kilian W (1973) Datenschutz in Wirtschaftsunternehmen [Data Protection in Economic Enterprises]. In: Kilian W, Lenk K, Steinmüller W (eds) Datenschutz [Data Protection]. S. Toeche-Mittler, Darmstadt, pp. 289–309.

Kingreen T (2016a) AEUV [TFEU] Art. 16. In: Calliess C, Ruffert M (eds) EUV/AEUV Kommentar [TEU/TFEU Commentary] 5th edn. C.H. Beck, Munich.

Kingreen T (2016b) EU-GRCharta [EU CFR] Art. 7. In: Calliess C, Ruffert M (eds) EUV/AEUV Kommentar [TEU/TFEU Commentary], 5th edn. C.H. Beck, Munich.

Kingreen T (2016c) EU-GRCharta [EU CFR] Art. 8. In: Calliess C, Ruffert M (eds) EUV/AEUV Kommentar [TEU/TFEU Commentary], 5th edn. C.H. Beck, Munich.

Kokott J, Sobotta C (2014) The Distinction between Privacy and Data Protection in the Jurisprudence of the CJEU and the ECtHR. In: Hijmans H, Kranenborg H (eds) Data Protection 2014: How to Restore Trust? Contributions in Honour of Peter Hustinx. Intersentia, Cambridge, pp. 83–95.

Korff D (1998) Study on the protection of the rights and interests of legal persons with regard to the processing of personal data relating to such persons. Cambridge. http://ssrn.com/abstract=1288583. Accessed 28 July 2021.

Kranenborg H (2014) Article 8. In: Peers S, Hervey T, Kenner J, Ward A (eds) The EU Charter of Fundamental Rights – A Commentary. Hart Publishing, Oxford.

Kühling J (2014) Rückkehr des Rechts: Verpflichtung von "Google & Co." zu Datenschutz [Return of the Law: Data Protection Obligations of Google & Co.]. EuZW 527–532.

Kühling J, Heberlein J (2016) EuGH "reloaded": "unsafe harbor" USA vs. "Datenfestung" EU [ECJ reloaded: unsafe harbor USA vs data fortress EU]. NVwZ 7–12.

Kuner C (2015) The Court of Justice of the EU Judgment on Data Protection and Internet Search Engines. In: Hess B, Mariottini C (eds) Protecting Privacy in Private International and Procedural Law and by Data Protection. Nomos, Baden-Baden, pp. 19–44.

Kuner C (2017a) Data Protection, Data Transfers and International Agreements. Verfassungsblog. https://verfassungsblog.de/data-protection-data-transfers-and-international-agreements-the-cjeus-opinion-115/. Accessed 28 July 2021.

Kuner C (2017b) Reality and Illusion in EU Data Transfer Regulation Post Schrems. GLJ 18:881–918.

Kuner C (2018) International agreements, data protection, and EU fundamental rights on the international stage. CMLRev 55:857–882.

Kuner C (2020) The Schrems II judgment of the Court of Justice and the future of data transfer regulation. European Law Blog. https://europeanlawblog.eu/2020/07/17/the-schrems-ii-judgment-of-the-court-of-justice-and-the-future-of-data-transfer-regulation/. Accessed 28 July 2021.

Kunnert G (2014a) Das Ende der Vorratsdatenspeicherung? [The End of Bulk Data Retention?]. DuD 103–108.

Kunnert G (2014b) EuGH zur Vorratsdatenspeicherung [ECJ on Bulk Data Retention]. DuD 774–784.

Lavrijssen S, Ottow A (2011) The Legality of Independent Regulatory Authorities. In: Besselink L, Pennings F, Prechal S (eds) The Eclipse of the Legality Principle in the European Union. Kluwer Law, Alphen aan den Rijn, pp. 72–96.

Lawrence H M (2021) Siri Disciples. In: Mullaney T S, Peters B, Hicks M, Philip K (eds) Your Computer is On Fire. MIT Press, Cambridge, MA, USA, pp. 178–197.

Lazaro C, Le Métayer D (2015) Control over Personal Data: True Remedy or Fairy Tale? SCRIPTed 12:3–34.

Leczykiewicz D (2013) Horizontal Application of the Charter of Fundamental Rights. ELRev 38:479–497.

Lenaerts K (2019) Limits on Limitations: The Essence of Fundamental Rights in the EU. GLJ 20:779-793.

Lenk K (1973) Datenschutz in der öffentlichen Verwaltung [Data Protection in Public Administration]. In: Kilian W, Lenk K, Steinmüller W (eds) Datenschutz [Data Protection]. S. Toeche-Mittler, Darmstadt.

Lynskey O (2014a) The Data Retention Directive is incompatible with the rights to privacy and data protection and is invalid in its entirety: Digital Rights Ireland. CMLRev 51:1789–1812.

Lynskey O (2014b) Deconstructing Data Protection: the 'Added-Value' of a Right to Data Protection in the EU Legal Order. ICLQ 63:569–597.

Lynskey O (2015a) Control over Personal Data in a Digital Age. MLR 78:522–548.

Lynskey O (2015b) The Foundations of EU Data Protection Law. OUP, Oxford.

Lynskey O (2017) The 'Europeanisation'of Data Protection Law. CYELS 19:252-286.

Lynskey O (2018) The Power of Providence. In: Moore M, Tambini D (eds) Digital Dominance. OUP, Oxford, pp. 176–201.

Lyon D (2003) Introduction. In: Lyon D (ed) Surveillance as Social Sorting: Privacy, risk, and digital discrimination. Routledge, London/New York, NY, USA, pp. 1–8.

Macenaite M (2017) The "Riskification" of European Data Protection Law through a two-fold Shift. EJRR 8:506–540.

Mantelero A (2016) Personal data for decisional purposes in the age of analytics: From an individual to a collective dimension of data protection. CLSLR 32:238–255.

Marauhn T, Thorn J (2013) Privat- und Familienleben [Private and Family Life]. In: Dörr O, Grote R, Marauhn T (eds) EMRK/GG Konkordanzkommentar [ECHR/Basic Law Commentary], 2nd edn, Band 2. Mohr Siebeck, Tübingen, pp. 253–286.

Marks S (1995) The European Convention on Human Rights and its 'Democratic Society'. BYIL 66:209–238.

Marsch N (2018) Das europäische Datenschutzgrundrecht [The European Fundamental Right to Data Protection]. Mohr Siebeck, Tübingen.

Marwick A, boyd d (2018) Understanding Privacy at the Margins. International Journal of Communication 12:1157–1165. https://ijoc.org/index.php/ijoc/article/view/7053 Accessed 29 September 2021.

Masing J (2014) RiBVerfG Masing: Vorläufige Einschätzung der "Google-Entscheidung" des EuGH [Judge Masing of the Bundesverfassungsgericht: Preliminary Assessment of the Google Judgment of the ECJ]. Verfassungsblog. https://verfassungsblog.de/ribverfg-masing-vorlaeufige-einschaetzung-der-google-entscheidung-des-eugh/. Accessed 28 July 2021.

Matzner T, Masur P, Ochs C, von Pape T (2016) Do-It-Yourself Data Protection—Empowerment or Burden? In: Gutwirth S, De Hert P, Leenes R (eds) Data Protection on the Move. Springer, Dordrecht, pp. 277–305.

Maxwell W J (2015) Principles-based regulation of personal data: the case of 'fair processing'. IDPL 5:205–216.

Mayer-Schönberger V (1997) Generational Development of Data Protection in Europe. In: Agre P E, Rotenberg M (eds) Technology and Privacy: The New Landscape. MIT Press, Cambridge, MA, USA, pp. 219–241.

Milanovic M (2021) The Grand Normalization of Mass Surveillance: ECtHR Grand Chamber Judgments in Big Brother Watch and Centrum för rättvisa. EJIL:Talk! https://www.ejiltalk.org/the-grand-normalization-of-mass-surveillance-ecthr-grand-chamber-judgments-in-big-brother-watch-and-centrum-for-rattvisa/. Accessed 28 July 2021.

Møller Pedersen A, Udsen H, Sandfeld Jakobsen S (2018) Data retention in Europe – the Tele2 case and beyond. IDPL 8:160–174.

Muir E (2011) Of Ages in – and Edges of – EU Law. CMLRev 48:39–62.

Mysegades J (2019) Rechtsstaat sticht Software. Verfassungsblog. https://verfassungsblog.de/rechtsstaat-sticht-software/. Accessed 28 July 2021.

Nas S, Roosendaal A (2018) DPIA Diagnostic Data in Microsoft Office Ministerie van Justitie en Veiligheid. https://www.rijksoverheid.nl/binaries/rijksoverheid/documenten/rapporten/2018/

11/07/data-protection-impact-assessment-op-microsoft-office/DPIA+Microsoft+Office+2016+and+365+-+20191105.pdf. Accessed 28 July 2021.

Nettesheim M (2014) § 9 Privatleben und Privatsphäre [Private Life and Privacy]. In: Grabenwarter C (ed) Enzyklopädie Europarecht [Encyclopedia of European Law] Band 2: Europäischer Grundrechteschutz. Nomos, Baden-Baden, pp. 387–415.

Nettesheim M (2015) The CJEU's decision on the Data Retention Directive. In: Hess B, Mariottini C (eds) Protecting Privacy in Private International and Procedural Law and by Data Protection. Nomos, Baden-Baden, pp. 57–69.

Ni Loideain N, Adams R (2019) From Alexa to Siri and the GDPR: The Gendering of Virtual Personal Assistants and the Role of EU Data Protection Law. CILJ 241–257.

Noble S U (2021) Your Robot Isn't Neutral. In: Mullaney T S, Peters B, Hicks M, Philip K (eds) Your Computer is On Fire. MIT Press, Cambridge, MA, USA, pp. 199–212.

Nocun K (2018) Datenschutz unter Druck [Data Protection under Pressure]. In: Roßnagel A, Friedewald M, Hansen M (eds) Die Fortentwicklung des Datenschutzes [The Development of Data Protection]. Springer Fachmedien, Wiesbaden, pp. 39–58.

Ohler C (2017) EUV [TEU] Art. 48. In: Grabitz E, Hilf M, Nettesheim M (eds) Das Recht der Europäischen Union [The Law of the European Union] 63rd EL. C.H. Beck, Munich.

Ojanen T (2014) Privacy Is More Than Just a Seven-Letter Word: The Court of Justice of the European Union Sets Constitutional Limits on Mass Surveillance. EuConst 10:528–541.

Ojanen T (2016) Making the Essence of Fundamental Rights Real: The Court of Justice of the European Union Clarifies the Structure of Fundamental Rights under the Charter [Case Note]. EuConst 12:318–329.

Pechstein M (2011) EU-Prozessrecht [EU Procedural Law], 4th edn. Mohr Siebeck, Tübingen.

Petri T (2009) EuGH: Rechtsgrundlage der EG-Richtlinie zur Vorratsdatenspeicherung [ECJ: Legal Basis of the EC Directive on Data Retention]. EuZW 214 et seq.

Petri T (2019) Artikel 9. In: Simitis S, Hornung G, Spiecker gen. Döhmann I (eds) Datenschutzrecht [Data Protection Law]. Nomos, Baden-Baden.

Podlech A (1970) Verfassungsrechtliche Probleme öffentlicher Datenbanken [Constitutional Implications of Public Databases]. DÖV 473–475.

Podlech A (1973a) Datenschutz im Bereich der öffentlichen Verwaltung [Data Protection in the Sector of Public Administration]. DVR Beiheft 1.

Podlech A (1973b) Prinzipien des Datenschutzes in der öffentlichen Verwaltung [Principles of Data Protection in Public Administration]. In: Kilian W, Lenk K, Steinmüller W (eds) Datenschutz [Data Protection]. S. Toeche-Mittler, Darmstadt, pp. 3–13.

Podlech A (1982) Individualdatenschutz – Systemdatenschutz [Individual Data Protection – Structural Data Protection]. In: Brückner K, Dalichau G (eds) Festgabe für Hans Grüner. R.S. Schulz, Percha am Starnberger See, pp. 451–462.

Podlech A (1987) Der Datenschutz und die Akzeptabilität unserer Gesellschaftsordnung [Data Protection and the Acceptability of our Societal Order]. In: Hohmann H (ed) Freiheitssicherung durch Datenschutz [Securing Political Freedom through Data Protection]. Suhrkamp, Frankfurt am Main, pp. 19–24.

Podlech A (1988) Unter welchen Bedingungen sind neue Informationssysteme gesellschaftlich akzeptabel? [Under Which Conditions Are New Information Systems Socially Acceptable?]. In: Steinmüller W (ed) Verdatet und Vernetzt [Registered and Networked]. Fischer Taschenbuch, Frankfurt am Main, pp. 118–126.

Pohle J (2014) Die immer noch aktuellen Grundfragen des Datenschutzes [The Still Pressing Fundamental Questions of Data Protection]. In: Garstka H, Coy W (eds) Gedächtnisschrift für Wilhelm Steinmüller: Wovon – für wen – wozu, Systemdenken wider die Diktatur der Daten [Whereof – for Whom – Why, Systems Thinking against the Tyranny of Data]. Helmholtz-Zentrum für Kulturtechnik, Humboldt-Universität zu Berlin, Berlin, pp. 45–58.

Pohle J (2018) Datenschutz und Technikgestaltung [Data Protection and Technology Design]. Berlin. https://edoc.hu-berlin.de/bitstream/handle/18452/19886/dissertation_pohle_joerg.pdf. Accessed 28 July 2021.

Pötters S (2017) Art. 5. In: Gola P (ed) Datenschutz-Grundverordnung Kommentar [General Data Protection Regulation Commentary]. C.H. Beck, Munich.

Purtova N (2012) Property Rights in Personal Data. Wolters Kluwer, Alphen aan den Rijn.

Quelle C (2017) The 'risk revolution' in EU data protection law: We can't have our cake and eat it, too. In: Data Protection and Privacy: The Age of Intelligent Machines. Hart Publishing, Oxford/Portland, OR, USA, pp. 33–62.

Rauhofer J (2015) Of Men and Mice: Should the EU Data Protection Authorities' Reaction to Google's New Privacy Policy Raise Concern for the Future of the Purpose Limitation Principle? EDPL 5:5–15.

Richardson R, Schultz J, Crawford K (2019) Dirty Data, Bad Predictions: How Civil Rights Violations Impact Police Data, Predictive Policing Systems, and Justice. N.Y.U. L. Rev. Online 94:192–233. https://papers.ssrn.com/sol3/papers.cfm?abstract_id=3333423. Accessed 28 July 2021.

Röben V (2013) Grundrechtsberechtigte und -verpflichtete, Grundrechtsgeltung [Subjects and Addressees of Fundamental Rights, Application of Fundamental Rights]. In: Dörr O, Grote R, Marauhn T (eds) EMRK/GG Konkordanzkommentar [ECHR/Basic Law Commentary] 2nd edn, Band 1. Mohr Siebeck, Tübingen, pp. 253–286.

Robrahn R, Bock K (2018) Schutzziele als Optimierungsgebote [Protection Goals as Optimisation Requirements]. DuD 7–12.

Robrahn R, Bremert B (2018) Interessenskonflikte im Datenschutzrecht [Conflicts of Interest in Data Protection Law]. ZD 291–297.

Roßnagel A (2014) Neue Maßstäbe für den Datenschutz in Europa – Folgerungen aus dem EuGH-Urteil zur Vorratsdatenspeicherung [New Standards for Data Protection in Europe – Consequences from the ECJ Judgment on Bulk Data Retention]. MMR 372–377.

Roßnagel A (2017) Datenschutzaufsicht nach der EU-Datenschutz-Grundverordnung [Enforcing the EU General Data Protection Regulation]. Springer Fachmedien, Wiesbaden.

Roßnagel A (2019) Artikel 5. In: Simitis S, Hornung G, Spiecker gen. Döhmann I (eds) Datenschutzrecht [Data Protection Law]. Nomos, Baden-Baden.

Rost M (2013) Zur Soziologie des Datenschutzes [On the Sociology of Data Protection]. DuD 85–91.

Rost M (2017) Bob, es ist Bob! [Bob, it is Bob!]. FifF-Kommunikation 4:63–66.

Rost M (2018a) Die Ordnung der Schutzziele [The System of Protection Goals]. DuD 13–17.

Rost M (2018b) Risiken im Datenschutz [Risks in Data Protection]. vorgänge 221/222:79–91.

Rouvroy A, Poullet Y (2009) The Right to Informational Self-Determination and the Value of Self-Development: Reassessing the Importance of Privacy for Democracy. In: Gutwirth S, Poullet Y, De Hert P, de Terwangne C, Nouwt S (eds) Reinventing Data Protection? Springer, Dordrecht, pp. 45–76.

Sajfert J (2020) Bulk data interception/retention judgments of the CJEU – A victory and a defeat for privacy. European Law Blog. https://europeanlawblog.eu/2020/10/26/bulk-data-interception-retention-judgments-of-the-cjeu-a-victory-and-a-defeat-for-privacy/. Accessed 28 July 2021.

Sandhu A (2017) Die Tele2-Entscheidung des EuGH zur Vorratsdatenspeicherung in den Mitgliedstaaten und ihre Auswirkungen auf die Rechtslage in Deutschland und in der Europäischen Union [The Tele2 Decision of the ECJ on the Bulk Data Retention Regimes in the Member States and its Consequences for the German and European Union's Legal Orders]. EuR 453–470.

Schmitz B (2018) Der Abschied vom Personenbezug [Farewell to Personal Data]. ZD 5–8.

Schneider J (1971) Datenschutz – Datensicherung [Data Protection – Data Security]. C.F. Müller, Munich.

Schneider J (1973) Technische Möglichkeiten des Datenschutzes [Technical Approaches to Data Protection]. In: Kilian W, Lenk K, Steinmüller W (eds) Datenschutz [Data Protection]. S. Toeche-Mittler, Darmstadt, pp. 223–233.

Schneider J (2017) Schließt Art. 9 DS-GVO die Zulässigkeit der Verarbeitung bei Big Data aus? [Does Art. 9 GDPR Preclude Big Data Processing?]. ZD 303–308.

Schorkopf F (2014) § 3 Grundrechtsverpflichtete [Addressees of Fundamental Rights]. In: Grabenwarter C (ed) Enzyklopädie Europarecht [Encyclopedia of European Law] Band 2: Europäischer Grundrechteschutz. Nomos, Baden-Baden, pp. 137–159.
Schröder M (2018) AEUV [TFEU] Art. 16. In: Streinz R (ed) Kommentar EUV/AEUV [Commentary TEU/TFEU], 3rd edn. C.H. Beck, Munich.
Scudiero L (2017) Bringing Your Data Everywhere: A Legal Reading of the Right to Portability. EDPL 3:119–127.
Siemen B (2004) Grundrechtsschutz durch Richtlinien / Die Fälle Österreichischer Rundfunk u.a. und Lindqvist [Fundamental Rights Protection Through Directives / The Cases of Österreichischer Rundfunk and Others and Lindqvist]. EuR 306–321.
Siemen B (2006) Datenschutz als europäisches Grundrecht [Data Protection as European Fundamental Right]. Duncker & Humblot, Berlin.
Simitis S (1970) Konsequenzen der Datenverarbeitung für die Rechtsordnung [Consequences of Data Processing for the Legal Order]. In: Ständige Deputation des Deutschen Juristentages (ed) Verhandlungen des Achtundvierzigsten Deutschen Juristentages [Proceedings of the 48. German Lawyer Association Conference], Band 2. C.H. Beck, Munich, pp. T 35–T 43.
Simitis S (1971) Chancen und Gefahren der elektronischen Datenverarbeitung [Chances and Risks of Electronic Data Processing]. NJW 673–682.
Simitis S (1973) Datenschutz – Notwendigkeit und Voraussetzungen einer gesetzlichen Regelung [Data Protection – Exigency and Requirements of Legal Regulation]. DVR 2:138–189.
Simitis S (1986) Von der Amtshilfe zur Informationshilfe [From Administrative Assistance to Information Assistance]. NJW 2795–2805.
Simitis S (1990) "Sensitive Daten" – Zur Geschichte und Wirkung einer Fiktion ["Sensitive Data" – On the History and Effects of a Legal Fiction]. In: Brem E, Druey N J, Kramer E A, Schwander I (eds) Festschrift zum 65. Geburtstag von Mario M. Pedrazzini. Stämpfl & Cie, Bern, pp. 469–493.
Simitis S (2009) Der EuGH und die Vorratsdatenspeicherung oder die verfehlte Kehrtwende bei der Kompetenzregelung [The ECJ and Bulk Data Retention or the Misguided Turnaround in the Allocation of Jurisdiction]. NJW 1782–1786.
Simitis S (2014) Einleitung [Introduction]. In: Simitis S (ed) Bundesdatenschutzgesetz [Federal Data Protection Act], 8th edn. Nomos, Baden-Baden.
Simitis S, Hornung G, Spiecker gen. Döhmann I (2019) Einleitung [Introduction]. In: Simitis S, Hornung G, Spiecker gen. Döhmann I (eds) Datenschutzrecht [Data Protection Law]. Nomos, Baden-Baden.
Sobotta C (2017) AEUV [TFEU] Art. 16. In: Grabitz E, Hilf M, Nettesheim M (eds) Das Recht der Europäischen Union [The Law of the European Union], 63rd EL. C.H. Beck, Munich.
Spindler G (2014) Durchbruch für ein Recht auf Vergessen(werden)? – Die Entscheidung des EuGH in Sachen Google Spain und ihre Auswirkungen auf das Datenschutz- und Zivilrecht [Breakthrough for a Right to be Forgotten? – The ECJ Decision in the Google Spain Case and its Consequences for Data Protection and Civil Law]. JZ 981–991.
Steinmüller W (1971) Rechtsinformatik [Legal Informatics]. JR 1–9.
Steinmüller W (1972a) Rechtstheorie, Rechtsinformatik und Rechtspolitik [Legal Theory, Legal Informatics and Legal Policy]. In: Albert H, Luhmann N, Maihofer W, Weinberger O (eds) Rechtstheorie als Grundlagenwissenschaft der Rechtswissenschaft [Legal Theory as Foundational Science of Jurisprudence]. Bertelsmann Universitätsverlag, Dusseldorf, pp. 373–389.
Steinmüller W (1972b) Stellenwert der EDV in der Öffentlichen Verwaltung und Prinzipien des Datenschutzrechts [The Significance of Electronic Data Processing in Public Administration and Principles of Data Protection Law]. ÖVD(11):453–462.
Steinmüller W (1973) Objektbereich "Verwaltungsautomation" und Prinzipien des Datenschutzes [Object Area "Administrative Automation" and Principles of Data Protection]. In: Kilian W, Lenk K, Steinmüller W (eds) Datenschutz [Data Protection]. S. Toeche-Mittler, Darmstadt, pp. 51–76.
Steinmüller W (1975) Datenschutz als Teilaspekt gesellschaftlicher Informationskontrolle [Data Protection as Facet of Societal Information Control]. In: Deutsche Sektion der Internationalen

Juristen-Kommission (ed) Datenschutz und Datensicherung [Data Protection and Data Security]. C.F. Müller, Karlsruhe, pp. 35–95.
Steinmüller W (1981) Die Zweite industrielle Revolution hat eben begonnen [The Second Industrial Revolution Has Just Begun]. Kursbuch 66(4):152–188.
Steinmüller W (1993) Informationstechnologie und Gesellschaft [Information Technologies and Society]. Wissenschaftliche Buchgesellschaft, Darmstadt.
Steinmüller W (2007) Das informationelle Selbstbestimmungsrecht [The Right to Informational Self-Determination]. RDV(4):158–161.
Steinmüller W, Lutterbeck B, Mallmann C, Harborth U, Gerhard K, Schneider J (1971) Grundfragen des Datenschutzes [Fundamental Questions of Data Protection], BT-Drs. VI/3826 Anlage 1, pp. 5–193.
Streinz R (2018) EU-Grundrechte-Charta [EU Fundamental Rights Charter] 2000 Artikel 8. In: Streinz R (ed) Kommentar EUV/AEUV [Commentary TEU/TFEU], 3rd edn. C.H. Beck, Munich.
Streinz R, Michl W (2011) Die Drittwirkung des europäischen Datenschutzgrundrechts (Art. 8 GRCh) im deutschen Privatrecht [The Horizontal Effect of the European Fundamental Right to Data Protection (Art. 8 CFR) in German Civil Law]. EuZW 384–388.
Szydlo M (2017) The Independence of Data Protection Authorities in EU Law: Between the Safeguarding of Fundamental Rights and Ensuring the Integrity of the Internal Market. ELRev 42:369–387.
Terhechte J P (2009) Rechtsangleichung zwischen Gemeinschafts- und Unionsrecht – die Richtlinie über die Vorratsdatenspeicherung vor dem EuGH [Approximation of Laws between Community and Union Law – the Directive on Bulk Data Retention before the ECJ]. EuZW 199–204.
Theilen J T, Hassfurther I, Staff W (2017) Guest Editor's Introduction: Towards Utopia – Rethinking International Law. GYIL 60:315–334.
Tracol X (2015) Back to basics: The European Court of Justice further defined the concept of personal data and the scope of the right of data subjects to access it. CLSLR 31:112–119.
Tracol X (2016) "Invalidator" strikes back: The harbour has never been safe. CLSLR 32:345–362.
Tridimas T, Gentile G (2019) The Essence of Rights: An Unreliable Boundary? GLJ 20:794–816.
Tzanou M (2017) The Fundamental Right to Data Protection. Hart, Oxford/Portland, OR, USA.
Ursic H (2018) Unfolding the New-Born Right to Data Portability: Four Gateways to Data Subject Control. SCRIPTed 15:42–69.
Van Alsenoy B, Koekkoek M (2015) Internet and jurisdiction after Google Spain. IDPL 5:105–120.
van der Sloot B (2015) Do privacy and data protection rules apply to legal persons and should they? A proposal for a two-tiered system. CLSLR 31:26–45.
van der Sloot B (2017) Legal Fundamentalism: Is Data Protection Really a Fundamental Right? In: Leenes R, van Brakel R, Gutwirth S, De Hert P (eds) Data Protection and Privacy: (In)visibilities and Infrastructures. Springer, Cham, pp. 3–30.
Varju M (2014) European Union Human Rights Law. Edward Elgar, Cheltenham.
Vedaschi A (2018) Privacy and data protection versus national security in transnational flights: the EU–Canada PNR agreement. IDPL 8:124–139.
Vogiatzoglou P (2019) Mass Surveillance, Predictive Policing and the Implementation of the CJEU and ECtHR Requirement of Objectivity. EJLT 10.
Vogiatzoglou P (2020) One more time with feeling: the latest AG Opinions on data retention and national security. CiTiP Blog. https://www.law.kuleuven.be/citip/blog/one-more-time-with-feeling-the-latest-ag-opinions-on-data-retention-and-national-security/. Accessed 28 July 2021.
Vogiatzoglou P, Fantin S (2019) National and Public Security Within and Beyond the Police Directive. In: Veddor A, Schroers J, Ducuing C, Valcke P (eds) Security and Law. Legal and Ethical Aspects of Public Security, Cyber Security and Critical Infrastructure Security. Intersentia, Cambridge/Antwerp/Chicago, pp. 27–61.
von Arnauld A, Theilen J T (2020) Rhetoric of Rights: A Topical Perspective on the Functions of Claiming a "Human Right to...". In: von Arnauld A, von der Decken K, Susi M (eds) The Cambridge Handbook on New Human Rights. CUP, Cambridge, pp. 34–49.

von Danwitz T (2014) § 6 Gerichtlicher Schutz der Grundrechte [Judicial Protections of Fundamental Rights]. In: Grabenwarter C (ed) Enzyklopädie Europarecht [Encylopedia on European Law] Band 2: Europäischer Grundrechteschutz. Nomos, Baden-Baden, pp. 255–301.

von Danwitz T (2015) Die Grundrechte auf Achtung der Privatsphäre und auf Schutz personenbezogener Daten [The Fundamental Rights to the Protection of Privacy and of Personal Data]. DuD 581–585.

von Lewinski K (2009) Geschichte des Datenschutzrechts von 1600 bis 1977 [History of Data Protection Law from 1600 to 1977]. In: Arndt F, Betz N, Farahat A, Goldmann M, Huber M, Keil R, Láncos P L, Schaefer J, Smrkolj M, Sucker F, Valta S (eds) Freiheit – Öffentlichkeit – Sicherheit. Nomos, Baden-Baden, pp. 196–220.

Wagner L-J (2013) Assoziative Anmerkungen zu den Schlussanträgen von Generalanwalt Villalón in Sachen Vorratsdatenspeicherung [Associate Remarks on the Opinion of Advocate General Villalón in the Case on Bulk Data Retention]. JuWissBlog. http://www.juwiss.de/127-2013/. Accessed 28 July 2021.

Wagner L-J (2015) Der Datenschutz in der Europäischen Union [Data Protection in the European Union]. Jan Sramek Verlag, Vienna.

Ward A (2014) Article 51. In: Peers S, Hervey T, Kenner J, Ward A (eds) The EU Charter of Fundamental Rights – A Commentary. Hart, Oxford/Portland, OR, USA.

Weichert T (2018a) DS-GVO [GDPR] Art. 9. In: Kühling J, Buchner B (eds) Datenschutz-Grundverordnung/BDSG [General Data Protection Regulation/Federal Data Protection Act], 2nd edn. C.H. Beck, Munich.

Weichert T (2018b) DSGVO [GDPR] Art. 5. In: Däubler W, Wedde P, Weichert T, Sommer I (eds) EU-Datenschutz-Grundverordnung und BDSG-neu [EU General Data Protection Regulation and the New Federal Data Protection Act]. Bund-Verlag, Frankfurt am Main.

Woods L (2017) Transferring personal data outside the EU. EU Law Analysis. https://eulawanalysis.blogspot.com/2017/08/transferring-personal-data-outside-eu.html. Accessed 28 July 2021.

Woods L (2019) The AG Opinion in Schrems II: Facebook, national security and data protection law. EU Law Analysis. http://eulawanalysis.blogspot.com/2019/12/the-ag-opinion-in-schrems-ii-facebook.html. Accessed 27 July 2021.

Zalnieriute M (2021) Procedural Fetishism and Mass Surveillance under the ECHR. Verfassungsblog. https://verfassungsblog.de/big-b-v-uk/. Accessed 28 July 2021.

Zanfir-Fortuna G (2016) Analysis of the AG Opinion in the "PNR Canada" Case: unlocking an "unprecedented and delicate" matter. pdpEcho. https://pdpecho.com/2016/09/12/analysis-of-the-ag-opinion-in-the-pnr-canada-case-unlocking-an-unprecedented-and-delicate-matter/. Accessed 28 July 2021.

Zerdick T (2012) Art. 16 AEUV [TFEU]. In: Lenz C O, Borchardt K D (eds) EU-Verträge Kommentar [EU Treaties Commentary], 6th edn. Bundesanzeiger Verlag, Cologne.

Zuboff S (2015) Big other: surveillance capitalism and the prospects of an information civilization. Journal of Information Technology 30:75–89.

Zuiderveen Borgesius F, Hallinan D (2020) Article 5 GDPR, 'Principles relating to processing of personal data. In: Cole M, Boehm F (eds) Commentary on the General Data Protection Regulation. Edward Elgar, Cheltenham.

Zysset A (2016) Searching for the Legitimacy of the European Court of Human Rights: The Neglected Role of 'Democratic Society'. Global Constitutionalism 5:16–47.

Table of Cases: Council of Europe

ECtHR, Klass and Others v. Germany, App. No. 5029/71, Judgment of 6 September 1978.

ECtHR, Young, James and Webster v. the United Kingdom, App. Nos. 7601/76 and 7806/77, Judgment of 13 August 1981.

ECtHR, Leander v. Sweden, App. No. 9248/81, Judgment of 26 March 1987.
ECtHR [GC], Chassagnou and Others v. France, App. Nos. 25088/94, 28331/95 and 28443/95, Judgment of 29 April 1999.
ECtHR [GC], Amann v. Switzerland, App. No. 27798/95, Judgment of 16 February 2000.
ECtHR [GC], Rotaru v. Romania, App. No. 28341/95, Judgment of 4 May 2000.
ECtHR, Pretty v. the United Kingdom, App. No. 2346/02, Judgment of 29 April 2002.
ECtHR, Peck v. the United Kingdom, App. No. 44647/98, Judgment of 28 January 2003.
ECtHR [GC], Sørensen and Rasmussen v. Denmark, App. Nos. 52562/99 and 52620/99, Judgment of 11 January 2006.
ECtHR, Weber and Saravia v. Germany, App. No. 54934/00, Decision of 29 June 2006.
ECtHR [GC], S. and Marper v. the United Kingdom, App. Nos. 30562/04 and 30566/04, Judgment of 4 December 2008.
ECtHR, Iordachi and Others v. Moldova, App. No. 25198/02, Judgment of 10 February 2009.
ECtHR, Kennedy v. the United Kingdom, App. No. 26839/05, Judgment of 18 May 2010.
ECtHR, Uzun v. Germany, App. No. 35623/05, Judgment of 2 September 2010.
ECtHR, M.M. v. the United Kingdom, App. No. 24029/07, Judgment of 13 November 2012.
ECtHR [GC], Von Hannover v. Germany (No. 2), App. Nos. 40660/08 and 60641/08, Judgment of 7 February 2012.
ECtHR [GC], Roman Zakharov v. Russia, App. No. 47143/06, Judgment of 4 December 2015.
ECtHR [GC], Baka v. Hungary, App. No. 20261/12, Judgment of 23 June 2016.
ECtHR [GC], Karácsony and Others v. Hungary, App. Nos. 42461/13 and 44357/13, Judgment of 17 May 2016.
ECtHR, Szabó and Vissy v. Hungary, App. No. 37138/14, Judgment of 12 January 2016.
ECtHR [GC], Regner v. the Czech Republic, App. No. 35289/11, Judgment of 19 September 2017, Partly Dissenting Opinion of Judge Serghides.
ECtHR, Big Brother Watch and Others v. the United Kingdom, App. Nos. 58170/13, 62322/14 and 24960/15, Judgment of 13 September 2018.
ECtHR [GC], Big Brother Watch and Others v. the United Kingdom, App. Nos. 58170/13, 62322/14 and 24960/15, Judgment of 25 May 2021.

Table of Cases: EU

ECJ, Case 26/62 Van Gend en Loos v Administratie der Belastingen, Judgment of 5 February 1963, ECLI:EU:C:1963:1.
ECJ, Case 29/69 Stauder v Stadt Ulm, Judgment of 12 November 1969, ECLI:EU:C:1969:57.
ECJ, Case 136/79 National Panasonic (UK) Limited v Commission of the European Communities, Judgment of 26 June 1980, ECLI:EU:C:1980:169.
ECJ, Case 145/83 Stanley George Adams v Commission of the European Communities, Judgment of 7 November 1985, ECLI:EU:C:1985:448.
ECJ, Case 78/85 Group of the European Right v European Parliament, Order of 4 June 1986, ECLI:EU:C:1986:227.
ECJ, Case 294/83 Parti écologiste "Les Verts" v European Parliament, Judgment of 23 April 1986, ECLI:EU:C:1986:166.
ECJ, Case 140/86 Gisela Strack v Commission of the European Communities, Judgment of 7 October 1987, ECLI:EU:C:1987:427.
ECJ, Case C-366/88 French Republic v Commission of the European Communities, Judgment of 9 October 1990, ECLI:EU:C:1990:348.
ECJ, Case C-260/89 Elliniki Radiophonia Tiléorassi AE and Panellinia Omospondia Syllogon Prossopikou v Dimotiki Etairia Pliroforissis and Sotirios Kouvelas and Nicolaos Avdellas and Others, Judgment of 18 June 1991, ECLI:EU:C:1991:254.

ECJ, Case C-159/90 The Society for the Protection of Unborn Children Ireland Ltd v Stephen Grogan and Others, Judgment of 4 October 1991, ECLI:EU:C:1991:378.
ECJ, Case C-155/91 Commission of the European Communities v Council of the European Communities – Framework Directive on Waste, Judgment of 17 March 1993, ECLI:EU:C:1993:98.
ECJ, Case C-280/91 Finanzamt Kassel-Goethestrasse v Viessmann KG, Judgment of 18 March 1993, ECLI:EU:C:1993:103.
ECJ, Case C-404/92 P X v Commission of the European Communities, Judgment of 5 October 1994, ECLI:EU:C:1994:361.
ECJ, Case C-404/92 P X v Commission of the European Communities, Opinion of AG Gerven of 5 October 1994, ECLI:EU:C:1994:172.
ECJ, Case C-334/95 Krüger GmbH & Co. KG v Hauptzollamt Hamburg-Jonas, Judgment of 17 July 1997, ECLI:EU:C:1997:378.
ECJ, Case C-369/98 The Queen and Minister of Agriculture, Fisheries and Food, ex parte Trevor Robert Fisher and Penny Fisher, Judgment of 14 September 2000, ECLI:EU:C:2000:443.
ECJ, Case C-369/98 The Queen and Minister of Agriculture, Fisheries and Food, ex parte Trevor Robert Fisher and Penny Fisher, Opinion of AG Alber of 10 February 2000, ECLI:EU:C:2000:79.
ECJ, Case C-101/01 Criminal proceedings against Bodil Lindqvist, Opinion of AG Tizzano of 19 September 2002, ECLI:EU:C:2002:513.
ECJ, Joined Cases C-465/00, C-138/01 and C-139/01 Rechnungshof (C-465/00) v Österreichischer Rundfunk and Others and Christa Neukomm (C-138/01) and Joseph Lauermann (C-139/01) v Österreichischer Rundfunk, Opinion of AG Tizzano of 14 November 2002, ECLI:EU:C:2002:662.
ECJ, Case C-101/01 Criminal proceedings against Bodil Lindqvist, Judgment of 6 November 2003, ECLI:EU:C:2003:596.
ECJ, Joined Cases C-465/00, C-138/01 and C-139/01 Rechnungshof (C-465/00) v Österreichischer Rundfunk and Others and Christa Neukomm (C-138/01) and Joseph Lauermann (C-139/01) v Österreichischer Rundfunk, Judgment of 20 May 2003, ECLI:EU:C:2003:294.
ECJ, Joined Cases C-317/04 and C-318/04 European Parliament v Council of the European Union (C-317/04) and Commission of the European Communities (C-318/04) – PNR, Opinion of AG Léger of 22 November 2005, ECLI:EU:C:2005:710.
ECJ, Case C-144/04 Werner Mangold v Rüdiger Helm, Judgment of 22 November 2005, ECLI:EU:C:2005:709.
ECJ, Case C-408/03 Commission of the European Communities v Kingdom of Belgium, Judgment of 23 March 2006, ECLI:EU:C:2006:192.
ECJ, Joined Cases C-317/04 and C-318/04 European Parliament v Council of the European Union (C-317/04) and Commission of the European Communities (C-318/04) – PNR, Judgment of 30 May 2006, ECLI:EU:C:2006:346.
ECJ, Case C-438/05 International Transport Workers' Federation and Finnish Seamen's Union v Viking Line ABP and OÜ Viking Line Eesti, Judgment of 11 December 2007, ECLI:EU:C:2007:772.
ECJ, Case C-275/06 Productores de Música de España (Promusicae) v Telefónica de España SAU Opinion of AG Kokott of 18 July 2007, ECLI:EU:C:2007:454.
ECJ, Case C-524/06 Heinz Huber v Bundesrepublik Deutschland, Judgment of 16 December 2008, ECLI:EU:C:2008:724.
ECJ, Case C-524/06 Heinz Huber v Bundesrepublik Deutschland, Opinion of AG Poiares Maduro of 3 April 2008, ECLI:EU:C:2008:194.
ECJ, Case C-301/06 Ireland v European Parliament and Council of the European Union, Opinion of AG Bot of 14 October 2008, ECLI:EU:C:2008:558.
ECJ, Case C-275/06 Productores de Música de España (Promusicae) v Telefónica de España SAU Judgment of 29 January 2008, ECLI:EU:C:2008:54.
ECJ, Case C-73/07 Tietosuojavaltuutettu v Satakunnan Markkinapörssi Oy and Satamedia Oy, Judgment of 16 December 2008, ECLI:EU:C:2008:727.

ECJ, Case C-73/07 Tietosuojavaltuutettu v Satakunnan Markkinapörssi Oy and Satamedia Oy, Opinion of AG Kokott of 8 May 2008, ECLI:EU:C:2008:266.
ECJ, Case C-553/07 College van burgemeester en wethouders van Rotterdam v M. E. E. Rijkeboer, Judgment of 7 May 2009, ECLI:EU:C:2010:662.
ECJ, Case C-553/07 College van burgemeester en wethouders van Rotterdam v M. E. E. Rijkeboer, Opinion of AG Ruiz-Jarabo Colomer of 22 December 2008, ECLI:EU:C:2008:773.
ECJ, Case C-518/07 European Commission v Federal Republic of Germany, Opinion of AG Mazàk of 22 October 2009, ECLI:EU:C:2009:694.
ECJ, Case C-28/08 P European Commission v The Bavarian Lager Co. Ltd., Opinion of AG Sharpston of 15 October 2009, ECLI:EU:C:2009:624.
ECJ, Case C-301/06 Ireland v European Parliament and Council of the European Union, Judgment of 10 February 2009, ECI:EU:C:2009:68.
ECJ, Case C-557/07 LSG-Gesellschaft zur Wahrnehmung von Leistungsschutzrechten GmbH v Tele2 Telecommunication GmbH, Order of 19 February 2009, ECLI:EU:C:2009:107.
ECJ, Case C-28/08 P European Commission v The Bavarian Lager Co. Ltd., Judgment of 29 June 2010, ECLI:EU:C:2010:378.
ECJ, Case C-518/07 European Commission v Federal Republic of Germany, Judgment of 9 March 2010, ECLI:EU:C:2010:125.
ECJ, Case C-555/07 Seda Kücükdeveci v Swedex GmbH & Co. KG, Judgment of 19 January 2010, ECLI:EU:C:2010:21.
ECJ, Joined Cases C-92/09 and C-93/09 Volker und Markus Schecke GbR (C-92/09) and Hartmut Eifert (C-93/09) v Land Hessen, Opinion of AG Sharpston of 17 June 2010, ECLI:EU:C:2010:353.
ECJ, Joined Cases C-92/09 and C-93/09 Volker und Markus Schecke GbR (C-92/09) and Hartmut Eifert (C-93/09) v Land Hessen, Judgment of 9 November 2010, ECLI:EU:C:2010:662.
ECJ, Joined Cases C-468/10 and C-469/10 Asociación Nacional de Establecimientos Financieros de Crédito (ASNEF) (C-468/10) and Federación de Comercio Electrónico y Marketing Directo (FECEMD) (C-469/10) v Administración del Estado, Judgment of 24 November 2011, ECLI:EU:C:2011:777.
ECJ, Case C-461/10 Bonnier Audio AB and Others v Perfect Communication Sweden AB, Opinion of AG Jääskinen of 17 November 2011, ECLI:EU:C:2011:753.
ECJ, Case C-534/09 Deutsche Telekom AG v Bundesrepublik Deutschland, Judgment of 5 May 2011, ECLI:EU:C:2011:279.
ECJ, Case C-282/10 Maribel Dominguez v Centre informatique du Centre Ouest Atlantique and Préfet de la région Centre, Opinion of AG Trstenjak of 8 September 2011, ECLI:EU:C:2011:559.
ECJ, Case C-70/10 Scarlet Extended SA v Société belge des auteurs, compositeurs et éditeurs SCRL (SABAM), Opinion of AG Cruz Villalón of 14 April 2011, ECLI:EU:C:2011:255.
ECJ, Case C-70/10 Scarlet Extended SA v Société belge des auteurs, compositeurs et éditeurs SCRL (SABAM), Judgment of 24 November 2011, ECLI:EU:C:2011:771.
ECJ, Case C-360/10 Belgische Vereniging van Auteurs, Componisten en Uitgevers CVBA (SABAM) v Netlog NV, Judgment of 16 February 2012, ECLI:EU:C:2012:85.
ECJ, Case C-461/10 Bonnier Audio AB and Others v Perfect Communication Sweden AB, Judgment of 19 April 2012, ECLI:EU:C:2012:219.
ECJ, Case C-614/10 European Commission v Republic of Austria, Opinion of AG Mazàk of 3 July 2012, ECLI:EU:C:2012:406.
ECJ, Case C-614/10 European Commission v Republic of Austria, Judgment of 16 October 2012, ECLI:EU:C:2012:631.
ECJ, Case C-282/10 Maribel Dominguez v Centre informatique du Centre Ouest Atlantique and Préfet de la région Centre, Judgment of 24 January 2012, ECLI:EU:C:2012:33.
ECJ, Case C-617/10 Åklagaren v Hans Åkerberg Fransson, Judgment of 26 February 2013, ECLI:EU:C:2013:105.
ECJ, Case C-176/12 Association de médiation sociale v Union locale des syndicats CGT and Others, Opinion of AG Cruz Villalón of 18 July 2013, ECLI:EU:C:2013:491.

ECJ, Joined Cases C-293/12 and C-594/12 Digital Rights Ireland Ltd (C-293/12) v Minister for Communications, Marine and Natural Resources and Others and Kärntner Landesregierung (C-594/12) and Others, Opinion of AG Cruz Villalón of 12 December 2013, ECLI:EU:C:2013:845.
ECJ, Case C-288/12 European Commission v Hungary, Opinion of AG Wathelet of 10 December 2013, ECLI:EU:C:2013:816.
ECJ, Case C-131/12 Google Spain SL and Google Inc. v Agencia Española de Protección de Datos (AEPD) and Mario Costeja González, Opinion of AG Jääskinen of 13 April 2014, ECLI:EU:C:2013:424.
ECJ, Case C-473/12 Institut professionnel des agents immobiliers (IPI) v Geoffrey Englebert and Others, Judgment of 7 November 2013, ECLI:EU:C:2013:715.
ECJ, Case C-426/11 Mark Alemo-Herron and Others v Parkwood Leisure Ltd, Judgment of 18 July 2013, ECLI:EU:C:2013:521.
ECJ, Case C-291/12 Michael Schwarz v Stadt Bochum, Judgment of 17 October 2013, ECLI:EU:C:2013:670.
ECJ, Case C-291/12 Michael Schwarz v Stadt Bochum, Opinion of AG Mengozzi of 13 June 2013, ECLI:EU:C:2013:401.
ECJ, Case C-283/11 Sky Österreich GmbH v Österreichischer Rundfunk, Judgment of 22 January 2013, ECLI:EU:C:2013:28.
ECJ, Joined Cases C-141/12 and C-372/12 YS (C-141/12) v Minister voor Immigratie, Integratie en Asiel and Minister voor Immigratie, Integratie en Asiel (C-372/12) v M and S, Opinion of AG Sharpston of 12 December 2013, ECLI:EU:C:2013:838.
ECJ, Case C-176/12 Association de médiation sociale v Union locale des syndicats CGT and Others, Judgment of 15 January 2014, ECLI:EU:C:2014:2.
ECJ, Joined Cases C-293/12 and C-594/12 Digital Rights Ireland Ltd (C-293/12) v Minister for Communications, Marine and Natural Resources and Others and Kärntner Landesregierung (C-594/12) and Others, Judgment of 8 April 2014, ECLI:EU:C:2014:238.
ECJ, Case C-288/12 European Commission v Hungary, Judgment of 8 April 2014, ECLI:EU:C:2014:237.
ECJ, Case C-212/13 František Ryneš v Úřad pro ochranu osobních údajů, Judgment of 11 December 2014, ECLI:EU:C:2014:2428.
ECJ, Case C-212/13 František Ryneš v Úřad pro ochranu osobních údajů, Opinion of AG Jääskinen of 10 July 2014, ECLI:EU:C:2014:2072.
ECJ, Case C-131/12 Google Spain SL and Google Inc. v Agencia Española de Protección de Datos (AEPD) and Mario Costeja González, Judgment of 13 April 2014, ECLI:EU:C:2014:317.
ECJ, Joined Cases C-141/12 and C-372/12 YS (C-141/12) v Minister voor Immigratie, Integratie en Asiel and Minister voor Immigratie, Integratie en Asiel (C-372/12) v M and S, Judgment of 17 July 2014, ECLI:EU:C:2014:2081.
ECJ, Case C-580/13 Coty Germany v Stadtsparkasse Magdeburg, Judgment of 16 July 2015, ECLI:EU:C:2015:485.
ECJ, Case C-580/13 Coty Germany v Stadtsparkasse Magdeburg, Opinion of AG Cruz Villalón of 16 April 2015, ECLI:EU:C:2015:485.
ECJ, Case C-362/14 Maximillian Schrems v Data Protection Commissioner, Judgment of 6 October 2015, ECLI:EU:C:2015:650.
ECJ, Case C-362/14 Maximillian Schrems v Data Protection Commissioner, Opinion of AG Bot of 23 September 2015, ECLI:EU:C:2015:627.
ECJ, Case C-201/14 Smaranda Bara and Others v Casa Naţională de Asigurări de Sănătate and Others, Judgment of 1 October 2015, ECLI:EU:C:2015:638.
ECJ, Joined Cases C-446 to C-449/12 W. P. Willems and Others v Burgemeester van Nuth and Others, Judgment of 16 April 2015, ECLI:EU:C:2015:238.
ECJ, Avis 1/15, Opinion of AG Mengozzi of 8 September 2016, ECLI:EU:C:2016:656.
ECJ, Case C-15/15 New Valmar BVBA v Global Pharmacies Partner Health Srl, Judgment of 21 June 2016, ECLI:EU:C:2016:464.

ECJ, Joined Cases C-203/15 and C-698/15 Tele2 Sverige v Post- och telestyrelsen (C-203/15) and Secretary of State for the Home Department v Tom Watson, Peter Brice and Geoffrey Lewis (C-698/15), Judgment of 21 December 2016, ECLI:EU:C:2016:970.

ECJ, Joined Cases C-203/15 and C-698/15 Tele2 Sverige v Post- och telestyrelsen (C-203/15) and Secretary of State for the Home Department v Tom Watson, Peter Brice and Geoffrey Lewis (C-698/15), Opinion of AG Saugmandsgaard Øe of 19 July 2016, ECLI:EU:C:2016:572.

ECJ, Case C-484/14 Tobias Mc Fadden v Sony Music Entertainment Germany GmbH, Judgment of 15 September 2016, ECLI:EU:C:2016:689.

ECJ, Case C-191/15 Verein für Konsumenteninformation v Amazon EU Sàrl, Judgment of 28 July 2016, ECLI:EU:C:2016:612.

ECJ, Avis 1/15, Opinion of 26 July 2017, ECLI:EU:C:2017:592.

ECJ, Case C-434/16 Peter Nowak v Data Protection Commissioner, Opinion of AG Kokott of 20 July 2017, ECLI:EU:C:2017:582.

ECJ, Case C-434/16 Peter Nowak v Data Protection Commissioner, Judgment of 20 December 2017, ECLI:EU:C:2017:994.

ECJ, Case C-73/16 Peter Puškár v Finančné riadite'stvo Slovenskej republiky and Kriminálny úrad finančnej správy, Judgment of 27 September 2017, ECLI:EU:C:2017:725.

ECJ, Case C-210/16 Unabhängiges Landeszentrum für Datenschutz Schleswig-Holstein v Wirtschaftsakademie Schleswig-Holstein GmbH, Opinion of AG Bot of 24 October 2017, ECLI:EU:C:2017:796.

ECJ, Case C-40/17 Fashion ID GmbH & Co.KG v Verbraucherzentrale NRW eV, Judgment of 29 July 2019, ECLI:EU:C:2019:629.

ECJ, Case C-684/16 Max-Planck-Gesellschaft zur Förderung der Wissenschaften eV v Tetsuji Shimizu, Judgment of 6 November 2018, ECLI:EU:C:2018:874.

ECJ, Case C-207/16 Ministerio Fiscal, Opinion of AG Saugmandsgaard Øe of 3 May 2018, ECLI:EU:C:2018:300.

ECJ, Case C-207/16 Ministerio Fiscal, Judgment of 2 October 2018, ECLI:EU:C:2018:788.

ECJ, Joined Cases C-569/16 and C-570/16 Stadt Wuppertal v Maria Elisabeth Bauer and Volker Willmeroth v Martina Broßonn, Judgment of 6 November 2018, ECLI:EU:C:2018:871.

ECJ, Case C-25/17 Tietosuojavaltuutettu – Jehovan todistajat, Judgment of 10 July 2018, ECLI:EU:C:2018:551.

ECJ, Case C-210/16 Unabhängiges Landeszentrum für Datenschutz Schleswig-Holstein v Wirtschaftsakademie Schleswig-Holstein GmbH, Judgment of 5 June 2018, ECLI:EU:C:2018:388.

ECJ, Case C-414/16 Vera Egenberger v Evangelisches Werk für Diakonie und Entwicklung e.V., Judgment of 17 April 2018, ECLI:EU:C:2018:257.

ECJ, Case C-673/17 Bundesverband der Verbraucherzentralen und Verbraucherverbände - Verbraucherzentrale Bundesverband e.V. v Planet49, Opinion of AG Szpunar of 21 March 2019, ECLI:EU:C:2019:246.

ECJ, Case C-673/17 Bundesverband der Verbraucherzentralen und Verbraucherverbände - Verbraucherzentrale Bundesverband e.V. v Planet49, Judgment of 1 October 2019, ECLI:EU:C:2019:801.

ECJ, C-311/18 Data Protection Commissioner v Facebook Ireland Ltd. and Maximillian Schrems – Schrems II, Opinion of AG Saugmansgaard Øe of 19 December 2019, ECLI:EU:C:2019:1145.

ECJ, Case C-496/17 Deutsche Post AG v Hauptzollamt Köln, Judgment of 16 January 2019, ECLI:EU:C:2019:26.

ECJ, Case C-18/18 Eva Glawischnig-Piesczek v Facebook Ireland Limited, Judgment of 3 October 2019, ECLI:EU:C:2019:821.

ECJ, Case C-507/17 Google LLC v Commission nationale de l'informatique et des libertés (CNIL), Judgment of 24 September 2019, ECLI:EU:C:2019:772.

ECJ, Case C-354/17 Sergejs Buivids, Judgment of 14 February 2019, ECLI:EU:C:2019:122.

ECJ, Case C-354/17 Sergejs Buivids, Opinion of AG Sharpston of 27 September 2018, ECLI:EU:C:2018:780.

ECJ, Case C-746/18 Criminal proceedings against H. K. – Prokuratuur, Opinion of AG Pitruzzella of 21 January 2020, ECLI:EU:C:2020:18.
ECJ, C-311/18 Data Protection Commissioner v Facebook Ireland Ltd. and Maximillian Schrems – Schrems II, Judgment of 16 July 2020, ECLI:EU:C:2020:559.
ECJ, Joined Cases C-511/18, C-512/18 and C-520/18 La Quadature du Net and Others v Premier ministre and Others, Judgment of 6 October 2020, ECLI:EU:C:2020:791.
ECJ, Joined Cases C-511/18, C-512/18 and C-520/18 La Quadature du Net and Others v Premier ministre and Others, Opinion of AG Campos Sànchez-Bordona of 15 January 2020, ECLI:EU:C:2020:6.
ECJ, Case C-520/18 Ordre des barreaux francophones and germanophone and Others, Opinion of AG Campos Sànchez-Bordona of 15 January 2020, ECLI:EU:C:2020:7.
ECJ, C-623/17 Privacy International v Secretary of State for Foreign and Commonwealth Affairs and Others, Judgment of 6 October 2020, ECLI:EU:C:2020:790.
ECJ, C-623/17 Privacy International v Secretary of State for Foreign and Commonwealth Affairs and Others, Opinion of AG Campos Sànchez-Bordona of 15 January 2020, ECLI:EU:C:2020:5.
ECJ, Case C-746/18 Criminal proceedings against H. K. – Prokuratuur, Judgment of 2 March 2021, ECLI:EU:C:2021:152.
ECJ, Case C-645/19 Facebook Ireland Limited and Others v Gegevensbeschermingsautoriteit, Opinion of AG Bobek of 13 January 2021, ECLI:EU:C:2021:5.
ECJ, Case C-645/19 Facebook Ireland Limited and Others v Gegevensbeschermingsautoriteit, Judgment of 15 June 2021, ECLI:EU:C:2021:483.
ECJ, Case C-401/19 Poland v Parliament and Council, Opinion of AG Saugmandsgaard Øe of 15 July 2021, ECLI:EU:C:2021:613.
ECJ, Case C-401/19 Poland v Parliament and Council, pending.
CFI, Case T-194/04 The Bavarian Lager Co. Ltd v Commission of the European Communities, Judgment of 8 November 2007, ECLI:EU:T:2007:334.
GC, Case T-738/16 La Quadrature du Net and Others v European Commission, Order of 14 December 2020, ECLI:EU:T:2020:638.

Table of Cases: National

Bundesverfassungsgericht, BVerfGE 7, pp. 198–230—Lüth, Judgment of 15 January 1958.
Bundesverfassungsgericht, BVerfGE 65, pp. 1–71—Volkszählung, Judgment of 15 December 1983.
Bundesverfassungsgericht, BVerfGE 113, pp. 29–63—Anwaltsdaten, Judgment of 12 April 2005.
Bundesverfassungsgericht, NJW 2019, pp. 827–842—Automatisierte Kennzeichenerfassung, Order of 18 December 2018.
Verfassungsgerichtshof, KR 1/00-33 Rechnungshof v Österreichischer Rundfunk, Judgment of 28 November 2003.

Other Documents: EU

Article 29 Working Party Opinion 4/2007 on the concept of personal data of 20 June 2007. WP 136.
Article 29 Working Party Opinion 3/2010 on the principle of accountability. WP 173.
Article 29 Working Party Opinion 15/2011 on the definition of consent of 13 July 2011. WP 187.
Article 29 Working Party Opinion 03/2013 on purpose limitation of 2 April 2013. WP 203.
Article 29 Working Party Opinion 06/2014 on the notion of legitimate interests of the data controller under Article 7 of Directive 95/46/EC of 9 April 2014. WP 217.

Article 29 Working Party Guidelines on the right to data portability of 13 December 2016. WP 242 rev.01.
Article 29 Working Party Guidelines on Data Protection Impact Assessment (DPIA) and determining whether processing is "likely to result in a high risk" for the purposes of Regulation 2016/679. WP 248 rev.01.
Article 29 Working Party Guidelines on transparency under Regulation 2016/679. WP 260 rev. 01.
ENISA Recommendations on shaping technology according to GDPR provisions (2018). https://www.enisa.europa.eu/publications/recommendations-on-shaping-technology-according-to-gdpr-provisions-part-2/at_download/fullReport. Accessed 28 July 2021.
European Data Protection Board Endorsement 1/2018 of 25 May 2018.
European Union Agency for Fundamental Rights 2018 #BigData: Discrimination in data-supported decision making. Vienna. https://fra.europa.eu/sites/default/files/fra_uploads/fra-2018-focus-big-data_en.pdf. Accessed 28 July 2021.
European Union Agency for Fundamental Rights, Council of Europe, European Data Protection Supervisor 2018 Handbook on European data protection law. Luxembourg. https://fra.europa.eu/sites/default/files/fra_uploads/fra-coe-edps-2018-handbook-data-protection_en.pdf. Accessed 16 June 2021.
Expert Group on Fundamental Rights Affirming Fundamental Rights in the European Union – Time to Act (Simitis Report) (1999). https://ftp.infoeuropa.eurocid.pt/database/000038001-000039000/000038827.pdf. Accessed 28 July 2021.

Other Documents: National

Autoriteit Persoonsgegevens Summary of Investigation Report on Microsoft Windows 10 Home and Pro (2017). https://autoriteitpersoonsgegevens.nl/sites/default/files/atoms/files/public_version_dutch_dpa_informal_translation_summary_of_investigation_report.pdf. Accessed 28 July 2021.
Information Commissioner's Office (2018) Investigation Into the Use of Data Analytics in Political Campaigns. https://ico.org.uk/media/action-weve-taken/2259371/investigation-into-data-analytics-for-political-purposes-update.pdf. Accessed 28 July 2021.
Konferenz der unabhängigen Datenschutzaufsichtsbehörden des Bundes und der Länder (2018) Kurzpapier Nr. 18 – Risiko für die Rechte und Freiheiten natürlicher Personen [Short Paper No. 18 – Risk to the Rights and Freedoms of Natural Persons]. https://www.datenschutzzentrum.de/uploads/dsgvo/kurzpapiere/DSK_KPNr_18_Risiko.pdf. Accessed 28 July 2021.
Konferenz der unabhängigen Datenschutzaufsichtsbehörden des Bundes und der Länder (2020) The Standard Data Protection Model – V.2.0b. https://www.datenschutz-mv.de/datenschutz/datenschutzmodell/. Accessed 28 July 2021.

Index

© T.M.C. ASSER PRESS and the author 2022

F. Bieker, *The Right to Data Protection*, Information Technology and Law Series 34,
https://doi.org/10.1007/978-94-6265-503-4

GPSR Compliance
The European Union's (EU) General Product Safety Regulation (GPSR) is a set of rules that requires consumer products to be safe and our obligations to ensure this.

If you have any concerns about our products, you can contact us on

ProductSafety@springernature.com

In case Publisher is established outside the EU, the EU authorized representative is:

Springer Nature Customer Service Center GmbH
Europaplatz 3
69115 Heidelberg, Germany

www.ingramcontent.com/pod-product-compliance
Ingram Content Group UK Ltd.
Pitfield, Milton Keynes, MK11 3LW, UK
UKHW020241290926
15470UKWH00002B/674

9789462655027